Mixed Race in Asia represents an important advance in both our theorizing and documentation of the multiple and varied forms of 'mixing' in a non-Western context. While Asia – in all its diversity – cannot be understood without reference to its colonial histories, this volume illuminates the pressing need to learn about what mixed race and mixing mean today in societies grappling with social change.
      Miri Song, *Professor of Sociology, School of Social Policy, Sociology,*
            & Social Research, University of Kent, UK

In the context of Asia where 'race' often holds considerable salience as a sociopolitical category, this volume turns the spotlight on the lived experiences of mixed race identities. Across a broad range of Asian societies from those that bear the marks of postcolonial plurality such as Singapore and Malaysia to those where nationhood is predicated on claims to racial homogeneity such as Japan and Korea, the authors provide us rare insight into both the pathologies and privileges of racial mixing.
      Brenda S.A. Yeoh, *National University of Singapore, Singapore*

This is a breakthrough volume for mixed race studies. It opens up a new set of regional perspectives, to provide us with fascinating insights into aspects of mixedness in the Asian context. Rocha and Fozdar are to be congratulated on putting together a unique contribution to the field.
    Rosalind Edwards, *Professor of Sociology, University of Southampton, UK*

Mixed Race in Asia

Mixed racial and ethnic identities are topics of increasing interest around the world, yet studies of mixed race in Asia are rare, despite its particular salience for Asian societies.

Mixed Race in Asia seeks to reorient the field to focus on Asia, looking specifically at mixed race in China, Japan, Korea, Indonesia, Malaysia, Singapore, Vietnam and India. Through these varied case studies, this collection presents an insightful exploration of race, ethnicity, mixedness and belonging, both in the past and present. The thematic range of the chapters is broad, covering the complexity of lived mixed race experiences, the structural forces of particular colonial and post-colonial environments and political regimes, and historical influences on contemporary identities and cultural expressions of mixedness.

Adding significant richness and depth to existing theoretical frameworks, this enlightening volume develops markedly different understandings of, and recognizes nuances around, what it means to be mixed: practically, theoretically, linguistically and historically. It will appeal to undergraduate and postgraduate students, as well as postdoctoral and other researchers interested in fields such as Race and Ethnicity, Sociology and Asian Studies.

Zarine L. Rocha is the Managing Editor of Current Sociology and the Asian Journal of Social Science

Farida Fozdar is Associate Professor in Anthropology and Sociology, at The University of Western Australia

Routledge Research in Race and Ethnicity

10 **Making Diaspora in a Global City**
South Asian Youth Cultures in London
Helen Kim

11 **A Moral Economy of Whiteness**
Four Frames of Racializing Discourse
Steve Garner

12 **Race and the Origins of American Neoliberalism**
Randolph Hohle

13 **Experiences of Islamophobia**
Living with Racism in the Neoliberal Era
James Carr

14 **Immigration, Assimilation, and the Cultural Construction of American National Identity**
Shannon Latkin Anderson

15 **Blackness in Britain**
Edited by Lisa Palmer and Kehinde Andrews

16 **The End of Black Studies**
Conceptual, Theoretical, and Empirical Concerns
Clovis E. Semmes

17 **Contemporary African American Families**
Achievements, Challenges, and Empowerment Strategies in the Twenty-First Century
Edited by Dorothy Smith-Ruiz, Sherri Lawson Clark and Marcia Watson

18 **Return Migration and Psychosocial Wellbeing**
Edited by Zana Vathi and Russell King

19 **Mapping the New African Diaspora in China**
Race and the Cultural Politics of Belonging
Shanshan Lan

20 **Doing Violence, Making Race**
Mattias Smangs

21 **Critical Reflections on Migration, 'Race' and Multiculturalism**
Australia in a Global Context
Edited by Martina Boese and Vince Marotta

22 **Mixed Race in Asia**
Past, Present and Future
Edited by Zarine L. Rocha and Farida Fozdar

Mixed Race in Asia
Past, Present and Future

Edited by
Zarine L. Rocha
and Farida Fozdar

LONDON AND NEW YORK

First published 2017
by Routledge
2 Park Square, Milton Park, Abingdon, Oxon OX14 4RN

and by Routledge
711 Third Avenue, New York, NY 10017

Routledge is an imprint of the Taylor & Francis Group, an informa business

© 2017 selection and editorial matter, Zarine L. Rocha and Farida Fozdar; individual chapters, the contributors

The right of Zarine L. Rocha and Farida Fozdar to be identified as the authors of the editorial matter, and of the authors for their individual chapters, has been asserted in accordance with sections 77 and 78 of the Copyright, Designs and Patents Act 1988.

All rights reserved. No part of this book may be reprinted or reproduced or utilized in any form or by any electronic, mechanical, or other means, now known or hereafter invented, including photocopying and recording, or in any information storage or retrieval system, without permission in writing from the publishers.

Trademark notice: Product or corporate names may be trademarks or registered trademarks, and are used only for identification and explanation without intent to infringe.

British Library Cataloguing in Publication Data
A catalogue record for this book is available from the British Library

Library of Congress Cataloging in Publication Data
A catalog record for this book has been requested

ISBN: 978-1-138-28267-4 (hbk)
ISBN: 978-1-315-27057-9 (ebk)

Typeset in Times New Roman
by Wearset Ltd, Boldon, Tyne and Wear

Contents

Notes on contributors   x
Acknowledgements   xv

Introduction: mixed race in Asia   1
ZARINE L. ROCHA AND FARIDA FOZDAR

PART I
China and Vietnam   17

1 'A class by themselves': battles over Eurasian schooling in late-nineteenth-century Shanghai   19
   EMMA J. TENG

2 Mixing blood and race: representing *Hunxue* in contemporary China   35
   CATHRYN H. CLAYTON

3 *Métis* of Vietnam: an historical perspective on mixed-race children from the French colonial period   52
   CHRISTINA FIRPO

PART II
South Korea and Japan   65

4 Developing bilingualism in a largely monolingual society: Southeast Asian marriage migrants and multicultural families in South Korea   67
   MI YUNG PARK

viii *Contents*

5 *Haafu* identity in Japan: half, mixed or double?   82
   ALEXANDRA SHAITAN AND LISA J. McENTEE-ATALIANIS

6 Claiming *Japaneseness*: recognition, privilege and status in
   Japanese-Filipino 'mixed' ethnic identity constructions   98
   FIONA-KATHARINA SEIGER

PART III
Malaysia and Singapore   115

7 Being 'mixed' in Malaysia: negotiating ethnic identity in a
   racialized context   117
   CARYN LIM

8 Chinese, Indians and the grey space in between: strategies
   of identity work among Chindians in a plural society   132
   RONA CHANDRAN

9 'Our Chinese': the mixedness of Peranakan Chinese
   identities in Kelantan, Malaysia   147
   PUE GIOK HUN

10 Eurasian as multiracial: mixed race, gendered categories
   and identity in Singapore   162
   ZARINE L. ROCHA

PART IV
India and Indonesia   177

11 Is the Anglo-Indian 'identity crisis' a myth?   179
   ROBYN ANDREWS

12 Performing Britishness in a railway colony: production of
   Anglo-Indians as a railway caste   195
   ANJALI GERA ROY

13 Sometimes white, sometimes Asian: boundary-making
   among transnational mixed descent youth at an
   international school in Indonesia   211
   DANAU TANU

14 **Class, race and being Indo (Eurasian) in colonial and postcolonial Indonesia** 224
ROSALIND HEWETT

Afterword 239
PAUL SPICKARD

Index 245

Contributors

Robyn Andrews is Senior Lecturer in the Social Anthropology Programme at Massey University, New Zealand. Her PhD, *Being Anglo-Indian: Practices and Stories from Calcutta* (2005) was her first of a number of Anglo-Indian Studies projects in India and the diaspora. She published *Christmas in Calcutta: Anglo-Indian Stories and Essays* (2014) and writes articles and book chapters for both academic and community publications. She co-edits the *International Journal of Anglo-Indian Studies*.

Rona Chandran holds a PhD in Anthropology from the University of Malaya. She is an Applied Anthropologist and Senior International Consultant. She has over 17 years of experience in the social sciences spanning education, anthropology and development facilitation. She has experience as a planner, focal point, advisor and trainer for the Governments of Malaysia, Bhutan, Philippines and Laos on initiatives supported by the European Union, Japan International Cooperation Agency, World Bank, UNESCO and ASEAN Secretariat. She has undertaken consultancy and research focusing on ethnic identity and cultural heritage sustainability in Asia. This includes substantial work on Education for Sustainable Development focusing on environmental and socio-cultural sustainability. She has also worked on developing effective intervention plans and frameworks for the sustainability of culture and heritage in development activity, such as tourism. Her work has resulted in publications with several international organizations.

Cathryn H. Clayton is a cultural anthropologist and Associate Professor in the Asian Studies Program at the University of Hawai'i at Mānoa. Her teaching and research explore questions of Chineseness – how and why it becomes a compelling form of collective subjectivity (be it nationalist, diasporic, regional, civilizational) at different points in time and space. Her first book, *Sovereignty at the Edge: Macau and the Question of Chineseness*, won the 2010 Francis L.K. Hsu Award for best new book on East Asia from the Society for East Asian Anthropology in the American Anthropological Association. She has a forthcoming monograph about the Cultural Revolution-style protests in Macau in 1966 that nearly toppled the Portuguese colonial administration. She has studied at Williams College, Stanford

University, and the University of California at Santa Cruz; held an An Wang Postdoctoral Fellowship at Harvard University's Fairbank Center; and taught at the University of Macau from 2001–2005.

Christina Firpo earned a PhD in Southeast Asian History at the University of California – Los Angeles. She is currently Associate Professor of Southeast Asian Studies at California Polytechnic State University in San Luis Obispo, in the United States. She spent more than ten years researching the history of Franco-Vietnamese children in seven archives in Vietnam, Cambodia, and France. She is the author of *The Uprooted: Race, Children, and Imperialism in Indochina, 1890–1980* (University of Hawai'i Press, 2016). She has published articles on race, childhood, prostitution, and human trafficking in the *Journal of Social History, Journal of Vietnamese Studies, Tạp Chí Nghiên cứu Lịch sử, Le Vigntième Siècle, French Historical Studies, Historical Reflections/Réflections Historiques* and *French Colonial History*. She is currently writing a book on clandestine prostitution in late-colonial Vietnam.

Farida Fozdar (aka Tilbury) is Associate Professor at the University of Western Australia. She is a leading researcher on issues of race relations in Australia. She has published over 60 articles and book chapters, including two on 'mixed race'. Her co-authored 'Antipodean Mixed Race' appeared in the groundbreaking 2014 collection *Global Mixed Race*. She also has three books, including *Race and Ethnic Relations* (co-authored), which focuses on issues of race, culture and nationalism in Australia and New Zealand; and the co-edited 2016 volume *Mixed Race Identities in Australia, New Zealand and the Pacific Islands*. Her research focuses on migrant settlement, citizenship, nationalism, social exclusion, religion and issues to do with refugees and asylum seekers. She has recently completed an ARC Future Fellowship, exploring national, transnational and postnational identities.

Rosalind Hewett is a PhD candidate in Pacific and Asian History at the College of Asia and the Pacific, Australian National University. She has published articles on the history of Eurasians in Indonesia and the Netherlands, disability activism in Indonesian politics and ethnic violence in Indonesia. Her research interests include Asian history, modern Indonesian history, race and ethnicity, colonialism, memory and mass violence. She speaks fluent Indonesian and Manado Malay and reads Dutch.

Caryn Lim is a PhD candidate at the School of Arts and Social Sciences, Monash University Malaysia. She is currently working on her thesis, which is an ethnographic study of death spaces and practice in the Klang Valley, Malaysia. In the past, she has also worked on issues of identity politics and the negotiation of ethnic identity amongst 'mixed race' Malaysians. Her honours research on this subject has been presented at international conferences and published in two other edited volumes. Though her current research focuses on death and the social transformations thereof, she remains interested in the politics of ethnic and racial identity particularly as it unfolds in her home country.

Lisa J. McEntee-Atalianis is Senior Lecturer in Applied Linguistics and Communication at Birkbeck, University of London. In recent years, her research has focused on issues of 'identity' at micro- and macro-linguistic levels. Her breadth of interest is evidenced in her forthcoming book: *Language and Identity* (Bloomsbury/Continuum), and articles and chapters which have focused on different sites and communities, including Greek-Cypriot communities in Cyprus and London; the autochthonous Greek-Orthodox community of Istanbul, Turkey; European NGOs and the United Nations.

Mi Yung Park (PhD, University of Hawai'i at Mānoa) is a lecturer in Korean at the University of Auckland. Her research interests include language and identity, sociolinguistics, and multilingualism. She has been investigating the relationship between second language acquisition and identity construction among marriage-migrant women in South Korea. While researching this topic, she became interested in the language-learning experiences of their multi-ethnic children, which led her to study heritage language development in multicultural families. She is now extending this work to a study on bilingualism and identity formation among heritage learners of Korean in New Zealand. She has published in *Journal of Pragmatics*, *Language and Intercultural Communication*, *Classroom Discourse*, *Japanese/Korean Linguistics*, and *The Korean Language in America*, and has contributed to other edited volumes.

Pue Giok Hun is Research Fellow and Head of Quality Assurance at Institute of Ethnic Studies (KITA), Universiti Kebangsaan Malaysia (UKM). A social anthropologist by training, her research focus has been on identity formation and negotiation among ethnic minority groups with mixed heritage roots, particularly the Peranakans. She graduated with a BA (Hons.) in Anthropology and Sociology (2002) and Master in Environmental Management (2003) from UKM. In 2012, she obtained her PhD in Ethnic Studies at UKM with her thesis 'Peranakan sebagai fenomena sosial dengan tumpuan kepada komuniti Cina Peranakan di Kelantan' (*Peranakan as social phenomenon with a focus on the Peranakan Chinese community in Kelantan*). Her latest publications include 'Perkahwinan campur dan fenomena Peranakan di Semenanjung Malaysia' *(Mixed marriage and the Peranakan phenomenon in Peninsular Malaysia)* (2015) and *Peranakan as plural identity: cases from Peninsular Malaysia* (2016).

Zarine L. Rocha is a sociologist, and the Managing Editor of *Current Sociology* and the *Asian Journal of Social Science*. She has a PhD from the National University of Singapore, an MSc from the London School of Economics and Political Science, and a BA from the University of Canterbury, New Zealand. Zarine specializes in issues of mixed race/mixed ethnic identity, narratives of belonging, multiculturalism, diversity and social conflict in Asia and the Pacific. She has worked as a researcher at the United Nations Research Institute for Social Development, the United Nations Environment Programme and the World Economic Forum. Zarine has published chapters and articles on issues of identity, belonging and race/ethnicity, including journal articles in *Identities: Global Studies of Culture and Power* and *Ethnicities*. Her first monograph *"Mixed Race" Identities in Asia and the Pacific: Experiences from Singapore and New Zealand* was published by Routledge in 2016.

Anjali Gera Roy is Professor in the Department of Humanities and Social Sciences at the Indian Institute of Technology Kharagpur. She has published 100 essays in literary, film and cultural studies in reputed journals and anthologies. She is the author of *Cinema of Enchantment: Perso-Arabic Genealogies of the Hindi Masala film* (Hyderabad: Orient Blackswan, 2015) and *Bhangra Moves: From Ludhiana to London and Beyond* (Aldershot: Ashgate, 2010). In addition, she has edited *Imagining Punjab, Punjabi, Punjabiyat in the Digital Era* (New York: Routledge, 2015) and *The Magic of Bollywood: At Home and Abroad* (Delhi: Sage, 2012) and co-edited (with Chua Beng Huat) *The Travels of Indian Cinema: From Bombay to LA* (Delhi: OUP, 2012) and (with Nandi Bhatia) *Partitioned Lives: Narratives of Home, Displacement and Resettlement* (Delhi: Pearson Longman, 2008). Recently, she has co-edited (with Ajaya K. Sahoo) a special issue of the *South Asian Diaspora* on the 'Journey of the Komagata Maru: National, Transnational, Diasporic'.

Fiona-Katharina Seiger received her PhD in Sociology from the National University of Singapore in 2014. She recently completed her post-doctoral fellowship at the Center for Southeast Asian Studies, Kyoto University in Japan. Her work focuses on Japanese-Filipino Children in the Philippines and their claims for paternal acknowledgment and Japanese nationality. Her research interests lie in the area of migration studies, with a particular focus on notions of belonging and identity politics, as well as on young migrants.

Alexandra Shaitan is a Doctoral student at Birkbeck, University of London investigating mixed-race identity in the context of Japan. She is currently employed as an Adjunct English Lecturer at the Gakushuin University, Tokyo, Japan.

Paul Spickard teaches history, Black studies, and Asian American studies at the University of California, Santa Barbara. He has taught at 15 universities in the United States and abroad. He is author/editor of 19 books and over 80 articles on race, mixed race, and related topics, including: *Race in Mind* (University of Notre Dame Press, 2015); *Global Mixed Race* (New York University Press, 2014); *Almost All Aliens: Immigration, Race and Colonialism in American History and Identity* (Routledge, 2007); *Is Lighter Better? Skin-Tone Discrimination among Asian Americans* (Rowman and Littlefield, 2007); and *Mixed Blood: Intermarriage and Ethnic Identity in 20th-Century America* (University of Wisconsin Press, 1989).

Danau Tanu is an Endeavour Research Fellow and the Commissioning Editor of Inside Indonesia. She has a PhD from the University of Western Australia in Anthropology and Asian Studies. Danau has published journal articles and chapters on issues of migration, identity, youth, global citizenship, international education and soft-diplomacy, as well as on the irregular migration of asylum seekers and refugees in Asia. She has also worked as a public relations consultant for the Embassy of Japan in Indonesia and Mission of Japan to ASEAN. Danau will publish her monograph in 2017 based on her dissertation 'Unpacking "Third Culture Kids": The Transnational Lives of Young People at an International School in Indonesia'.

Emma J. Teng is the T.T. and Wei Fong Chao Professor of Asian Civilizations at MIT, with a dual appointment on the Global Studies and Languages, and History Faculties. Teng earned her PhD in East Asian Languages and Civilizations at Harvard University. Her publications include: *Taiwan's Imagined Geography: Chinese Colonial Travel Writing and Pictures, 1683–1895* (2004); *Eurasian: Mixed Identities in the United States, China and Hong Kong, 1842–1943* (2013); and articles in both US and international academic journals. In 2013, Teng was named a MacVicar Faculty Fellow for her contributions to undergraduate teaching at MIT. Continuing her trajectory of work on migration, diaspora, and transculturation, her current projects include an exhibit on the early history (1877–1931) of Chinese students at MIT, and a study of pioneering Chinese culinary author, Buwei Yang Chao (1889–1981).

Acknowledgements

The editors and authors would like to thank all participants in the research projects that formed the basis of the various chapters. Their input was invaluable, and provided us with fascinating, rich data about mixed race and identity in Asia.

The editors also thank their families, for their patience and support.

Introduction
Mixed race in Asia

Zarine L. Rocha and Farida Fozdar

Race, ethnicity, identity and belonging are key topics of academic interest. Identity remains a complicated field of study, connecting micro processes of personal negotiation with macro-level institutions and structures at national, and supranational, levels. Research into identity and race has been further complicated over the past decades, as the idea of 'mixed race'[1] has been increasingly recognized and thus included in academic and policy debates. Processes of globalization have increased human mobility, bringing into contact peoples of different cultural and racial backgrounds, and drawing attention to the increasing numbers of individuals of mixed heritage. Combined with historical processes of colonization, mobility and change, mixed race is now a particularly important topic for scholars of identity, multiculturalism and social cohesion in all diverse, and not-so-diverse, societies.

Mixed-race identities have been the subject of growing interest, both popular and scholarly, over the past three decades. In many multicultural societies, increasing numbers of people of complex ancestries are identifying themselves outside of traditional racial categories, challenging both historical systems of classification and established sociological understandings of 'race'. However, the vast majority of the research has focused on 'Western' societies, particularly the United Kingdom (UK) and the United States of America (US), and within these countries, on black/white mixes. Works such as *Global Mixed Race* (King-O'Riain *et al.*, 2014) and *International Perspectives on Racial and Ethnic Mixing* (Edwards *et al.*, 2012) have sought to take the focus off these key players, and to consider the different experiences of being mixed around the world. However, both volumes lack contributions on mixed race in Asia. This huge section of the world's population remains relatively unexamined, leaving a significant proportion of diverse, intermingling populations unstudied.

This book seeks to reorient, or at least extend, the field of study to look directly at Asia. Race, mixed race and identity are topics that are particularly salient for Asian societies, nations with great diversity in terms of histories, ethnic groups, and patterns of migration and change. Research looking specifically at the meanings of mixedness in Asia is rare, with much work reinforcing the bias towards Western research by focusing on mixed Asian identities in other contexts, particularly North America (see, for example, Chang, 2015; Williams-León and

Nakashima, 2001). This volume, in contrast, looks specifically at mixed race in a range of national contexts in Asia, exploring both the past and the present. The thematic range of the chapters is broad, covering the complexity of lived mixed-race experiences, the structural forces of particular colonial and post-colonial environments and political regimes, and historical influences on contemporary identities and cultural expressions of mixedness. Issues around transmigration, multiculturalism, cosmopolitanism, state classification and gender are also discussed, as well as the ways that these interact with each other.

This introductory chapter lays out the key issues explored in the book. After considering definitions of race and ethnicity, the introduction puts the experiences of mixed race in Asia into a global context, while also examining the unique features of the Asian region in generating different experiences of racial mixing. It draws out the intersections between race and power that often accompany colonial pasts, and questions the assumption that race and heritage are understood in the same way across the world. In engaging with international theorizing around mixed race, this introduction highlights the particular importance of the Asian region in enriching current theoretical approaches. It offers a brief summary of the unique geographic, cultural and historical contexts of the various countries, as each chapter draws out the ways in which these factors have influenced the development of mixed race identities, opportunities and challenges.

Race, ethnicity and mixed race

Understanding mixed race requires engagement with the concept of race itself: recognizing both the constructed nature of race and its continued social importance in everyday life. Within the social sciences, race is frequently understood as socially and politically constructed: a way to organize the population along lines of phenotype and ancestry, fundamentally linked to personal and social qualities and intrinsic worth (Spickard, 1992; Winant, 2000, 2001). Historically, European racial theory emphasized purity and blood descent as a means to stratify society and disempower certain groups (Perkins, 2005; Brace, 2005; Parker and Song, 2001; Ali, 2012). Different discourses around race and heritage also developed outside of Europe and North America, as several of the chapters in this book show. In nineteenth-century China, for example, notions of patrilineal descent, lineage and blood fed into an influential discourse of racialized belonging and national identity, with widespread impacts in the region (Dikotter, 1992, 1996, 1997).

Despite the discrediting of Western biological theories of race following World War II (UNESCO, 1951; Lewontin, 1972; American Anthropological Association, 1998;), the assumptions behind these understandings of race lingered (Guillaumin, 1995). The practical power of race remains, and continues to structure social and political institutions and everyday interactions, particularly in post-colonial societies (Omi and Winant, 1994). The diverse hierarchies, oppressions and identities which rely on racially-based understandings of the world remain salient, and it is this interdependency which underpins the contemporary strength of race in many parts of the world (Gilroy, 2004).

In an attempt to move away from the history and power of race, some researchers and policymakers have rejected its use in social analysis.[2] Ethnicity is used instead, aiming to describe the positive aspects of a voluntary group identity, rather than the negative aspects of race as ascribed (Nagel, 1994; Weber, 1996), and focusing more on culture than phenotypical features. However, although analytical distinctions can promote the positive and dynamic aspects of ethnicity as a group identity, the lines between race and ethnicity are blurred and shifting (Gunew, 2004; Song, 2001, 2003). Both categories are socially constructed (see Spickard, 1992), and, in reality, each relies on a combination of external and internal classifications and identification. The concepts of mixed-race and mixed-ethnic identity highlight these contradictions. Mixedness provides an important lens through which to view and understand existing racial paradigms and notions of ethnic belonging, illuminating the everyday permeability of racial and ethnic boundaries.

The idea of racial mixing[3] is not new. However, reflecting the legacies of racial hierarchies and inequalities of power, the children of interracial relationships have historically been either ignored, absorbed into singular groupings, or seen in a particularly negative light (Shih and Sanchez, 2005; King O'Riain *et al.*, 2014): norms, and sometimes laws, around miscegenation were common in many places. More recently, in many diverse societies, increasing numbers of people have begun to identify with more than one racial or ethnic group, positioning themselves outside of traditional categories. It is this flexible identification of these new generations which is markedly different, and such fluidity is increasingly recognized at the state level, with a number of countries now including mixed race identifications in racial classificatory frameworks.[4] However, attempts to recognize or assert mixed identities have frequently been met with institutional resistance and social resentment. Notions of racial purity, historically strong but waning, continue to generate imperatives to identify solely as a member of one racial category or another. While social norms around racial purity are changing, and indeed mixedness is valorized in some contexts, there remains a level of suspicion of racial miscegenation across many countries in both Asia and the West, associated with strong racial hierarchies with colonial and cultural inflections.

Research on mixed race has a long and varied history. It has shifted from early pathologies of 'mixed blood' and the 'marginal man', through mid-century models of 'correct' racial identity development, to the current Western-centric plethora of multiracial research, autobiography and even advocacy. The most recent wave of research is notably interdisciplinary, with perspectives from psychology, sociology, geography, political science, history, cultural studies and social work providing a diverse set of theoretical frameworks and experiences (see, for example, Root, 1996; Parker and Song, 2001; Spickard, 2001; Rockquemore *et al.*, 2009; Edwards *et al.*, 2012; King-O'Riain *et al.*, 2014; Mahtani, 2014; McGavin and Fozdar, 2017). Drawing on this intellectual heritage, in the current international literature, people of mixed race are often represented as either 'marginal' individuals, the embodiments of cultural and psychological tensions, or alternatively as harbingers of an integrated, post-racial, cosmopolitan world (Edwards *et al.*, 2012). Theoretical approaches to mixed race tend to be grounded in the idea of difference, setting apart mixed identities and experiences: pathologized as the worst of both worlds, or celebrated as the best of both (Haritaworn, 2009; Nakashima, 1992).

Such dichotomies ignore the complex realities of the lived experience of being mixed. These can include 'passing' as a member of one or another group, seeing oneself as 'multiracial', dealing with the challenges of embracing a cultural identity not reflected in one's embodied reality, and so on (see Jones, 2011; Paradies, 2006; Perkins, 2007; Song and Aspinall, 2012). It is also vital to recognize that these lived experiences of being 'mixed' are strongly influenced by the political and social contexts in which individuals find themselves (Luke and Luke, 1999; Song, 2003). The changing meanings of mixed race across time provide key insights into the sociological concepts of race and ethnicity, as well as how these relate to personal experiences of identity and belonging. Within increasingly multicultural and mixed populations, identities which transcend racial boundaries reveal the weaknesses of classification structures, and the blurred edges of ethnic and racial groups, particularly in the face of dynamic social change (Parker and Song, 2001).

Mixed race remains a difficult category for academic study. Some frame it as self-evident, others as problematic. Some see it as a dangerous fabrication, given that race itself has been soundly disproved as a scientific concept, arguing that racial categories should be dispensed with entirely (see Gilroy, 1998; Zack, 1993, 1995). Others argue that because of its wide use and very real effects, mixed race must be acknowledged as a social reality. This highlights a key contradiction in the field: researchers seek to make sense of *what it means to be mixed*, without reifying the idea that separate races *exist to be mixed*. Hence, research on mixed race is often contradictory, given different histories of racialized oppression and the inconsistencies of contemporary theories of race (Rockquemore *et al.*, 2009). Theories of mixed race do not always match individual and social understandings, often leading to dissonance between theoretical frameworks, state conceptualizations, popular understandings, and individual experiences.

What's in a name? Classificatory systems and terminology

Histories of classification, contemporary naming practices and self-identification generate a range of terminologies that provide interesting insights into the ways in which race and mixed race are understood. Such categorization, in both Asia and the West, is highly contextualized, and reflects past racial ideology, colonial legacies of measurement (Hirschman, 1986) and current forms of racialization (Bonilla-Silva, 2000), often treating race as an objective characteristic to be reported (Morning, 2008). Classification is particularly significant for individuals of mixed descent, as the available racial categories rarely match the complexity of the lived identities of individuals. This lack of symbolic recognition can have significant effects, and can even work to erase 'mixedness' as a legitimate identity claim (Teng, 2010).

Classification has developed in different ways around the world. Britain measures ethnicity rather than race, and recently included 'mixed ethnicity' as a category in the census (Aspinall, 2003). Brazil classifies individuals by colour: from white and yellow to brown and black (preto, pardo, amarelo and branco): categories which change according to socio-economic status (Telles and Lim, 1998). New Zealand has allowed the selection of multiple ethnic groups on the census for several decades, recognizing the fluidity and multiplicity of identities (Callister, 2004). A strong racial ideology can be seen in the American context, both in the recent shift towards the selection of multiple racial groups on the census, and in advocacy for a multiracial category (Snipp, 2003).

In Asia, Singapore has structured much social policy around racial classification, as defined by the Chinese–Malay–Indian–Other (CMIO) system, originally designed along gendered, patrilineal lines (Chua, 2003). Malaysia uses a similar system, with Malay taking first place in the hierarchy, and with the added complication of defining *Bumiputra* status (see Lim, Chapter 7). Racial categories in India owe much to British colonialism and European racial thinking, with some groups designated by the colonizers as 'martial races' – of stronger and more noble stock (see Roy, Chapter 12). Race is approached from a different angle in Korea and Japan, which are often perceived as less diverse, and where national identity, ethnic belonging and ancestry are closely intertwined (see Park (Chapter 4), Seiger (Chapter 6) and Shaitan and McEntee-Atalianis (Chapter 5)). Race in China has a complicated history, and is related in intricate ways to particular understandings of blood and lineage (see Teng (Chapter 1) and Clayton (Chapter 2)).

Worldwide, there are a range of different terms used to refer to those of mixed race, and there is no general consensus on which is most appropriate (Aspinall, 2009; Ifekwunigwe, 2004). Terms such as 'mixed race', 'multiracial' and 'biracial' are frequently used in North America, while in the UK 'mixed ethnicity' or 'mixed heritage' are more common (colloquial, and often derogatory, terms are also plentiful in both contexts) (Aspinall, 2003, 2009). In Asia, terminology is even more diverse, often reflecting specific histories of intermixing or colonial hierarchies of power: Eurasian in Singapore, China and Malaysia, *Hunxue* in China, *Métis* in Vietnam, Indos in Indonesia (a term with multiple meanings in contemporary discourse), *Damunhwa* and *Honhyeol* in Korea, Anglo-Indian in India, Chindian and Peranakan in Malaysia, *haafu* (and 'double') in Japan. These terms are discussed in detail in the chapters that follow. Each of the terms carries with it historical and theoretical assumptions, reinforcing ideas of binary racialization and the purity of race, imputing identities to heritage, or even focusing on the concept of 'mixed' as confused, in-between and somehow less than whole.

Mixed race in Asia

While research on mixed race is increasing in many parts of the world, work in Asia has lagged behind. This book begins to fill this gap, with chapters exploring dilemmas around race, mixed race, identity and classification in a wide selection of countries from the Asian region. Asia is an area unique in its diversity of cultures, ethnicities, languages and histories, with rich histories and contemporary experiences of mixed race. A focus on this region highlights how previous understandings of race and belonging may not be applicable in all contexts, and demonstrates that theories derived primarily in Western contexts may not necessarily be generalizable across the world.

Much previous work which touches on race, ethnicity and mixed race in Asia has a historical dimension. This includes histories of Anglo-Indians (Blunt, 2002, 2005), discussions of mixed race and gender (Jayawardena, 2007), analyses of race and colonialism (Pomfret, 2009), the history of the construction of "Eurasian" in Singapore (Pereira, 1997), and explorations of racial discourse in China (Dikotter, 1992, 1996, 1997). Contemporary work includes examinations of mixed identities for young people in Japan (Burkhardt, 1983; Murphy-Shigematsu, 2001; Oikawa and Yoshida, 2007), Anglo-Indian identity today (James, 2003), and photographic essays about Eurasian identity in South East Asia (Zimmern, 2010). Older work includes Hirschman's seminal work on colonialism, population management and race in Singapore and Malaysia (Hirschman, 1986, 1987), van der Veur's study of Eurasians in Indonesia (van der Veur, 1968), and smaller studies such as Lamson's, looking at Eurasian identity in Shanghai (Lamson, 1936). These contributions all present fascinating insights into the history of race and mixed race in the region, but often remain disconnected from contemporary theorizing.

In many countries in Asia, racial, ethnic and cultural mixing has a long and fascinating history, and narratives around mixed race have developed in vastly different ways. From established collective identities such as Anglo-Indians in India (Blunt, 2005), Eurasians in Singapore (Pereira, 1997) and Peranakans in Southeast Asia (Tan, 1993), to newer identities such as *haafus* in Japan (Reicheneker, 2011), individuals of mixed heritage have diverse experiences across the region. These experiences have been shaped by a range of historical circumstances (colonial regimes, military occupations, or more peaceful intercultural engagements), political contexts (monarchies, democracies, authoritarian dynasties), and by the type of mixedness, as well as different levels of political, cultural and social acceptance.

In a number of countries, including India, Singapore and Malaysia, the privileging of certain groups by colonial authorities has carried down through generations, offering greater opportunities for those from some mixed backgrounds, as opposed to others. Classification systems feed into this privileging, as do gender hierarchies. Those who have benefited from these structures have greater opportunities for transmigration and the development of cosmopolitan identifications. However, other mixes, such as Chinese/Indian 'Chindians' in Malaysia, challenge the presumption that it is whiteness alone (even partial whiteness) that brings power. On the other hand, different forms of 'purity' are desired in countries such as Japan, China and Korea, illustrating distinct historical legacies, and potentially leading to the marginalisation of those of mixed backgrounds. Some mixed groups have established names and even some form of institutional organization (including Eurasians in Singapore, *haafus* in Japan and Anglo-Indians in India), while others have not, generating different degrees of collective identification and solidarity (such as identification through NGO (non-profit organization) involvement, as in the Philippines). The chapters in this book attempt to tease out these connections, offering insights into mixed race at both individual and structural levels.

Contributors come from a wide range of backgrounds, disciplines and career stages. We sought to include as many contributors from Asia as possible, and we found scholars of Asia from all over the world. Unintentionally, we have put together a collection authored solely by women, an interesting reflection of those working in the field. Some authors are of mixed descent themselves, some are from the national context about which they are writing, and others are external observers, with a great deal of knowledge about their country of specialization. The editors of the volume are of mixed descent themselves: coincidentally, both of mixed Indian and European parentage, and both having been born, studied, worked and lived in the Asia-Pacific region.

Chapter overviews

The 14 chapters in this book cover a wide range of countries, which each have diverse histories in relation to nation-building and forms of belonging. Each chapter draws out the ways in which unique geographic, historical, cultural and political contexts have influenced the development of mixed-race identities, and have shaped the contemporary opportunities and challenges in each setting. While many take a nationwide approach, a number focus on much more local contexts (town or region specific), offering a counterpoint to the methodological nationalism that often characterizes studies of mixed race. Different disciplines and methodologies are used, from historical studies and linguistic analysis, to anthropological and sociological explorations of mixed race. For the reader's convenience, these chapters are divided geographically, rather than thematically, highlighting the thematic overlaps between country case studies.

The first section focuses on mixed race in China and Vietnam, and has a significant historical dimension. Teng's paper looks at the history of the founding of the Eurasian School in Shanghai in the late nineteenth century, and the discourses surrounding the 'Eurasian problem' in China during this time. It explores the tension between notions of hybrid degeneracy and hybrid vigour in representations of the Chinese Eurasian as an embodiment of East–West union. Clayton's paper brings the focus forward, looking at *hunxue jiating*, or mixed-blood households, in contemporary China. She uses Critical Mixed-Race Theory to explore the relationship between the media and how processes of globalization and immigration are sparking reconceptualizations of who counts as Chinese, and why, in mainland China today. Importantly, she argues that the Chinese notion of *hunxue* does not map easily on to the concept of mixed race, highlighting a key contextual difference and significantly contributing to the theoretical development of the concept. Firpo's chapter on Vietnam looks both backwards and forwards, starting with the colonial legacy of mixed race of *métis* children, and the ways in which these children were separated from their mothers or ostracized as children of the colonizers. She explores the historical context in which four children were born and raised, and their experiences of living in France after decolonization or remaining in Vietnam.

The second section looks at experiences in South Korea and Japan, two countries with national narratives focusing on homogeneity, at least historically. Park focuses on developing bilingualism in the largely monolingual society of Korea, highlighting key issues of socioeconomic status, gender roles, migration and power. She draws out the challenges of the multicultural family in the face of significant discrimination, particularly the experiences of mothers, and explores the strategies used to resist derogatory perceptions of heritage and to promote bilingualism. The concept of '*haafu*' identity in Japan is presented by Shaitan and McEntee-Atalianis, looking at how discourses around mixedness affect the image of Japan as a homogeneous and/or monoethnic race/society. This chapter explores the marginalization experienced by individuals of mixed descent, who, despite their native linguistic and cultural repertoires, are often treated as *gaijin* (foreigners). Seiger's chapter looks at migrant Japanese-Filipino youth, their relationships with international NGO advocacy, and the ways in which context affects identification. Born to Filipino mothers and Japanese fathers, and largely deemed Japanese in the Philippines, Japanese-Filipino youth experience complicated identifications upon arrival in their 'other homeland': Japan. Using these experiences, she teases out ideas of what makes a person Japanese, as those considered 'Japanese' in the Philippines do not correspond to ideas and ideals of Japaneseness in Japan.

Section three groups together Malaysia and Singapore, both ex-British colonies located on the Malay Peninsula. These two countries have an interesting shared history, and significant differences in their contemporary trajectories of nation-building. Both are diverse and multicultural, with significant histories of intermixing, and each uses race and ethnicity as ways to manage the population. Lim provides a useful overview of race, ethnicity and 'mixed race' in Malaysia, with background on the politicization and institutionalization of 'race' in the Malaysian context. She looks at how 'mixed' Malaysians negotiate their ethnic identity, and how this differs from Malaysians who regard themselves as 'pure' Malay, Indian or Chinese. Individuals of Chinese/Indian descent in Malaysia, Chindians, are the focus of Chandran's chapter, which emphasizes the colonial history and the lack of official recognition given to mixed groups. It looks at the identity work carried out by these individuals, as they develop a sense of identity within a racially structured society. Pue looks at yet another mixed group in Malaysia, the Peranakan Chinese in Kelantan. This group is notable for its ethnic diversity in descent, and the chapter draws out the historical consequences of interethnic interaction, the long-term impacts of resinicization and the ways in which enacted ethnicity can shift over time. Eurasian ethnicity in Singapore is then explored by Rocha in the following chapter. She looks at the official and social category of Eurasian, examining how discourses of race and mixed race have developed over time in colonial and post-colonial Singapore. The chapter draws out how the label of Eurasian has developed and changed over time, providing an official space for mixedness, yet masking much complexity in everyday life.

Section four looks at India and Indonesia; very different countries with different colonial experiences. The first chapter explores the identities of Anglo-Indians, suggesting that although Anglo-Indian identity is fluid and changing, it is not in a state of crisis. Andrews draws out what it means for a group to experience an identity crisis, while arguing that Anglo-Indians form a strong and distinct ethnic group in India. Roy then focuses on a case study of Anglo-Indian experiences in Kharagpur, an Indian railway town, examining what it means to be Anglo-Indian in postcolonial India. She looks at how the performance of Britishness through sports, music, dancing, and other forms of sociality, not only accorded colonial Anglo-Indians honorary Britishness, but also contributed to a specifically Anglo-Indian subjectivity. The final two chapters look at mixed race in Indonesia, from very different perspectives. The chapter by Hewett presents a historical overview of mixing in Indonesia, focusing on the 1930s to the present. It looks at the colonial privileging of mixedness, and the developing identity politics around belonging and national identity in the postcolonial era. Tanu looks at the contemporary experience of being mixed race in an international school in Indonesia, focusing on transnational youth of mixed descent, demonstrating the impact of class and multiple migration experiences on the development of identity. She finds that students' identifications are often ambiguous and situational, highlighting how their experiences bring into relief the colonial discourse that continues to permeate even the way we define being 'international'.

Mixed race in Asia and the world

A number of themes of significance arise from these chapters, both drawing and building on existing theorizing around mixed race. For a volume with a strong geographical focus, context is shown to be crucial. Mixed race does not mean the same thing, in terms of histories, experiences or identities, across the world. The importance of socio-political structures and historical context is highlighted repeatedly throughout the case studies. The strength of the colonial past, in Singapore, Malaysia, Vietnam, China and India, illustrates the powerful legacies of colonial categories and racial theories. Colonial boundaries in effect crystallized lines to be crossed, giving rise to a host of new identities and understandings of belonging.

The effects of colonialism in the region can thus be mapped through investigations of mixed race, exploring the racial hierarchies and differential access to power based on the physical and cultural capital associated with mixedness. As well as the more obvious structural and socio-political legacies, post-colonial studies should therefore, we argue, also focus on racial legacies. Several chapters illustrate the ways in which regime change has had fundamental effects on the status of those of mixed race, and on classification, with concomitant effects on life chances and recognition, such as for the Anglo-Indians in India, and the *Métis* in Vietnam. In both colonial and non-colonial contexts, hierarchies of race exist, and persist. Histories of conflict and oppression have at times seen those of mixed backgrounds the targets of categorical prejudices and sanctions, such as in Indonesia.

However, this is also the case for those societies which historically have been largely homogenous, or at least have constructed a sense of their national identity as homogenous and monocultural. Japan and Korea are the most obvious examples, where there is a conflation of national identity and descent, leaving those of mixed backgrounds not only racially but nationally suspect. While mixed race is often examined against a background of multiculturalism, these two cases highlight the particular difficulties and negotiations required in less diverse contexts. Phenotype and language are key factors here, being even more visible in countries where sameness is strongly emphasized. This adds an important dimension to the existing literature, extending the reach of current theories by factoring in the diversity and social history of the national context.

Transnational identities also add a further dimension to understanding mixed race, illustrating how identities and histories can both cross and encompass national boundaries and types of citizenship. Stories of students at an international school in Indonesia, and narratives of belonging as Japanese Filipinos, bring this dynamic to the fore, showing how hierarchies of race and citizenship can overlap and disconnect. Histories of mobility in the region generate ongoing connections, often across multiple nations, again challenging the methodological nationalism inherent in some studies of mixedness.

This collection also highlights how intersectionality affects the lived experiences of individuals. All chapters recognize that hierarchies of colour, but also gender and class, feed into access to power and significantly influence perceptions and opportunities.

Cultural factors are equally important. For example, each country has its own, often unique, understandings of race/blood/heritage, often embedded in language. Exploring mixedness in these different contexts highlights the ways in which current work on mixed race is fundamentally grounded in Western concepts of race. Clayton's chapter on China particularly illustrates these linguistic and cultural differences in understandings of the essence of what exactly is being mixed: blood, life essence, or heritage? Such nuances significantly affect the ways in which mixedness is understood and experienced, both for individuals and for the wider societies. Roy's discussion of Anglo-Indians highlights race as performative for identities drawing on Britishness in India, while Lim, Chandran and Pue all tease out the ways in which race and belonging are played out through actions and deliberate negotiation in Malaysia.

Introduction 11

The role of language, custom and culture is also a significant feature influencing the degree of 'visibility' of those of mixed backgrounds – those who share languages and customs tend to be seen as less different compared to those who do not. Language is an important cultural marker, and many papers discuss the effects of linguistic proficiency (or lack thereof) on belonging. Does an individual need to speak multiple languages to be authentically mixed race? The chapters on Japan highlight the importance of language in everyday interaction and identity construction, while Park on Korea looks at language from the perspective of the mother, indicating that linguistic knowledge is a powerful tool in creating a sense of belonging, or deliberately fostering a more singular identity. Clayton's discussion of the linguistic nuances of race and blood in China takes this further, illustrating that the construction of the language itself can influence what it means to be mixed.

An interesting feature of some Asian countries is that populations of mixed race descent have formed their own communities, yet these communities are inclusive in different ways, and to different ends. Many chapters highlight what appears to be the development of 'new' ethnic identities, based around a history of mixedness. For Eurasians, Anglo-Indians and Peranakans, what began as a way to describe and classify hybridity and mixedness has become a new ethnic label in and of itself, with specific, recognizable cultural traits and practices which can be passed down through generations. In the case of Eurasians in Singapore (and to some degree, Malaysia), Eurasian is both an historical and a contemporary label for mixed race, with 'new' and 'old' Eurasians both experiencing commonality in ancestry and significant differences in culture and feelings of belonging. For Anglo-Indians, the term is very much historically based, and there are not 'new' community members in the same way – rather, it is an ethnicity which can be inherited. This perhaps reflects the different legacies of colonialism across Asia, highlighting the strength of the post-colonial construction of identities. It is as yet unclear what social and political factors generate the development of mixed race communities with shared physical and cultural features, as opposed to mixedness remaining largely an individual identification. However, these chapters seem to suggest that a strong base of racial categorization, together with an emphasis on racial grouping as linked to practical (sometimes material) outcomes (as in Malaysia, Singapore and India, as well as in the Philippines) lends itself to the formation of institutionalized groups around mixedness.

Most importantly, this volume illustrates the immense diversity in contexts, experiences and histories in the Asian region, and the ways in which race, ethnicity, mixedness and belonging play out in similar and in different ways. Each chapter presents a new starting point from which to approach mixed identities, and shows clearly how different historical contexts have led to situations of both continuity and change around mixedness. Identities can be overarching and transnational, or specific and regionalized, such as the Peranakans, Chindians and Indos. The case studies illustrate the complexity of these different mixes, and highlight that there are alternative ways to be mixed and multicultural. An identity based around multiplicity does not necessarily involve conflict and crisis.

Conclusion

Looking at mixed race in the Asian region is key to understanding race and mixedness from a more comprehensive perspective. Moving away from privileging Western experiences and notions of belonging, this volume draws on this richness of diversities and histories, to bolster the field of mixed race studies.

We hope that this book is the first of many projects looking at mixed race and different ways to belong across the globe. There remains much left to explore: different national contexts in Asia and around the world, more detailed analyses of classificatory systems and linguistic nuances around mixedness, the contexts in which mixed communities form and flourish, the relationship between mixed race and cultural formations, and further theorizing based around non-Western concepts of race, ethnicity, ancestry and belonging.

Notes

1 From this point, we do not use scare quotes around the term mixed race. Recognising race, like class, gender, sexuality and so on, is a social construct, and mixed race likewise, we also recognize that race and mixedness have real social effects, and are engaged with by social actors in the process of interaction. We see no value in signalling the social construction of race and mixed race over other constructs.
2 This can be seen in research from the US and many parts of Asia, which uses race, compared with research from New Zealand, Australia and the UK, which tends to use ethnicity when discussing similar concepts and situations.
3 The idea of race and racial mixing is used cautiously, describing race as socially constructed, and racial mixing based on social concepts of difference.
4 Notably, in the Western context, the US and UK sought to incorporate mixed identities in the 2000/2001 census round.

Bibliography

Ali, S. (2012). 'Situating Mixed Race Politics'. In Rosalind Edwards, Suki Ali, Chamion Caballero and Miri Song (eds), *International Perspectives on Racial and Ethnic Mixedness and Mixing*. London: Routledge, pp. 169–183.

American Anthropological Association. (1998). 'American Anthropological Association Statement on Race'. Available at: www.aaanet.org/stmts/racepp.htm (accessed: 10 December 2016).

Aspinall, P. (2003). 'The Conceptualisation and Categorisation of Mixed Race/Ethnicity in Britain and North America: Identity Options and the Role of the State'. *International Journal of Intercultural Relations* 27, pp. 269–296.

Aspinall, P. (2009). '"Mixed Race", "Mixed Origins" or What?: Generic Terminology for the Multiple Racial/Ethnic Group Population'. *Anthropology Today* 25(2), pp. 3–8.

Blunt, A. (2002). '"Land of our Mothers": Home, Identity, and Nationality for Anglo-Indians in British India, 1919–1947'. *History Workshop Journal* 54, pp. 49–72.

Blunt, A. (2005). *Domicile and Diaspora: Anglo-Indian Women and the Spatial Politics of Home*. Malden, MA: Blackwell Publishing.

Bonilla-Silva, E. (2000). '"This is a White Country": The Racial Ideology of the Western Nations of the World-System'. *Sociological Inquiry* 70(2), pp. 188–214.

Brace, C. (2005). *'Race' is a Four-Letter Word: The Genesis of the Concept.* Oxford: Oxford University Press.

Burkhardt, W. R. (1983). 'Institutional Barriers, Marginality, and Adaptation Among the American-Japanese Mixed Bloods in Japan'. *The Journal of Asian Studies* 42(3), pp. 519–544.

Callister, P. (2004). 'Ethnicity Measures, Intermarriage and Social Policy'. *Social Policy Journal of New Zealand* 23, pp. 109–140.

Chang, S. H. (2015). *Raising Mixed Race: Multiracial Asian Children in a Post-Racial World.* London: Routledge.

Chua, B. H. (2003). 'Multiculturalism in Singapore: An Instrument of Social Control'. *Race and Class* 44(3), pp. 58–77.

Dikotter, F. (1992). *The Discourse of Race in Modern China.* London: Hurst & Company.

Dikotter, F. (1996). 'Culture, "Race" and Nation: The Formation of National Identity in Twentieth Century China'. *Journal of International Affairs* 49(2), pp. 590–605.

Dikotter, F. (1997). 'Racial Discourse in China: Continuities and Permutations'. In *The Construction of Racial Identities in China and Japan*, Frank Dikotter (ed.). Honolulu: University of Hawai'i Press, pp. 12–33.

Edwards, R., Ali, S., Caballero, C., and Song, M. (eds) (2012). *International Perspectives on Racial and Ethnic Mixedness and Mixing.* London: Routledge.

Gilroy, P. (1998). 'Race Ends Here'. *Ethnic and Racial Studies* 21(5), pp. 838–847.

Gilroy, P. (2004). *After Empire: Melancholia or Convivial Culture?* Oxfordshire: Routledge.

Guillaumin, C. (1995). *Racism, Sexism, Power, and Ideology.* London: Routledge.

Gunew, S. (2004). *Haunted Nations: The Colonial Dimensions of Multiculturalisms.* London: Routledge.

Haritaworn, J. (2009). 'Hybrid Border-Crossers? Towards a Radical Socialisation of "Mixed Race"'. *Journal of Ethnic and Migration Studies* 35(1), pp. 115–132.

Hirschman, C. (1986). 'The Making of Race in Colonial Malaya: Political Economy and Racial Ideology'. *Sociological Forum* 1(2) pp. 330–361.

Hirschman, C. (1987). 'The Meaning and Measurement of Ethnicity in Malaysia: An Analysis of Census Classifications'. *The Journal of Asian Studies* 46(3), pp. 555–582.

Ifekwunigwe, J. O. (2004). 'Notes on Terminology'. In *'Mixed Race' Studies: A Reader.* London: Routledge, pp. xix–xxii.

James, S. P. (2003). 'The Anglo-Indians: Aspirations for Whiteness and the Dilemma of Identity'. *Counterpoints* 3(1), pp. 50–60.

Jayawardena, K. (2007). *Erasure of the Euro-Asian: Recovering Early Radicalism and Feminism in South Asia.* Colombo: Social Scientists' Association.

Jones, J. A. (2011). 'Who Are We? Producing Group Identity Through Everyday Practices of Conflict and Discourse'. *Sociological Perspectives* 54(2), pp. 139–161.

King-O'Riain, R. C., Small, S., Mahtani, M., Song, M., and Spickard, P. (eds) (2014). *Global Mixed Race.* New York: NYU Press.

Lamson, H. D. (1936). 'The Eurasian in Shanghai'. *The American Journal of Sociology* 41(5), pp. 642–648.

Lewontin, R. C. (1972). 'The Apportionment of Human Diversity'. *Evolutionary Biology* 6, pp. 381–398.

Luke, A., and Luke, C. (1999). 'Theorizing Interracial Families and Hybrid Identity: An Australian Perspective'. *Educational Theory* 49(2), pp. 223–249.

Mahtani, M. (2014). *Mixed Race Amnesia: Resisting the Romanticization of Multi-raciality.* Vancouver: UBC Press.

McGavin, K., and Fozdar, F. (eds) (2017 forthcoming) *Mixed Race Identities in Australia, New Zealand and the Pacific Islands*. Abingdon: Routledge.

Morning, A. (2008). 'Ethnic Classification in Global Perspective: A Cross-National Survey of the 2000 Census Round'. *Population Research Policy Review* 27, pp. 239–272.

Murphy-Shigematsu, S. (2001). 'Multiethnic Lives and Monoethnic Myths: American-Japanese Amerasians in Japan'. In Teresa Williams-Leon and Cynthia L. Nakashima (eds), *The Sum of Our Parts: Mixed Heritage Asian Americans*. Philadelphia: Temple University Press, pp. 207–216.

Nagel, Joane. (1994). 'Constructing Ethnicity: Creating and Recreating Ethnic Identity and Culture'. *Social Problems* 41(1), pp. 152–176.

Nakashima, C. L. (1992). 'An Invisible Monster: The Creation and Denial of Mixed-Race People in America'. In *Racially Mixed People in America*, Maria P. P. Root (ed.). Newbury Park: Sage Publications, pp. 162–178.

Oikawa, S., and Yoshida, T. (2007). 'An Identity Based on Being Different: A Focus on Biethnic Individuals in Japan'. *International Journal of Intercultural Relations* 31, pp. 633–653.

Omi, M., and Winant, H. (1994). *Racial Formation in the United States: From the 1960s to the 1990s (Second Edition)*. New York: Routledge.

Paradies, Y. (2006). 'Beyond Black and White: Essentialism, Hybridity and Indigeneity'. *Journal of Sociology* 42(4), pp. 355–367.

Parker, D., and Song, M. (2001). 'Introduction: Rethinking "Mixed Race"'. In David Parker and Miri Song (eds), *Rethinking 'Mixed Race'*. London: Pluto Press, pp. 1–22.

Pereira, A. (1997). 'The Revitalization of Eurasian Identity in Singapore'. *Southeast Asian Journal of Social Science* 25(2), pp. 7–24.

Perkins, M. (2005). 'Thoroughly Modern Mulatta: Rethinking "Old World" Stereotypes in a "New World" Setting'. *Biography* 28(1), pp. 104–116.

Perkins, M. (2007). 'Visibly Different: Face, Place and Race in Australia'. In Maureen Perkins (ed.), *Visibly Different: Face, Place and Race in Australia*. Bern: Peter Lang, pp. 9–29.

Pomfret, D. M. (2009). 'Raising Eurasia: Race, Class, and Age in French and British Colonies'. *Comparative Studies in Society and History* 51(2), pp. 314–343.

Reicheneker, S. (2011). 'The Marginalization of Afro-Asians in East Asia: Globalization and the Creation of Subculture and Hybrid Identity'. *Global Tides: Pepperdine Journal of International Studies* 5, pp. 1–15.

Rockquemore, K. A., Brunsma, D. L., and Delgado, D. J. (2009). 'Racing to Theory or Retheorizing Race? Understanding the Struggle to Build a Multiracial Identity Theory'. *Journal of Social Issues* 65(1), pp. 13–34.

Root, M. P. P. (ed.) 1996. *The Multiracial Experience: Racial Borders as the New Frontier*. London: Sage.

Shih, M., and Sanchez, D. T. (2005). 'Perspectives and Research on the Positive and Negative Implications of Having Multiple Racial Identities'. *Psychological Bulletin* 131(4), pp. 569–591.

Snipp, C. M. (2003). 'Racial Measurement in the American Census: Past Practices and Implications for the Future'. *Annual Review of Sociology* 29, pp. 563–588.

Song, M. (2001). 'Comparing Minorities' Ethnic Options: Do Asian Americans Possess "More" Ethnic Options than African Americans?' *Ethnicities* 1(1), pp. 57–82.

Song, M. (2003). *Choosing Ethnic Identity*. Cambridge: Polity Press.

Song, M., and Aspinall, P. (2012). 'Is Racial Mismatch a Problem for Young "Mixed Race" People in Britain? The Findings of Qualitative Research'. *Ethnicities* 12(6), pp. 730–753.

Spickard, P. R. (1992). 'The Illogic of American Racial Categories'. In Maria P. P. Root (ed.), *Racially Mixed People in America*. Newbury Park: Sage Publications, pp. 12–23.

Spickard, P. R. (2001). 'The Subject is Mixed Race: The Boom in Biracial Biography'. In David Parker and Miri Song (eds), *Rethinking 'Mixed Race'*. London: Pluto Press, pp. 76–98.

Tan, C. B. (1993). *Chinese Peranakan Heritage in Malaysia and Singapore*. Kuala Lumpur: Fajar Bakti.

Telles, E. E., and Lim, N. (1998). 'Does it Matter Who Answers the Race Question? Racial Classification and Income Inequality in Brazil'. *Demography* 35(4), pp. 465–474.

Teng, E. J. (2010). 'Naming the Subject: Recovering "Euro-Asian" History'. *Journal of Women's History* 22(4), pp. 257–262.

UNESCO. (1951). 'Statement on Race'. Paris: United Nations Educational, Scientific and Cultural Organization.

van der Veur, P. W. (1968). 'The Eurasians of Indonesia: A Problem and Challenge in Colonial History'. *Journal of Southeast Asian History* IX(2), pp. 191–207.

Weber, M. (1996). 'The Origins of Ethnic Groups'. In John Hutchinson and Anthony D. Smith (eds), *Ethnicity*. Oxford: Oxford University Press, pp. 35–40.

Williams-León, T., and Nakashima, C. L. (2001). *The Sum of our Parts: Mixed-heritage Asian Americans*. Philadelphia: Temple University Press.

Winant, H. (2000). 'Race and Race Theory'. *Annual Review of Sociology* 26, pp. 169–185.

Winant, H. (2001). *The World is a Ghetto: Race and Democracy Since World War II*. New York: Basic Books.

Zack, N. (1993). *Race and Mixed Race*. Philadelphia: Temple University Press.

Zack, N. (ed.) (1995). *American Mixed Race: The Culture of Microdiversity*. Lanham, MD: Rowman & Littlefield.

Zimmern, K. (2010). *The Eurasian Face*. Hong Kong: Blacksmith Books.

Part I
China and Vietnam

1 'A class by themselves'
Battles over Eurasian schooling in late-nineteenth-century Shanghai

Emma J. Teng

Introduction

The contemporary multiracial movement in places such as the US and Britain has often focused on the demand for recognition of 'mixed' identities that fall outside of or supersede the dominant monoracial/monoethnic categories, with their roots in binary modes of understanding race. As noted in the introduction to this volume, the new generation's 'flexible identification' is markedly different and is moreover gaining state recognition, with a number of countries now including 'multiracial' or 'mixed' identifications in updated racial classificatory frameworks. Yet, the degree to which recognition of mixed identities actually challenges established structures of racial binaries and dominant notions of racial purity remains an open question. Indeed, historical examples suggest that the mere fact of recognition, in and of itself, cannot be equated with empowerment.

One question taken up by this volume is why recognized collective identities for those of 'mixed' heritage historically emerged in some sites in Asia – Anglo-Indians in India, Eurasians in Singapore, and Peranakans in Southeast Asia – but not in others. Cedric Dover (1937) early on also raised this issue in noting that Sino-European 'half-castes' in colonial Hong Kong largely identified with the Chinese population, but in Shanghai were conversely merging into the 'cosmopolitan' foreign community.[1] These different outcomes suggest the specificity of the socio-political conditions that support collective identities, and prompt us to further query the degree to which such identifications are empowering. How have those of mixed heritage in Asia historically navigated systems of racial classification and hierarchy in order to make claims for rights and recognition? In order to probe these questions, this chapter examines two episodes in the history of schooling for Eurasians in nineteenth-century Shanghai in relation to efforts to define Eurasians as 'a class by themselves'. As this history reveals, institutional recognition of distinct identities for those of mixed heritage does not necessarily lead to empowerment or inclusion, but may actually reinforce their marginalization within established racial structures.

A class by themselves?

In September 1870, advertisements recruiting pupils for a new school in Shanghai's International Concession began to appear in the *North-China Herald*. The notice promised students an education based on the English Home Schools curriculum, Chinese tutoring, and 'maternal care exercised over the manners and habits of the Scholars' (Bonney, 1870, p. 213). Prospective students were advised that European dress and food were preferred, but pupils who wished to maintain their Chinese dress could take their meals at a separate table. Although the advertisement suggested the school was 'for Chinese Children', in fact, it was specifically intended for Eurasians, chiefly defined in this context as the children of European fathers and Asian mothers. The notice soon attracted attention, and on September 19, 1870, the first boarder entered the institution that would become known as Shanghai's 'Eurasian School'.

The school was founded by American missionary Catharina Van Rensselaer Bonney (1817–1891), with the backing of prominent Anglo-American business and missionary figures (Bonney, 1875, pp. 522–523; Teng, 2013, pp. 147–148). The need for such an institution had been discussed for some years within Shanghai's International Settlement, with the *North-China Herald* calling for a solution to an emerging 'problem' – what to do with the growing numbers of Eurasian children, those who could not be sent 'Home' for schooling, but lacked local opportunities other than the 'native' schools. The foreign community had a duty, the newspaper argued, to provide adequate training for these children, lest they be permanently handicapped by their mixed parentage. Such training, the school's founders argued, was best provided in a separate school, as had been done elsewhere in Asia:

> There are many reasons for dealing with Eurasian children as a class by themselves, at least during the earlier years of their education; and it has always been felt that, wherever such children exist in considerable numbers, schools for them are a necessity....
> (First Yearly Report, 1871, p. 772)

Nearly three decades after the school's founding, the issue of Eurasian education once more surfaced as a 'problem' for the settlement, with the perfunctory expulsion of Eurasian pupils from the Shanghai Public School in February 1897. Quite remarkably, given the earlier conviction of the necessity for separate education for Eurasians, the ratepayers of the International Settlement voted overwhelmingly in favour of reinstating their rights to attend this 'high-class' public school. This controversy, dubbed the 'Eurasian battle', made dramatically evident the tension between exclusionary practices and inclusive impulses that Ann Stoler has theorized as one of the fundamental 'tensions of empire', at work in semi-colonial Shanghai (Stoler, 1997, p. 199). It further demonstrates that whereas demographic changes in Shanghai between 1870 and 1897 prompted some expatriates to draw a tighter line against the racially 'mixed', Eurasians

'A class by themselves' 21

nonetheless proved able in this case to defend their claims, largely through the advocacy of powerful white men, undermining attempts to relegate them to the 'Eurasian School'.

Juxtaposing these two episodes in the history of the schooling of Shanghai's Eurasians, this chapter examines evolving Anglo-American discourses on the city's 'Eurasian Problem', and education as an arena for delineating, and re-delineating, their place in the highly fraught racial hierarchy of late-nineteenth-century Shanghai. As David Pomfret has argued, across Asia in European colonies such as Hong Kong, Vietnam, and Singapore, 'European [colonial] elites reworked civilising projects and reimagined racial intermediacy through the lens of childhood' (Pomfret, 2016, p. 276). The struggles over Eurasian schooling in Shanghai demonstrate the parallels in this semi-colonial milieu, where the [hyper] visible emergence of Eurasian children similarly raised 'difficult questions of moral responsibility in empire' (Pomfret, 2016, p. 249). Through an examination of debates on schooling, this chapter aims to elucidate the rhetorical grounds on which the struggle for Eurasian inclusion, in an era of racial exclusiveness, could be waged within the inner circles of power. To use the words of Audre Lorde: is it possible for the master's tools to dismantle the master's house (Lorde, 1984, p. 110)? Whereas Stoler's analysis of the 'tensions of empire' focused on the legal treatment of mixed race in French and Dutch colonies, I seek to understand the dynamic of exclusion/inclusion beyond the strictly juridical arena, and in a setting that was not, strictly-speaking, colonial. I argue that whereas the movement for the Eurasian School built on commonplace stereotypes of Eurasians as objects of rescue – orphans or 'gutter children' – the later Public School controversy demonstrated the successful contestation of these stereotypes in favour of Eurasian 'respectability', and the mobilization of [elite] Eurasian claims through recourse to Anglo-American discourses of rights, justice, fair play, and dependent citizenship. I further contrast the maternalistic discourses evident in advocacy for the Eurasian School with the emphasis on paternal care and affiliation in negotiating a place for Eurasians at Shanghai's Public School.

The founding of Shanghai's Eurasian school

Although the Eurasian population in Shanghai had been expanding since the 1840s, when Shanghai was first established as a Treaty Port, for decades no special provision was made for their schooling. By the late 1860s, however, the *North-China Herald* alerted readers to a looming 'problem' that could be ignored no longer. As an editorial cautioned in 1869: 'One of the most important questions, and one that is daily thrusting itself before us into greater prominence, is that of the position of Eurasians' ('Eurasians', 1869, p. 69). The paper warned that a 'Eurasian Problem', akin to that in India, was on the horizon.

The 'Eurasian Problem' was produced in British India from the 1780s onward as racial hierarchies became increasingly rigid, and the liminality of Eurasians disrupted the notional divide between Europeans and 'natives', colonizers and colonized. Impoverished Eurasians reduced to living like natives, or perhaps compelled to turn to begging, prostitution, or petty crime, were considered a blight on white prestige, and many feared disgruntled Eurasians would become a source of unrest. By the late nineteenth century, anxieties over the Eurasian Problem had spread across Asia, with various local permutations (Dover, 1937; Saada, 2012; Stoler, 1997). As Ann Stoler notes, racial mixing in French Indochina and the Dutch East Indies was 'conceived as a dangerous source of subversion' and 'seen as a threat to white prestige, an embodiment of European degeneration and moral decay' (Stoler, 1997).

As I have argued elsewhere, the 'Eurasian Problem' exposed a fundamental contradiction in the status of Eurasians, who were despised and feared, on one hand, but also desired, needed, and partially privileged, on the other. Insofar as Eurasians embodied the crossing of the colour line, they were regarded as threatening or potentially destabilizing to the racial hierarchies of the era. At the same time, Eurasians were also regarded as indispensable to the degree that they served to *stabilize* imperialist interests by *bridging* racial distance and playing the role of intermediary (Teng, 2013).

Alluding to this intermediary role, the *North-China Herald* conceded that Eurasians in India had partially 'bridged over the gulf between Europeans and natives', but warned that 'their anomalous position between the two races, belonging as it were to neither and in a manner despised by both, has developed a mixed breed, wanting in the best qualities both of Europeans and Hindoos' (Eurasians, 1869, p. 69). The *Herald* thus invoked scientific notions of hybrid degeneracy to cast Eurasians as objects of intervention.

Scientific theories of hybrid degeneration lent legitimacy to colonial representations of Eurasians as biologically, mentally, and morally inferior (Stepan, 1991; Teng, 2013, p. 95; Young, 1995). As Dr H. N. Ridley declared in a paper on the 'Eurasian Problem' in 1895:

> Taking the race as a whole they are weak in body, short-lived, deficient in energy and feeble in morals. Even a little admixture of native blood seems to result in an individual who possesses the bad qualities of both races.
> (Ridley, 1913, p. 54)

In this manner, scientific discourses on hybrid degeneration gave credibility to the long-standing cultural taboos against miscegenation.

Whereas the notion of racial degeneration featured in the *Herald*'s characterization of the 'Eurasian Problem', it primarily identified social, and not biological, factors for their 'stunted growth'. The *Herald* blamed boarding schools placing Eurasians and 'Europeans of pure blood' together for this stunting, as Eurasians were daily reminded of their subordinate status and subjected to the 'depressing stigma of [their] birth'. The only solution was to remove Eurasians from such environments, unleashing their potential for 'perfectly free, unconstrained and manly development' (Eurasians, 1869, p. 70). If an elaborate argument was made to justify the segregation of Eurasians from 'Europeans of pure blood', it was taken for granted that they required rescue from detrimental

Chinese influences. Consigning Eurasians to the care of Chinese mothers and to Chinese schools, the paper argued, was to relinquish 'any prospect of making civilized men and women of them' (Eurasians, 1869, p. 70). Thus, whereas Eurasians were on one hand subjected to segregation and exclusion, the inclusive notion that Eurasians were of 'their own blood' also prompted Europeans to assert a special sense of duty toward them. The paper called on Shanghai's expatriate community to establish a separate school for Eurasians, as the only feasible solution. In keeping with the assumption that China was 'home' for the mixed population, it proposed that Eurasians be civilized through a European education, but also taught Chinese, thereby training them as valuable intermediaries to advance Anglo-American interests: 'we would be raising up an intermediate race as a civilized link between Foreigners and Chinese, and we would have the satisfaction of doing our duty, and of introducing among the Chinese a valuable civilizing influence' (Eurasians, 1869, p. 70). With this idea of a 'civilized link', the problematic 'anomalous position' of Eurasians is transformed into the positive and productive notion of an 'intermediate race' that could bridge 'over [the gulf] that separates the two races'. Yet, such an intermediate race would only be valuable under Western guidance:

> ... is it not well that we should direct the lives of the intermediate race that is rising ... rather than allow them to remain under the almost unbroken influences of native mothers, and the surrounding circumstances of Chinese ignorance and superstition?
>
> (Eurasians, 1869, p. 70)

Appealing to notions of duty and justice, the *Herald* exhorted expatriates to recognize 'half-caste' children fathered by European men as their communal responsibility (Eurasians, 1869, p. 70). As the *Herald* chastized readers, refusing to recognize such children was to 'commit a manifest and grievous injustice towards an increasing race, who have distinct and unimpeachable claims on our sense of duty, and highest title to our assistance and co-operation, on grounds of humanity and religion' (Eurasians, 1869, p. 70). Hence, parental responsibility and Christian ethics produced claims for Eurasian standing, though not on equal footing with 'Europeans of pure blood'.

The *Herald*'s call to action was taken up by several prominent members of the Shanghai business community, including Britisher (later Sir) Thomas Hanbury (1832–1907), who donated a house for the school's use. R. S. Gundry, editor of the *North-China Herald*, became Secretary of the school committee. Of the initial group, it was Hanbury who would play the central role in the school's history, eventually lending it his name. Having made his fortune in Shanghai, Hanbury was a renowned philanthropist, but his generosity in this endeavor may not have been entirely disinterested, for he was rumoured to have fathered Eurasian children himself (Cranley, 2015).

Beginning with its first boarder in September 1870, the new school rapidly increased its enrolment to over a dozen by November (Summary of News,

1870b, p. 371). By the end of its first year, Shanghai's Eurasian School had taken in 20 day-students and 12 boarders, so it was judged to be an excellent success. Reports on the school marvelled at the progress made by children who had entered without any knowledge of English, and praised Mrs Bonney for instilling order and organization among the pupils, even as she showered them with motherly attention (First Yearly Report, 1871). The imperialist civilizing project thus assumed a maternalistic guise as it sought to remake Eurasian children in the image of their European fathers. The disciplining nature of this institution was thereby masked, taking on the form of 'maternal care' as affective labour. Mrs Bonney ardently embraced the role of school mistress and surrogate mother, referring to herself as her pupils' 'mamma'. Replacing formality with intimacy, and structuring the teacher–pupil relationship as a mother–child relationship, the school advanced the civilizing mission of supplanting the denigrated figure of the native mother. In doing so, it followed an imperialist pattern also evident in programs directed at 'abandoned' Eurasians in Vietnam, Hong Kong and other colonial possessions (Firpo, 2010; Pomfret, 2009; Saada, 2012; Stoler, 2002).

To put the school on a more permanent footing, the trustees began a fundraising appeal, and Hanbury stepped up with the promise of a new building. In this effort, the school reaffirmed the rationale for segregated education for Eurasians, reiterating that this model was being implemented across Asia (First Yearly Report, 1871). The notion of Eurasians as 'a class by themselves' reinforced their intermediate status between Europeans and Chinese, and ultimately served expatriate self-interest in producing a group of intermediaries. Hanbury explained this rationale in a letter dated 16 June 1871, detailing his construction of a building:

> for an Eurasian school, an institution also very much required here, there being many half-caste children who are but little cared for, but who might be trained for useful members of society, and form a good link to promote a more kindly feeling between Europeans and Chinese.
> (Hanbury, 1913, p. 223)

Hanbury's letter indicates that he viewed 'half-caste' children as objects of rescue who could be recuperated through training as 'useful members of society' and racial intermediaries. Indeed, the Eurasian School would come to provide Shanghai's mercantile firms and others with a useful pool of bilingual labour (*Report and Budget*, 1889, p. 182, The Children's Home, 1889, p. 778). William Rowe shows that by the turn of the twentieth century, Eurasians constituted a significant source of labour, filling low-paying jobs as clerks, bookkeepers, and secretaries (Rowe, 2009, p. 141; The Telephone Report, 1908).

The merger with the children's home

Despite auspicious beginnings, the school struggled to become self-sustaining. The committee continually appealed for financial support and pupil recruitment, often using the spectre of the Eurasian Problem to drum up donations. As the report of 1875 asserted, Eurasians' 'education should be attended to, in order to prevent them becoming a burdensome and possibly troublesome class in the future' (Hongkew School Report, 1875).[2] To stabilize the school, in 1882, Hanbury offered to transfer the property in trust to the Municipal Council, on the condition that it should be called 'The Hanbury School for Eurasians' and admission reserved for this group. The Municipal Council declined responsibility for the school, but began making annual grants to keep it afloat (*Report and Budget*, 1884, p. 124). In 1889, Hanbury brokered an agreement to merge the Eurasian School with the newly established Children's Home, launched in 1887 under a charitable committee led by Cornelius Thorne (The Thomas Hanbury School and Children's Home, 1907; Wright and Cartwright, 1908, p. 489). As the 'Thomas Hanbury School and Children's Home', the new institution was to admit 'Eurasian boys and girls and destitute children of all nationalities' (Summary of News, 1889, p. 711). The mission was understood to be the training of pupils 'to be efficient and useful members of society – not to be "ladies and gentlemen"' (The Children's Home, 1889, p. 778).

The merger placed the Thomas Hanbury School and Children's Home on a solid footing, but the decreased reliance on tuition fees had some unfortunate consequences, since the Committee 'thought desirable … that the boys should consist of Eurasians only, and so the Chinese were not admitted'. This resulted in the expulsion of approximately 40 Chinese students, all long-time scholars of good record (Muirhead *et al.*, 1892, p. 200). Hence, even as the institution opened its doors to 'destitute children of all nationalities', it drew a rigid line against the Chinese. While furthering efforts to distance Eurasians from 'natives', this move effectively promoted their association with 'poor whites' instead, marking it as a 'charity school' – with repercussions down the road.

The Shanghai Public School controversy

In 1897, a bitter controversy erupted over the question of Eurasian children attending the Shanghai Public School (The Shanghai Public School, 1897a), ignited by a headmaster's letter sent to the parents of Eurasian children in February, bluntly informing them that the school would no longer 'continue to receive scholars except such as are of Western parentage on both sides' (Lanning, 1897). No reason was given for their children's expulsion, and the parents were subsequently outraged. A number were influential members of the International Settlement and soon rallied supporters to their side, convening a meeting at the Royal Asiatic Society (Summary of News, 1897, p. 328).

Presiding over this meeting was Brodie Clarke (1844–1931), who would come to play a pivotal role in the ensuing 'Eurasian battle'. One of the most prominent businessmen in Shanghai, Clarke had wealth and prestige, and was considered a 'leading resident' (Wright and Cartwright, 1908, p. 517). While prominent in public life, Clarke was also married, privately and discreetly, to Chan Ah Yuen (c.1837–1907), with a daughter, Louisa Augusta Clarke, born in 1872. It is no surprise, then, that Clarke was significantly interested in the matter of Eurasian education (Hall, 2012, pp. 12–17).

As controversy mounted, letters soon began to fly into the *North-China Daily News*. The paper published a communication on the question on 26 February, leading up to the annual ratepayers' meeting scheduled for 9 March (The Shanghai Public School, 1897a). Laying out the history behind the Public School's founding in 1894, it asserted the committee's rationale for excluding Eurasian students (20 students out of 200, plus ten in the kindergarten) to make way for more 'Westerns' as the expatriate population grew. Shanghai was indeed in the midst of a demographic shift produced by the increase of Western women coming out to China after 1880, establishing settled families in the place of the 'bachelor society' of the settlement's founding decades. Asserting that the Public School was established to educate 'the children of foreign, i.e. Western, residents', Eurasian children were urged to attend one of 'three prominent Eurasian schools' (Thomas Hanbury, St. Xavier's, or Ecole de La Providence; The Shanghai Public School, 1897a, p. 355).

An editorial further defended the actions of the Education Committee as a reflection of public intent and on the grounds that the school's constitution empowered it 'to refuse admission or to expel any children whose presence might be or is considered by them detrimental to the School': the presence of Eurasian children being determined 'detrimental' (The Shanghai Public School, 1897b, p. 336). It argued that differences in English-language competency, family background, and future roles in society warranted the separate education of Eurasian and 'European' children. As in 1869, then, schooling Eurasians as a 'class by themselves' was once again advocated. However, in sharp contrast to earlier arguments that co-education was detrimental *to Eurasians*, the focus now shifted to the detrimental effects on Europeans. Attempting to bury the racial prejudices at the heart of this controversy, the editorial declared:

> The Eurasian Question is a much too large and important one to be entered upon now, and we should hope that it will be put altogether on one side when this question comes up for discussion at the Ratepayers' Meeting.
> (The Shanghai Public School, 1897b, p. 336)

The editorial concluded by expressing confidence that the Committee's action would be supported by all but a small minority of the ratepayers.

This minority, however, was determined to make its voice heard. On 5 March, the father of two young Eurasian girls, J. Chambers, wrote a letter to the editor protesting the expulsion of his daughters (Chambers, 1897, p. 458). Decrying the headmaster's letter to parents as an insult, Chambers argued that the committee's actions were illegal, narrow-minded, and cowardly. He accused them of overstepping their power, arguing that their right to exclude children was limited to individual cases of bad conduct or offensiveness. Their narrow-minded action in attempting to 'grab' a tax-funded school for the interests of 'one class only', he argued, insulted Eurasians and raised 'race animosities which heretofore did not exist and which will take years to smooth over again'. Finally, he called the committee cowardly in making an 'unprovoked attack on innocent and helpless children', casting a slur on these children where they would not 'have dared to attack their parents or try to ostracize them from society so long as they had wealth and position' (Chambers, 1897, p. 458).

Another letter was received from a writer, identified only as 'A Eurasian Ex-Pupil of the Shanghai Public School'. Calling the actions of the committee unwise and indiscreet, the writer asserted the rights of Eurasian children to attend a public school. As did Chambers, s/he invoked the image of innocent Eurasian children, unfairly penalized for the sins of their fathers:

> If we are Eurasians, it is by no fault of our own; and not a small section of our class are children of old and respectable residents ... and so long as we are well cared for, and our moral character remains untarnished, I contend that we ought to be accorded the right of attending a public school....
> (The Public School Question, 1897, p. 459)

In defending Eurasians, the writer asserted their claims on the basis of their 'respectability', their moral character, and their filial connection to 'old and respectable residents', that is: white men of status recognized as the founding fathers of the International Settlement. Against the rumour that Eurasian children lived in 'alleyways, and places hardly reputable', and were therefore 'detrimental to the interests of the school', s/he challenged the headmaster to identify a single pupil living in a disreputable neighbourhood (The Public School Question, 1897, p. 459). Implicit was a call to distinguish two sets of Eurasians: a 'respectable' group that was fit to attend the public school ('towards the support of which [their] parents [were] contributing'); and another fit only for the charity schools.

The 'Eurasian battle' finally came to a head at the general meeting of ratepayers on 9 March. With 201 in attendance, the lengthy debate raised fundamental questions concerning concepts of 'public' versus 'private', and 'European' versus 'native'. Supporters of the Committee defended their action as necessitated by the public good, whereas the opposition denounced it as *ultra vires*, unjust, and divisive (Meeting of Ratepayers, 1897; *Report and Budget*, 1898, pp. 253–254).

Supporters argued it was the clear public will to limit the Public School to Europeans. Invoking the slippery slope argument, they warned that if Eurasians were not debarred, then Chinese and Japanese would demand admittance. Declaring Eurasians detrimental, they trotted out stereotypes of mixed-race children as 'guttersnipes', the illegitimate offspring of disreputable Chinese mothers and irresponsible Western fathers. Advocates of exclusion, who included powerful men like E. A. Probst and E. F. Alford, further claimed that the lack of European cultural influences and English-language at home (hinting at absentee fathers) rendered Eurasians unsuited for public schools (Meeting of Ratepayers, 1897, pp. 440–454).

The opposition countered these arguments by turning the notion of public, as an inclusive ideal, to serve their ends. Led by Francis Ellis, who had been deputized to speak on behalf of Eurasians, and Brodie Clarke, they pointed to the school's charter as an institution open to 'all classes of children' (Meeting of Ratepayers, 1897, p. 448). Being a 'Public School, governed by public men and supported by public funds for the public good', Ellis argued, 'the children of every ratepayer represented on the Constitution of the Settlement' were entitled to education (Meeting of Ratepayers, 1897, p. 448). Ellis refused the distinction between 'Westerns' and 'Eurasians', referring to the latter as the 'children of ratepayers' to stake their claims in the expatriate community.

Clarke condemned the Committee's letter as a direct attack on the 'privacy of domestic life' – drawing an enthusiastic 'hear, hear'. By debarring Eurasian children, Clarke argued, the Committee was passing judgment on the individual conduct of domestic life, violating the sacredness of a man's 'own hearth and home' (Meeting of Ratepayers, 1897, p. 449). Clarke nimbly turned the issue to a defence of European men's rights, and the sanctity of the home as a private domain of individual freedom. The 'Eurasian battle' brought to the fore a tension between a new ideal of expatriate family life and bourgeois domestic values, and the old order of expatriate 'bachelorhood' that characterized Shanghai's founding era (Pomfret, 2016). Indeed, historians like Elizabeth Buettner have demonstrated how the arrival of European women in the colonies mapped onto increased hostility toward interracial unions (Buettner, 2004; Stoler, 2002).

In casting the attack on Eurasians as an insult to European fathers, their defenders warned of divisiveness. Ellis declared the policy would 'work great injustice to so many worthy members of this community', and 'sever that unity which has been for so long the cause of the progress and prosperity of this Settlement' (Meeting of Ratepayers, 1897, p. 448). Ellis thus appealed to the material self-interest of the Anglo-American community. Repeatedly alluding to the fact that 'worthy members' of the community were themselves the fathers of Eurasian children, Ellis and Clarke effectively deflected the issue of race and put in play the honour and standing of white men.

The debate furthermore showed the effective mobilization of appeals to justice and fair play as core Anglo-American values, central to expatriate identity as exponents of 'civilization' in China. For some, the principles of fair play and common justice were held above one's personal opinion on miscegenation. As one ratepayer wrote to the *Herald*: 'Personally I deplore the existence of legitimate Eurasians, but think they should not be excluded for the reason of birth only' (The Public School Question, 1897, p. 459). While Ellis called on 'men of sturdy independence and lovers of fair play' to support his position, he also pulled no punches in labelling the Committee's action 'an attempt to stir up racial prejudices which will produce evil effects, the extent of which you cannot gauge'. Clarke declared that the 'unpleasantness' of the 'separating of one race from another' was 'directly opposed to our [British] teaching' (Meeting of Ratepayers, 1897, p. 449). Through these rhetorical moves, the pro-Eurasian camp undercut their opponents as bigots.

Challenging stereotypes of mixed children as guttersnipes, they asserted instead the 'respectability' of Eurasians at the Public School. Cornelius Thorne, President of the Thomas Hanbury school committee, decried the attempt to expel Eurasians as a class, reminding his audience that:

> Their fathers are mostly members of our community. Some of them are most respectably married, and although they may have married Chinese wives, I do not see where we can look down upon these women so long as they behave themselves in a manner which would reflect credit upon any lady....
>
> (Meeting of Ratepayers, 1897, p. 450)

Thorne argued that since these wives mixed socially with the expatriate community, there were no grounds to debar their children on account of those 'few who think that their children are too good to mix with Eurasians in the Shanghai public school' (Meeting of Ratepayers, 1897, p. 450). Garnering applause, Thorne invoked class-based notions of 'respectability' to counter negative images of Eurasian illegitimacy and Chinese mothers as 'bad women'.

Whereas detractors emphasized the detrimental influences of Chinese mothers, defenders of the Eurasian cause highlighted the beneficial inheritance from European fathers. As Dr J. Ward Hall declared: 'One constantly hears of the good conduct and cleverness of Eurasian children, partly as if it were a wonder'. Yet, such intelligence was only natural, Hall asserted, since these children had 'inherited their cleverness from their fathers', who included the 'cleverest men' who had lived in Shanghai (Meeting of Ratepayers, 1897, p. 454). Conceding that the Public School was founded for children 'of European nationality', Ellis boldly posed the rhetorical question: 'Of what other nationality, I should like to know, of what nationality are the children concerned?' Affirming the exclusion of 'natives', Ellis again challenged his audience: 'Are the children concerned native?' (Meeting of Ratepayers, 1897, p. 448). Without contesting the racially exclusive nature of the school, Ellis thus placed Eurasians on the European side of the European/native divide. Thorne supported this position by reminding ratepayers that the international legal principle of dependent citizenship conferred married women and minor children the nationality of their husbands and fathers, respectively – a point met with a resounding 'hear, hear' (Meeting of Ratepayers, 1897, p. 452).

The pro-Eurasian camp furthermore argued that this group had an important role to play in Shanghai's future. Whereas their opponents emphasized the necessity of shoring up boundaries, they emphasized the necessity of forging ties between the foreign and Chinese communities to ensure the settlement's future economic prosperity. Thorne, for example, asserted that Eurasians would play important roles in building the Settlement into a model community for the Chinese to emulate. Pointing to their future role, they alluded to colonial discourses concerning Eurasians as a new intermediate race in the making. Rejecting the thesis of hybrid degeneration, they advanced instead the idea of Eurasians as a productive amalgamation of European and Asian. Indeed, such notions of 'constructive miscegenation' (Stepan, 1991) circulated in Shanghai alongside worries over the Eurasian Problem. In 1896, for example, *Mesny's Chinese Miscellany* called Eurasians a 'coming race', a eugenic 'breed' that would 'do more to bring about the reformation of China than anything else' (Mesny, 1896, p. 292).

After lengthy debate, much of it focused on the powers of the Education Committee and the definition of a 'public school', Mr W. V. Drummond 'cut the knot' by bringing the discussion back to the heart of the matter: 'shall Eurasian children, who are now in the school be allowed to remain there; and shall Eurasian children in the future be admitted, or refused admission?' Thorne seconded Drummond's resolution, and the amendment was passed by the meeting, 'carried by a considerable majority, amidst applause' (Meeting of Ratepayers, 1897, p. 454).

Conclusion

These two episodes demonstrate the contestations over the place of Eurasians in Shanghai's racial hierarchy, and the 'tensions of empire' at play in the struggle between inclusive impulses and exclusionary practices, and further reveal certain sharp contrasts. Whereas the call to establish the Eurasian School was dominated by philanthropic voices, the Public School controversy of 1897 saw a dramatic shift as the voices of European fathers, and to a lesser extent Eurasians themselves, came to the fore. In championing the rights of Eurasians as members of Shanghai's expatriate community, and not mere objects of rescue, these advocates placed primacy on concepts of justice, fair play, and equality, while the earlier notions of humaneness, duty and religious charity took a backseat. Their successful overturning of attempts to exclude Eurasian pupils, hailed in later years as a triumph of 'good sense and right feeling' against 'social injustice', demonstrates the degree to which white allies were able to challenge stereotypes of Eurasians as 'guttersnipes' and assert the respectability of a middle-class cohort (Couling, 1917, p. 170). The notions of European paternal inheritance, and of continuing care and attention from European fathers, proved central in this regard.

Yet, although Eurasians were able to successfully defend their claims in the Public School controversy, it was largely through their white allies that they secured representation before the Municipal Council. As Dr J. Ward Hall reminded ratepayers on 9 March: 'Those who are really interested, who are not here, and who cannot properly be heard, are Eurasian children of to-day and of the future' (Meeting of Ratepayers, 1897, p. 454). Similarly, the Chinese mothers of Eurasian children remained voiceless and virtually invisible from the record. Indeed, Eurasian claims to European status depended on the *erasure* of these native mothers and a rhetorical emphasis on filiation with European fathers

– consistent with the gender-biased principle of dependent citizenship. Although often obliquely articulated, class played a vital role in the Public School controversy, expressed through notions of 'respectability' and 'worthiness', and the repudiation of the Thomas Hanbury as a 'charity school'.

In 1930, the Thomas Hanbury School and Children's Home merged with the Shanghai Public School, thus bringing to an end the former's history of educating Eurasians 'as a class by themselves'. Shanghai today is a much different place, freed from the semi-colonial yoke, yet the influx of foreign expatriates since China's liberalization is once again reshaping this cosmopolitan port city as a contact zone for those of diverse heritage. 'Eurasian' is no longer a stigmatized label, but a badge of honour, though the pressure to serve as racial intermediaries has taken on new guises under globalization. How will today's mixed heritage children navigate the tensions between inclusion and exclusion, between claims of distinctiveness and those of equality? Even as Eurasians are now celebrated as the 'best of both worlds', to what degree are the doors of 'Chineseness' and 'whiteness' closed to them? The legacy of the 'Eurasian Battle' may be instructive to us today, as the struggle to forge post-racial societies, in Asia and the West, continues.

Notes

1 On Shanghai, Dover followed the work of Robert E. Park.
2 Eurasians in Shanghai were not always separately enumerated on the census, and were likely undercounted even when they were (Teng, 2013, pp. 238–239).

Bibliography

Bonney, C. V. R. (15 September 1870). 'Boarding and Day School'. *The North-China Herald and Supreme Court & Consular Gazette*, p. 213. Shanghai.
Bonney, C. V. R. (1875). *A Legacy of Historical Gleanings*. Albany, NY: J. Munsell.
Buettner, E. (2004). *Empire Families: Britons and Late Imperial India*. Oxford; New York: Oxford University Press.
Chambers, J. (12 March 1897). 'The Public School Question'. *The North-China Herald and Supreme Court & Consular Gazette*, p. 458. Shanghai.
Clark, J. D. (1894). *Sketches in and Around Shanghai etc.* Shanghai: Printed at the 'Shanghai Mercury' and 'Celestial Empire' Offices.
Couling, S. (1917). *The Encyclopaedia Sinica, by Samuel Couling*. London: Oxford University Press.
Cranley, W. P. (20 April 2015). 'Old Shanghai: The Thomas Hanbury School'. *Timeoutshanghai.com*. Available at: www.timeoutshanghai.com/features/Blog-Rediscovering_old_Shanghai/26689/Old-Shanghai-The-Thomas-Hanbury-School.html (accessed: 18 June 2016).
Dover, C. (1937). *Half-caste*. London: Martin Secker and Warburg.
Education in Shanghai. (11 May 1878). *The North-China Herald and Supreme Court & Consular Gazette*, p. 480. Shanghai.
Eurasians. (6 February 1869). *The North-China Herald and Market Report*, pp. 69–70. Shanghai.

Eurasian School – Report. (1 June 1872). *The North-China Herald and Supreme Court & Consular Gazette*, pp. 431–432. Shanghai.

Eurasian School – Report. (31 October 1883). *The North-China Herald and Supreme Court & Consular Gazette*, pp. 431–432. Shanghai.

Firpo, C. (2010). 'Crises of Whiteness and Empire in Colonial Indochina: The Removal of Abandoned Eurasian Children from the Vietnamese Milieu, 1890–1956'. *Journal of Social History* 43(3), pp. 587–613.

First Yearly Report of the Shanghai Eurasian School – Established September 1870. (11 October 1871). *The North-China Herald and Supreme Court & Consular Gazette*, p. 772. Shanghai.

Hall, P. (2012). *In the Web*. Birkenhead, UK: Appin Press.

Hanbury, T. (1913). 'Shanghai Revisited'. In *Letters of Sir Thomas Hanbury*. London: West, Newman & Co.

Hanbury, T. and Hanbury, K. A. (Pease). (1913). *Letters of Sir Thomas Hanbury*. London: West, Newman & Co.

Hongkew School Report. (4 February 1875). *The North-China Herald and Supreme Court & Consular Gazette*, p. 101. Shanghai.

Lanning, G. (12 March 1897). 'The Shanghai Public School'. *The North-China Herald and Supreme Court & Consular Gazette*, p. 448. Shanghai.

Lorde, A. (1984). *Sister Outsider: Essays and Speeches*. Trumansburg, NY: Crossing Press.

Meeting of Ratepayers. (12 March 1897). *The North-China Herald and Supreme Court & Consular Gazette*, pp. 440–454. Shanghai.

Mesny, W. (1896). *Mesny's Chinese Miscellany: A Text Book of Notes on China and the Chinese, in Two Volumes*. China Gazette Office.

Mesny, W. (1897). *Mesny's Chinese Miscellany*. China Gazette Office.

Muirhead, W. M., Hodges, H. C., and Moule, A. E. (1892). 'Report of the Eurasian, now Thomas Hanbury School, for the Year 1891'. In *Report and Budget*, pp. 199–200.

Pomfret, D. M. (2009). 'Raising Eurasia: Race, Class, and Age in French and British Colonies'. *Comparative Studies in Society and History* 51(2), pp. 314–343.

Pomfret, D. M. (2016). *Youth and Empire: Trans-colonial Childhoods in British and French Asia*. Stanford, CA: Stanford University Press.

Pott, F. L. H. (1928). *A Short History of Shanghai: Being an Account of the Growth and Development of the International Settlement*. Shanghai: Kelly & Walsh Ltd.

Report for the Year 1930 and Budget for the Year 1931. (1931). Kelly & Walsh Ltd.

Report for the Year ended 31st December 1883 and Budget for the Year ending 31st December 1884. (1884). Shanghai: Kelly & Walsh Ltd.

Report for the Year ended 31st December 1888 and Budget for the Year ending 31st December 1889. (1889). Nanking: Kelly & Walsh Ltd.

Report for the Year ended 31st December 1897 and Budget for the Year ending 31st December 1898. (1898). Nanking: Kelly & Walsh Ltd.

Ridley, H. N. (1913). 'The Eurasian Problem'. In *Noctes Orientales: Being a Selection of Essays Read Before the Straits Philosophical Society Between the Years 1893 and 1910*. Singapore: Kelly & Walsh Ltd, pp. 54–56.

Rowe, W. T. (2009). *China's Last Empire: The Great Qing*. Cambridge, MA: Harvard University Press.

Saada, E. (2012). *Empire's Children: Race, Filiation, and Citizenship in the French Colonies*. Chicago: The University of Chicago Press.

Shanghai Municipal Council. (1892). *Report for the Year ended 31st December 1891 and Budget for the Year ending 31st December 1892*. Shanghai.
Stepan, N. (1991). *The Hour of Eugenics: Race, Gender, and Nation in Latin America*. Ithaca, NY: Cornell University Press.
Stoler, A. L. (1992). 'Sexual Affronts and Racial Frontiers: European Identities and the Cultural Politics of Exclusion in Colonial Southeast Asia'. *Comparative Studies in Society and History* 34, pp. 514–551.
Stoler, A. L. (1997). 'Sexual Affronts and Racial Frontiers: European Identities and the Cultural Politics of Exclusion in Colonial Southeast Asia'. In *Tensions of Empire: Colonial Cultures in a Bourgeois World*. Berkeley, CA: University of California Press, pp. 198–237.
Stoler, A. L. (2002). *Carnal Knowledge and Imperial Power: Race and the Intimate in Colonial Rule*. Berkeley, CA: University of California Press.
Summary of News. (15 September 1870a). *The North-China Herald and Supreme Court & Consular Gazette*, pp. 202–204. Shanghai.
Summary of News. (22 November 1870b). *The North-China Herald and Supreme Court & Consular Gazette*, pp. 370–371. Shanghai.
Summary of News. (28 December 1870c). *The North-China Herald and Supreme Court & Consular Gazette*, pp. 458–459. Shanghai.
Summary of News. (1 June 1872). *The North-China Herald and Supreme Court & Consular Gazette*, pp. 426–427. Shanghai.
Summary of News. (31 October 1883). *The North-China Herald and Supreme Court & Consular Gazette*, pp. 490–493. Shanghai.
Summary of News. (13 December 1889). *The North-China Herald and Supreme Court & Consular Gazette*, pp. 710–712. Shanghai.
Summary of News. (26 February 1897). *The North-China Herald and Supreme Court & Consular Gazette*, pp. 326–332. Shanghai.
Teng, E. (2013). *Eurasian: Mixed Identities in the United States, China, and Hong Kong, 1842–1943*. Berkeley, CA: University of California Press.
The Children's Home. (27 December 1889). *The North-China Herald and Supreme Court & Consular Gazette*, pp. 777–778. Shanghai.
The Education Report. (1 July 1911). *The North-China Herald*, pp. 28–29. Shanghai.
The Late Mr Cornelius Thorne. (20 July 1906). *The North-China Herald and Supreme Court & Consular Gazette*, p. 170. Shanghai.
The Public School Question. (12 March 1897). *The North-China Herald and Supreme Court & Consular Gazette*, pp. 458–459. Shanghai.
The Ratepayers' Meeting. (12 March 1897). *The North-China Herald and Supreme Court & Consular Gazette*, pp. 428–429. Shanghai.
The Shanghai Public School. (26 February 1897a). *The North-China Herald and Supreme Court & Consular Gazette*, p. 355. Shanghai.
The Shanghai Public School. (26 February 1897b). *The North-China Herald and Supreme Court & Consular Gazette*, p. 336. Shanghai.
The Telephone Report. (3 April 1908). *The North-China Herald and Supreme Court & Consular Gazette*, pp. 21–22. Shanghai.
The Thomas Hanbury School and Children's Home. (8 March 1907). *The North-China Herald and Supreme Court & Consular Gazette*, p. 497. Shanghai.
Wallace, K. E., and Dover, C. (1930). *The Eurasian Problem, Constructively Approached*. Calcutta and Simla: Thacker, Spink & Co.

Wright, A., and Cartwright, H. A. (1908). *Twentieth Century Impressions of Hongkong, Shanghai, and Other Treaty Ports of China: Their History, People, Commerce, Industries, and Resources* (Vol. 1). London: Lloyds Greater Britain Publishing Company.

Young, R. (1995). *Colonial Desire: Hybridity in Theory, Culture, and Race.* London; New York: Routledge.

2 Mixing blood and race
Representing *Hunxue* in contemporary China

Cathryn H. Clayton

Introduction

In China in 2009, a young woman named Lou Jing represented Shanghai in a nationally televised talent show entitled *Go! Oriental Angel*. Her performance sparked a controversy of international proportions, not because of her talent, but because of her family background: fathered by an African-American man she never met, Lou Jing was raised in a single-parent household in Shanghai by her Chinese mother. In the wake of the broadcast, the Chinese internet exploded with bigoted attacks on Lou, many of which claimed she was not a 'real Chinese' and should 'get out of China'. These attacks in turn sparked a series of impassioned defences of Lou's beauty, her character, and her Chineseness (BBC World Service, 2009; Leung, 2015; Teoh, 2011; Vines, 2009). Lou's detractors castigated her mother, who allegedly had conceived Lou Jing during an extramarital affair, as an adulteress and a traitor who had destroyed the good name and career of her ex-husband (a local party secretary) by sleeping with a foreigner and refusing to abort the pregnancy that resulted.[1] They mocked Lou herself as the 'ugly' product of 'shameful' behaviour, whose claim to Chineseness was fraudulent and who should not be paraded on national television. Others countered this outburst with equally passionate statements of support for Lou, pointing to the deep love and care she showed to her mother, and calling her a 'good daughter and a good student' whose hard work, maturity, positive outlook and love of country – Lou Jing is proud to call herself 'a native Chinese' – could only have been the result of good parenting (Zhou, 2009). They suggested that Lou Jing was precisely the kind of young Chinese person China needs more of these days.

At first glance, it may seem there is little that can be learned from this incident: it appears to be just another example of the entrenched anti-black racism in China that has been discussed by several scholars (Cheng, 2011; Dikötter, 1992; Sautman, 1994; Sullivan, 1994). The fact that the most vicious invective – and the most effusive praise – was reserved for ways in which Lou and her family members violated, or adhered to, the normative ideals of womanly virtue, ethnic solidarity and patriotism seems to simply confirm the well-established observation that the logics of race, nation, kinship, gender and sexuality are intimately related (Balibar, 1990; Borneman, 1992; Cook, 1996; Parker *et al.*, 1992; Sullivan, 1994; Williams, 1995). The debate over the legitimacy of Lou Jing's claim to Chineseness seems merely to replay long-standing debates about whether Chineseness is a racial or cultural category, and to reflect the role that discourses of patrilineal kinship have played in structuring national identity since the early twentieth century. The revulsion towards mixed-race individuals – especially those with dark skin – echoes similar sentiments in Japan and South Korea, and seems to confirm the view that East Asian national identities are based on 'a strong idea of racial purity' (Small and King-O'Riain, 2014, p. x; see also Lie, 2009). Because both Lou's supporters and her detractors drew attention to the darkness of her skin in tropes familiar to, but no longer acceptable in, the US American public sphere (her fans called her 'Chocolate Angel' and 'Black Pearl') the Anglophone media and blogosphere portrayed the entire episode as yet another example of China's racist backwardness (see Chang, 2009; Steve, 2009), feeding straight into centuries-old Western narratives of China as quintessentially and unrepentantly xenophobic.

In this chapter, I suggest that the reason it may seem there is little to be learned from Lou Jing's story is that the conceptual frameworks most often used to describe it, such as those outlined above, share unexamined assumptions about the universality of ideas about race and monoraciality that keep us trapped in the same questions and observations about race, gender and nation in China today. The insights of Critical Mixed-Race Studies can open up new questions by placing China's current debates about mixing in global and historical perspective. Simultaneously, closer ethnographic attention to the specific metaphors through which mixing is represented in the Chinese language can suggest more nuanced and robust conceptual frameworks through which to pursue the cross-cultural study of mixing that many proponents of Critical Mixed-Race Studies have advocated.

By suggesting that what the online attacks on Lou Jing expressed was not precisely the universality of ideas about anti-black racism, I do not mean to dismiss the severity of the hurtful, plainly racist statements, the worst of which were reported by incredulous observers both in China and elsewhere (see Leung, 2015). Some of the most outrageous of these may be dismissed as mere trolling. But the more serious debates these trolls sparked focused not so much on Lou Jing's blackness as her mixedness: the questions that her mixed parentage (and the conditions under which that mixture came about) raised about who counts as Chinese and why.

It is here that the insights of Critical Mixed-Race Studies – which puts mixing, not race per se, at the centre of inquiry, and asks why, how and what kinds of 'mixedness' become visible, acceptable, even prideworthy (Daniel *et al.*, 2014, p. 8) – can raise new questions, not just about the prospects for Lou Jing and others like her, but about how conceptions of Chineseness itself may be changing. In recent years, 'China's rise' to world prominence has entailed rising numbers of foreigners settling in China, rising ethnic tensions in its border regions, and a renarrativization of its relationship to the globe and global capitalism. These processes have sparked new debates about various kinds of mixing across various kinds of borders, as well as about the continuing relevance of the long-standing official representations of China as a multi-ethnic nation comprised of 56 distinct, autochthonous ethno-national groups that have been united since ancient times. Yet focusing on the newness of this challenge obscures the fact that narratives of mixing – both across and within the shifting boundaries of Chineseness – have been instrumental in conceptualizing and cementing the subject of 'China' and its place in the world since the late nineteenth century. In the first half of the chapter, I briefly trace this history, showing how, alongside the questions about 'who counts as Chinese?' that are raised by contemporary representations of mixing, it is important to raise the converse question: who counts as 'mixed' when it comes to representing Chineseness?

Yet thinking critically about 'mixedness' in Asia also invites us to take seriously the resilience and recombinant nature of indigenous concepts and classifications. Many of the Chinese friends and scholars I spoke with about the Lou Jing incident averred that the term 'racism' was a conceptual misfit: not that the Chinese are not prejudiced against people with dark skin, but that this prejudice stems from a different history, a different logic, than does racial prejudice in the West, and thus functions in a sociologically different way. They suggested that what appears to Americans to be 'racism' is a distinct system of social classification that involves bodily markers of wealth, occupation, and 'civilization' which are at least partly mutable and which, crucially, apply as much to the Han Chinese as to individuals of different races.[2] Although it is possible to dismiss such protestations as ignorance about how racism 'really' works, in this chapter I suggest that we take seriously this assertion that the concept of race does not do analytical justice to the controversy sparked by the televised appearance of a Chinese woman with African-American and Chinese parentage.

At its simplest, this is a linguistic argument: in Chinese, for Lou Jing and others like her, what is being mixed is not race, but blood. The Chinese word most often glossed as 'mixed race' is 'hunxue' (混血) or 'mixed-blood'. According to Chinese Wikipedia, 'hunxue'er' refers to 'a person with different racial, ethnic or national backgrounds' (有不同人种、民族或国族背景的人); in other words, it does imply the bridging, in one individual, of two or more groups that are defined as distinct. But these groups are not necessarily races, if by that we mean the classification of humanity into discrete groups based on distinctive biological traits within each group. In Chinese, it is possible to refer to the Chinese people as a race (indeed, at times during the twentieth century the idea of 'the Chinese race' has been an important political construct), and Western theories and discourses of scientific race and racism have made their mark on Chinese social sciences and popular opinion (see Dikötter, 1992). Nonetheless, the Chinese term for race (种族) is a relative neologism coined by scholars translating the works of European social scientists in the early twentieth century (Liu, 1995), one that sits in an uneasy relationship with older constructs of shared substance and belonging based on metaphors of blood (*xue* 血, and its cognates, *xuetong* 血统 or bloodline, and *xuemai* 血脉 or blood vessels). In the People's

Republic of China (PRC) today, *xuetong* is a more powerful and commonsensical term than race for expressing the 'myth of consanguinity' (Chow, 1993) that unites family members, PRC citizens, and ethnic Chinese around the world.

Although several scholars writing under the rubric of Critical Mixed-Race Studies have noted that their research communities do not use the word 'race' (see Nandi and Spickard, 2014; Ualiyeva and Edgar, 2014), few have argued that such terminological differences make a difference. In the second half of the paper, I draw on recent work in anthropology to argue that the difference between 'xue' and 'race' does matter. Ultimately, I argue, the cross-cultural project of Critical Mixed-Race Studies will be better served by paying attention to the culturally specific histories and metaphors through which groups categorize, naturalize, and assign meaning to various aspects of human diversity, without reifying 'race' as an object of study.[3]

Mixing in view

The 2009 debates over Lou Jing's Chineseness formed one node in a broader conversation about the place of mixed Chinese families and individuals in Chinese society that has emerged since the turn of the twenty-first century. On one hand, the streets and shopping malls of urban China, as well as the internet, are rife with positive representations of *hunxue'er*. Eurasian models and performers, deemed more attractive than mono-ethnics, adorn billboards and television programmes; there are websites dedicated to cataloguing mixed beauties (Wang, 2012) and others to collecting images of mixed families and commenting on the attractiveness of their offspring (Xie, 2012). Social networking sites such as cn.Xihalife.com provide spaces for Chinese-speakers of mixed descent nationwide to compare experiences, share insights, and establish communities. After the city of Macau, which had been ruled by Portugal for more than 400 years, was returned to Chinese administration in 1999, there was a surge of interest in the Macanese – the small minority of that city's population who lay claim to a mixed ethnocultural heritage including Chinese, Portuguese, Malay, Japanese and Indian origins – and whose hybrid language, cuisine, and looks attracted attention from journalists, tourists, and scholars alike. The Chinese government began promoting the image of certain kinds of mixed families as the epitome of the 'ideal citizens' it hoped to cultivate: beautiful, intelligent, modern, educated, upwardly mobile, cosmopolitan, small nuclear families that are firmly rooted in China and Chinese cultural practice (see NewsGD.com, 2012; Guangzhou Daily, 2011). By the early 2010s, in the southern city of Guangzhou the topic of mixing seemed to be everywhere: on one hand, as the population of foreigners from all around the world – including, most famously, a resident population of tens of thousands of Africans – had soared in the early 2000s, the sight of interracial families (including those whose members were European, North American, African and Middle Eastern) who had chosen to settle in China for the long term had become routine. On the other hand, I had lengthy conversations with Cantonese friends who had become fascinated by recent research proving that, linguistically, genetically and culturally, the Cantonese people were a mix of northern Chinese and the indigenous Yue peoples they had displaced through successive waves of southward migration.

Yet as public representations of mixedness in China have proliferated since the turn of the twenty-first century, ambivalence toward the place of mixed individuals and groups in the 'great family of the Chinese nation' (中华民族大家庭 *Zhonghua minzu da jiating*) has only increased. Emma Teng notes an antimixing rant that online columnist Shangguan Tianyi published in 2001, criticizing the 'fashionable' view that 'the mixed-blood hybrid' should be 'a figure of admiration' (see Teng, 2006). While Eurasians are often praised as more beautiful, Blasians (individuals with African and Asian ancestry) such as Lou Jing and Ding Hui, a member of the national men's volleyball team of South African and Chinese parentage, are more often reviled as freakish and un-Chinese (CCTV-5, 2009). Although mixed children are viewed as desirable (smarter, healthier, and more attractive), there are often misgivings about the parents who produce them: while best-selling self-help books teach aspiring cosmopolites 'how to marry a foreigner' and chronicle the lives of glamorous Chinese celebrities who have found familial bliss with their foreign spouses and adorable children (Xinhuanet, 2013), the blogosphere is rife with posts warning young Chinese women against the folly of trying to marry foreign men (Anonymous, 2010), or denigrating Chinese men *and* women with foreign partners as degenerate, traitorous, hypersexed, unattractive losers whom no self-respecting Chinese person would accept as a spouse (see McGeary, 2013). Although state media outlets celebrate *hunxue'er* as evidence of China's openness and cosmopolitanism, Chinese citizens are prevented from officially identifying themselves as 'mixed' on their state-issued national identification cards, which list just one ethnic category per person. And the proposal, debated for a number of years in the 1990s and 2000s, that the Macanese – viewed by some as a literal incarnation of European imperialism in China – should be incorporated into the Chinese nation-state as an official ethnic minority (*shaoshu minzu*), on a par with Tibetans and Uyghurs, was greeted gleefully by some bloggers but with derision and incredulity by others.

What is striking are the very different ways that, in media reports, chatrooms, and passing conversations, these different 'mixed' groups and their individual members are positioned – as fully Chinese, halfway Chinese, completely foreign, potential Chinese-in-the-making, or more like a *shaoshu minzu*. In this sense, the figure of the *hunxue'er* has become a lightning rod for a budding nationwide conversation not just about the unanticipated consequences of globalization, immigration, and 'China's rise', but about the nature and limits of Chineseness.

Mutts like us

The emerging field of Critical Mixed-Race Studies can help make sense of this ambivalence as part of a global phenomenon. A 2014 volume entitled *Global Mixed Race* suggests that, while mixing has always occurred, recent trends in globalization (labour migration, study abroad, tourism, online dating, and the transnational reach of social media) have created unprecedented opportunities for the genesis of new mixed-race populations as well as the 'increasing recognition and visibility of mixed people and identities within contemporary societies' across the globe (Small and King-O'Riain, 2014, p. viii). Thus, it is not just that people of mixed descent are more numerous than they were before, but that the increasing social acceptability of being 'mixed' has allowed many people who once felt compelled to choose one or another identity to openly identify as both (here they cite the figure of Barack Obama, who famously referred to himself as a 'mutt'). Although they are careful not to homogenize the experience of mixed-race people around the world, these scholars do suggest that there are 'the beginnings of a commonality of experience ... that spans the globe with increasing efficiency and speed' (King-O'Riain, 2014, p. 277). They highlight the interplay of transnational flows and technologies, on one hand, and individual state policies, on the other, as key forces that shape the experiences and identities of mixed people across the globe. They also argue that there has been a global convergence of *ideas* about race and mixing, as states and scholars borrow from other parts of the world ideas about how to classify, think about, and govern 'difference' in their own localities (King-O'Riain, 2014, p. 272).

In this sense, the essays in *Global Mixed Race* suggest that China is similar to the UK, Germany, Kazakhstan, Mexico, or the US where in recent decades the category 'mixed', the phenomenon of mixing, and the individuals who call themselves mixed have posed a challenge to dominant monoracial notions of citizenship and cultural or ethnic authenticity. In this way, the insights of Critical Mixed-Race Studies provide an analytical framework, some useful theoretical vocabulary, as well as a plethora of case studies for comparison and contrast.

But to my mind, simply positing the increased visibility of mixed groups as the end result of globalization misses an important opportunity to explore how this visibility itself is a way for communities to grapple with the meaning and outcomes of globalization – which, after all, is short-hand not just for increasing deterritorialization and hybridization, but for the often-wrenching process of economic integration into a transnational capitalist order that is far from egalitarian. Similarly, although recent decades have ushered in unprecedented opportunities for, and celebrations of, transnational mobility and hybridity, highlighting the 'newness' of mixed identities misses the opportunity to historicize this trend: examining how and why certain kinds of mixing become visible in different ways, to different groups, at particular moments in time.

This becomes especially clear in the case of China, where intimacies across national and racial lines have long been an especially charged locus for the expression of desires and anxieties surrounding China's various modes of engagement with the transnational capitalist economic order. As Emma Teng has shown, in the late nineteenth century, when that mode of engagement involved China's forcible inclusion into the global economy through gunboat diplomacy and 'unequal treaties', Chinese subjects marrying European, American or Japanese spouses were depicted by some Chinese authors as engaging in a form of 'cultural treason' that symbolized China's 'national humiliation' (国耻). Others, though, hailed intermarriage as a way of saving the Chinese nation by literally domesticating the agents of a threatening alien power (Teng, 2013). During the Maoist period, when the socialist state equated global economic integration with Western imperialism (or later, with Soviet revisionism) and did its best to rid China of its influence, many mixed families and individuals report being treated with suspicion; the few mixed families lauded by the state were those of high-profile 'friends of China' who married Chinese spouses and settled in China (like American communist George Hatem) and thus could be hailed as evidence of the universal appeal of Chinese Marxism (Brady, 2003).

This changed in the decades following the initiation of economic reforms that opened China to cautious interaction with capitalist economies. In 1983, the state legalized international and interracial marriages, hailing this step as a measure of 'social progress' in China (X. Chen, 2001). The many legal handbooks and sociological studies on the increase in both marriage and divorce between PRC citizens and foreigners published in the 1980s and early 1990s all begin with the assertion that marriage between Chinese and foreigners has a long history and is, under normal circumstances, the best way to achieve mutual understanding among nations (Li, 1989; Lu et al., 1987; Zhou, 1992). But the authors remained concerned that China's contemporary circumstances were not 'normal', since the characteristics of the vast majority of international marriages they studied flouted the Chinese state's ideals of appropriate companionate marriage, namely: 'first marriage for both sides; no appreciable age difference; compatible physical and health conditions and appearance; and a better occupation on the part of the men' (Lu et al., 1987). The pattern of older, well-off, unattractive foreign men marrying young, poor, lovely Chinese women (who then proceeded to leave China as quickly as possible) was, according to these analyses, due to the wide gap in standards of living between China and the men's home countries, and to the orientalist perception that PRC women, given their poverty and ignorance of the outside world, were less demanding and more easily taken advantage of than their foreign counterparts – in short, evidence of the continuing inequities in the global capitalist system and the ever-present potential for China to be exploited by that system.

What is noteworthy here is that these shifting views on the desirability of mixing *across* national and racial borders correspond to shifts in mainstream ideas about the relative purity or hybridity of the Chinese people themselves. Early twentieth-century revolutionaries who fought to bring down the Qing Dynasty (in which ethnic Manchus had ruled over a vast, multi-ethnic empire) deliberately developed a narrative of ethnic purity: in the words of revolutionary writer Zou Rong, the Han Chinese were the 'unsullied descendants of the Yellow Emperor' who for thousands of years had been engaged in battle with the non-Chinese barbarians on their borders (Chow, 2001, pp. 61–62). Once these revolutionaries succeeded in toppling the Qing, the problem became one of constructing a discourse of Chineseness that could incorporate both Manchus and the other heretofore non-Chinese groups inhabiting the vast territories conquered by the Qing that the new Republic did not wish to relinquish.

In the 1920s, some scholars melded kinship ideologies with the scientific discourse of paleoarchaeology to argue that newly discovered hominid fossils near Beijing (dubbed 'Peking Man') represented the apical ancestor of all Chinese peoples, and that Mongols and Tibetans and Han Chinese corresponded to different branches of a single lineage (Leibold, 2006). After the establishment of the PRC, the Maoist view – which Edward Friedman describes as 'the mythos ... that a people from the northern plain had assimilated all would-be conquerors' by the sheer charisma of their superior civilization (Friedman, 1994, p. 72) – replaced both narratives with one of cultural assimilation, and located the enduring unity of China's peoples not in shared kin ties but in shared experiences of class oppression.[4] But it still posited a single point of origin, a self-generating superior civilization that arose in the Yellow River basin and spread outwards, exerting a civilizing influence on the 'backwards' minorities it encountered (see Harrell, 1995).

In the post-Mao period of 'opening up', this narrative began to give way to one about the fundamental hybridity of the Chinese people. New archaeological research provided evidence that 'the genesis of China's civilization did not come from one source but from many, that were scattered ... throughout different regions', and of 'the importance of foreign contacts in the development of Chinese civilization ... and the relative impact of non-Han peoples on the Han' (Guldin, quoted in Friedman, 1994, pp. 70–71). In 1988, China's most famous anthropologist, Fei Xiaotong, advanced the 'snowball' theory of Han Chineseness, which, as later elucidated by Xu Jieshun, likens the Han Chinese to 'a snowball fusing many other ethnicities as it coagulated and formed' (Xu Jieshun cited in Leibold, 2012, p. 211). In this view, the Han are irreducibly plural in origins, yet firmly bound together through a process of mixing: 'people lived in mixed communities, assimilated and blended, and each time infused new blood into the Han, making them stronger' (Fei, 2015, p. 105). While American scholars have criticized this approach as a primordialist and teleological view of identity (and one that coincides too neatly with the state's efforts to promote 'ethnonational unity' in contentious regions like Tibet and Xinjiang), it nonetheless does legitimate the idea that Han Chineseness is at heart a hybrid identity: the result of thousands of years of intermarriage and borrowing between dozens of ethnic groups.

These narrative shifts in the discourse of mixing both within and across the category 'Chinese' follow political shifts in how Chinese elites conceptualize China's place in the world. As the narrative of global-capitalism-as-imperialist-exploitation is slowly supplanted by the narrative of 'China's rise', the valorization of mixing has everything to do with the state's attempts to foster national unity in the face of increasing inequality and to justify China's re-engagement with global capitalism by demonstrating the long history of China's 'openness' to the world. Yet this new vision of Chinese hybridity stands in tension with the narrative (which continues to be politically useful) of patrilineal purity that needs to be protected against threats from without and traitors from within (see Leibold, 2010).

This context is crucial to understanding how Lou Jing made it onto national television in 2009 in the first place, as well as the passions expressed both in support of and against her. More importantly, it is a reminder that definitions of what and who is 'mixed' can shift radically over time. From this perspective, what is most interesting about the Lou Jing case was not the racist invective, nor her supporters who argued that a person could be a 'good Chinese' *despite* having a foreign parent; rather, it was the surprising frequency with which interlocutors shifted seamlessly from talking about Lou Jing and mixed-race people in China to talking about the endless hybridizations that had produced the Chinese people themselves. Where a few decades ago, *hunxue'er* like author Han Suyin (the daughter of a Belgian mother and Chinese father) who identified as Chinese found themselves relegated to the 'wrong' side of a dichotomy in which hybridity signified Otherness, today the question is: which kinds of hybridity can count as Chinese?

Bloodwork

What is significant about the narratives I have traced above is that these diverse constructions of Chineseness – as pure kin group, multi-ethnic nation, or set of distinct ethnicities unified through time by intermarriage – are all underpinned by reference to the metaphor of shared blood (*xue*). Blood is a powerful and commonsensical metaphor of relatedness in the US no less than in China: it is the corporeal substance that lends naturalizing power to interrelated notions of race, kinship and nation (Schneider, 1968; Weston, 2001). Yet for blood to work as a metaphor of social cohesion, work must be done on blood: to be made compelling, it must be articulated to other categories of identification and to assumptions about bodies and personhood, health and vitality, sexual and social reproduction, and humans' relationship to nature and the cosmos (Carsten, 2001 and 2011; Tapper, 2001; Copeman, 2009). This means that, despite the apparent similarity across cultural contexts, the symbolics of *xue* and biological blood are different. In the rest of the chapter, I suggest that tracing the symbolic workings of *xue* through a variety of domains – such as medicine, kinship, and the law – has implications for how it functions as a metaphor of relatedness, and gives rise to different discourses, logics, and mythologies of mixing.

In the US, blood as a substance – the red liquid that circulates throughout the body – is a symbol par excellence of nature: given at birth, the qualities of blood and the connections it creates are largely seen as unalterable by human effort. In contrast, in Chinese medicine, *xue* is not so much a red liquid as it is a function or principle of nourishment that mediates between nature, the social, and the metaphysical. *Xue* is classed as yin in contrast to *qi*, its yang counterpart, and can be manifest in the human body as blood, menses, placenta, breast milk, and semen. Together with *qi*, it links individual vitality, reproductive potential, and cosmic generative forces. *Xue* is a natural endowment, but must be replenished and reinvigorated by deliberate human effort. Since blood is derived from 'the purified essence of food', careful regulation of diet, the emotions, and sexual activity are all necessary to maintain the vitality and proper function of blood, and to prevent its viscosity from becoming altered, its volume depleted, its circulation blocked (Furth, 2002; Wilms, 2005; Neeb, 2007).

In late imperial China, the 'blood tie' between parents and children was similarly seen as a complex and fluid interplay between nature and nurture, in which deliberate human action had the capacity not just to prevail over nature, but to transform it. On one hand, the blood of parents and children was understood to be literally the same substance – the standard paternity test in late imperial China involved placing drops of blood from two persons (or, in some cases, a bone fragment from one person and a drop of blood from the other) into a basin of water: if the drops commingled, the individuals were blood relatives. On the other hand, it was widely accepted that, for example, expectant parents could shape the looks, character, and even the sex of their unborn children through virtuous acts, and wet-nurses could transmit both physical and behavioural characteristics through their milk. There was open debate as to whether husbands and wives could be identified using the blood test – opinions were divided as to whether the exchange of care, food, and other bodily fluids was enough to fundamentally alter the physical properties of a married couple's blood to the point that, over time, they too would become 'blood relatives' (Waltner, 1990). In this sense, 'blood ties' were not only a key vector through which a wide range of economic, social, ritual and emotional investments, responsibilities, and rewards were apportioned among humans, blood itself was also a key substance through which the multiple close ties between social, natural and supernatural worlds could be apprehended and manipulated.[5]

Patricia Ebrey shows how in imperial China, the metaphor of blood connection was expanded to describe the Chinese people as a 'giant patrilineal descent group made up of intermarrying surname groups' (Ebrey, 1996, p. 20). Ebrey argues that this notion of Chinese identity as kinship does not map easily onto Western assumptions about race and ethnicity: the Chinese conception was far more flexible, in that the plausible assertion of a single Han Chinese ancestor could be enough for thousands of patrilineal descendants to legitimately claim a Chinese identity if they so desired, and genealogies asserting the existence of such an ancestor could be 'discovered, invented, fabricated or otherwise artfully produced for those who came to be socially accepted as Chinese' (Ebrey, 1996, p. 30; see also Szonyi, 2002). As Ebrey notes, this meant that, unlike Western theories of race and ethnicity, assertions of 'blood kinship' bore no relationship to phenotype, mother tongue or place of origin.

Indeed, Ebrey argues that the interest that Chinese intellectuals in the late nineteenth century showed in the Western race theory was a major departure in their thinking. Yet as Kai-wing Chow demonstrates, there was enough overlap between Chinese notions of blood kinship and the Western discourse of biological race that it was possible for some of these same intellectuals to commandeer the language of race and evolution to imbue their anti-Manchu ethnic nationalism with an aura of scientific legitimacy: the importance of blood kinship as a metaphor of social cohesion and political loyalty made it easier to posit the entire Chinese people as a distinct 'race' that should govern its own affairs (K. Chow, 1997). It bears emphasis that although this early twentieth century invention of 'the Chinese race' drew rhetorical power equally from Chinese kinship discourse and Western racial discourse, it completely upended key tenets of both: for example, in Western scientific racial discourse, Manchus and Chinese both belonged to the 'Mongol' race; and in conventional Chinese kinship discourse, the idea of linking thousands of lineages together into a giant über-lineage would have seemed absurd and downright unfilial. Yet given the political context in China at the time, it took little work to popularize and naturalize this new understanding of Chinese self and alien other, and of the significance of blood as a hard boundary dividing them.

As historian Shao Dan notes, it was around this time that the term *xuetong* came into wide usage. Separately, the two characters mean 'blood' and 'govern, command, unite', thus connoting cohesion, political legitimacy, and control. Prior to the nineteenth century, the word more often used to refer to the importance of blood lineage was *xuemai* (血脉), which, not unlike the English term 'arteries', referred to ' "circuits of blood" in medical texts, kinship or genealogy in history texts, and watercourses in geography texts' (Shao, 2009, p. 14) – metaphors not of singularity and exclusivity, but of multiplicity and interconnectedness, implicitly linking humans and nature in flows of life-sustaining fluids.

In highlighting the culturally and historically specific meanings of *xue*, I do not mean to suggest that they have existed unchanged for centuries in an isolated and hermetically sealed cultural system. However, without understanding these earlier concepts of relatedness, much of the Chinese discourse about mixing and *hunxue'er* does not make sense. For example, as Emma Teng points out, early twentieth-century reformer Kang Youwei advocated for the creation of the perfect 'Eurasian' race; but in his view, perfection would come about only partly by intermarriage. The rest would come from deliberate human action: dietary change, exercise, and the migration of southerners – not just blacks and browns but southern Europeans and Cantonese *like himself* – to more northerly climes. As Teng points out, Kang saw whiteness not as a sign of purity or superiority that was exclusive to the 'white race', but as simply a desirable physical characteristic that was attainable by individuals of all races through purposeful effort. While Kang's ideas make little sense from the perspective of scientific race theory, with its assumptions about the immutability of nature and the determinism of biology, they become comprehensible when we consider that Kang and others like him were most likely reading eugenics theory through their own commonsensical understandings of *xue*.

Many of the constructions of interracial mixing (both positive and negative) in China today – especially the idea that some kinds of *hunxue'er* are stronger, healthier, and more attractive than monoracials – stem precisely from this early twentieth-century eugenic discourse. But the term *hunxue* is not limited to racial mixing: *hunxue* is a more fluid concept that can be used to describe, usually positively, a wide variety of 'hybrids', both human and non-human.[6] Because *xue* is at heart a kinship metaphor rather than a racial one, the offspring of marriages between a whole range of socially distinct groups – national, ethnic, regional – can be called *hunxue'er*. I heard one man who identifies as Han assert, jokingly and in public, that he should be considered a *hunxue'er* because his father was from Henan and his mother from Anhui – two adjacent provinces in a part of the central plain (*zhongyuan*, 中原) that has been dubbed the 'cradle of Chinese civilization'. The joke worked because Henan and Anhui are core parts of the Chinese heartland, whose populations are 99 per cent Han Chinese; the differences that do exist in local culture and dialect would not normally be thought of as ones that need bridging. In this sense, unlike 'mixed race', which tends to reinscribe 'race' or 'ethnicity' as the most important social boundary that can be bridged, the term *hunxue* can be used reflexively and ironically to question why certain categories have become socially significant, and to subtly point out that, in one way or another, everyone is 'mixed'.

More specifically, however, the imagined properties of flexibility, connectivity and mutability entailed in the *xue* metaphor can also help explain details about Lou Jing's story that may sound ridiculous or implausible to those accustomed to thinking about race in the US American context. Consider the following: (1) when Lou Jing was a girl, her grandmother told her that her skin was dark because her mother had had to take Chinese herbal medicine while she was pregnant, while her friends surmised (apparently plausibly) that it was because she ate too much chocolate or soy sauce;[7] (2) it was widely reported that Lou defended her mother's dignity by emphasizing that her father was 'American, not African', implying that his place of birth (a wealthy, powerful, majority white nation) trumped the colour of his skin; and (3) despite the fact that Lou Jing has 'Chinese blood' and is a Chinese citizen according to the *jus sanguinis* principle enshrined in Chinese nationality law, some bloggers demanded that her citizenship be revoked because of her foreign father, her un-Chinese looks, and her 'shameless' flouting of Chinese moral norms (by appearing in public despite her 'base' origins).

In these details, we see ideas about phenotype, national origin, social status, hypergamy, patriline, diet, medicine, morality and the mutability of nature all circulating uneasily around the symbol of the *hunxue'er*. Rather than trying to apprehend this complexity under the overdetermined sign of 'race' – or simply using the nominal adjective 'mixed', as I have done in this chapter – I suggest that we need conceptual frameworks that can do justice to both the specificity and elasticity of the blood metaphor, as it combines and recombines with other corporealized categories of identity like race and nation, and is put to work in the service of a wide range of political and ideological agendas. More work remains to be done to develop such conceptual frameworks and understand how they impact the lives and prospects of *hunxue* people in China today. Doing so would not only deepen our understanding of Chinese society in a period of rapid and destabilizing change, it would also help the field of Critical Mixed-Race Studies to imagine new and broader ways of conceptualizing its subject of inquiry.

Conclusion

By digging out aspects of the discourse on *hunxue* that do not fit the rubric of race, I am not trying to exonerate the Chinese from the charge of racism or to downplay the experiences of discrimination, exclusion, and othering that many *hunxue'er* (or their parents) report. I simply mean to suggest that if such exclusionary attitudes are to be challenged, they must be understood and addressed on their own terms. While the terms of the debate about Lou Jing's Chineseness can be taken as a sign that the discursive terrain is starting to shift, what remains to be seen is whether the emerging narrative of Han Chinese as a hybrid people will in fact facilitate new ways of thinking about blood and mixing and Chineseness. There is some urgency to this question: if China's relatively robust economy and rising standards of living continue to attract young, single foreigners to move to China and settle there long term, and if the unintended consequences of the state's successful birth-planning policies – a rapidly shrinking labour force, a rapidly growing proportion of citizens over age 65, and a rapidly diverging sex ratio that ensures that by 2020, nearly 30 million more men than women will reach marriageable age (Hesketh, 2009) – continue to reshape labour and marriage markets, it is likely that the PRC will, like its East Asian neighbours, witness an explosion in the numbers of *hunxue* families in the next few decades.

Ann Morning, in an essay that advocates for a comparative perspective on 'the multiracial experience', argues that 'close examination of specific cultures in order to trace the development of local notions of "who" or "what" racially mixed people are' is a useful but limited way of approaching the study of multiraciality. Instead, she suggests, it is necessary to ask 'what we might gain from international exploration of the multiracial experience' (Morning, 2014, pp. 1–2). The Lou Jing case, this chapter has suggested, can provide one answer to this question: it is precisely through close examinations of the cultural and historical contexts that have given rise to specific conceptual vocabularies of and attitudes toward mixing that we can gain a more theoretically rigorous framework for thinking globally about mixing. This in turn will move us closer toward the goal of challenging the political, social, academic and aesthetic hierarchies structured around assumptions of race and monoraciality.

Notes

1 Both Lou Jing and her mother Sun Min denied that Sun was married at the time Lou was conceived.
2 Journalist Raymond Zhou published an article defending Lou Jing, denouncing racism in China, and subscribing to precisely this view. See Zhou, 2009.
3 Here I am paraphrasing Kath Weston, who, in discussing the 'new kinship studies' in anthropology, suggests the need to 'attend closely to matters of relatedness, without reifying kinship as an object of study' (Weston, 2001, p. 152).
4 Baranovitch (2010) discusses some of the ambivalences and changes in this Maoist narrative.

5 Historian Sun Jiang points out that in ritual practice, too, blood was 'the medium through which men and spirits (ancestors) communicated'; its purpose in rituals of swearing brotherhood (in which men of different lineages swore loyalty to each other by drinking blood mixed with wine or smearing blood on the mouth) was not to create bonds of fictive kinship, but to attract the attention of the ancestors and 'let the spirits bear witness to the bonds that have been forged and punish those who dared to violate them' (Sun, 2005, p. 25).
6 Literature, music, business practices: I have seen all of these described as *hunxue*, even though other words for 'hybrid' do exist.
7 www.cnn.com/2009/WORLD/asiapcf/12/21/china.race/

Bibliography

Anonymous. (2010). 'Chinese Women, Please Do Not Sleep with Foreigners (中国女人，请不要和老外上床)'. *Netease Forum (*网易论坛*)*. Available at: http://bbs.news.163.com/bbs/society/ 178165755.html (accessed: 6 December 2013).

Balibar, E. (1990). 'The Nation Form: History and Ideology'. *Review: Fernand Braudel Center* 13(3), pp. 329–361.

Baranovitch, N. (2010). 'Others No More: The Changing Representation of Non-Han Peoples in Chinese History Textbooks, 1951–2003'. *The Journal of Asian Studies* 69(1), pp. 85–122.

BBC World Service. (2009). 'Oriental Angel'. *BBC World Service*. 18 November. Available at: www.bbc.co.uk/worldservice/programmes/2009/11/091118_outlook_chinese_singer.shtml (accessed: 3 March 2017).

Borneman, J. (1992). *Belonging in the Two Berlins: Kin, State, Nation*. Cambridge; New York: Cambridge University Press.

Brady, A. (2003). *Making the Foreign Serve China: Managing Foreigners in the People's Republic*. Lanham, MD: Rowman & Littlefield.

Carsten, J. (ed.) (2000). *Cultures of Relatedness: New Approaches to the Study of Kinship*. Cambridge, UK and New York: Cambridge University Press.

Carsten, J. (2001). 'Substantivism, Antisubstantivism, and Anti-Antisubstantivism'. In S. Franklin and S. McKinnon (eds), *Relative Values: Reconfiguring Kinship Studies*. Durham and London: Duke University Press, pp. 29–53.

Carsten, J. (2011). 'Substance and Relationality: Blood in Contexts'. *Annual Review of Anthropology* 40(1), pp. 19–35.

CCTV-5. (2009). 'My Olympics: Ding Hui' [我的奥林匹克 丁慧]. *Tudou*. Uploaded by Hai nabian de sinian [还那边的思念], 25 May. Available at: www.tudou.com/programs/view/Z2YZDzfPe_4/ (accessed: 5 March 2017)

Chang E. (2009). 'TV Talent Show Exposes China's Race Issue'. *CNN.com*, 22 December. Available at: www.cnn.com/2009/WORLD/asiapcf/12/21/china.race/ (accessed: 31 May 2016).

Chen X. (2001). 'Marriage Law Revisions Reflect Social Progress in China'. *China Today* 50(3), pp. 12–17.

Cheng Y. (2011). 'From Campus to Cyber Racism: Discourse of Race and Chinese Nationalism'. *The China Quarterly* 207, pp. 561–579.

Chow Kai-wing. (1997). 'Imagining Boundaries of Blood: Zhang Binglin and the Invention of the Han "Race" in Modern China'. In Frank Dikötter (ed.), *The Construction of Racial Identities in China and Japan: Historical and Contemporary Perspectives*, pp. 34–52. Honolulu: University of Hawai'i Press.

Chow K. (2001). 'Narrating Nation, Race and Culture'. In K. Chow, K. Doak, and P. Fu (eds), *Constructing Nationhood in Modern East Asia*. Ann Arbor: University of Michigan Press, pp. 47–84.
Chow R. (1993). *Writing Diaspora: Tactics of Intervention in Contemporary Cultural Studies*. Bloomington: Indiana University Press.
Cook, J. (1996). 'Penetration and Neocolonialism: The Shen Chong Rape Case and the Anti-American Student Movement of 1946–47'. *Republican China* 22(1), pp. 65–97.
Copeman, J. (2009). *Veins of Devotion: Blood Donation and Religious Experience in North India*. Studies in Medical Anthropology. New Brunswick, NJ: Rutgers University Press.
Daniel, G. R., Kina, L., Dariotis, W.M., and Fojas, C. (2014). 'Emerging Paradigms in Critical Mixed-Race Studies'. *Journal of Critical Mixed-Race Studies* 1(1), pp. 6–65.
Dikötter, F. (1992). *The Discourse of Race in Modern China*. Stanford, CA: Stanford University Press.
Ebrey, P. (1996). 'Surnames and Han Chinese Identity'. In M. Brown (ed.), *Negotiating Ethnicities in China and Taiwan*. Berkeley: Institute of East Asian Studies, University of California, Berkeley, Center for Chinese Studies, pp. 11–36.
Fei X. (2015). *Globalization and Cultural Self-awareness*. Berlin: Springer.
Friedman, E. (1994). 'Reconstructing China's National Identity: A Southern Alternative to Mao-Era Anti-Imperialist Nationalism'. *Journal of Asian Studies* 53(1), pp. 67–91.
Furth, C. (2002). 'Blood, Body, and Gender: Medical Images of the Female Condition in China, 1600–1850'. In S. Brownell and J. Wasserstrom (eds), *Chinese Femininities, Chinese Masculinities: A Reader*. Berkeley: University of California Press, pp. 291–314.
Guangzhou Daily. (2011). 'Special Report: Hunxue'er Wins "Guangzhou's Little Mayor" Semi-Finals'. (记者专访：广州小事长半决赛混血儿拿第一名) Available at: http://gzdaily.dayoo.com (accessed: 23 October 2013).
Harrell, S. (1995). 'Introduction: Civilizing Projects and the Reaction to Them'. In S. Harrell (ed.), *Cultural Encounters on China's Ethnic Frontiers*. Seattle: University of Washington Press, pp. 3–36.
Hesketh, T. (2009). 'Too Many Males in China: The Causes and the Consequences'. *Significance* 6(1), pp. 9–13.
King-O'Riain, R. (2014) 'Global Mixed Race: A Conclusion'. In R. King-O'Riain, S. Small, M. Mahtani, M. Song, and P. Spickard (eds), *Global Mixed Race*. New York: New York University Press, pp. 263–280.
Leibold, J. (2006). 'Competing Narratives of Racial Unity in Republican China: From the Yellow Emperor to Peking Man'. *Modern China* 32(2), pp. 181–220.
Leibold, J. (2010). 'More Than a Category: Han Supremacism on the Chinese Internet'. *The China Quarterly* (203), pp. 539–559.
Leibold, J. (2012). 'Searching for Han: Early Twentieth-Century Narratives of Chinese Origins and Development'. In T. Mullaney, J. Leibold, S. Gros, and E. Bussche (eds), *Critical Han Studies*. Berkeley, CA: University of California Press, pp. 210–233.
Leung W. (2015). 'Who Could Be an Oriental Angel? Lou Jing, Mixed Heritage and the Discourses of Chinese Ethnicity'. *Asian Ethnicity* 16(3), pp. 294–313.
Li Shuangyuan 李双元. (1989). *International Marriage Inheritance Law* (涉外婚姻继承法). China Politics and Law University Press (中国政法大学出版社).
Lie J. (2009). *Multiethnic Japan*. Cambridge: Harvard University Press.
Liu L. (1995). *Translingual Practice: Literature, National Culture, and Translated Modernity – China, 1900–1937*. Stanford: Stanford University Press.

Lu H., Cao N., and Mei X. (1987). 'Mixed Marriages Between Guangzhou Girls and Hong Kong or Macao Compatriots, Overseas Chinese, or Foreign Nationals'. *Chinese Sociology & Anthropology* 20(2), pp. 76–87.

McGeary, K. (2013). 'Shenzhen Woman Urges Chinese to Avoid Marrying American Men'. *Nanfang Insider*. Available at: www.thenanfang.com/blog/shenzhen-woman-derided-for-airport-gesture/ (accessed: 16 December 2016).

Morning, A. (2014). 'Multiraciality and Census Classification in Global Perspective'. In R. King-O'Riain, S. Small, M. Mahtani, M. Song, and P. Spickard (eds), *Global Mixed Race*. New York: New York University Press, pp. 1–15.

Nandi, M., and Spickard, P. (2014). 'The Curious Career of the One-Drop Rule: Multiraciailty and Membership in Germany Today'. In R. King-O'Riain, S. Small, M. Mahtani, M. Song, and P. Spickard (eds), *Global Mixed Race*. New York: New York University Press, pp. 188–212.

Neeb, G. (2007). *Blood Stasis: China's Classical Concept in Modern Medicine*. Edinburgh: Churchill Livingstone/Elsevier.

NewsGD.com. (2012). 'International Marriage: Enjoy Typical Chinese Family Ties'. *NewsGD.com*, 21 December. Available at: www.newsgd.com/culture/CultureTravel-Highlights/content/ 2012-12/21/content_60622017.htm (accessed: 13 June 2016).

Parker, A., Russo, M., Sommer, D., and Yaeger, P. (eds) (1992). *Nationalisms and Sexualities*. New York: Routledge.

Sautman, B. (1994). 'Anti-Black Racism in China'. *China Quarterly* 138, pp. 413–437.

Schneider, D. (1968). *American Kinship: A Cultural Account*. Englewood Cliffs, NJ: Prentice-Hall.

Shao D. (2009). 'Chinese by Definition: Nationality Law, Jus Sanguinis, and State Succession, 1909–1980'. *Twentieth-Century China* 35(1), pp. 4–28.

Small, S., and King-O'Riain, R. (2014). 'Global Mixed Race: An Introduction'. In R. King-O'Riain, S. Small, M. Mahtani, M. Song, and P. Spickard (eds), *Global Mixed Race*. New York: New York University Press, p. vii–xxii.

Steve (2009) 'Lou Jing: Racism Gone Wild?' *Fool's Mountain: Blogging for China*. Available at: www.blog.foolsmountain.com/2009/10/21/lou-jing-racism-gone-wild/ (accessed: 3 March 2017).

Sullivan, M. (1994). 'The 1988–89 Nanjing Anti-African Protests: Racial Nationalism or National Racism?' *The China Quarterly* 138(June 1994), pp. 438–457.

Sun Jiang. (2005). 'Imagined Blood: The Creation of a Community of Memory Through Sworn Brotherhood'. *Chinese Sociology and Anthropology* 37(2–3), pp. 9–52.

Szonyi, M. (2002). *Practicing Kinship: Lineage and Descent in Late Imperial China*. California: Stanford University Press.

Tapper, M. (2001). 'Blood/Kinship, Governmentality, and Cultures of Order in Colonial Africa'. In S. Franklin and S. McKinnon (eds), *Relative Values: Reconfiguring Kinship Studies*. Durham and London: Duke University Press, pp. 329–354.

Teng E. (2013). *Eurasian: Mixed Identities in the United States, China, and Hong Kong, 1842–1943*. Berkeley, CA: University of California Press.

Teng E. (2006). 'Eurasian Hybridity in Chinese Utopian Visions: From "One World" to "A Society Based on Beauty" and Beyond'. *Positions: East Asia Cultures Critique* 14(1), pp. 131–163.

Teoh, S. K. (2011). 'Developing Critical Race Theory to Study Race and Racism in China's Media: A Case Study of the Chocolate Girl's Bittersweet Stardom on Go Oriental Angel'. M.A. Thesis in Communication Studies, Sacramento, CA: California State University.

Ualiyeva, S. K., and Edgar, A. (2014). 'In the Laboratory of Peoples' Friendship: Mixed People in Kazakhstan from the Soviet Era to the Present'. In R. King-O'Riain, S. Small, M. Mahtani, M. Song, and P. Spickard (eds), *Global Mixed Race*. New York: New York University Press, pp. 68–90.

Vines, S. (2009). 'China's Black Pop Idol Exposes Her Nation's Racism'. *Guardian*. 1 November. Available at: www.theguardian.com/world/2009/nov/01/lou-jing-chinese-talent-show (accessed: 3 March 2017).

Waltner, A. (1990). *Getting an Heir: Adoption and the Construction of Kinship in Late Imperial China*. Honolulu, Hawaii: University of Hawai'i Press.

Wang Q. (2012). 'Beauty That Will Take Your Breath Away: Ten Mixed-Blood Actresses (美到令人窒息的10大混血女星)'. *Xinhua Shequ* 新华社区. Available at: http://news.xinhuanet.com/forum/2012–09/26/c123760704.htm (accessed: 3 March 2017).

Weston, K. (2001). 'Kinship, Controversy, and the Sharing of Substance: The Race/Class Politics of Blood Transfusion'. In S. Franklin and S. McKinnon (eds), *Relative Values: Reconfiguring Kinship Studies*. Durham and London: Duke University Press, pp. 148–174.

Williams, B. (1995). 'Classification Systems Revisited'. In S. Yanagisako and C. Delaney (eds), *Naturalizing Power*. New York and London: Routledge, pp. 201–236.

Wilms, S. (2005). ' "Ten Times More Difficult to Treat": Female Bodies in Medical Texts from Early Imperial China'. *Nan Nü: Men, Women and Gender in Early and Imperial China* 7(2) (October), pp. 182–215.

Xie C. (2012). 'The Mixed-Blood Offspring of Chinese Men Married to Foreign Women in the Past Few Years (More Than a Thousand Photographs) – Chinese Blood Overseas! (最近几年中国男人和外国女人的混血孩子（上千张照片）–海外的中华血脉！)'. Available at: http://bbs.tianya.cn/post-funinfo-3107012–1.shtml (accessed: 3 March 2017).

Xinhuanet. (2013). 'Shen Danping's Beautiful Mixed-Blood Daughter Takes Stock of the Joys and Sorrows of Celebrities' Foreign Love Lives (沈丹萍漂亮混血女儿惊艳盘点明星悲喜异国恋-港澳频道-新华网)'. *News.china.com.cn*. Available at: http://news.china.com.cn/live/2013–05/23/content_ 20116067.htm (accessed: 10 October 2014).

Zhou Xingkai 周杏开. (1992). *Handbook on International Marriage (*涉外婚姻指南*)*. Guangzhou: Sun Yat-sen University Press (中山大学出版社).

Zhou R. (2009). 'Seeing Red over Black Angel'. *China Daily.com*, 18 September. Available at: www.chinadaily.com.cn/showbiz/2009–09/18/content_8707573.htm (accessed: 16 December 2013).

3 *Métis* of Vietnam

An historical perspective on mixed-race children from the French colonial period

Christina Firpo

Introduction

Gerard Addat, a *métis* (mixed-race) Franco-Vietnamese septuagenarian, stepped onto the stage, adjusted his hat and listened while the first few Orientalized notes of a tune began to play. His eyes scanned the studio audience as he began to sing: '*I remember Saigon* …', reminiscing about the city he had left in the middle of his 'tender childhood'. As the music continued, the screen began displaying 1950s photos of *métis* children posing with their siblings or mothers. 'Pierre Hermitte, seeking sister Marie Therese Hermite, born October 10, 1935 in Quy Nhơn, father was a French soldier', the screen read in Vietnamese. The screen cut to Robert Vaeza, a handsome *métis* adolescent in a dress shirt and freshly ironed pants, one hand in his pocket and head held proudly, and then to a photo of a mother lovingly cradling her infant daughter, Jaqueline Louise Richard. Between photos, the screen flashed a phone number for viewers to call with information that could connect these *métis* with their maternal families.

In December 2013, Addat and his childhood friend, Jacques Roger, also *métis*, travelled from France to Ho Chi Minh City to appear on the Vietnamese television show 'As Though Never Separated' ['Như chưa hè có cuộc ly']. Wildly popular, the show reunites loved ones who had been separated by the many wars of the twentieth century. Sixty years ago, when the men were boys, they were separated from their mothers and sent to France during the last years of French colonial rule in Vietnam. Jacques, the son of an Indian soldier of the colonial army, pleaded with viewers to help him find his Vietnamese mother. He struggles to maintain his composure as he tells Thu Uyên, the show's host, that he yearns to see his mother one last time.[1]

Gerard Addat, the Hermite children, Robert Vaeza, and Jaqueline Louise Richard were just a handful of the thousands of *métis* children of French soldiers removed from the Vietnamese milieu to be raised by colonial French child welfare agencies. After the 1954 defeat of the French at Diện Biên Phủ – the battle that brought colonial rule to an end – French childcare organizations evacuated more than 1,000 *métis* children to France, where they were raised as middle-class French children. With few exceptions, the *métis* evacuees never saw their mothers again. Six decades later, Gerard, Jacques, and dozens of other *métis* evacuees are returning to Vietnam to find the mothers they left behind.

Vietnamese media has focused a great deal of attention on stories of *métis* from the colonial period. In 2014, *Thanh Niên* newspaper published a series of articles titled 'Mixed-race Children' featuring, among many others, the stories of Lường Thị Lao and Lương Văm Đăm. Like Gerard and Jacques, both were *métis* children of soldiers fighting for the colonial army. However, unlike the other two boys, Lao, the daughter of an ethnic minority woman and a North African soldier for the colonial army, and Đăm, the son of a Vietnamese woman and a sub-Saharah African soldier, remained in Vietnam after decolonization. In May 2014, the Vietnamese newspaper *Thanh Niên* ran a story about the pair, who were rejected by Vietnamese society and denied an education. Today, the two are a topic of interest for Vietnamese media.[2]

The case of mixed-race children in colonial Vietnam follows similar patterns to those of the colonies in the Anglophone world of the US, Great Britain, and South Africa, where mixed-race people came to be seen as potentially problematic to the colonial social order (Furedi, 2001). As David Parker and Miri Song argue, the very existence of mixed-race children casts doubt on colonial claims of racial difference (Parker and Song, 2001). In colonial situations where the colonized population greatly outnumbered colonizers, the status of mixed-race children was determined by the social and political exigencies of the time (Ifekwunigwe, 2004).

This chapter explores the complicated colonial history and legacy of Franco-Vietnamese, Indian-Asian, and Afro-Asian mixed-race children who were associated with the colonial empire. I argue that the racial categorization of mixed-race individuals in twentieth-century Vietnam depended on multiple factors, including the marital status of their parents, the race of the father, and the political environment of the time. In the early decades of colonial rule, although Eurasian children of married French men and Vietnamese were seen as French, both Vietnamese and French colonial society rejected the children of unmarried couples. This changed during World War I, when French colonists made the case that all Eurasian children – legitimate or illegitimate – were racially French. Yet the colonial state ignored illegitimate Afro-Asian and Indian-Asian illegitimate mixed-race children until after World War II, when the state also incorporated them into the French racial imagination. In the process of decolonization, colonial officials sent mixed-race Eurasian and Afro-Asian children to France with the claim of protecting them from a Vietnamese population that French administrators thought had become virulently anti-French. In recent years, however, some of these individuals, now adults, have returned to Vietnam to reconnect with their past. Long shunned by Vietnamese society, *métis* like Gerard, Jacques, Lao and Đăm are now being welcomed with open arms.

Franco-Vietnamese *métis*

Although the French presence in Vietnam dates back to the early missionary and trading activity of the seventeenth century, the *métis* population did not become substantial until the late nineteenth century. In the late nineteenth century, the influx of French soldiers sent to Indochina to fight in colonial wars resulted in mixed-race births.[3] The ensuing colonization of Indochina was initially a male endeavour. Historian Charles Meyer calculated that in 1888, there were 12,308 French troops in Tonkin, 2,348 in Annam, 2,090 in Cochinchina, and 614 in Cambodia, as well as roughly 40,000 troops from North Africa stationed throughout the area. In the city of Hanoi alone, there were 356 men and 73 women, meaning one European woman to 4.8 European men (Meyer, 1985). In the countryside, where most of the military battles took place, there were almost no European women. European men thus took local wives and paramours, resulting in mixed-race births. In the early twentieth century, the French colonial government attempted to rectify these ratios and developed various programs in conjunction with the metropolitan government to send white French women to Indochina (Ha, 2014).

No comprehensive statistics exist for the colony's entire population of *métis* – neither recognized nor unrecognized. Statistics on *métis* births are impossible to estimate because the colonial census rarely recorded *métis* by ethnicity, but instead by citizenship. While the categories changed over time, generally speaking, the census accounted for French citizens, European nationals, indigenous, and 'other Asians'. Legally speaking, *métis* who had been recognized by their French fathers were French; those who had not been recognized were Asian (Ha, 2014). As a result, the census classified *métis* as either French/European or indigenous. Those *métis* born to parents who had registered their marriage with the colonial state inherited their father's French citizenship (Saada, 2011).

For the most part, Eurasian *métis* whose French fathers remained with the family became integrated into the French colonial sphere, and, if born to wealthy or politically connected fathers, some even led privileged lives. *Métis* often served in the colonial police, and, by the 1920s, *métis* journalists like Henri Chavigny de la Chevrotière and Eugène Dejean De Batie had become household names (Langlois, 1967; Peycam, 2012; Trần, 1961). Of course, the degree to which French colonists accepted Eurasians raised with their fathers depended on a multitude of factors, including class, racial characteristics, and fluency (or lack thereof) in French language and culture. Vietnamese society came to regard Eurasians who had become integrated into the French cultural sphere as racially French.

In cases where parents were unmarried at the time of their *métis* child's birth, the child inherited its mother's status as a colonial subject and was thus denied the rights and privileges of a French citizen. This could change if the father legally recognized the child as his offspring. This only happened, however, if the father remained part of his child's life – and most relationships were temporary. In some cases, the father's military unit moved on, and he went with it; in other cases, the father had been serving as a functionary and was called back to the metropole. Some fathers deliberately evaded the responsibility of fatherhood, while others, having impregnated the mothers through prostitution or rape, remained oblivious to their paternity. The result was that many *métis* were abandoned by their French fathers and raised with their Vietnamese mothers in the

Vietnamese cultural milieu. Without the cultural influence of their French fathers, these *métis* followed their mothers' cultural practices, and few learned to speak French or understand French cultural norms. From the early years of colonization until the first years of World War I, French colonial society regarded fatherless *métis* as racial Others: as Vietnamese or as an ambiguous non-French racial outsider.

For its part, Vietnamese society likewise regarded *métis* children as outsiders, regardless of their citizenship status. The outsider status of *métis* in Vietnamese society is best understood in terms of family lineage. As is the case today, mid-twentieth-century Vietnamese society was patrilineal. Under this social structure, the paternal lineage is referred to as the 'inside family' (*gia đình bên nội*) and the maternal lineage is referred to as the 'outside family' (*gia đình bên ngoại*). This patrilineal structure manifested in various ways. For one thing, after marrying, a couple typically moved into the groom's family home. The bride and her new family did maintain relations with her parents but now considered them part of the 'outside family'; as for the bride's parents themselves, they likewise considered their daughter's family to be outside of their lineage – though they most certainly loved her family nonetheless. The connection to the paternal line was not just physical but also spiritual, with children performing worship rites in honour of their paternal, but not maternal, ancestors. *Métis* children, lacking the important paternal line within Vietnamese society, could not fulfil their social duties of performing ancestor rites. Because *métis* traced their paternal line to France, they were widely regarded as being French (Hy Van Luong, 1984).

Although *métis* lacked a paternal line, they were not necessarily physically abandoned to fend for themselves or unloved. Judging from correspondence between mothers and the colonial government, it is evident that many Vietnamese mothers and grandparents loved their *métis* children and considered them part of their families. Nonetheless, because many of the mothers of *métis* children were unmarried, they were often assumed to be prostitutes, and their children were stigmatized as a result. The most infamous writing on mixed-race relationships was a series of reportage articles published in 1934 by Vũ Trọng Phụng. Phụng's articles portrayed the mothers of *métis* children as conniving women who went looking for 'Sugar Daddies' among the French soldiers and cold-heartedly gave birth to *métis* children in the hope of getting wealthy off the support that the fathers would presumably pay to support their children (Vũ, 2004).

Seeing *métis* children rejected by both French and Vietnamese society, in the 1890s, French colonists organized welfare societies to 'protect' Eurasian *métis* children who lacked a French paternal influence. These 'protection societies', as they were called, were based off the Dutch model of Eurasian welfare institutions in the Netherlands Indies.[4] Although in many cases, the organizers of these societies were genuinely concerned about the welfare of these children, their motivations were not merely altruistic. They also feared that abandoned Eurasian children would become social deviants (sex workers, rebels, or poor whites) and thus potential threats to French prestige and colonial authority.[5] Protection societies tracked down fatherless Eurasian children in the Vietnamese countryside and took custody of them. While some mothers voluntarily gave up custody, others were coerced – or even forced – to separate from their children (Firpo, 2016). Protection societies used the French 1889 law on parental neglect to make the case that impoverished Vietnamese mothers could not properly care for their children. For example, the 1906 policy handbook of the Society for Protection of Abandoned *Métis* Children in Tonkin states:

> The association takes in *métis* children who have been abandoned by their father or mother.... For children abandoned by their father, in cases where the attitude of the mother justifies such measure, [the society will see to] the divestment of parental power in the terms of the 24 July 1889 law, promulgated in Indochina on 8 August 1891.[6]

Similar to cases of the 'Stolen Generation' in Australia, Indian Boarding Schools in the United States, and the First Nation Schools in Canada, the French colonial government collaborated with protection societies throughout the colonial period to systematically remove children from their mothers and the indigenous cultural milieu. Protection societies raised wards in institutions where they were educated in the French language and culture, with the aim of reintegrating them into the colony as French men and women loyal to the colonial government.

Although protection societies and the colonial state accepted fatherless Eurasians as French, it was not until World War I that the general colonial public came to regard them as such. As massive war deaths led to demographic concerns about the decline of the French race, French colonists began to focus on the white ancestry of fatherless Eurasians and to consider these young people as a potential means of revitalizing the French population in the colony as well as strategic areas of the metropole.[7] It was within this context that protection societies increased efforts to remove Eurasian children from the Vietnamese milieu and worked with colonial officials to apply laws that promoted granting French citizenship to fatherless Eurasians.[8]

After the war, protection societies worked with the colonial state to use wards to populate strategic areas of Annam and villages in France that had experienced high levels of war deaths. The state devised a four-part program to integrate fatherless Eurasians into the colonial population. The colonial government established a military school for *métis*, L'École des Enfants de Troupe Eurasiens, to train them as officers to lead the Indochinese troops.[9] The state continued to fund settlement programs in Annam[10] and introduced a new program to use Eurasians to populate the city of Dalat, the site of the proposed new colonial capital, with white French men and women.[11] The aim of the plan was for Eurasians to become the permanent French population of the colony and to form a new elite to counterbalance the Vietnamese, Cambodian, and Lao elite.[12]

Afro-Asian and Indian-Asian *métis*

Jacques Roger, mentioned in the introductory paragraph as one of the guests on the television show 'As Though Never Separated', was born in 1952 to Lê Thị Nghĩa and an Indian soldier fighting for the French army. Roger's birth name was Lê văn Janot. In 1958, his father returned to India and Roger was sent to France. While the US–Vietnam War raged in his maternal homeland, Roger grew up in a protection society institution in France. He remained in France through his adulthood, but always longed for the mother he left behind in Vietnam.[13]

Jacques Roger's story reflects a shift in the racial imaginings of *métis* children that occurred among French colonists after World War II. Until the end of World War II, protection societies and the colonial government were mainly interested in Eurasians: the *métis* children of white fathers. Even when mothers of Indian or African children willingly offered to give up custody of their children, protection societies refused these children of non-white men.[14] Protection society archives reveal a handful of cases in which low-ranking administrators did give aid to children of Indian or African soldiers, only to be reprimanded by superiors who explained, 'We do not concern ourselves with Hindu children'.[15] At the end of World War II and the start of the Vietnamese Revolution (1946–1954), protection societies, now operating under the umbrella name Fédération des Ouvres de l'Enfance Francaise d'Indochine (FOEFI), changed their policy to include the *métis* children of Asian and African soldiers, like Jacques Roger. The FOEFI worked with the French military to prevent abandoned Afro-Asian children from being used as propaganda by the Việt Minh rebel forces. This change in policy signalled a shift in the racial imagination of the French nation, which French colonists came to see as incorporating the greater French empire. FOEFI's members, most of whom were *métis* themselves, began working with organizations in other French colonies, specifically French West Africa and French Equitorial Africa, to secure rights for biracial children. The close relationship and frequent correspondence among groups concerned with mixed-race children in other colonies speaks to the emergence of a transnational French imperial identity among mixed-race individuals. The groups found solidarity among peoples with familial ties to the French colonies. The metaphors of family and neglected children were frequently employed when discussing mixed-race children in the empire.[16] By the late 1940s, when protection societies began using Afro-Asian and Indian-Asian children with no white French heritage to further the colony's demographic plans, it was clear that the 'French race' was no longer about whiteness; instead, it was associated with the empire (Firpo, 2016). For example, adult members of a *métis* organization, many members of which also served as the administrators of *métis* protection societies, described themselves as belonging to part of an empire-wide 'family' in which the Eurafricans of Africa and the Eurasians of Indochina were brothers and sisters.

In 1954, severe losses at the battle of Điện Biên Phủ led France to concede the colony at the Geneva Convention. The resulting Geneva accords ended

French colonization and shifted governance of the area south of the seventeenth parallel to the Republic of Vietnam (RVN). Although the RVN opened Vietnamese citizenship to the *métis* of Vietnamese mothers, once they had reached adulthood,[17] FOEFI administrators feared that *métis*, being the children of former colonizers, would become targets for violence. The FOEFI evacuated almost 1,000 Eurasian, Afro-Asian, Caribbean Asian, and Indian-Asian wards. Jacques Roger, Gerard Addat, and the others were among those sent to France.

Gerard Addat and his brother were evacuated in 1955 or 1956 – he is not sure of the year. 'We were lucky to have a second chance at life', he told Thu Uyên, host of 'As Though Never Separated', adding that 'the separation from Vietnam was painful, very painful'. In France, the FOEFI raised wards in group homes located throughout the country. The FOEFI separated Gerard and his brother, sending the boys to different group homes, as per FOEFI policy. Recounting the separation from his brother, Addat became emotional. 'It was cruel', he said.[18]

In France, Gerard, Jacques, and other wards integrated into French culture and enrolled in French schools. Yet the FOEFI did not completely erase their *métis* identity. Although the directors of the FOEFI institutions forbade wards from speaking Vietnamese, many continued to do so on the sly (Roustan, 2011). Meanwhile, FOEFI president William Bazé, himself a *métis* from Saigon, carefully cultivated in his wards a racial identity that allowed them to see themselves as simultaneously French and mixed-race. Decades later, former FOEFI wards identified themselves as both, and they specifically described themselves as 'FOEFIen' (Roustan, 2011).

The majority of FOEFI wards who were raised in France grew up to be quite successful. Many attended university, medical school or law school. Unfortunately, however, some wards faced difficulties adjusting to the separation from their families and their new life in France; a few even committed suicide.[19] Although the majority of the wards sent to France never reconnected with their mothers back in Vietnam, some lucky ones did manage to do so.[20]

Métis who stayed in Vietnam

Lường Thị Lao and Lương Văm Đăm had a very different experience from Gerard Addat and Jacques Roger. Both Lao, the child of an ethnic minority woman and a north African soldier for the colonial army, and Đăm, the child of a Vietnamese woman and a sub-Saharan African soldier, remained in Vietnam after decolonization and have continued to live there ever since. Both Lao and Đăm had difficult lives due to their mixed heritage.[21]

Lao and Đăm grew up as outcasts in communist North Vietnam. Initially, the Democratic Republic of Vietnam allowed *métis* to take DRV citizenship – and some did.[22] Aside from basic facts gleaned from citizenship files and a few anecdotal stories about *métis* fighting for the DRV, historians know little about DRV policies towards *métis*. In April 1954, as the battle of Điện Biên Phủ raged nearby, Lường Thị Khón, an ethnic Tai woman, found North African-Vietnamese *métis* baby Lường Thị Lao abandoned by the roadside.

After decolonization, young Lao remained in communist North Vietnam. Her appearance made her stand out among the villagers. Like many *métis*, her foreign background barred her from school and she grew up illiterate. For his part, Lường Văn Đăm, also from the Điện Biên Phủ region, was born of a love affair that his ethnic Tai mother had with a sub-Saharan African soldier in the French colonial army. When a Việt Minh victory became imminent, his father left in a rush, crying as he scribbled some foreign words on a piece of paper. His mother, pregnant at the time, never saw his father again – and never learned the meaning of the note. When the baby was born, she named him Đăm, which means 'black' in the Tai language. Like Lao, Đăm's mixed heritage left him excluded from schools and employment.[23] Today, Đăm still lives in the region of his birth and makes a meagre living as a farmer.

In war-torn South Vietnam, life was difficult for the children of the former colonizers, and popular culture portrayed *métis* as outcasts.[24] Wealthier *métis* adults migrated to France for fear of being punished as the children of colonizers.[25] Those who came from impoverished backgrounds had to remain where they were, and few finished grade school.[26] *Métisse* girls and their mothers were sexualized for their 'exotic' looks and presumed association with prostitution. Rumours abounded about *métisse* seductresses robbing hapless men or about innocent *métisse* girls lured into the sex industry.[27]

In April 1975, the army of the Democratic Republic of Vietnam invaded Saigon, thereby ending the war and unifying the country. Upon taking over, the communist state established a provisionary government in the South that punished the mothers of mixed-race children on the grounds that they had worked as prostitutes for the French or American enemy (Duiker, 1989). Franco-Vietnamese *métis* and their mothers flooded the FOEFI office in Saigon, begging for passage to France.[28] Initially, the provisionary government in Saigon denied their requests to emigrate.[29] Later, in 1979, the DRV adopted a policy to allow the emigration of people deemed 'difficult to assimilate' – a move that provided children of Frenchmen with the necessary exit visas.[30] Yet, for unknown reasons, the French government stalled immigrations, thus leaving the now-adult children of Frenchmen in Vietnam.[31]

In November 1979, a group of Franco-Vietnamese *métis* adults gathered at the French consulate in Ho Chi Minh City, as Saigon was now known, to demand that the French government follow through with promises to allow *métis* immigration into France. The crowd became impatient with the consulate's refusal to hear their cases. Crowd members broke through the security barrier, into the consulate grounds. Consulate guards fired on the crowd and beat protesters.[32] While the story appeared in the French newspapers, it was overshadowed by the catastrophic events resulting from the Khmer Rouge takeover in neighbouring Cambodia, and thus received little international coverage.

Unable to go to France, some *métis* descendants of Frenchmen managed to emigrate from Vietnam by passing themselves off as the children of American soldiers. With the end of the US-Vietnam War, the US Congress had attempted to legislate a means for the children of American soldiers to immigrate to the

United States. After a series of failed acts, in 1988, Congress passed the Amerasian Homecoming Act to allow Amerasian children born between 1962 and 1976 to immigrate to the United States. Because the Amerasian Homecoming Act was specifically designed to provide aid to the mixed-race children of American soldiers whose fathers never officially recognized them, the criteria for determining American parentage was subjective and often relied on racial phenotypes. Ideally, children or their mothers could provide the name of the father, his military unit, or provide a time and place of conception that would enable the US government to identify his military unit. Mixed-race individuals born of French or Franco-African fathers sometimes succeeded in passing for children of American soldiers born in the early years of the American intervention (Yarborough, 2005; DeBonis,1995).

Conclusion

Mixed-race children of the colonial era have historically been excluded from the Vietnamese national imagination, as these children were an uncomfortable reminder of the women who had sexual relations with the colonizer. Today, the Vietnamese historical memory is revisiting the war-torn twentieth century and the mixed-race children born during the late colonial era. Stories of *métis* left behind in Vietnam have begun appearing in the news, with major Vietnamese newspapers covering stories of *métis* returning to Vietnam after many decades away.[33] Meanwhile, 'As Though Never Separated' has chronicled more than 30 cases of *métis* evacuees returning to Vietnam to find their maternal families. The unparalleled popularity of this television show, which uses family histories to address the complicated politics of the twentieth century wars, has led the Vietnamese public to reconsider *métis* people from the colonial period. Once viewed as outsiders, the television show presents them as long-lost family members who suffered along with the Vietnamese nation. Whereas during the colonial period discourse on *métis* focused on their French heritage, in its efforts to connect *métis* with their Vietnamese families 'As Though Never Separated' shifted the focus to the Vietnamese side of their identity. As a result, this television show is encouraging viewing audiences to reconsider *métis* as sharing in the national and racial identity. Popular culture has thus played a significant role not just in framing the history of *métis* removals within the broader context of Vietnamese history, but also in including, however belatedly, *métis* people within the Vietnamese nation.

Notes

1 'Như chưa hề có cuộc chia ly', episode 69, 15 December 2013.
2 'Chuyện những người con lính lê dương tại Việt Nam–Kỳ 3: Nỗi buồn ven trời Tây Bắc', *Thanh Niên*, 9 May 2014.
3 One of the first memoirs believed to be written by a Franco-Vietnamese man was Chaigneau, Michel Đức. *Souvenirs de Hué*. Paris: L'Imprimerie Impériale, 1857.

4 Letter, signed G.C.C., 10 December 1903, VNNA 1, GGI 3823; 'Rapport sur le paupérisme à Java', 3 October 1903, French National Archives, Centre des Archives d'Outre Mer [hereafter CAOM], GGI 54225.
5 'Note', 29 February 1904, CAOM, GGI 7701; 'Société de protection des enfants métis abandonnés du Tonkin, Statuts revises à l'assemblée générale du 18 Mars 1904', VNNA 1, RST 5545; 'Rapport de la chamber de commerce de Hanoi regardant la Proposition de loi relative à l'abrogation de l'article 340 du code civil (Reconnaîssance Legale de la Paternité Naturelle)', 26 December 1910, VNNA 1, RST 41624; Stoler, 'Making Empire Respectable', 361.; Letter, signed G.C.C., January 10, 1903, VNNA 1, GGI 3823.
6 Article II, Section II, 'Société de Protection des Enfants Métis Abandonnés, Statuts', 13 July 1906. Hanoi National Archives, Center 1, Files of the Resident Superior of Tonkin 5545.
7 Minister of Colonies to GGI, 18 October 1926, VNNA 1, RST 48972.
8 See laws on the retroactively legitimate children of fallen French soldiers and 'pupille de la nation'. Minister of War to Minister of Colonies, 16 June 1917, CAOM, GGI 26921; 'Petit Guide pour l'Application de Loi du 27 Juillet 1917 Institutant les Pupilles de la Nation', CNA, RSC 37339.
9 Arrêté by GGI Jules Brévié, 10 October 1938, VNNA 4, RSA 3864.
10 Goucoch to GGI, 3 November 1941, VNNA I, GGI 4806.
11 RSA to GGI, 9 March 1939, VNNA 1, GGI 76.
12 'Rapport sur l'activité de la Fondation Jules Brévié pendant l'année 1943', 1944, VNNA I, GGI 482.
13 'Như chưa hề có cuộc chia ly', episode 69, 15 December 2013.
14 For example, see the case of Franco-Senegalese children. Rivière to Aumont, 18 November 1944, VNNA 1, GGI 495.
15 Aumont to Rivière, 28 September 1944, VNNA 1, GGI 495; Aumont to Rivière, 7 October 1944, VNNA 1, GGI 495; Aumont to Rivère, 7 November 1944, VNNA 1, GGI 495; Rivière to Aumont, 18 November 1944, VNNA 1, GGI 495.
16 For more on the Eurafrican community, see Owen White, *Children of the French Empire: Miscegenation and Colonial Society in French West Africa 1895–1960*; Bazé, 'L'Indispensable Solidarité'; 'Retour Vers Le Passé'; 'Position Juridique des Métis', *L'Eurafricain*, 1952.
17 Under the terms of the 1955 Franco-Vietnamese Convention on citizenship, unless recognized by their fathers, *métis* minors inherited their mothers' Vietnamese citizenship. The Vietnamese policy allowed for those *métis* who inherited their fathers' citizenship to, upon passing through adolescence into adulthood, choose Vietnamese citizenship. 'Convention sur la Nationalité' reprinted in 'Féderation des Oeuvres de l'Enfance Francais d'Indochine, Exercice 1955, Assemblée Général Ordinaire des 19, 20, 21 Mars 1956' (Saigon: Imprimerie Francais Outre Mer, 1956).
18 'Như chưa hề có cuộc chia ly', episode 69, 15 December 2013.
19 'FOEFI, Exercice 1959, Assemblée Générale Ordinaire des 5 et 6 Aout 1960'; 'FOEFI, Exercice 1963, Assemblée Générale Ordinaire du 11 Aout 1964'; 'Rapport sur les Activites de la FOEFI', 10 September 1965, CAC 0019960015, ART 22.
20 Photographic evidence from the FOEFI archives shows a few mothers reunited with their children in Paris. CAOM, FOEFI album 48.
21 'Chuyện những người con lính lê dương tại Việt Nam–Kỳ 3: Nỗi buồn ven trời Tây Bắc', *Thanh Niên*, 9 May 2014.
22 For example, see the citizenship requests in CAOM, Files of the Gouvernement Fait 9.
23 'Chuyện những người con lính lê dương tại Việt Nam–Kỳ 3: Nỗi buồn ven trời Tây Bắc', *Thanh Niên*, 9 May 2014.

24 See for example, the popular saying '*Métis* eat sweet potatoes with the skin, they eat dog meat with the fur, and they eat persimmons with the seeds'. ['Tây lai ăn khoai cả vỏ, ăn chó cả lông, ăn hồng cả hột']. Conversation with PNL, October 2011, San Luis Obispo, California.; The operetta 'Những đứa Métis' chronicles their struggles. Xuân Triêm, 'Nhận xét khái quát qua ca kịch phẩm xã hội trên sân khấu TMTN Những đứa Métis', *Miền Nam*, 22 December 1967.
25 In 1968, reportage journalist Hoàng Thị Thư interviewed a *métis* named René who left because he feared that *métis* lives would be difficult under the Diệm Regime. Thư, 'Người Việt trên đất Pháp'. Thư, 'Người Việt trên đất Pháp'; ibid.
26 Conversation with PNL October 2011, San Luis Obispo, California.
27 For example, see the story of 15-year-old MTL also known as AD. Mai Anh and Thanh Xuân, 'Quanh vụ La-thoại-Tân bị thưa dụ dỗ gái vị thành niên cô Mai Thị Liễu đã trở về gia đình vào tối 16–2', Mai Anh and Thanh Xuân, *Saigon Mới*, 18 February 1963.; VNNA 2: Phông Phủ thủ tướng việt nam cộng hoà: HS 29839.
28 Letter, Le Sous Directeur de la Famille et de l'Enfance Péchabrier to Ministre des Affaires Étrangèrs, direction des conventions administratives et des affiares consulaires, 18 June 1975. CAC 0019960015 ART 22.
29 Letter, signed Beauvais, 23 June 1975. CAC 0019960015 ART 22.
30 At the time of this policy, the Vietnamese government had just finished a two-decade project to classify Vietnam into 54 ethnic groups, as well as encourage Vietnam's ethnic Chinese and Khmer populations to emigrate. Patricia Pelley argues that the classification process homogenized Vietnamese society and created a new national culture. Patricia Pelley, ' "Barbarians" and "Younger Brothers": The Remaking of Race in Post Colonial Vietnam', *Journal of Southeast Asian Studies* 29(2) (1998); Van Tinh Nguyen, Hoang Van Nguyen, and Van Than Thai, 'Les difficulties des *métis* franco-Vietnamiens à émigrer en France et l'attitude de Paris', *Le Monde*, 18 September 1980; Conversations with PNL, October 2011, San Luis Obispo, CA.
31 Nguyen, Van Tinh, Hoang Van Nguyen, and Van Than Thai, 'Les difficulties des métis Franco-Vietnamiens à émigrer en France et l'attitude de Paris', *Le Monde*, 18 September 1980.
32 'Les difficultés des *métis* Franco-Vietnamiens à emigrer en France et l'attitude de Paris' (reprint of an unlabelled source, most likely *Le Monde*, 18 September 1980); FOEFI private archives.
33 'Những người Métis Pháp ở Điện Biên', *Tài nguyên và Môi Trường*, 11 April 2014. Available at: http://baotainguyenmoitruong.com.vn/suc-khoe-doi-song/201404/nhung-nguoi-con-lai-phap-o-dien-bien-518330,.html (accessed 27 January 2015); 'Người Métis Pháp 20 năm viết đơn tìm cha', *Báo Mới*, 17 July 2014. Available at: www.baomoi.com/Nguoi-con-lai-Phap-20-nam-viet-don-tim-cha/139/14330861.epi (accessed: 27 January 2014); 'Mihagui: Trong máu tôi ... có nước mắm?'; 'Robert Vaeza "coi như là Pháp" '; 'Tìm di ảnh', *Tuổi Trẻ*, 3 March 2012; 'Chuyện những người con lính lê dương tại Việt Nam–Kỳ 2: Những dòng họ cô đơn', *Thanh Niên Online*, 8 May 2014. Availble at: www.thanhnien.com.vn/doi-song/chuyen-nhung-nguoi-con-linh-le-duong-tai-viet-nam-ky-2-nhung-dong-ho-co-don-393882.html (accessed: 27 January 2015).

Bibliography

Báo Mới. (17 July 2014). Người con lai Pháp 20 năm viết đơn tìm cha. *Báo Mới*. 'Như chưa hề có cuộc chia ly'. Episode 69, 15 December 2013.

Bazé, W. (1952). L'indispensable Solidarité. *L'Eurafricain*.

Chaigneau, M. Đ. (1857). *Souvenirs de Hué*. Paris: L'Imprimerie Impériale.

DeBonis, S. (1995). *Children of the Enemy: Oral Histories of Vietnamese Amerasians and Their Mothers*. London: McFarland.
Duiker, W. (1989). *Vietnam Since the Fall of Saigon*. Athens: Ohio University Press.
Firpo, C. (2016) *The Uprooted: Race, Childhood, and Imperialism in French Indochina, 1890–1980*. Honolulu: University of Hawai'i Press.
FOEFI. (1956). 'Féderation des Oeuvres de l'Enfance Francais d'Indochine, Exercice 1955, Assemblée Général Ordinaire des 19, 20, 21 Mars 1956'. Saigon: Imprimerie Francais Outre Mer.
Furedi, F. (2001). 'How Sociology Imagined "Mixed-Race"'. In *Rethinking "Mixed-Race"*. London: Pluto Press.
Ha, M.-P. (2014). *French Women and the Empire: The Case of Indochina*. London: Oxford University Press.
Hoàng, T. T. (14 May 1968). Người Việt Trên Đất Pháp. *Miền Nam*.
Hy, V. L. (1984). 'Brother' and 'Uncle': An Analysis of Rules, Structural Contradictions and Meaning in Vietnamese Kinship. *American Anthropologist* 86, pp. 290–315.
Ifekwunigwe, J. O. (2004). 'Introduction: Rethinking Mixed-race Studies'. In Jayne O. Ifekwunigwe (ed.), *'Mixed-race' Studies: A reader*. New York: Routledge, pp. 1–29.
L'Eurafricain. (1949). 'Position Juridique des Métis'. *L'Eurafricain*.
Langlois, W. (1967). *André Malraux: The Indochina Adventure*. New York: Praeger.
Mai Anh and Thanh Xuân. (18 February 1963). 'Quanh vụ La-thoại-Tân bị thưa dụ dỗ gái vị thành niên cô Mai Thị Liễu đã trở về gia đình vào tối'. 16–2. *Saigon Mới*.
Meyer, C. (1985). *La Vie Quotidienne des Français en Indochine 1860–1910*. Paris: Hachette Littérature.
Nguyen, V. T., H. V. Nguyen, and V. T. Thai. (18 September 1980). Les difficulties des métis Franco-Vietnamiens à émigrer en France et l'attitude de Paris. *Le Monde*.
Parker, D., and M. Song, (2001). 'Introduction'. In *Rethinking "Mixed-Race"*. London: Pluto Press, pp. 1–22.
Pelley, P. (1998). ' "Barbarians" and "Younger Brothers": The Remaking of Race in Post Colonial Vietnam'. *Journal of Southeast Asian Studies* 29(2), pp. 374–391.
Peycam, P. M. F. (2012). *The Birth of Vietnamese Political Journalism: Saigon, 1916–1930*. New York: Columbia University Press.
Roustan, F. (2011). *Inconnu, Presumé Français* (documentary).
Saada, E. (2011). *Empire's Children: Race, Filiation, and Citizenship in the French Colonies*. Chicago: University of Chicago Press.
Tài Nguyên và Môi Trường. (11 April 2014). 'Những người con lai Pháp ở Điện Biên'. *Tài Nguyên và Môi Trường*.
Thanh Niên. (8 May 2014). 'Chuyện những người con lính lê dương tại Việt Nam–Kỳ 2: Những dòng họ cô đơn'. *Thanh Niên*. Available at: www.thanhnien.com.vn/doi-song/chuyen-nhung-nguoi-con-linh-le-duong-tai-viet-nam-ky-2-nhung-dong-ho-co-don-393882.html (accessed: 27 January 2015).
Thanh Niên. (9 May 2014). 'Chuyện những người con lính lê dương tại Việt Nam–Kỳ 3: Nỗi buồn ven trời Tây Bắc'. *Thanh Niên*.
Trần Huy Liệu. (1961). *Đảng Thanh Niên 1926–1927: Tập tài liệu và hồi ký*. Hà Nội: Nhà Xuất Bản Sử Học.
Tuổi Trẻ Cuối Tuần. (26 July 2009). Robert Vaeza 'Coi Như Là Pháp'. *Tuổi Trẻ Cuối Tuần*.
Tuổi Trẻ. (3 March 2012). 'Tìm di ảnh'. *Tuổi Trẻ*.
Việt Báo. (7 October 2006). 'Mihagui: Trong Máu Tôi … Có Nước Mắm?' *Việt Báo*.

Vũ Trọng Phụng. (2004). 'Kỹ nghệ lấy tây'. In *Kỹ nghệ lấy tây & cơm thầy cơm cô*, by Vũ Trọng Phụng, 9–101. Hà Nội: Nhà xuất bản văn học.

White, O. (1999). *Children of the French Empire: Miscegenation and Colonial Society in French West Africa 1895–1960*. Oxford: Oxford University Press.

Xuân Triêm. (22 December 1967). 'Nhận xét khái quát qua ca kịch phẩm xã hội trên sân khấu TMTN Những đứa Métis'. *Miền Nam*.

Yarborough, T. (2005). *Surviving Twice: Amerasian Children of the Vietnam War*. Washington, DC: Potomac Books.

Part II
South Korea and Japan

4 Developing bilingualism in a largely monolingual society
Southeast Asian marriage migrants and multicultural families in South Korea

Mi Yung Park

Introduction

In recent years, the number of international marriages has increased substantially in East Asian countries (Jones and Shen, 2008), including South Korea (hereafter 'Korea'). International marriage in Korea, predominantly between foreign women and Korean men, is especially common in rural communities (Kim, 2008). The number of female marriage migrants in Korea has risen from 111,834 in 2007 to 253,791 in 2015, an increase of approximately 130 per cent (Korean Ministry of Gender Equality and Family, 2015). This has contributed to rapid diversification in the country's ethnic composition. This new diversity is usually described as *damunhwa*, meaning 'multicultural'. Families that include marriage migrants are often categorized as *damunhwa gajeong* ('multicultural families'). This term refers to families with 'one or both spouses ... of different ethnic or cultural backgrounds from mono-cultural Koreans' (Kang, 2010, p. 293). The growth in international marriage has led to increasing numbers of Korean children of mixed heritage, who are often referred to as *damunhwa* children ('multicultural children'), even when they are born and raised in Korea.

Damunhwa is a derogatory label and evokes low socio-economic status (Kim and Kim, 2015). Koreans maintain a strong sense of ethnic homogeneity, which many consider fundamental to the nation's stability (Shin, 2012). This ideology of monolithic nationalism creates very rigid boundaries in which migrants and their children are often defined as outsiders. Pride in ethnic homogeneity can cause discrimination and prejudice against migrant women and their children who do not look or speak like 'pure Koreans'. Although marriage migrants' children are Korean citizens, their status is often challenged by ethnic Koreans because of their mixed-race heritage (Lee *et al.*, 2015). In the conceptualization of Koreans as a single people, with a single language and a single culture, marriage migrants may be viewed as a triple threat with their different ethnicities, languages, and cultures. Marriage migrants' children face pressure to assimilate linguistically and culturally – perhaps to help mitigate the fact of their biological heritage and the threat their ethnicity and appearance pose to the imagined ideal. Marriage-migrant women are generally working class, from developing countries, and darker skinned than many Koreans (Kim, 2008), and their Korean husbands are often perceived as lower-class individuals who are unable to marry locally (Bélanger et al., 2010). These elements all feed into the derogatory nature of the term *damunhwa* and its evocation of low socio-economic status.

Previous studies have consistently shown a positive relationship between heritage language proficiency and the development of ethnic identities. Not only does heritage language proficiency enhance a multicultural child's sense of self (Pao et al., 1997; Shin, 2010), but ethnic minority children with higher levels of heritage language proficiency also develop bicultural identities and more positive attitudes toward both heritage and mainstream groups (Jo, 2001; Lee, 2002; Soto, 2002). Identity building among multicultural children is facilitated by supporting their knowledge of two languages and cultures (Kim and Kim, 2015). Depriving them of either language does 'injustice to their sense of identity because it is through language that one constructs an identity defined in collective terms of a shared culture' (Lee and Suarez, 2009, p. 142).

Multicultural children who are raised in Korea are usually exposed to two languages at home: Korean, which is usually their dominant language, and their heritage language, which is spoken by their mothers. For children, whose mothers are from Southeast Asia, their heritage languages such as Vietnamese, Cambodian, and Tagalog are not only minority languages, but are considered to represent low status and to be of limited use in education, media, and business (Park, 2017). This perceived low status is an additional burden within the context of largely monolingual Korea.

Korea's classroom instruction does not yet incorporate the linguistic and cultural backgrounds of multicultural children. Most elementary, middle, and high schools in Korea do not teach any Southeast Asian language as a foreign or heritage language. Currently, the only foreign language taught in most elementary schools is English. High schools usually offer three or four foreign languages, but only a couple of 'Special Purpose Foreign Language High Schools' provide elementary Vietnamese language classes (Ipsikorea, 2015).

This study explores whether and to what extent children of Southeast Asian marriage-migrant women learn, develop, and maintain their heritage language. In particular, it focuses on the views and behaviour of these women regarding their children's heritage language maintenance and the challenges they encounter in teaching their children their mother language in Korea's relatively monolingual society. By examining the complex interplay of these views and the impact they have on minority heritage language learning, the study offers insight into how multiculturalism and multilingualism can develop in a largely monocultural and monolingual society.

Language learning and discrimination against multi-ethnic children in Korea

As diversity in Korea has increased, multi-ethnic children's experiences have attracted researchers' interest. For example, Kim and Kim's (2015) study shows that the linguistic resources and cultural diversity of multi-ethnic children in

Korea are undervalued and not maintained. The children in their study were losing their heritage language proficiency because they had no heritage language community or were uninterested in learning the language. Lee et al.'s (2015) examination of Southeast Asian migrant women's childrearing practices discusses the women's ambivalent feelings about passing on their mother languages due to high expectations for their children's Korean proficiency. They sometimes avoided using their mother language because they worried about delaying their children's Korean language development and making them more vulnerable to discrimination. Kim (2010) found that the unfavourable environment for heritage language maintenance in Korea led some Filipino migrant women to send their children to the Philippines to learn their heritage language. This transnational mobility resulted in rapid development of the children's heritage language skills and helped build their Filipino identity. However, as Kim noted, these effects were probably transitory because the children avoided revealing their ethnic identities in Korean schools due to bullying or teasing.

In some cases, children from multicultural families suffer from academic and social problems, reportedly due to insufficient Korean language proficiency. Previous studies indicate that their academic performance tends to be poor, and their school dropout rates are much higher than those of children with two native Korean parents (Cho, 2006; Jo et al., 2008; Lee et al., 2008). There is a discourse in Korea that the educational problems of multi-ethnic children are caused by their foreign mothers' lack of Korean language proficiency (Kim, 2010). Bélanger et al. (2010) argue that the Korean government views migrant women as potentially problematic mothers whose limited language skills cause them difficulty in raising their children. From the perspectives of both migrant women and the dominant Korean society, language might be viewed – whether positively or negatively – as a proxy for other aspects of culture, heritage, and ethnicity.

To ease their integration into Korean society and the educational system, the Korean government provides Korean language programs for children from multicultural families. Children between three and 12 can receive in-home Korean language tutoring, where instructors visit the child's home weekly for one-to-one lessons on the language and culture. The program's objective is to make it easier for the children to adapt to school life and help prevent them from dropping out (Seoul Metropolitan Government, 2014). Elementary schools also provide after-school Korean language and culture lessons for multi-ethnic children, with the primary goal of improving the children's Korean literacy skills and cultural knowledge. These efforts have been criticized as assimilationist projects (Shin, 2012).

Despite various government efforts to assist multi-ethnic children's integration, the children often experience discrimination and prejudice. According to one survey of multi-ethnic children (Seol et al., 2005), 31 per cent of respondents reported that they felt excluded from their peer groups because their mothers were foreigners. Many respondents also reported the belief that their different attitudes or appearances (18.3 per cent) and language barriers (20.7 per cent) caused their experiences of isolation. The findings from Kim and Kim's 2015 study show that race played a major role in the children's socialization in schools. Lighter skinned children were welcomed whereas darker skinned children experienced bullying by their classmates. However, Kang (2010) argues that even children whose mothers are from other East Asian countries, and who have little or no difference from Koreans in their skin colour, have difficulty socializing with their Korean peers. He also asserts that after-school programs for multicultural children draw attention to their mixed heritage, prompting other Korean students to treat them differently.

Taken together, these studies suggest that Korean-born multi-ethnic children with Southeast Asian backgrounds may be stigmatized and subjected to discrimination based on their race, language, and culture. This may in turn discourage their development of a sense of belonging and pride in their family. In addition, due to little institutional or societal support for promoting minority languages, it is challenging for migrant women to teach their children their heritage language. This study examines Southeast Asian migrant women's attitudes and behaviour regarding their children's heritage language development, an aspect of their identity to which much attention is drawn by their mothers, the wider Korean society, and the state itself, and discusses the challenges they face in teaching their children their heritage languages within this context.

The study

This study's data come from fieldwork conducted from June to July 2014 and from December 2014 to January 2015 in a rural city in North Gyeongsang Province (also known as Gyeongbuk), in the southeast of the Korean peninsula. Semi-structured interviews, open-ended questionnaires, and field notes were the main data sources. Five women from Southeast Asia who had children between the ages of three and 15 participated. Their residency in Korea ranged from eight to 13 years, with a mean of ten years, six months. The ages of the participants were between 27 and 34 with a mean age of 31.8. All the participants reported that their child(ren)'s native or strongest language was Korean, and that they understood their heritage language better than they spoke it. Only two of the five participants reported that their children had basic literacy skills in the heritage language. Tables 4.1 and 4.2 summarize the backgrounds of the participants and their children, respectively. All names are pseudonyms.

At the first meeting, the participants were asked to complete background information sheets and open-ended questionnaires on their families and life histories, including decisions about migration, educational and work experiences, and future goals. Each participant was interviewed twice, with each interview session lasting from one to two hours. The interview questions covered the women's childrearing practices and beliefs and attitudes toward their heritage language and Korean, the challenges of teaching their mother language to their children, and their children's heritage language use and identities. These questions were used as a guide; the participants were encouraged to talk about their

Table 4.1 Participant profiles

Name	Age	Country of origin	Length of residence in Korea	Highest level of education	Occupation	Korean language proficiency[a]
Hyesoo	30	Cambodia	8 years	High school	Interpreter	Level 4
Jeong	34	Vietnam	12 years	High school	Salesperson	Level 3
Kyung	34	Vietnam	13 years	3-year college	Farmer	Level 4
Sooah	34	Vietnam	13 years	2-year college (in Korea)	Housewife	N/A[b]
Yumi	27	Vietnam	8 years	High school	Interpreter	Level 4

Notes

a Based on the participants' TOPIK test results. Test takers receive a level between 1 (the lowest) and 6 (the highest). Levels 3 and 4 are considered intermediate.

b Sooah had not taken the TOPIK; however, her Korean language proficiency seemed to be advanced given that she had graduated from a two-year college in Korea.

Table 4.2 Participants' children's backgrounds

Family	Age	Birthplace	Length of residence in Korea	Proficiency in heritage language	Parents' income[a]
Hyesoo's family	4 and 6	Korea	4 and 6	Beginner	Significantly below average
Jeong's family	9	Korea	9	Beginner	Above average
Kyung's family	9 and 11	Korea	9 and 7[b]	Beginner	Below average
Sooah's family	5, 9 and 11	Korea	5, 9 and 11	Beginner	Significantly below average
Yumi's family	4 and 6	Korea	4 and 6	Beginner	Significantly below average

Notes

a Estimated household income in relation to the average monthly household income of a Korean family (about 4.193 million won or approximately US$3,546; Statistics Korea 2015).

b Kyung's oldest child lived in Vietnam between the ages of one and four.

opinions and experiences freely. Korean was used throughout the interviews because all the participants could express themselves easily in Korean. All interview data were transcribed in Korean after each interview and translated into English by the author. The findings were analysed qualitatively and were checked with the participants for accuracy.

Findings

The findings are reported here in two broad sections. The first section illustrates the women's attitudes and behaviour in regard to heritage language maintenance. The second section focuses on the challenges they have encountered in teaching their children their mother language in the relatively monolingual environment of Korea.

Mothers' attitudes and behaviour in regard to heritage language development

The participants in this study generally had positive attitudes toward their children maintaining their heritage language. They felt that it was important for their children to develop their heritage language skills because the language was the children's main connection to their heritage and family back in their mothers' home country. However, the participants did not view their native languages as having high social capital in Korea, noting that the languages are neither taught in schools nor recognized by Korean society as having value.

Jeong explained that her son was not interested in learning his heritage language because he did not want to stand out from his Korean peers as a child of a multicultural family. In the hope that he would change his attitude toward his heritage language and culture, Jeong continued to encourage his heritage language learning by reading Vietnamese storybooks, watching Vietnamese movies, and taking him on trips to Vietnam. She mentioned her belief that speaking his heritage language would allow him to build closer relationships with his grandparents in Vietnam and strengthen his ethnic identity. She also took her son to Vietnamese events held in Korea so that he would be exposed to cultural activities such as singing, dancing, and cooking. However, she was unable to speak Vietnamese freely to her son at home, because her mother-in-law, with whom they lived, discouraged her from teaching him the language. By not accepting the use of Vietnamese, Jeong's mother-in-law overtly conveyed her negative attitude regarding the child's heritage language.

Hyesoo reported her belief that mothers should help their children learn their heritage languages, given that they do not otherwise receive bilingual education that values their linguistic and cultural background. She believed that the use of the heritage language at home is the most important factor in a child's heritage language maintenance. In response to a question regarding her children's heritage language development, Hyesoo said:

> My children's Cambodian proficiency is about 30 per cent of their Korean proficiency. My older daughter is especially interested in learning Cambodian. At first she laughed whenever I spoke Cambodian and was reluctant to learn, saying that the language sounded strange. Now my children can even sing Cambodian songs. I ask them many questions in Cambodian, pointing to various things. On the weekend, I also read Cambodian books with them and have them repeat and use important words in conversations so that I can teach them how to pronounce them correctly.

When I asked what type of vocabulary she taught, she said, 'I teach verbs and nouns including food, body parts, and clothes'. Although Hyesoo could not spend much time with her children because of her busy work schedule, she made sure to teach them Cambodian after work or on the weekend, and her constant efforts had slowly changed at least her eldest child's attitude from negative to positive.

Although all participants attached at least some importance to maintaining and developing their children's heritage language skills, many did not actually translate their beliefs into action. They faced a conflict between their wish to pass on their language and heritage to their children and Korean society's expectation that their children master Korean quickly. In order to help their children become fluent Korean speakers, some of the women promoted a Korean-speaking home environment. For example, Yumi, who initially used both Vietnamese and Korean at home, allowed her children to gradually move toward using only Korean:

> I spoke Vietnamese at home, but my children didn't understand. I wanted to teach it, but they didn't want to learn. I don't use Vietnamese anymore because they live in Korea and have to learn Korean, which is more important for their future. I want them to do well in school. When they get older, and if they want to learn [Vietnamese], I will teach them so that they can travel around in Vietnam.

Having little access to a heritage language community or opportunities for acquiring literacy skills made heritage language maintenance difficult for Yumi's children. Moreover, Yumi did not expect her children to learn Vietnamese for reasons of identity development, and she did not see it as useful for her children's future. Unlike Jeong's child, who visited Vietnam to see his grandparents, Yumi's children had never visited Vietnam, and thus did not feel an immediate need to learn Vietnamese for personal reasons. As a consequence of the language shift, Yumi's children 'speak very little Vietnamese'.

Similarly, Kyung was concerned that using the heritage language would negatively impact her children's Korean language development and adjustment to school life. She therefore only used Korean at home. Kyung's eldest child was born in Korea but was raised by her grandparents in Vietnam until Kyung got settled in Korea. After Kyung brought her daughter back to Korea, she placed a great deal of emphasis on Korean language learning. Whereas Yumi simply did not promote the heritage language, Kyung went further by prohibiting the use of Vietnamese at home. Her reasons for doing so include societal pressure and fears of the consequences of her child being marked as a linguistic and cultural other.

> I didn't use Vietnamese. My daughter lived in Vietnam until she was four. She can speak Vietnamese a little. I want to teach her Vietnamese, but it is too late. I should have taught it when she was younger. Because she lived in Vietnam for four years, after she moved to Korea, I taught her Korean only, as if life depended on it. I was really worried that she would be behind in school and get bullied. Now I regret it. No one told me about the benefits of learning Vietnamese. Every Korean around me said it would not be useful.

Because there was no Vietnamese community in her city at that time, Kyung could not foresee any future benefits of developing Vietnamese language skills in her children. The shift from the native language to Korean at home had an impact on her daughter's fluency in Vietnamese. Kyung explained, '[My daughter] uses very simple language – just words to communicate in Vietnamese. She can't communicate with me in Vietnamese as effectively as she would like'. Koreans' negative perceptions of their native language together with Kyung's concern over her children's Korean ability and social integration led to the family abandoning the heritage language for Korean.

After her children entered elementary school, Kyung was exposed to a discourse supporting bilingualism and realized the benefits of teaching the heritage language. She gradually adopted a more positive attitude toward heritage language teaching, and came to view Vietnamese as an important component in the formation of her children's ethnic identity as Korean-Vietnamese. Kyung started teaching her children basic Vietnamese conversation skills and phrases used in everyday situations. She also encouraged her children to have regular contact with their grandparents and relatives in order to keep their links to their heritage. In order to provide Vietnamese-speaking opportunities outside the home, she decided to send her daughter to a Vietnamese language camp held in Korea. The camp, designed for multicultural children with Vietnamese parents, was being held for the first time in her province. Its goal was to provide an immersion experience. When I asked Kyung why she decided to send her daughter to the camp, she said, 'Exposure to this type of program will help her appreciate Vietnamese more and build a closer relationship with her family and the Vietnamese community'. Kyung appreciated that the teachers valued the language ability the children brought with them from home, but acknowledged that the situation was by no means perfect:

> I sent my daughter to a Vietnamese camp last winter for two weeks, where 25 teenagers attended and learned the Vietnamese language. They also learned about Vietnamese popular culture including songs. However, two weeks were not sufficient for them to improve their language skills. Also, the teachers were not properly trained in language education and spoke a regional dialect rather than standard Vietnamese.

Challenges in maintaining and developing heritage languages

Public school support for teaching minority languages is rare; none of the participants' children received bilingual education or heritage language education in school. Responsibility for the maintenance and development of their heritage languages is left to the family. The lack of mainstream school support is one of the barriers Southeast Asian marriage-migrant women experience in fostering their children's positive attitudes toward heritage language learning.

Passing their mother languages on to their children is also challenging because their Korean family members and acquaintances tend to consider their linguistic and cultural backgrounds a problem rather than a resource. Moreover, the participants saw their lack of Korean language skills as having prevented them from obtaining high-paying jobs in Korea; thus, to them, their children's fluent command of Korean was a top priority.

Sooah held positive attitudes toward heritage language maintenance; however, she was not successful in fostering Vietnamese language skills in her children. Sooah's family told her not to teach her children Vietnamese because it did not have any extrinsic value and would only impede their learning of Korean. Sooah said, 'My mother-in-law didn't let me teach Vietnamese. It took many years for her to change her attitude toward Vietnamese. She's now okay with teaching it. But it's too late'. Sooah felt that her Korean family members' negative attitudes had a significant impact on her children's interest in learning the heritage language. She further indicated that the language attitudes of the older siblings influenced the youngest sibling's perception of the language. She explained, 'My youngest child is five years old. He doesn't want to learn [Vietnamese]. He pretends he doesn't understand anything whenever I speak in Vietnamese. He doesn't want to learn Vietnamese because his older sisters don't want to'.

Similarly, Jeong placed great value on teaching Vietnamese to her son, but it became a source of tension with her Korean family and her son. Jeong recalled:

> I tried to teach him Vietnamese, but my son was not interested because Koreans, including my acquaintances, look down on the Vietnamese people. In their minds, people with dark skin are poor and uneducated. My son also thinks the same. It's not easy to teach. Even my mother-in-law scolded me, 'Why are you teaching him Vietnamese? His Korean is not good because of you'. I got so upset that I sent my son to Vietnam for three months.

Jeong's son had absorbed Korean people's negative views not only of the language, but also of his ethnicity. Thus, Jeong faced opposition from all quarters: from her family in the form of her mother-in-law, from the wider Korean society, and from her son himself as a product of his environment. In an act of resistance, Jeong sent her son to Vietnam over the winter break to learn Vietnamese in a comfortable, immersion environment. In going to Vietnam, Jeong's son moved from a context in which he was an ethnic, linguistic, and cultural outsider to one where the qualities that had marked him as other were shared by his immediate social group. After he returned, Jeong noticed her son's attitude toward Vietnam and the Vietnamese language changing from negative to more positive because he had enjoyed spending time with his peers in Vietnam.

Kyung also wanted to take her children to Vietnam during a school vacation in order to surround them with Vietnamese speakers to improve their heritage language skills. However, her idea was not supported by her Korean family members, especially her in-laws.

> I wanted to take my children to Vietnam for their Vietnamese language studies. However, my in-laws strongly objected to the idea, saying, 'Why do

> you spend money on unnecessary things?' They did not support me and misunderstood my intentions. They believed that the actual reason why I wanted to go to Vietnam with my children is because I wanted to bring all their resources and money to my parents in Vietnam.

Her in-laws' reaction suggests a lack of openness to Kyung's heritage and to her wish to pass elements of that heritage on to her children, especially at a material cost. But another element of her in-laws' response appears to be the negative stereotypes prevalent in Korean society that marriage migrants only marry Korean men to financially support their needy parents back home (Kim, 2008; Freeman, 2011). Eventually, Kyung received financial support from her parents in Vietnam, which enabled her to take her children there while proving to her in-laws that their assumptions were false.

Another challenge related to heritage language maintenance is the discriminatory treatment faced by multi-ethnic children in Korea. The Southeast Asian women in this study felt that they needed to avoid using their mother language with their children in public because doing so would reveal their own status as foreigners, especially from Southeast Asia, which could lead to prejudice against the children. Hyesoo described this concern:

> I don't use Cambodian with my children in public because people would look down on my children. Korean children say things like 'Hey, your mom is a foreigner. She can't speak like a Korean'. I'm really worried that my children will get bullied like my [foreign] friends' children when they enter school. Korean people treat us badly not just because we're foreigners, but because we're from a poor country. They accept western people whereas they look down on Southeast Asians.

When I asked her what parents of multi-ethnic children could do to resolve this problem, Hyesoo suggested that foreign mothers need to become Korean themselves. She said, 'We need to speak Korean fluently, change our name to a Korean name, obtain Korean citizenship, and try to look like Koreans'. She believed that multi-ethnic children would be accepted by Koreans if they and their mothers were fully assimilated into Korean society, not only linguistically, but in every possible way.

Southeast Asian mothers' concerns about their children's education pose challenges for heritage language maintenance. One of the reasons why many marriage-migrant women decide to move to Korea is to gain financial stability (Kim, 2008). However, they usually work long hours and struggle to make ends meet. As a result, the women are determined to see their children excel in school so that they will have career opportunities in mainstream Korean society and a better life (Lee et al., 2015). The women perceive mastery of Korean as having a direct influence on the children's academic success, and mastery of the heritage language as largely irrelevant, or even detrimental, to success. This is not only the case for the children, but also for the migrant women themselves, as discussed by Yumi:

I'm very concerned about my children's education because I'm a foreign mother. Korean mothers pay a lot of attention to their children and teach them many things. I want to raise my children like a Korean mother, but I don't know how to. One time, I wanted to teach my children a song learned in kindergarten, but I couldn't because I don't know the Korean song. And I can't even tell how well my children speak Korean. I'm practicing Korean so hard so that I can teach them Korean and raise them well.

Watching the middle-class Korean mothers around her, Yumi came to believe that providing a good education is an essential part of Korean mothering (Lee et al., 2015). Yumi viewed herself as an unskilled mother who was unable to provide adequate educational support to her children, having internalized the messages conveyed by the wider society that migrant women have limited capabilities in child rearing as a consequence of their foreignness and lack of Korean proficiency. As with Hyesoo, Yumi appeared to view success in terms of becoming Korean, matching her Korean peers and models in their linguistic and child-rearing practices, which naturally made her home a Korean-speaking environment.

Discussion and conclusion

The participants' narratives support the findings of Kim and Kim (2015) that the younger generations of ethnic minority groups in Korea are losing knowledge of their heritage languages and undergoing a language shift in the process of assimilation. Without adequate support from schools and society, the task of maintaining and developing heritage languages is left to the individual child and family. Heritage language maintenance provides a basis for a child's strong bicultural identity development (Jo, 2001; Lee, 2002; Lee and Suarez, 2009; Shin, 2010). However, the participants' children experienced tremendous pressure to abandon their heritage languages in favour of Korean. Their heritage languages were undervalued and considered inferior to the Korean language, and even detrimental to their education and future (Park, 2017). For example, Jeong's, Sooah's, and Kyung's family members regarded Vietnamese as an obstacle to the children's acquisition of Korean, disapproved of the mothers' attempts to transmit their cultural heritage, and discouraged the children's development of a multi-ethnic identity. This finding is also consistent with the findings of Kim's (2008) study on Filipino migrant women in Korea, whose Korean families discouraged them from teaching their mother languages to their children.

In addition to the low status of their heritage languages in Korean society, the Southeast Asian mothers' desire to see their children succeed academically and become well-integrated into Korean society led them to promote Korean within the household. Their strong desire for their children to assimilate is shaped by the mainstream society in which multi-ethnic children are vulnerable to discrimination against their ethnicity and language (Kim, 2010; Shin, 2012). Kyung and Yumi reinforced their children's Korean identities by choosing not to teach them their mother language. Even Hyesoo, who was deeply engaged in teaching the heritage language at home, avoided interacting with her children in Cambodian in public in order to protect the children from social prejudice. In addition, the Southeast Asian mothers perceived themselves as unqualified to provide a good education for their children due to their lack of Korean language skills, and they struggled to do what they felt was expected of them as Korean mothers (Lee *et al.*, 2015). Their emphasis on their children's educational and societal success contributed to their children's heritage language loss.

In spite of these unfavourable educational and sociocultural circumstances, some of the women in this study made attempts to support their children's heritage language development. The reasons behind these efforts included enabling the children to communicate with family, to stay connected with their heritage, and to build a positive ethnic identity. The Southeast Asian mothers' attitudes toward the heritage language impacted the ways in which their children viewed and used it. The ways in which they socialized their children consequently influenced whether the children became bilingual or monolingual (Shin, 2005). For example, Hyesoo valued both Korean and Cambodian and actively involved her children in home literacy practices; this resulted in more successful intergenerational transmission of the heritage language. In contrast, Yumi assigned more importance to Korean ability and integration into the mainstream society, and chose to use only Korean with her children; this contributed greatly to an overall shift to Korean in her family. Moreover, due to the difficulty of teaching their mother language to their children in Korea, some of the women invested in sending their children to their home country to provide a comfortable, immersion environment for language learning. Yet as Kim (2010) noted, the positive effects of such study abroad experiences may be short-lived unless the children continue to be surrounded by a rich linguistic environment which encourages them to speak their heritage languages.

Without systematic and long-term efforts to maintain and promote linguistic diversity at the governmental, educational, and familial levels, minority language loss eventually occurs (Baker, 2011; Shin, 2013). It is even more difficult for multicultural children with one heritage-language-speaking parent to develop their heritage language skills than for children whose parents are both native heritage-language speakers. All participants reported that their husbands knew only a few commonly used expressions in their wives' mother language and that their co-habiting parents-in-law did not speak their mother language at all. Thus, multicultural children's exposure to their heritage language is much less than their exposure to Korean, and this decreases further as they start receiving schooling through the medium of the dominant language. Supportive home and social environments are necessary if multicultural children are to continue to develop as bilingual.

Educating all children to respect different cultures serves as an important first step to promote linguistic diversity and vice versa. Thus, it is crucial to integrate heritage languages into the regular curriculum of the schools by offering bilingual and heritage language programs (Jeon, 2008; Shin, 2013). Furthermore, it is essential to promote greater awareness of the benefits of bilingualism and biliteracy and of the importance of preserving minority languages and cultures, through holding information sessions and cultural events with parents, community members, and teachers (Shin, 2006). As a result of common misconceptions about bilingualism (Baker, 2011), parents are often influenced by public opinion and are uncertain about whether or not they should teach their children their heritage language (Shin, 2005). Convincing both minority- and majority-language parents of the benefits of multilingualism and multiculturalism is key to the success of maintenance-oriented bilingual programs (Baker, 2011). The benefits of promoting and increasing multiculturalism, multilingualism, and heterogeneity within Korean society are many and varied, at both the societal and individual levels. Similarly, the challenges to achieving these goals need to be met not only by the government, schools, and wider society, but also within the family and indeed within the individual.

Funding

This research was supported by an Arts Faculty Research Development Fund grant from the University of Auckland and by an Academy of Korean Studies Grant funded by the Korean Government (MEST) (AKS-2012-BAA-2101).

Bibliography

Baker, C. (2011). *Foundations of Bilingual Education and Bilingualism*. Clevedon, UK: Multilingual Matters.

Bélanger, D., Lee, H.-K., and Wang, H.-Z. (2010). 'Ethnic Diversity and Statistics in East Asia: "Foreign Brides" Surveys in Taiwan and South Korea'. *Ethnic and Racial Studies* 33(6), p. 1108–1130.

Cho, Y. (2006). *Survey on Education of the Children of Multicultural Families*. Seoul: Policy Report of Ministry of Education and Human Resources.

Freeman, C. (2011). *Making and Faking Kinship: Marriage and Labor Migration Between China and South Korea*. Ithaca, NY: Cornell University Press.

Ipsikorea. (2015). The Phenomenon of More Students Choosing Arabic and Vietnamese for the University Entrance Exam. *Ipsikorea*. Available at: http://m.ipsikorea.com/magazine/focus_view?ma_idx=3631 (accessed: 1 March 2016).

Jeon, M. (2008). 'Korean Heritage Language Maintenance and Language Ideology'. *Heritage Language Journal* 6(2), pp. 153–172.

Jo, H.-Y. (2001). '"Heritage" Language Learning and Ethnic Identity: Korean Americans' Struggle with Language Authorities'. *Language, Culture, and Curriculum* 14(1), pp. 26–41.

Jo, H.-Y., Seo, D. H., and Kwon, S. H. (2008). 'An Ethnographic Study on the Academic Performance of Children of Migrants'. *Korean Journal of Sociology of Education* 18(2), pp. 105–134.

Jones, G., and Shen, H. H. (2008). 'International Marriage in East and Southeast Asia: Trends and Research Emphases'. *Citizenship Studies* 12(1), pp. 9–25.

Kang, S.-W. (2010). 'Multicultural Education and the Rights to Education of Migrant Children in South Korea'. *Educational Review* 62(3), pp. 287–300.

Kim, M. (2008). *Gendering Marriage Emigration and Fragmented Citizenship Formation: 'Korean' Wives, Daughters-in-law, and Mothers from the Philippines*. Unpublished doctoral dissertation. Albany: State University of New York.

Kim, M. (2010). 'Gender and International Marriage Migration'. *Sociology Compass* 4(9), pp. 718–731.

Kim, M., and Kim, T.-Y. (2015). 'A Critical Study of Language Minority Students' Participation in Language Communities in the Korean Context'. *Language and Intercultural Communication* 15(2), pp. 224–239.

Korean Ministry of Gender Equality and Family. (2015). *Statistics on Multicultural Families in Korea*. Available at: www.mogef.go.kr/korea/view/policy/policy02_05a.jsp?func=view&currentPage=0&key_type=&key=&search_start_date=&search_end_date=&class_id=0&idx=696898 (accessed: 1 December 2015).

Lee, E., Kim, S.-K., and Lee, J. K. (2015). 'Precarious Motherhood: Lives of Southeast Asian Marriage Migrant Women in Korea'. *Asian Journal of Women's Studies* 21(4), pp. 409–430.

Lee, J.-B., Kang, S.-W., and Kim, H. (2008). *Research on the Educational Status of the Children from Multicultural Families*. Seoul: Korea Educational Development Institute.

Lee, J. S. (2002). 'The Korean Language in America: The Role of Cultural Identity in Heritage Language Learning'. *Language, Culture, and Curriculum* 15(2), pp. 117–133.

Lee, J. S., and Suarez, D. (2009). 'A Synthesis of the Roles of Heritage Languages in the Lives of Immigrant Children'. In T. G. Wiley, J. S. Lee, and R. Rumberger (eds), *The Education of Language Minority Immigrants in the United States*. Clevedon, UK: Multilingual Matters, pp. 136–171.

Pao, D. L., Wong, S. D., and Teuben-Rowe, S. (1997). 'Identity Formation for Mixed-Heritage Adults and Implications for Educators'. *TESOL Quarterly* 31(3), pp. 622–631.

Park, M. Y. (2017). 'Resisting Linguistic and Ethnic Marginalization: Voices of Southeast Asian Marriage-migrant Women in Korea'. *Language and Intercultural Communication*, doi: 10.1080/14708477.2016.1165240.

Seol, D., Seol, D.-H., Kim, Y.-T., Kim, H. M., Yoon, H. S., Lee, H.-K., Yim, K. T., Chung, K. S., Ju, Y., and Han, G.-S. (2005). *Foreign Wives' Life in Korea: Focus on the Policy of Welfare and Health*. Seoul: Ministry of Health and Welfare.

Seoul Metropolitan Government. (2014). *Seoul Supports Home Tutoring for Multicultural Children*. Available at: http://woman.seoul.go.kr/archives/23608 (accessed: 1 March 2016).

Shin, G.-W. (2012). 'Racist South Korea? Diverse but not Tolerant of Diversity'. In R. Kowner and W. Demel (eds), *Race and Racism in Modern East Asia: Western and Eastern Constructions*. Boston, MA: Brill, pp. 369–390.

Shin, S. J. (2005). *Developing in Two Languages*. Clevedon, UK: Multilingual Matters.

Shin, S. J. (2006). 'High-stakes Testing and Heritage Language Maintenance'. In K. Kondo-Brown (ed.), *Heritage Language Development: Focus on East Asian Immigrants*. Amsterdam: John Benjamins, pp. 127–144.

Shin, S. J. (2010). '"What About Me? I'm Not Like Chinese but I'm Not Like American": Heritage Language Learning and Identity of Mixed Heritage Adults'. *Language, Identity, and Education* 9(3), pp. 203–219.

Shin, S. J. (2013). *Bilingualism in Schools and Society: Language, Identity, and Policy*. London: Routledge.

Soto, L. D. (2002). 'Young Bilingual Children's Perceptions of Bilingualism and Biliteracy: Altruistic Possibilities'. *Bilingual Research Journal* 26(3), pp. 599–610.
Statistics Korea. (2015). *The Household Survey Data of the Third Quarter of 2015*. Available at: http://kostat.go.kr/portal/korea/kor_nw/2/4/3/index.board?bmode=read&bSeq=&aSeq=34 9861&pageNo=1&rowNum=10&navCount=10&currPg=&sTarget=title&sTxt= (accessed: 1 December 2015).

5 *Haafu* identity in Japan
Half, mixed or double?

Alexandra Shaitan and Lisa J. McEntee-Atalianis

Introduction

For many years, the Japanese government and its national media have depicted Japan as an ethnically and culturally homogeneous society (Burkhardt, 1983; Burgess, 2010). This is reinforced through a discourse of *Nihonjinron* (Befu, 2001), which incorporates an ideology based predominantly on the tenets of blood lineage, cultural competence and social participation. However, homogeneity based on ethnicity and language is an illusion, if not a myth (Jabar, 2013; Caltabiano-Miyamoto, 2009). A number of ethnically and linguistically diverse minority groups have existed in Japan for centuries, such as the Ainu, Okinawans, Chinese and Koreans (Gottlieb, 2005; Murphy-Shigematsu, 2004). Through various restrictive policies and forceful assimilation designed to attain cultural homogeneity, these minority groups have abandoned their native languages and culture to prevent themselves from being racially and ethnically marginalized in Japanese society (Htun, 2012). Moreover, in recent decades, a growing number of interracial marriages have contributed to the emergence of a new group of 'half-Japanese' people, most commonly referred to in the vernacular as *haafu* (half) or the 'Hapa'[1] community in Japan. Greer (2012) and Jabar (2013) report that approximately 22,000 multi-ethnic Japanese children are born in Japan each year.

Individuals of mixed parentage in Japan can experience ethnic and cultural marginalization. Despite their native linguistic and cultural repertoire and the fact that they have fully integrated into Japanese society, they report being treated as *gaijin* – the Japanese collective term for 'foreigner' or 'outsider'. Unless a person shares similar phenotypical features, blood lineage and conforms to Japanese cultural and social mores, he/she may face marginalization, and 'otherization' (Iino, 1996). These 'self' and 'other-ascribed' *haafu* often report experiencing an identity crisis as a consequence of the treatment they experience at the hands of the majority culture, including their outsider positioning as foreigners in both Japan and the country of their non-Japanese parentage. They often express feeling 'in-between' (Eckert, 1989) their cultures.

In this chapter, we explore how *haafu*[2] adults construct their identities with respect to circulating ethnic labels in Japanese society. This research contributes to discursive studies of identity construction, (such as Bucholtz and Hall, 2005; De Fina, 2010) drawing in particular on research which explores subjective and intersubjective positioning acts in identity construction in interaction (including Bamberg and Georgakopoulou. 2008; Korobov, 2013). Like Bamberg (2011, p. 16) we aim to 'scrutinise the inconsistencies, ambiguities, contradictions, moments of trouble and tension, and the teller's constant navigation ... between different versions of selfhood in local interactional contexts'. We specifically explore the role of stance in evaluating, aligning and positioning subjects, the linguistic features (including 'labels') used to encode positions, and their role in indexing, reproducing and contesting discourses about *haafu* identity. The rationale for this study is three-fold:

1 to contribute to recent sociolinguistic investigation of minority/contested identity construction in interaction (see Ladegaard, 2012; 2015);
2 to explore how dominant discourses of *Nihonjinron* and *gaijin* affect identity construction; and
3 to explore the under-researched experiences of Japanese *adults* of mixed parentage.

Whilst there has been some research investigating American-Japanese and Japanese-American adolescent/youth identity (see below), this study is one of the first to focus on the identity of mixed-race adults (other than American) in their late 30s, 40s and 50s in Japan.

We begin with a brief review of the research literature, initially focusing on the topic of the 'Hapa'/half-Japanese community and research on labelling, positioning and stance in sociocultural and social-psychological studies of identity construction and performance. This is followed by a methodological description and analysis of the interview data. The chapter concludes with a discussion of findings and recommendations for further research.

The 'Hapa'/half-Japanese community

The 'Hapa Community' unofficially formed in Tokyo, Japan, in 1991 as a social organization for mixed-race people, in response to feelings of social isolation and the need to share similar lived experiences with others. Membership is diverse, reflecting the different family backgrounds of its members. All have one Japanese parent, while some have one parent of Western ethnicity, others are of African descent (often referred to as 'Blackanese', Gaskins, 1999), and others are of Asian origin. Initially, meetings within the community were organized in the form of dinners, seasonal parties and monthly events, however activities have now extended to more political enterprises aimed at gaining recognition and equality for *haafu* people. For example, members have been motivated to give public talks in educational institutions throughout Japan to raise awareness amongst Japanese children and youth about *haafu* people and their experiences. It should be noted that not all mixed-race Japanese people refer to themselves using the referents of 'hapa' or *haafu*. For example, in 2001 mixed-race adults of the Kansai area formed another group of mixed-race members, referring to themselves as 'Mixed Roots', promoting their mixed-race backgrounds through a variety of academic and social events. Furthermore, groups called 'Halvsie', 'Half Japanese', and 'Over 30s *Haafu*' have emerged on Internet sites where biracial individuals are brought together to discuss their experiences of being 'half' in Japan. Despite these differing ascriptions, large communities of mixed-race Japanese people have evolved in recent decades (for example, Hapa has 1,000 members, Halvsie has 4,000 members) and they share a common desire to be understood on their own terms.

Self-ascribed versus externally ascribed ethnic referents/labels

The issue of 'self' versus 'other' ascription is salient in any discussion of individuals of mixed-race heritage in Japan. There has been widespread academic interest in 'self-' versus 'other–ascribed' reference or identity labels (see Eckert, 1989; Life, 1995; McCarty, 1996) with the complexity associated with this issue highlighted by many (including Asakawa, 2015; Caballero, 2014; Greer, 2005; Kamada, 2005, 2006; Oikawa and Yoshida, 2007). In Japan, the term *haafu* has become commonly used as a generic referent for those persons of mixed-race heritage despite differences in self-ascription. Luke and Luke (1998) note that naming, marking, and indexing are the definitive moments of displacement and 'othering'. While addressing the problematic issue of what to call multiracial children in Japan, Greer (2001, p. 14) warns, 'binary notions such as "half" and "double" are inadequate to describe the multiple selves that make up their multifaceted identities'. He reports that adolescent participants reacted differently to the term 'half', '... the word *haafu* is tolerated and ignored, assumed and ascribed, accepted and contested' (2003, p. 20) depending on the situation in which the participants find themselves. He notes that the term is associated with other negative ascriptions in English ('half-breed' and 'half-caste'). Greer (2003) also reports that not all multi-ethnic children necessarily position themselves using the referent 'daburu' or 'double' in English, and in his 2005 study found that participants reported being negatively positioned by Japanese people who often ascribed non-Japanese or novice attributes to them, which in turn implied *haafu*'s lack of 'normal' Japanese cultural proficiencies. Applying the yin yang metaphor aimed at theorizing the dualities of *haafu* ethnic identity, he concludes, 'being multiethnic is not an either/or choice but a both/and experience' (p. 16). More recently, Kittaka (2013) and Surdick (2013) report on self- versus other-ascribed referents for mixed-race individuals in Japan. Their findings reveal ongoing debates and disagreements between parents as to how to refer to their mixed-race children in Japan.

Taking up Greer's observation that identity ascriptions are contextually and interactionally-influenced, we now explore the concepts of positioning and stance in identity construction and performance before discussing our research questions.

Positioning and stance in identity construction

'Positioning' – 'the discursive process whereby people are located in conversations as observably and subjectively coherent participants in jointly produced storylines' (Davies and Harré 1999, p. 37) has become an important analytic category and descriptor in studies of identity construction (see Bucholtz and Hall, 2005). The term first emerged in socio-psychological accounts of self and identities in 'narratives in interaction' (Davies and Harré, 1990; Harré and van Langenhove, 1991, 1999) but has since been taken up by sociocultural/ linguistic researchers investigating the (agentive) discursive processes of identity construction (Korobov, 2013). Positioning can be a self-reflexive activity (self-positioning) and/or an interactive act (other-positioning), making salient the concept of participant role and alignment which uncovers the sociolinguistically constructed nature of identity. Claimed or ascribed subject positions may be fluid – contingent and temporarily fixed in time and space. What 'fuels positioning is accountability of participants' orientations to their setting and the emergent conversational activities' (Wetherell, 1998, p. 401). In conversation, positioning acts become open to scrutiny by interlocutors such that positions may be supported, contested or re-envisioned.

Positioning analysis aims to explore how speakers use discursive resources to construct and negotiate versions of social reality and self in the moment and also, via iterativity, more stable versions of the self and reality over time. Davies and Harré (1999, p. 46) argue that 'an individual emerges through the process of social interaction, not as a relatively fixed end product but as one who is constituted and reconstituted through the various discursive practices in which they participate'. In other words, 'fluid positioning' (van Langenhove and Harré, 1999) is what people usually use to cope with the sociocultural and context-dependent situations in which they find themselves. Every uttered word or other semiotic resource in a conversation has a mission to accomplish within an interaction – to align/disalign, resist/contest, persuade/negotiate. In short, people position themselves and others in any given conversation. This is what van Langenhove and Harré (1999, p. 15) call 'discursive practice', that is, 'within a conversation each participant always positions the other while simultaneously positioning himself or herself'. Additionally, they argue a conversation has a tripartite structure: consisting of positions, storylines and relatively determinate speech-acts. By means of this triad, conversations can be analyzed to uncover their episodic structure. However, neither storylines nor positions are freely constructed. Rather, they are jointly constructed, negotiated, contested, and initiated.

The concept of 'positioning' is invoked in studies of stance. For Du Bois (2007) stance consists of three acts in one – a triune, or tri-act. In taking a stance, the stance-taker simultaneously (1) evaluates the stance object, (2) positions a subject, and (3) aligns with other subjects.

> Stance is a public act by a social actor, achieved dialogically through an overt communicative means, of simultaneously evaluating objects,

positioning objects, positioning subjects (self and others), and aligning with other subjects, with respect to any salient dimension of the sociocultural field.

(Du Bois, 2007, p. 173)

Here, we use this framework to explore:

1 how *haafu* adults identify themselves, and what (if any) identity labels they use/align with;
2 the stances they take with respect to different stance objects and subjects – for example, their place of origin, heritage and the labels/discourses circulating and invoked in Japanese society/discourse about *haafu* identity.

Methodology: participants' background and data collection

Data was derived from ethnographically informed, semi-structured sociolinguistic interviews and focus group discussions with four male and five female *haafu* subjects. Due to limitations of space and the nature of the analysis, the data presented here focuses on two main subjects referred to using the pseudonyms Jack and Takao. The selection of Jack and Takao as case studies is based on the following criteria: Jack (aged 54) and Takao (aged 41) both live and work in Tokyo, Japan. Jack's father is American and his mother Japanese; Takao's mother is Russian and his father Japanese. Both Jack and Takao were born, raised, and educated in Japan and have lived there their entire lives. Both report having travelled to the country of their non-Japanese parent to attend summer language schools aimed at enhancing their knowledge of the language spoken by their non-Japanese parent. Both report using their bilingual/multilingual skills at work. However, whilst Jack has been a member of the 'Hapa'/*haafu* community for more than a decade or so, Takao has not joined, although he reports being aware of the community.

Informants were recruited using snowball sampling. The thematic content of the interviews was based on Kamada's (2010) questionnaire, although the questions were adapted and altered to match the age group of the study participants and included questions about: (1) identity labelling; (2) the pros and cons of being *haafu*; (3) experiences at school/work; (4) Japan's nationality law and choice of citizenship; (5) being born to a Japanese family; (6) language use at home; (7) affiliations (including with the 'Hapa' community); (8) their definition of ethnic identity; and (9) their beliefs about Japan as a single-race society.

Participants were offered the choice to be interviewed in English or Japanese. Jack chose to be interviewed in English whereas Takao's interview involved code-switching between three languages – Russian, Japanese and English – the languages also spoken by the interviewer.

Results

The analysis revealed subtle variations in the ways participants self-ascribed and defined their identity, with both intra- and inter-individual differences found. All participants identified context (including the participation frame) as a key variable in determining self-identification. They cited various influences on their self-determination, including: parental heritage; lived experiences; and their attitudes towards/alignments with the majority culture of their 'inherited' ethnicities. Many described the tensions and difficulties involved in self-ascription, as well as others' positioning of them, as evidenced in the extracts below. We begin with the case of Jack.

Case study 1: Jack

Jack prides himself in having attended a very prestigious International school, where he received his education in English. He is fluent in both English and Japanese and has applied his bilingual skills throughout his professional career. Jack holds an American passport and is issued with an alien registration card, which, according to a newly implemented Japanese law in 2012, must be carried at all times in case the police need to check his ID. Jack reported that he could not be granted Japanese citizenship in the 1960s due to a Japanese law which prevented the award of citizenship based on maternal nationality.[3] Jack is a very active member of the 'Hapa' community and regularly attends all events. In the interview a provocative question about his ethnicity prompted a response in relation to his outsider status within Japanese society (Excerpt 1).

Excerpt 1 (Jack)

INTERVIEWER: 001. Do you consider yourself a typical half, hybrid, double, or 'hapa'?
JACK: 002. NEITHER, really. I feel like just a human being, really. This
003. attitude.... It is just people classify me as different ... being ... half
004. or whatever, RIGHT? I just see myself as a human being.
INTERVIEWER: 005. But, for example, if people in Japan or in America ask you where
006. you are from, what do you tell them?
JACK: 007. In Japan, I usually say ... mo (well), first of all, if it is mendokusai
008. (troublesome), I just tell them I am from Okinawa. If I do not really
009. care, I really say that. But, most people, if they ask me, it is none
010. of their business; I tell them I am half. In Japan I say, I am half.
INTERVIEWER: 011. Oh, I see. All right. ((*silence*))
JACK: 012. But nobody would ask me in US, RIGHT? If I go to US, nobody
013. would ask me, RIGHT? Everybody is mixed, anyway. They often
014. mistake me for a Hispanic. They start talking to me in Spanish,
015. Portuguese or something. They think I am Spanish.

The initial question in which the interviewer presents an unequivocal stance about there being a 'typical' mixed-race identity, taps into a sensitive issue for Jack to which he takes a determined distal stance, marked through an emphatic rejection of the category labels suggested ('NEITHER'). He expresses his frustration with people who classify him as 'half', rejecting a positioning by others as 'different', as being an outsider and/or a foreigner – *gaijin*. He distances himself from their position, expressing a degree of contempt for any questioner who may suggest that he is outside the 'norm'. He reports 'playing' with them and in so doing confronts and contests the dominant ideology of *Nihonjinron* – including indices of belonging based on phenotypical characteristics. He subverts the question in his answer, responding that he is from Okinawa (line 6), (a Japanese island), refusing to acknowledge the possibility that his looks may suggest that he is anything but Japanese. He further explains that his answer actually depends on his attitude towards the interlocutor, (line 6) and the perceived motivation behind the question posed. If the exchange is perceived as 'troublesome' or he wishes to challenge his interlocutor, he aligns himself with other Okinawans, if not, he conforms to an evaluation and positioning which aligns with sociocultural norms – invoking the label of 'half'. As in Oikawa and Yoshida (2007), Jack regarded himself as non-Japanese only after others pointed it out to him.

Whilst the initial question (line 1) elicited a negative response, the follow up question to imagine labelling within contrasting national contexts (Japan and America) elicits a more nuanced response. Jack takes a different stance towards the imagined questioning by interlocutors in the US, and asserts that the notion of a 'mixed'/'other' would not be an issue for him because 'Everybody is mixed anyway' – and therefore such a question would not be asked. This echoes Jarnes's (2016) report on Yoshikawa's stance of being viewed as a non-Japanese in Japan. Jack uses extreme case formulations (Pomerantz, 1986) e.g. 'nobody' and 'everybody' (line 9) to present his justification of generalized assumptions about himself in the US context. Moreover, he seeks alignment from the interviewer of the position he expresses (repetition of 'RIGHT'). Here the interactional frame and story-telling are constructed differently – the narrative characters developed in the US context are positioned in juxtaposition to the inquiring Japanese context. In America, multi-ethnicity is argued to be 'normal', although he notes also being positioned as 'Hispanic', suggesting mono-ethnic interpretations are also common there.

When asked if there are any advantages to being a 'half', Jack (line 26) initially avoids answering the question and implies that he does not ascribe any pros or cons to being 'half', asserting that he had not even entertained ascribing positive value to his heritage.

Excerpt 2 (Jack – continued from Excerpt 1)

INTERVIEWER: 025. What is good about being *haafu*?
JACK: 026. I really never thought of it THAT way. But you know, at least I get
  027. exposed to different cultures. I mean,
  028. sometimes I do not fit in as either, I mean (*coughing*), I do not know
  029. how to say this, I am not Japanese and
  030. I am not American. Sometimes I am American, sometimes I am
  031. Japanese. You know what I mean?

INTERVIEWER:	032. So, what does it depend on?
JACK:	033. It depends on ... maybe when I see something negative, things about
	034. how the Japanese do things, THEN
	035. I think I am American. But say, if I go to States, or even, you know,
	036 between Americans, when I see some
	037. people that are OBNOXIOUS or something, like you know who I
	038. am talking about ...
INTERVIEWER:	039. (*laughing*) ... yeah, I know, I know what you mean. (*Jack mentions*
	040. *one American man known to the interviewer*)
JACK:	041. Then, I am GLAD I am Japanese ... uhm ... but ... uh ... I do not
	042. think I am Japanese to a point where ... I do not
	043. know ... like most Japanese people ... I am NOT American like
	044. most American people. I am MIXTURE!
	045. THAT'S what I am!

Jack apparently struggles to address the question: 'what is good about being *haafu*' (line 25) instead choosing to explain the negotiation of his identification according to circumstance. Using the demonstrative pronoun 'that' and emphatic stress, he suggests that he never considered being a 'half' as an advantage over the mainstream Japanese. Marked by the adversative marker 'but' he goes on to elaborate on the possible positive value of his bicultural experience. He sets himself apart experientially from the mono-ethnic mainstream Japanese and/or Americans, asserting in line 27 that he does 'not fit in as either'. Jack further asserts that his self-identification can depend on his evaluation (his stance) of the behaviour of those he 'classifies' as mono-ethnically Japanese or American. In particular, a negative evaluation of one nationality leads to a closer affiliation and alignment with the other. However, he finally provides a definitive self-label as a 'mixture' (line 35) – as neither a complete embodiment of one or the other but a partial and 'mixed' version of both – a synthesis constituted by the more favourable aspects of each culture.

Excerpt 3 (Jack – continued from Excerpt 2)

INTERVIEWER:	046. Yeah, but ... if ... uhm ... if someone asks you what your ethnicity
	047. is, what would you say?
	048. Would you say I am American or I am Japanese or I am Asian
	049. American or I am American-Asian? What is
	050. the first word that would come out of your mouth?
JACK:	051. I would say my mother is Japanese and my father is American of
	052. German decent. It is the EASIEST thing to
	053. say.

When pressed for an ethnic identification, Jack states that he would use the frame of his parentage and lineage to define himself (line 40). He acknowledges descent from two (or three) discrete (rather than mixed) nationalities: Japanese/

American-German. However, this statement complements and contrasts with his earlier definition of himself as a 'mixture'. This may be read as an acknowledgement of the importance of the ideology of 'purity' in Japan and preference for a definitive report (his parents' lineage, for all intents and purposes, were monoethnic). He therefore descends from two defined – or three, given his father's background – ethnicities. Another possible explanation for Jack's self-ascription arises from his rare German surname which is acknowledged as difficult to pronounce. He explains that he frequently has to explain that his father is of German descent and there are very few people left (even in Germany) with such a surname. He prides himself in having German 'roots' and multiple ethnic backgrounds compared to those with only a bicultural background.

Unlike Jack, our second participant (Case Study 2) appears, initially, to more comfortably align with the labels circulating in Japanese society, such as 'haafu' and 'double'. However, he subsequently takes a more agentive and reflective stance, noting the complexity and difficulty of others' ascriptions and their impact on his sense of self.

Case study 2: Takao

The second interview was conducted with a 41-year-old man, Takao, who was born to a Japanese father and Russian mother. The interview took place at the researcher's home. Like Jack, he was born, raised and educated in the Tokyo area. Takao attended Japanese public elementary and junior high school, and a private high school where English as a subject was given a high priority. Takao also reported attending summer school programmes in Russia to enhance his skills in the Russian language and also to experience Russian culture. Takao holds a Japanese passport and says that he was not aware of the fact that he could change his nationality at the age of 22. However, when asked a hypothetical question about a possibility of changing his nationality to Russian, he said that he would still choose to be Japanese rather than Russian due to the social and economic stability afforded to him in Japan. Takao's interview revealed that being 'half' is problematic for him, as illustrated below:

Excerpt 4 (Takao)

INTERVIEWER: 001. Do you consider yourself a typical half, hybrid, double or 'hapa'?
TAKAO: 002. Hm ... I do not consider myself, but because in Japan they use
003. HALF, so I think I am half. But my father
004. DOESN'T like the word half, so he uses double. There was even an
005. article in the media about it. So, really, I
006. do not know if I consider myself half or something.
INTERVIEWER: 007. Yes, but what if someone asks you? What do you say? Do you say
008. you are half?
TAKAO: 009. NO, I usually say I am half Japanese, half Russian.
INTERVIEWER: 010. Oh, ok, I see. So, you do not have any preferences, right?

TAKAO:	011.	Hm ... I think so.
INTERVIEWER:	012.	What is good about being half?
TAKAO:	013.	Hm.... Maybe ... ((*thinking*)) ... maybe it is that you can feel at
	014.	home in both cultures.
INTERVIEWER:	015.	Oh, ok, I see.

Takao initially ponders the question posed by the interviewer ('Hm') and appears to initially refute the suggestion that he is 'half, hybrid, double or "hapa"'. However, this incomplete initial response 'I don't consider myself' is truncated and followed by the adversative marker 'but'. The subsequent subordinate clause frames a different response to the interviewer's question than first articulated, marking a shift in perspective in real-time processing. Takao goes on to identify labels and ascriptions assigned by others. He appears to align with the labels ascribed to him by mainstream Japanese society – 'I think I am half' – although his use of the cognitive verb 'I think' marks his uncertainty. He further acknowledges his father's negative stance towards the dominant attribution of 'half' noting his preference for the term 'double'. Takao initially appears confused (line 4) as to what to call himself, apparently depending on the ascriptions and stances of others for his own identification. However, when pressed by the interviewer (line 5) to detail how he would describe himself if asked by others, he becomes more certain (line 6) asserting that he would not use the term 'half' without qualification, that is, he would refer to himself as 'half Japanese, half Russian', preferring to mark an affiliation with both Japanese and Russian identities.

When asked whether being 'half' is a good thing, he is at first hesitant to give a response but then responds that it is the ability to feel at home in both cultures (line 10) which is 'good'. However, he subsequently contradicts his earlier statement and highlights the difficulty of being either Russian or Japanese. To him, being 'half' is a problem, for he feels he does not belong to either culture/country.

Excerpt 5 (Takao – continued from Excerpt 4)

TAKAO:	016.	It is like ... I do not feel 100 per cent Japanese. Nor do I feel 100
	017.	per cent Russian. So, being in Japan ... I feel a bit different
	018.	from others. And being in Russia, I feel different too. So, THAT'S
	019.	the problem. ((*laughing*))
INTERVIEWER:	020.	That is the problem, yeah.
TAKAO:	021.	And ... uhm ... you know ... *haba ga aru* (you are broad-minded)
	022.	... you know ... *haba ga aru* ....
INTERVIEWER:	023.	Yes, I understand.
TAKAO:	024.	At least you understand both cultures.... But I feel bad at times,
	025.	'cause I do not really think I belong to any
	026.	culture or country 100 per cent. I always compare and weigh up
	027.	how would Russians and Japanese act in similar

	028.	situations. There is always something ... you know ... *hikakateiru*
	029.	(stands in the way/bothering me)....
	030.	Do you understand?
INTERVIEWER:	031.	Yes, something stands in the way.
TAKAO:	032.	Do you REALLY understand what I mean?
INTERVIEWER:	033.	Yes, of course.
TAKAO:	034.	That is why I sometimes feel BAD ... and LOST. It is really painful
	035.	not to belong anywhere ... 100 per cent.
INTERVIEWER:	036.	Oh, I see. Maybe it is because you have absorbed BOTH cultures?
TAKAO:	037.	Yes, I think so. 'Cause my mother is a typical representative of
	038.	Russia, and my dad is a typical
	039.	representative of Japan.

Takao goes further to elaborate on what he thinks is good about being 'half'. In line 17 he insists that it is the knowledge of both cultures, however, he quickly repositions himself and contradicts his statement yet again to dealign himself from any culture or country. An interesting stance is given in line 18 where he perceives Russian and Japanese as a 'stable'/'whole' identity, something against which to be measured. Similar to Jack, Takao also evaluates and weighs up how Russians and Japanese would behave or think in any given situation. In line 24 he touches on the theme of identity and belonging, suggesting that being 'half' denies access to a stable, complete, identity. Through the deployment of predicate adjectives 'feel bad', 'lost' and the adjective 'painful', which lexicalize his internal state in response to the external social context, Takao problematizes and dramatizes the issue of being 'half'. In lines 26 and 27 he refers to the fact that his parents are 'typical' of their national cultures as one of the reasons for him not 'belonging' to any culture or country, and being torn between being a true Japanese or Russian.

When asked about how he identifies himself, Takao does not give any definitive answer nor does he take an epistemic stance, rather he expresses an apparent paradox: that he is Japanese because he has lived in Japan all his life and yet 'at the same time [he] is not' (line 31).

Excerpt 6 (Takao – continued from excerpt 5)

INTERVIEWER:	040.	That is right. I think so. How do you identify yourself ethnically?
TAKAO:	041.	Well, I am often asked if I am half, right?
INTERVIEWER:	042.	Yes?
TAKAO:	043.	Well, since I have lived in Japan for so long, I say that I am Japanese.
	044.	But, at the same time, I am not. It is
	045.	like, I am 95 per cent Japanese and 5 per cent Russian, you can say,
	046.	95 per cent Japanese with a 5 per cent Russian flavour.
INTERVIEWER:	047.	((*laughter*)) ... Or Russian spices?
TAKAO:	048.	Especially recently, I feel ... I started to realize that I am NOT 100
	049.	per cent Japanese, and that is why I do not act

050. EXACTLY as a typical Japanese does. So ... that is what I feel
051. now ...
052. But I say Japanese, 'cause I have lived here for such a long time ...
053. you know.... It is easier for me to be here
054. than in Russia. I think because I have lived here all the time ... that
055. is the ONLY reason ... I do not know....
056. And you know, my students ask me if I am half ... and when I say
057. yes, they reply, ah, indeed, we thought so ...
058. So, it is like a reminder ... you know ...

In attempting to explain his sense of self, he invokes a numerical (percentage) referent in order to explain the stance he takes towards his Japanese and Russian identity. He asserts that he feels mostly Japanese (95 per cent) whilst marginally Russian (5 per cent). Like Jack, he positions himself along a binary pole – 'I am' versus 'I am not' – qualifying the latter in the assertion that 'I started to realize that I am NOT 100 per cent Japanese' (line 34), '[e]specially recently' – adverbially marking the moment when he realized he did not feel entirely Japanese, despite his upbringing in Japan (lines 34 and 35). There are moments, he notes, when his dual identity becomes particularly salient and perceptible, when he is confronted by the questions of others who probe his status as a *haafu* (line 38). It is at these times that he aligns with their suppositions, cognizant that he is not 100 per cent Japanese. He deploys adverbs 'especially' and 'exactly' (lines 34 and 35) to highlight an important moment in his life.

Discussion and conclusion

Whilst research on *haafu* children and adolescents has been undertaken in Japan, to date there has been limited research on *haafu* adults. In this chapter, we investigated how *haafu* adults construct their identities with respect to others' ascriptions, to dominant discourses about being 'half', and to the affiliations/ascriptions *haafu* individuals seek/invoke throughout their lived experiences. Like Greer (2001), our findings point to the salience of context in determining one's self-labelling and the indexical associations brought forth when using terms such as 'double', 'mixed' or 'half'. Alignments or dis-alignments with labels may be determined by the positive or negative stances invoked in their use and the meanings associated with them and carried within the context of interaction. Context may be multi-layered. It can be nationally framed (such as Jack's accounts of his self-ascription within the Japanese versus USA contexts) or dependent on a dialogic frame, a participation framework – according to whom the speaker is talking. We saw how informants may resist and/or negotiate fixed category-based provocations, instead drawing on personal, situated and contextual detail to self-ascribe in more complex, fluid and multiple ways, and often qualifying their ascriptions according to biological (e.g. lineage); social-psychological (e.g. attitudes) and socio-cultural influences. Identity construction in these accounts is borne out as a complex process and a product of localized practices, ideologies and lived experiences.

For some adults, (notably Takao, in the data presented here), labelling oneself or being labelled as 'half' within the Japanese context can be painful and associated with a lack of belonging. Being positioned as *haafu* has much in common with being positioned as *gaijin* and our more extensive data set reveals the difficulties and negative experiences suffered by many due to this positioning. For others, (such as Jack), the 'problem' of labelling is externalized: it is not something to dwell on or seek to determine, rather it is something others do or are concerned with. However, identifying with one culture over another may also be to one's advantage, as in Jack's disaffiliation with one culture and affiliation with another on seeing behaviour that he deems unacceptable.

While Kamada (2005, 2008, 2009), using the concept of 'ethnic embodiment' observed that multi-ethnic Japanese boys and girls engage in similar discursive practices enabling them to position themselves as powerful, rather than powerless, based on their looks, our study did not reveal similar findings.[4] Rather, our data revealed that for adults, being *haafu* does not necessarily mean being marked by exotic beauty, rather it afforded respondents other forms of capital, such as the ability to know two or more languages and cultures. It must be noted however that some also reported difficulties in 'knowing' the languages and cultures of both parents to the same extent. Our participants often expressed feelings of 'in-between-ness' (Eckert, 1989) and conflicting emotions when faced with the choice between countries/cultures. As one of the participants in this study asserted:

> I wish there was a country called 'Hapa' where only haafus lived. It would feel great, as nobody would ever ask you questions like 'where are you from' or about your ethnicity or nationality. Because all haafus share similar experiences and stories.

This eloquent quotation succinctly embodies the sentiments of many individuals with a mixed-raced background that we interviewed in Japan.

We have provided evidence that moments of contestation in externally versus self-ascribed labels can cause distress and difficulty for some mixed-race individuals in Japan. We have also demonstrated that some report an identity that is more positively framed and demonstrate the ability to negotiate a fluid rendering of the self. Whilst this chapter could only focus on a small selection of data, it highlights the necessity for further work on the discursive construction of *haafu* identity.

Notes

1 The term *hapa haole* is originally a Hawaiian term used to describe a person who was of half-white and half Hawaiian ancestry. These mixed-race children resulted from relationships between Hawaiian women and British sailors.

2 We use the term '*haafu*' generically to refer to individuals who self-ascribe as being of mixed-race heritage, with one Japanese and one 'other' parent.
3 Murazumi (2000) provides a detailed overview of Japan's law on dual nationality.
4 Although, this may be a consequence of our small sample size.

Bibliography

Asakawa, G. (2015). 'What are Words Worth: Hapa, Hafu, or Mixed-Race?' Available at: www.discovernikkei.org/en/journal/2015/3/9/what-are-words-worth (accessed: 14 July 2016).
Aspinall, P. J. (2009). '"Mixed Race", "Mixed Origins" or What? Generic Terminology for the Multiple Racial/Ethnic Group Population'. *Anthropology Today* 25(2), pp. 3–8.
Bamberg, M. (2011). 'Narrative Practice and Identity Navigation'. *Varieties of Narrative Analysis* pp. 99–124.
Bamberg, M., and Georgakopoulou, A. (2008). 'Small Stories as a New Perspective in Narrative and Identity Analysis'. *Text & Talk* 28(3), pp. 377–396.
Befu, H. (2001). *Hegemony of Homogeneity: An Anthropological Analysis of 'Nihonjinron'* (Vol. 5). Melbourne: Trans Pacific Press.
Bucholtz, M., and Hall, K. (2005). 'Identity and Interaction: A Sociocultural Linguistic Approach'. *Discourse Studies* 7(4–5), pp. 585–614.
Burgess, C. (2010). 'The "Illusion" of Homogeneous Japan and National Character: Discourse as a Tool to Transcend the "Myth" vs. "Reality" Binary'. *The Asia Pacific Journal: Japan Focus* 9, pp. 1–10.
Burkhardt, W. R. (1983). 'Institutional Barriers, Marginality, and Adaptation Among the American-Japanese Mixed Bloods in Japan'. *The Journal of Asian Studies* 42(3), pp. 519–544.
Caballero, C. (2014). 'Mixed Emotions: Reflections on Researching Racial Mixing and Mixedness'. *Emotion, Space and Society* 11, pp. 79–88.
Caltabiano-Miyamoto, Y. (2009). 'Negotiation of Multicultural and Multilingual Identities: An Ethnographic Study of a Cambodian Boy in Japan'. *Japan Journal of Multilingualism and Multiculturalism* 15(1), pp. 39–50.
Davies, B., and Harré, R. (1990). 'Positioning: The Discursive Production of Selves'. *Journal for the Theory of Social Behaviour* 20(1), pp. 43–63.
Davies, B., and Harré, R. (1999). 'Positioning and Personhood'. In R. Harré and L. van Lagenhove (eds), *Positioning Theory: Moral Contexts of Intentional Action*. Malden, MA: Blackwell, pp. 32–52.
De Fina, A. (2010). 'The Negotiation of Identities'. In M. A. Locher and S. L. Graham (eds), *Interpersonal Pragmatics*. New York: De Gruyter Mouton, pp. 32–52.
Du Bois, J. (2007). 'The Stance Triangle'. In R. Englebreston (ed.), *Stancetaking in Discourse*. Amsterdam: John Benjamins, pp. 139–182.
Eckert, P. (1989). *Jocks and Burnouts: Social Categories and Identity in the High School*. New York: Teachers College Press.
Eckert, P. (1993). 'Cooperative Competition in Adolescent "Girl Talk"'. In D. Tannen (ed.), *Gender and Conversational Interaction*. New York and Oxford: Oxford University Press, pp. 32–61.
Gamble, A. E. (2009). 'Hapas: Emerging Identity, Emerging Terms and Labels and the Social Construction of Race'. *Stanford Journal of Asian American Studies* II, pp. 1–20.
Gaskins, P. (1999). *What Are You? Voices of Mixed-race People*. New York: Henry Holt and Company.

Gottlieb, N. (2005). *Language and Society in Japan*. Cambridge: Cambridge University Press.

Greer, T. (2001). 'Half, Double or Somewhere In-between?' *Japan Journal of Multilingualism and Multiculturalism* 7(1), pp. 1–7.

Greer, T. (2003). 'Multi-ethnic Japanese Identity'. *Japan Journal of Multilingualism and Multiculturalism* 9(1), pp. 1–23.

Greer, T. (2005). 'The Multi-ethnic Paradox: Towards a Fluid Notion of Being "Haafu"'. *Japan Journal of Multilingualism and Multiculturalism* 11(1), pp. 1–18.

Greer, T. (2012). 'Accomplishing Multiethnic Identity in Mundane Talk: Half-Japanese Teenagers at an International School'. *Pragmatics* 23(3), pp. 371–390.

Haefelin, S. (2012). *Haafu ga bijin nante mousou desu kara: komatta jun japa to no tatakai no hibi*. [The Delusion of Haafu Being Beautiful. Daily Struggles with Pure Japanese People]. Tokyo: Chuko Shinsho La Clef.

Harré, R., and van Langenhove, L. (1991). 'Varieties of Positioning'. *Journal for the Theory of Social Behaviour* 21(4), pp. 393–407.

Harré, R., and van Langenhove, L. (1999). 'The Dynamics of Social Episodes'. In R. Harré and L. van Lagenhove (eds), *Positioning Theory: Moral Contexts of Intentional Action*. Malden, MA: Blackwell, pp. 1–12.

Htun, T. (2012). 'Social Identities of Minority Others in Japan: Listening to the Narratives of Ainu, Buraku and Zainichi Koreans'. *Japan Forum* 24 (1), pp. 1–22.

Iino, M. (1996). '"Excellent Foreigner!" Gaijinization of Japanese Language and Culture in Conflict Situations – An Ethnographic Study of Dinner Table Conversations Between Japanese Host Families and American Students'. Unpublished doctoral dissertation. University of Pennsylvania.

Jabar, M. A. (2013). 'The Identity of Children of Japanese-Filipino Marriages in Oita, Japan'. *Japan Journal of Multilingualism and Multiculturalism* 19(1), pp. 28–39.

Jarnes, M. (2016). 'Japan's Beauty Queens Rewrite Old Rules on Race and Nationality'. *Japan Times*. Available at: www.japantimes.co.jp/life/2016/09/19/language/japans-beauty-queens-rewrite-old-rules-race-nationality/#.V-EENYXKEnU (accessed: 19 September 2016).

Kamada, L. (2005). 'Celebration of Multi-ethnic Cultural Capital Among Adolescent Girls in Japan: A Post-structuralist Discourse Analysis of Japanese-Caucasian Identity'. *Japan Journal of Multilingualism and Multiculturalism* 11(1), pp. 19–41.

Kamada, L. D. (2006). 'Multiethnic Identity of "haafu/daburu" Girls in Japan'. In K. Bradford-Watts, C. Ikeguchi, and M. Swanson (eds), *JALT 2005 Conference Proceedings*, Tokyo: JALT, pp. 102–113.

Kamada, L. (2008). 'Discursive "Embodied" Identities of "Half" Girls in Japan: A Multiperspectival Approach'. In K. Harrington, L. Litosseliti, H. Saunston, and J. Sunderland (eds), *Gender and Language Research Methodologies*. London: Palgrave Macmillan, pp. 174–190.

Kamada, L. (2009). 'Mixed-ethnic Girls and Boys as Similarly Powerless and Powerful: Embodiment of Attractiveness and Grotesqueness'. *Discourse Studies* 11(3), pp. 329–352.

Kamada, L. (2010). *Hybrid Identities and Adolescent Girls: Being 'Half' in Japan*. Bristol, Buffalo and Toronto: Multilingual Matters.

Kittaka, L. G (2013). 'Prove You Are Japanese: When Being Bicultural Can Be a Burden'. Available at: www.japantimes.co.jp/community/2013/07/29/issues/prove-youre-japanese-when-being-bicultural-can-be-a-burden/ (accessed: 1 April 2015).

Korobov, N. (2013). 'Positioning Identities: A Discursive Approach to the Negotiation of Gendered Categories'. *Narrative Inquiry* 23(1), pp. 111–131.

Ladegaard, H. J. (2012). 'The Discourse of Powerlessness and Repression: Identity Construction in Domestic Helper Narratives'. *Journal of Sociolinguistics* 16(4), pp. 450–482.

Ladegaard, H. J. (2015). 'Coping with Trauma in Domestic Migrant Worker Narratives: Linguistic, Emotional and Psychological Perspectives'. *Journal of Sociolinguistics* 19(2), pp. 189–221.

Life, R. (1995). 'Doubles: Japan and America's Intercultural Children'. In R. Life (Producer): Video documentary available at: www.globalfilmnetwork.net (accessed: 5 December 2015).

Luke, C., and Luke, A. (1998). 'Interracial Families: Difference within Difference'. *Ethnic and Racial Studies* 21(4), pp. 728–754.

McCarty, S. (1996). 'Biculturals: Not "Half" but "Double"'. *Bilingual Japan* 5(1), p. 10.

Murazumi, M. (2000). 'Japan's Laws on Dual Nationality in the Context of Globalized World'. *Pacific Rim law and Policy Journal* 9(2), pp. 415–443.

Murphy-Shigematsu, S. (2004). 'Ethnic Diversity, Identity and Citizenship in Japan'. *Harvard Asia Quarterly* VIII(I), pp. 51–57.

Murphy-Shigematsu, S., and Willis, D. B. (2008). 'Transcultural Society'. In F. Coulmas, H. Conrad, A. Schad-Seifert, and G. Vogt (eds), *The Demographic Challenge: A Handbook about Japan*. Leiden: Brill Academic Publishers, pp. 293–315.

Noro, H. (2009). 'The Role of Japanese as a Heritage Language in Constructing Ethnic Identity Among HAPA Japanese Canadian Children'. *Journal of Multilingual and Multicultural Development* 30(1), pp. 1–18.

Oikawa, S., and Yoshida, T. (2007). 'An Identity Based on Being Different: A Focus on Bi-ethnic Individuals in Japan'. *International Journal of Intercultural Relations* 31(6), p. 633–653.

Pomerantz, A. (1986). 'Extreme Case Formulations: A Way of Legitimizing Claims'. *Human Studies* 9, pp. 219–229.

Singer, J. (2000). 'Japan's Singular "Doubles"'. *Japan Quarterly* 47(2), pp. 76–82.

Surdick, R. (2013). 'There Is More to My Son than the Fact He Is a "*half*"'. Available at: www.japantimes.co.jp/community/2013/07/29/issues/there-is-more-to-my-son-than-the-fact-hes-a-half/#.V4aPJ66yknV (accessed: 14 July 2016).

van Langenhove, L., and Harré, R. (1999). 'Introducing Positioning Theory'. In R. Harré and L. van Langenhove (eds), *Positioning Theory: Moral Contexts of Intentional Action*. Oxford: Blackwell Publishers, pp. 14–31.

Wetherell, M. (1998). 'Positioning and Interpretative Repertoires: Conversation Analysis and Post-structuralism in Dialogue'. *Discourse & Society* 9(3), pp. 387–412.

6 Claiming *Japaneseness*

Recognition, privilege and status in Japanese-Filipino 'mixed' ethnic identity constructions

Fiona-Katharina Seiger

Introduction

In the 1970s, the Philippine government started to actively attract foreign investors and vacationers to the country, increasing encounters between Filipino women and Japanese men, who made up a large proportion of the visitors to the country. This often led to the development of affective and sexual relationships. Relationships between Japanese men and Filipino women also flourished in Japan, as since the early 1980s, numerous women from the Philippines found employment in Japan's snack-bars and nightclubs. Barely a decade later, Filipina brides of rural Japanese bachelors joined the 'entertainers' and 'talents' in their Japan-bound migration. By 1995, women from the Philippines were among the top three foreign nationalities wed by Japanese men.[1] From 1995 to 2009, 33,210 Japanese-Filipino babies were born to Japanese-foreign couples in Japan, which is higher than any other Japanese-foreign couple grouping (Jabar, 2013). Numerous Filipino women also gave birth to children of Japanese fathers in the Philippines, but the total number of Japanese-Filipino offspring remains unknown as similar statistics are not available for the Philippines. Non-Governmental Organizations (NGOs) catering to Japanese-Filipino children from non-traditional, and sometimes difficult, family arrangements estimate the total number of Japanese-Filipinos in both Japan and the Philippines to range between 100,000 and 400,000.[2]

Claiming *Japaneseness*

Japanese-Filipinos in the Philippines present a case in the study of 'mixed' ethnic identities insofar as their identity claims are intertwined with the migration histories of their parents, with ongoing rights-claims towards the Japanese state, and are dependent upon the possibilities and implications of ethnic and 'racial' identification available in Philippine contexts. Historian Vicente Rafael (2000, 2015) contends that *mestizoness*[3] in the Philippines has always been about distinction through claiming access to an outside world which remains out of reach for many others. *Mestizos* in the Philippines are generally associated with modern privileged lifestyles, as a light skin-tone 'retains a certain

Claiming Japaneseness 99

socio-cultural caché' (Rafael, 2015). The prevalence of such connotations is well illustrated by an advertising campaign launched in 2012 by the Filipino fashion brand *Bayo*, titled 'What's your Mix?', inciting significant anger from netizens in the Philippines (ABS-CBN News, 2012; Rappler, 2012) for its aggressive equation of 'mixed' ancestry with high social status. The campaigns' posters featured 'mixed race' Filipino models whose genealogy was quantified in percentages and accompanied their photos. The text which supplemented one of the posters read 'Call it biased, but the mixing and matching of different nationalities with Filipino blood is almost a sure formula for someone beautiful and world class' (see Rappler, 2012). This drew criticism for insinuating the superiority of people of 'mixed' descent over 'regular' Filipinos. The widespread outrage caused by this campaign shows the sensitivity around the issue of race and its intricate link to matters of status and privilege in the Philippines, which remain painful reminders of the socio-economic and cultural pervasiveness of racial hierarchies that were established under the Spanish and US American colonial regimes.

Despite the absence of officially endorsed ethnic or racial classifications today, colonial categories and hierarchies linger, with race remaining a powerful practice of social differentiation. Persistent racial tensions surface again and again through enduring anti-Chinese sentiments (Hau, 2014), negative stereotypes towards South-Asians (Lorenzana, 2013), and ambivalent attitudes towards 'mixed' Filipino-foreign offspring. Skin colour, writes historian Vicente Rafael (2015), '... serves as the gauge of social difference and the sign of class inequality. Light skinned mestizos – whether Chinese and European – tend to be endowed with considerable cultural capital regardless of their actual economic standing'. Offspring of Filipino-Japanese couples also elicit cultural admiration (Satake and Da-anoy, 2006, p. 135). This attitude is tied to the largely positive image of Japan as a rich country with a long-standing, venerated culture. Thus, widespread imaginings of Japan, as well as a socio-historical context in which ancestral ties to wealthier countries tend to be associated with higher socio-economic status, form part of the backdrop against which Japanese parentage is made sense of by Japanese-Filipinos.

Claims to *Japaneseness* moreover need to be looked at in the context of advocacy on behalf of Japanese-Filipinos, as well as in view of potential opportunities for Japanese-Filipinos to migrate to Japan. This research found that far more Japanese-Filipino respondents in the Philippines actively claimed a Japanese or 'mixed' Japanese identity than respondents located in Japan. This not only shows that the ethnic identifications of Japanese-Filipinos are diverse, it also demonstrates that notions of ethnic identities as innate, static conditions fail to take into account the important influence of place and social space in the ongoing process of identity formation. Ethnic identity is supple and subject to change, as numerous scholars (including Alcoff, 1995; Jenkins, 2008; Morris-Suzuki, 2000) have argued, and 'people (and peoples) can and do shift their ethnic ascriptions in the light of circumstance and environment. The pursuit of political advantage and/or material self-interest is the calculus which is typically held to inform such behaviour' (Jenkins, 2008, p. 46). The meanings attached to ethnicity, and their various social consequences in a particular setting, will influence how much ethnicity matters to an individual and to a larger group. If the deployment of a particular ethnic identity engenders higher social status, access to resources, or cross-border mobility, then such benefits would make this particular ethnic affiliation more interesting to the individuals who are able to claim it.

The conception of ethnic identities as flexible, performable social identities tied to concerns over social status resonates with Goffman's (1963) notion of 'passing'. Goffman examines how individuals manage undisclosed discrediting information about themselves in order to gain acceptance in mainstream society and avoid social stigma. The notion of 'passing' has been discussed in the context of 'acting ethnic' (see Kachtan, 2015; Matsunaga, 2007; Song, 2003; Waters, 1990), wherein ethnic identities are performed in order to pass into mainstream society, to gain group membership, or to challenge harmful perceptions of certain ethnic groups (Kachtan, 2015). As will be discussed in more detail below, Japanese filiation is not always a source of privilege, but can lead to social stigma under certain circumstances. Claiming and asserting a 'mixed' Japanese ethnic identity is therefore intertwined with concerns over social status.

The concepts 'identity' and 'ethnic identity' are used in an effort to grasp an ongoing, fluid process at particular moments in time. This chapter looks at how and in what contexts certain affiliations are claimed, as well as how these claims are substantiated to become meaningful to respondents within a socio-cultural context that tends to prize *mestizoness*, within the context of advocacy and claims for Japanese citizenship, as well as in relation to their network of significant others,[4] including support organizations, peers, and family members who have great influence on how these children and youths learn to make sense of their Japanese filiation.

Methodology

This chapter is based on doctoral research conducted from 2008 to 2011, and fieldwork conducted in 2015/2016.[5] Data was collected through in-depth interviews, casual chats, and participant observation in multiple sites such as Metro Manila and the city's adjacent provinces, in different cities in Japan, as well as online through web-based research and social media. This chapter focuses on teenage and young adult respondents. Data has also been collected from NGOs (non-governmental organizations), including the Manila-based *Development Action for Women Network* (DAWN), *The Batis Center for Women*, The *Batis Youth Organization that Gives Hope and Inspiration* (Batis YOGHI), and *Maligaya House* as well as the Tokyo-based *Citizen Network for Japanese Filipino Children* (CNJFC). NGOs are important gate-keepers providing contacts for many respondents, as well as contributors to the discourse on Japanese-Filipino Children, who are commonly referred to as 'JFC' by NGO workers and in NGO publications.

The reliance on NGOs as gatekeepers in the Philippines has resulted in a limitation concerning the type of respondents that could be accessed. Interviewees tended to be of less privileged socio-economic backgrounds. The large majority of Philippine-based interviewees had Philippine passports only, at the time of the interview. Japanese-Filipinos from more affluent families do exist and most probably would have very different stories to tell, but since they do not join NGOs, they are thus harder to find.

> Before I came here to Japan, when I was growing up in the Philippines, I don't know if it's just my personality but, at home I would feel out of place. I don't know if I imposed that on myself. I am Filipina, but I feel I have to distinguish myself from my friends or other Filipinos. I would think of myself as having another culture. Because growing up I would have memories of eating Japanese food, traveling to Japan, being told by my mom to behave a certain way because of being in Japan.... But living here in Japan as an adult, I realized how I am more Filipino. Staying here and interacting with Japanese people, that's how [I realized].
> (Erika, 27)

> [I see myself] as a Japanese. Because most of people when I was in the Philippines, they always said that I look like a Japanese even though they didn't hear my name, like just in my face. They, they always said, 'are you a Japanese?' So, yeah, that's why I think I'm- I really belong here [to Japan].
> (Natsumi, 22)[6]

Erika and Natsumi are two young women of Japanese-Filipino parentage born during the 1980s. Both spent their formative years in the Philippines in the absence of their fathers. Erika was born in Japan and lived there until age five. When her parents divorced, she was sent to her maternal grandmother in Manila, while her mother returned to Japan to make ends meet. Erika remembers the large boxes filled with Japanese products sent to her by her mother and recalls travelling to Japan during her school holidays.

As an adult, Erika reflects more thoroughly upon her ideas of what it means to have a Japanese father. In the Philippines, the idea of being Japanese was largely driven by her access to cultural products and experiences less easily accessible to other Filipinos, the combination of her looks and name, which clearly suggested a link to Japan, and her migrant mother having made Japan her home, which Erika visited on a regular basis. But upon having resettled in Japan, Erika says that she sometimes feels embarrassed to tell people about having a Japanese father, mostly because she cannot live up to the expectations of linguistic and cultural fluency that she believes are directed towards Japanese '*hafu*'.[7]

Natsumi was born and raised in the Philippines. Her Filipino mother and Japanese father were married, but her birth was never registered in her father's family register in Japan. Thus, Natsumi acquired Filipino citizenship at birth, but not Japanese nationality.[8] She visited Japan once during her childhood, where she briefly met her father. The above extract is taken from an interview I conducted with Natsumi during her first trip to Japan as an adult. Natsumi had travelled to Tokyo to take part in a lawsuit against the Japanese government, aimed at removing the age-ceiling imposed on (re-) acquisitions of Japanese nationality for foreigners with Japanese fathers.[9] The interview was conducted shortly after the court hearing, where Natsumi had made her statement along with other Japanese-Filipino plaintiffs.

Based on Natsumi's statement in court and our subsequent conversation, her motives for participating in the lawsuit are manifold. On the one hand, Natsumi clearly indicates an identification as Japanese based on her imagination of Japanese attitudes and lifestyles as well as the validation of her claim by the people around her. On the other hand, Natsumi also harbours a hope to help create a pathway to Japan for herself and others. Her participation in this case was indeed a gamble; Natsumi told me that she had lost her job in the Philippines because she had to take time off to travel to Tokyo. Asked where she would see herself in the future, Natsumi replies that she would like to live and work in Japan.

Although some of my respondents, such as Erika, have maintained social and cultural ties to Japan through functional transnational family arrangements, Japanese-Filipino children in the Philippines usually grow up in cultural environments that are no different from environments in which other non-Japanese Filipino children and youth from similar socio-economic backgrounds are raised. Also, Japanese-Filipino children in the Philippines are, in most cases, non-migrants. These circumstances have led a Japanese NGO-volunteer to describe the 'JFC' he met in the Philippines as '100% Filipino linguistically and culturally' (Yuusuke, 2009). Yet, their Japanese lineage allows Erika and Natsumi, as well as numerous other children born to Japanese-Filipina couples in the Philippines, to develop a sense of distinction which is intertwined with concerns over social status.

Significant others

Support organizations

Since the early 1990s, NGOs in the Philippines and in Japan have raised awareness of the many children born to Filipino women and Japanese men without official paternal acknowledgment. The deliberate physical absence of many fathers from their children's lives and the frequent lack of paternal recognition have had numerous social and legal consequences for many children.[10] To counter these consequences, NGOs have engaged in a variety of activities in accordance with their respective expertise. These range from the provision of livelihood training to taking legal action against individual fathers.

Central to NGO advocacy on behalf of Japanese-Filipinos is their discursive construction as 'JFC'. The acronym 'JFC' is widely used by NGO-members, Filipino women and their children alike. In fact, all Philippine-based respondents, except one,[11] who were also members of advocacy groups referred to themselves as 'JFC' during our conversations. The term has provided a means for

Japanese-Filipino NGO members to encapsulate their many experiences and render them meaningful in relation to the various aspects of NGO advocacy. The learning of NGO-vernacular is an almost inevitable aspect of NGO-membership. The habitual use of the acronym 'JFC' – with all its implications – has thus gone hand in hand with processes of rights assertion.

As I have shown elsewhere (Seiger, 2014), the 'JFC' has become a category-like identity, through the creation of a grand narrative for the purpose of claims-making. NGOs have contributed to the *ethnicization* of the 'JFC' by making efforts to establish symbolic ties between their clients and the Japanese nation. In the absence of first-hand lived experiences in Japan, this tie is substantiated and made meaningful through the provision of 'imaginative resources' (Appadurai, 1996) pertaining to Japan: Japanese language classes, visits by Japanese volunteers and guests, study tours and theatre tours to Japan, home-stays and school visits in Japan, presentations about Japan, origami folding, rice-ball making, the learning of Japanese songs, and calligraphy. Another important characteristic of NGO activities are workshops, conducted during summer-camps or at NGO premises, which are directed at the discussion of children's 'mixed' backgrounds (DAWN, 2010). The rationale behind the assumption that 'JFC' should learn about Japan seems to be that this was a 'natural' desire. One NGO worker told me: 'If you knew that you are Japanese, or that your father is Japanese, wouldn't you be curious to know about Japan?'.

Another reason may be the desire to make their clients more relevant to a Japanese audience within the context of advocacy through the performance of *Japaneseness*. For instance, the play *The CraneDog*, written by a Japanese-Filipina playwright uses 'kabuki-inspired visuals' to show the Japanese audience 'that these kids are not different from them but are actually one of them' (E-mail from the play's author, 8 February 2012). At times, the effort of making the children relevant to a Japanese audience results in the conflation of biological with cultural lineage. In advocacy on behalf of 'JFC', Japanese-Filipinos who '... hail from failed *inter-racial* unions' (United Japanese Filipino Children, 2009, emphasis added) are generalized as individuals who are 'fortunate to be blessed with two cultures' (United Japanese Filipino Children, 2009). In describing the play *The Ugly Duckling*[12] performed by *Teatro Akebono* in 2001, the story is said to easily be one 'of every Japanese-Filipino child, who soon finds that being born of two cultures means never fitting in any of them' (DAWN, 2001, p. 4). These depictions of Japanese-Filipinos' experiences reiterate a common trope pertaining to people of 'mixed' heritage, considering the latter as marginal individuals caught between two worlds (see Erikson, 1968; Park, 1928; Stonequist, 1937) and draw upon theoretical approaches through which 'mixed race' identities are 'seen as linking separate worlds, pathologized as the worst of both worlds, or celebrated as the best of both worlds' (Rocha, 2013).

The metaphor used in the theatre production *The CraneDog* depicts its Japanese-Filipino lead as a hybrid animal (a mix of a dog and a crane) who can both bark and fly, thus tying abilities to biological heredity, not merely between parent and child, but between the individual and a 'race' (or nation: in the play, cranes are from crane-land, dogs are from dog-land). Some NGO-members too imagine their *Japaneseness* to be more than purely a matter of filiation. For Mifune, for instance, the distinction between biological and cultural heritability is not clear-cut:

> It's probably something that called through it, you know. I don't know if you believe that there is something like genetic psychology or what, it's probably a fallacious thing, but sometimes I just feel like I might have some, some behaviours that people might think it is Japanese, or I might think it is Japanese. It's something that I can't explain myself. Something that I struggle with, this unknown factor, this unknown variable. And so, yes, it's something that others have called to by acknowledging the physical thing [his looks]. But it's none the less present. Something that I tried to thresh up and discover.
>
> (Mifune, 34)

In trying to explain what made them Japanese, it seemed that it was often not clear, even to my respondents, where to draw the line between cultural and biological descent, thus explaining their interest in and affinity to Japan as natural consequences of their biological make-up. Yukari, who also took part in the same trial as Natsumi, explained that how she identified herself proved:

> ... quite confusing because I was born and raised in the Philippines and even though I'm – I haven't been to Japan when I was young, I still feel a bit Japanese ... some of my interests are more Japanese than Filipino so um, it's sort confusing, it's a, a little bit of both Japanese and Filipino.
>
> (Yukari, 22)

Asked which of her interests were 'Japanese', Yukari answered: 'A remake of Japanese songs, something like that, Japanese songs. And things like that and also, I like the discipline of Japanese people. I like the food'. Indeed, I encountered the tendency to explain preferences, interests or behaviour by linking these to parentage in more than one interview.

Advocacy groups and individual Japanese-Filipinos who conflate biological with cultural heredity draw upon primordial conceptions of ethnicity, which are also found in Japanese cultural nationalism. Post-war Japanese cultural nationalism has expressed itself in numerous academic and journalistic publications concerned with defining Japan, the Japanese, and doing things 'the Japanese way'. These publications, also referred to as *Nihonjinron* (literally: theories of the Japanese), commonly emphasize Japanese exceptionalism, the homogeneity of Japanese society, as well as the importance of shared blood, culture and language. With the majority of my Philippine-based respondents having spent a significant portion of their childhood and adolescence in the Philippines in the absence of their Japanese fathers, the emphasis on 'Japanese blood' becomes central to ethnic identity claims.

Erika is one of the few respondents who was raised in the Philippines with sustained access to Japan throughout her childhood and adolescence. Her Japanese cultural experiences and her familiarity with Japanese products made Erika feel additionally anchored in another cultural environment that her friends and classmates did not have access to. Asked what she thought made others perceive her as Japanese, Erika answered: 'Probably the way I look, and my name'. Then she continued:

> But what I thought made me Japanese was when I noticed some aspects of Filipino culture that I don't like. Maybe it was just at home where I saw many aspects of Filipino culture that I didn't like, so I started comparing. Maybe I would think, because I am half Japanese I like my privacy. I mistook these things that I perceived about myself as being Japanese.... That's when I was younger.
>
> (Erika, 27)

Erika reflects on her past ideas about what made her Japanese and deconstructs some of the simplistic links often made casually between biological lineage, behaviour, preferences and taste. A self-perception as Japanese or half-Japanese hinged upon 'Japanese blood' alone becomes complicated once Japanese-Filipinos resettle in their 'fathers' homeland'. There, the lack of linguistic abilities and cultural proficiency reveal migrant Japanese-Filipinos' foreignness and the limitations of primordial conceptions of belonging.

Family and friends

> The funny thing is when we were all growing up our mothers would always say you will go to Japan someday, because that's where you belong. There is that whole building of expectations so that suddenly you're romanticizing it. It's also some sort of like Shangri-la, or you know, some sort of mythological place ... that expectation I think mythologizes Japan in such a way that it becomes some sort of paradise for JFC.
>
> (Mifune, 34)

Mothers of Japanese-Filipino children play a crucial role in nurturing their offspring's self-perception as children of Japanese fathers by calling attention to their lineage and, in many cases, by establishing favourable associations with being Japanese. Only two interviewees mentioned that their mothers disliked talking about their experiences in Japan. The large majority shared that their mothers had introduced them to Japanese food, informed them about Japanese customs and had told them positive stories about their stay in Japan.

> I don't know if what my mother told me [is true] but Japanese give dolls to babies as gifts hoping to imbibe the characteristics of the doll in the child.
>
> (Mifune, 34)

> [I got interested in things Japanese] by just watching Japanese channels. From my mother, she offered me, takes me to Japanese restaurants, things like that.... But before going there [to Japan] I'll be studying I want to enrol in a Japanese [class] before moving there, 'cause my mom told me that if you don't know how to speak their language and you go there it will be very hard for you to live and socialize. Because Japanese are not that good in English that's why you can't just talk in English.
>
> (Kenta, 21)

In most cases,[13] Japanese-Filipino children's mothers are the first ones to let their children know about their Japanese lineage, and they are the first ones to create images of Japan for their children. This considerably contributed to Japanese-Filipinos' identification as half-Japanese. Many respondents who had their mothers with them whilst growing up mentioned that their mothers would make them aware of their *Japaneseness*, whether by commenting on their looks or interpreting their behaviour.

> ... it's just like what my mom always says that I am like a Japanese even though I have – I'm not with all these people.
>
> (Yukari, 22)

Fumiko and Erika, who both grew up in the Philippines, shared that friends and acquaintances have also contributed to their self-perception as Japanese. Erika and Fumiko revealed that as children they had experienced teasing, experiencing positive reactions only as they grew older. Fumiko told me that being recognized as half Japanese 'gives you a little privilege. Because when you are half Japanese some people ... some person will treat you different'.

Erika, who was taken care of by her maternal relatives in Manila while her mother stayed in Japan, recounts that her Japanese parentage was instrumentalized to discipline her.

> I was not very well behaved. So, when I misbehaved my aunt would say 'No wonder, it's because she's Japanese', because they had that image of Japanese people being mean and sadistic. Maybe from history.
>
> (Erika, 27)

By learning to associate their Japanese descent with particular behaviour and preferences, Japanese-Filipinos also internalize the essentialism underlying these conceptions of *Japaneseness*. Family and acquaintances are central in their self-perception as half-Japanese or Japanese. The mothers of Japanese-Filipino children greatly contribute to the construction of their children's ethnic identification through positive depictions of Japan but also through their presumed competence in identifying *Japaneseness*.[14]

One striking trend among Japanese-Filipino children is that the large majority are given Japanese first names (but not all carry their father's last names), presumably by their mothers who registered them with the Philippine authorities. Names as indicators of belonging to social groups have symbolic value (Bodenhorn and Vom Bruck, 2006). As ethnic markers, Japanese-Filipinos' names symbolically establish their link to Japan. In giving their children distinctively Japanese names, mothers of Japanese-Filipinos participate in identity politics; Japanese names often reveal, or emphasize, a person's Japanese lineage where appearance may not necessarily divulge it.

Recognition, privilege and status

In order to grasp how Japanese-Filipinos in the Philippines make sense of their 'mixed' Filipino-Japanese parentage it is vital to take into account forms of social difference which usually escape a narrow focus on lineage-based differentiations or cultural identifications. Some individuals thus develop a sense of who they are and where they belong in relation to their relative privilege, or their sense of deprivation.

The positive image of wealthy, technologically advanced, 'First World' Japan, as well as the popularity of Japanese popular culture among young people in particular, may explain why young Japanese-Filipinos like to associate themselves with these aspects of Japanese culture. Erika mentioned that her classmates in college were curious about Japan and often asked her about J-pop (Japanese popular music) and the Japanese language. Shizuka, a 13-year-old girl who recently resettled in Japan told me that her classmates in the Philippines would ask her to count in Japanese. Having a Japanese father has led some Japanese-Filipinos to assert a sometimes diffuse sense of difference and an awareness of opportunities, as these published statements show:

> What is it to be a JFC? Before, I did not know what a JFC was. I just know that my father is Japanese and my mother is a Filipino. But when we joined DAWN, I understood what it is to be a JFC. I am not alone. There are other children like me.
>
> (Kay Celine in DAWN, 2010, p. 61)

> I am proud to be a Japanese-Filipino child (JFC). A JFC is different from other children because a JFC has Japanese blood. Some JFC have Japanese names or have Japanese features. For me JFC are different from other children because they have the chance to find work in Japan when they grow up.
>
> (Jenny in DAWN, 2010, p. 66)

Jenny's statement particularly illustrates how 'Japanese blood' is appreciated as a source of privilege and thereby of distinction, reflecting the latent admiration in Philippine society for people with 'mixed' ancestry. Jenny then makes the link between descent and class: the boundaries separating 'us, JFC' from 'them, other Filipinos' are the many opportunities ideally provided by that filiation. De Dios

(2012, p. 31) similarly found that her Japanese-Filipino respondents set themselves apart from Filipinos without a Japanese parent through their ability to legally live and work in Japan.

While for individual Japanese-Filipinos, NGO-members and non-members alike, ethnic identity is linked to rights and privileges provided by – or expected from – Japanese lineage, these pragmatic reasons for claiming Japanese nationality are played down in NGO advocacy. The focus on non-economic motives deflects from the problematic association between claims for one's 'birthright', and expectations of 'a better life' by means of overseas migration. Instead, advocates have until recently limited their focus to the affective dimensions of belonging, such as the desire to be acknowledged by Japan, to experience life in Japan, and the efforts and sacrifices that Japanese-Filipinos would be ready to make if granted Japanese nationality. The now inactive group, *United Japanese-Filipino Children* (UJFC) released a statement[15] demanding Japanese citizenship for all Japanese-Filipinos in order 'to learn first hand the ways of our fathers' (United Japanese Filipino Children, 2009) and points out that '[t]he major hindrance for the full realization of a JFC's identity is the issue of Nationality' (United Japanese Filipino Children, 2009), thus fastening the demand for nationality to discourses on personal identities, rather than to the more practical objective of seeking paid employment in Japan.

Growing up in the Philippines, Japanese-Filipinos are aware of the widespread associations of having a foreign parent and living a wealthy lifestyle. For Sachiko and Yukari, their inability to display the expected 'socio-cultural caché' (Rafael, 2015) resulted in negative reactions from their peers. Sachiko, a girl in her late teens at the time of our interview, recounted how her *Japaneseness* was challenged by one of her classmates who asked her to name all the members of a Japanese boy-band. Sachiko failed the test. Consequently, she felt that she failed to 'do justice' to her Japanese lineage. Yukari too has experienced being treated with suspicion for her lack of cultural proficiency. Additionally, her apparent lack of wealth and the familial arrangement she grew up in made her a target for malicious comments:

> Growing up, I experienced a lot of awkward and embarrassing situations whenever my classmates would ask me why I am a Filipino citizen and not Japanese. They asked me where my father is and why I am not in Japan. They asked me why we don't observe Japanese practices at home. I was looked down upon and discriminated because being a Filipino, they thought I was an illegitimate child. Although it is true that my father left me and my mother, it happened for a reason different from what other people think. My mother tried to protect me from all the discrimination so she worked hard to show everyone that we all are well-provided for.
>
> (Yukari, 22)

Yukari has been subjected to the upsetting assumptions that she must have been an unwanted child born from an 'illegitimate' relationship, possibly from her mother's engagement in sex-work. In the Philippines, having a Japanese father can be evocative of numerous assumptions about the nature and thus the moral legitimacy of the parental relationship. The encounters of Filipino women and Japanese men occurred during a time of intensely feminized migration from the Philippines to Japan's entertainment industry, a migration which has misleadingly been equated with overseas prostitution. Moreover, being raised by a single mother still remains a social stigma in a society where women with children ought to be married and '[w]omen with a "past" or with children of an earlier marriage are sometimes viewed essentially as "damaged goods" in the strict Catholic society of the Philippines' (Bulloch and Fabinyi, 2009, p. 136). Japanese-Filipinos born from this contentious mobility can therefore find themselves confronted either with admiration for their presumed wealth, their connection and their knowledge of a 'First World' country, or with disdain. When the expectations of a wealthy, modern lifestyle are not met, genealogy and skin-colour no longer reveal privilege, but are instead construed as evidence of the Philippine nation's susceptibility to foreign money and power.

Indeed, the association of foreign parentage with wealth is a two-edged sword. Drawing attention to this problem, one Japanese-Filipino *Facebook* user reacted to the above-mentioned *Bayo* advertisement campaign:

> Our looks, our eyes, the color of our skin creates assumptions of where we come from and these are far from what the image the ad is selling. I tell you there is nothing really that fashionable about being a 'mix'. Perhaps the 'mixes' the ad is referring to are those children from upwardly mobile and happy families. When a child hails from a 'well bred' family and also happens to have a foreigner for a parent who is also well off, all stigma seems to be erased. This projection confirms a certain fantasy; one of being white and being rich.... I, personally, am not against intercultural marriages but what I am against is marrying somebody because of their ethnicity and their country's pecking order in the global capitalist structure. When people marry for economic reasons or use their better halves as passports to a better life, the foundation of the relationship itself is shallow and the marriage itself may be compromised. Should the split come, it is the children who suffer.

In his comment, this Japanese-Filipino *Facebook* user remarks that cross-border relationships can play out very differently, and that the motives for engaging in such relationships are subject to heightened suspicion, including his own, as they occur within the context of global inequalities. The espousal of a Japanese ethnic identity thus makes obtaining proof of official recognition as Japanese all the more important, especially where general knowledge of Filipinas' prominence in Japan's sex-industry would otherwise suggest unfavourable family backgrounds.

Conclusion

This chapter illustrates how Japanese-Filipinos' construction and reconstruction of a Japanese or 'mixed' Japanese ethnic identity depends on various factors including personal, economic and political circumstances, and shows the complexity of identifying as 'mixed' Japanese in the Philippines. Although the postcolonial context in the Philippines provides space for 'mixed' identities, the latter is frequently tied to expectations of heightened socio-economic status. In a society that tends to admire light-skinned *mestizos* (Rafael, 2015) for their presumed wealth and worldliness, the stigma managed by respondents pertains to their socio-economic and familial backgrounds as well their insufficient proficiency in things Japanese, rather than their ethnic or 'racial' ones.

The birth of the many children of Japanese men in the Philippines is cradled in pronounced income disparities within Philippine society, global economic inequalities, and a history of highly gendered migration from the Philippines to Japan. Significant others, including mothers, close relatives, classmates and NGO workers, have played their part in pointing out to Japanese-Filipinos that their Japanese parentage is worthy of attention. They have actively or unwittingly asked these children and young adults to take a stand regarding their Japanese filiation which, considering the frequent absence of Japanese fathers from their lives and the lack of lived experiences in Japan, has to be assembled through otherwise available information pertaining to Japan and *being Japanese*.

Commonly, racial ideologies conflating cultural with biological heritage remain unchallenged in personal narratives. Such racial ideologies buttress primordial conceptions of *Japaneseness*, which have also been deployed as a political tool in processes of rights-assertion towards the Japanese state. 'Mixedness' has indeed been expressed in conjunction with gaining the privilege, or rather the right, to cross-border mobility and paid employment in Japan primarily reserved to Japanese citizens. Besides this political expression of claiming *Japaneseness*, respondents frequently tied their sense of who they are to things of everyday life – food, music and other consumable goods – as well as stereotypical imaginations of Japanese dispositions. However, as Erika's narrative has shown, Japanese-Filipinos may be prompted to re-evaluate their understandings of what makes them Japanese upon migration to Japan, showing the importance of context in choosing among ethnic options. This study elaborates on the existing 'mixed race' literature, by foregrounding context and maintaining identity formation as a flexible and ongoing process.

Notes

1 According to Japan's Ministry of Health Labour and Welfare, the number of Filipina spouses of Japanese men was first recorded in 1995. That year 7,188 Filipino women married Japanese men, out of a total of 20,787 couples composed of a Japanese man and a foreign woman (original table available at www.mhlw.go.jp/english/database/db-hh/1–2.html).

Claiming Japaneseness 111

2 The NGO DAWN (2010) estimates 100,000 to 200,000 Japanese-Filipinos living in both Japan and the Philippines. In a statement given by Japanese-Filipino youth made in 2009, 300,000 Japanese-Filipino children were mentioned (United Japanese Filipino Children, 2009). Batis Center for Women (2009) counts 300,000 to 400,000 Japanese-Filipino children and youths currently living in the Philippines.
3 In the Philippines, the term *mestizo* denotes people of 'mixed' race and is most commonly used for Filipinos with one 'white' parent.
4 Cooley (1902) defines 'significant others' as people within a person's immediate environment who are of importance in their development of a sense of self.
5 I would like to thank the *Japan Foundation* for having funded my fieldwork in Japan in 2010/2011 through their Japanese Studies Fellowship Program. I would also like to express my sincere gratitude to the *Japan Society for the Promotion of Science* for funding my fieldwork in 2015/2016 in Japan through the Post-Doctoral Fellowship for foreign researchers.
6 All names are pseudonyms. The age indicated refers to the respondents' age at the time of the interview.
7 Erika used the term *hafu* in our conversation to refer to herself and others with one Japanese and one non-Japanese parent. Although *hafu* is controversial and has been considered demeaning, many persons of Japanese descent use it to refer to themselves without seeing it as a discriminatory term.
8 Full citizenship rights in Japan are tied to, and overlap with, Japanese nationality.
9 In 2008, the Japanese Supreme Court ruled the requirement of parental marriage for children of foreign women and Japanese men as codified in Japan's Nationality Law to be unconstitutional. However, after the ruling, retroactive acquisition of Japanese nationality was only possible for persons aged 21 or younger. Anyone beyond age 21 was deemed to have chosen his/her nationality. As numerous Japanese-Filipinos were beyond the cut-off age when the Nationality Law amendment came into force, they lost the opportunity to become Japanese nationals. Subsequently, the CNJFC supported Japanese-Filipino plaintiffs, including Natsumi and Yukari, in their lawsuit against the Japanese government. Eventually, they lost their case.
10 Usually, families who have joined NGOs face these problems, which is why they seek support in the first place. Indeed, the generalization of Japanese-Filipinos as a problem population partly grew out of NGO activism, which again is based on the cases and personal fates encountered by NGO workers. But not all offspring of Japanese-Filipina couples live financially strained, troubled lives. On the contrary, the children of expatriate Japanese fathers in the Philippines, or those with well-functioning transnational family arrangements, may be considered privileged.
11 The one person who refused to do so also challenged the idea of a shared set of issues, based on growing up as the child of a Japanese man in the Philippines. As Ubalde (2013) has noted, relatively privileged Japanese-Filipinos rarely use the label 'JFC' and resist being pigeonholed as abandoned, poverty-stricken offspring of their Filipino mother's failed relationship with a Japanese man.
12 The play is based on the classic by Hans-Christian Andersen (DAWN, 2001), but the author of the play remains unmentioned.
13 Some of my respondents did not learn of their Japanese father through their mothers but their relatives.
14 Numerous mothers of Japanese-Filipino children used to work and/or were married in Japan.
15 The statement was read by the Japanese-Filipino participant at a conference in Saitama in 2009, organized by the International Organization for Migration.

Bibliography

ABS-CBN News. (2012). *Bayo Draws Flak Over Mixed-race Campaign*. Available at: http://news.abs-cbn.com/lifestyle/06/06/12/bayo-draws-flak-over-mixed-race-campaign (accessed: 14 March 2017).

Alcoff, L. (1995). 'Mestizo Identity'. In *American Mixed Race: The Culture of Microdiversity*. Maryland: Rowman & Littlefield Publishers, pp. 257–278.

Appadurai, A. (1996). *Modernity at Large*. Minneapolis, London: University of Minnesota Press.

Batis Center for Women. (2009). *A Sneak Peek at Batis-YOGHI Development: A Handbook on the Learning Experiences of Japanese-Filipino Children*. Quezon City: Batis Center for Women, Inc.

Batis Center for Women; DAWN; Maligaya House. (2009). *Non-Government Organizations Joint Statement National Conference, Saitama, Japan*. Saitama, Japan.

Batis Center for Women, Batis-YOGHI, CNJFC, DAWN, Maligaya House. (2008). 'Unity Statement of Non-Government Organizations and Japanese-Filipino Children's Organization on the Japan Supreme Court Decision on Nationality'. *Sinag* July–September, pp. 2–3.

Batis, Y. (2012). *Statement of Japanese-Filipino Children on the Tokyo District Court Ruling: Rights Should not Have Any Expiry Dates!* Available at: www.facebook.com/batisyoghi (accessed: 24 October 2012).

Bodenhorn, B., and Vom Bruck, G. (2006). '"Entangled in Histories": An Introduction to the Anthropology of Names and Naming'. In G. Vom Bruck and B. Bodenhorn (eds), *An Anthropology of Names and Naming*. Cambridge; New York: Cambridge University Press, pp. 1–30.

Bulloch, H., and Fabinyi, M. (2009). 'Transnational Relationships, Transfoming Sleves: Filipinas Seeking Husbands Abroad'. *The Asia Pacific Journal of Anthropology* 10(2), pp. 129–142.

Cooley, C. H. (1902). *Human Nature and the Social Order*. New York: Charles Scribner's Sons.

DAWN. (2000). 'Theatre Tour Evaluated, Gets Positive Reviews'. *SINAG* October–December, pp. 6–7.

DAWN. (2001). 'Teatro Akebono Play Likens JFC to "Ugly Ducklings"'. *SINAG* April–June, p. 4.

DAWN. (2010). *We Are Your Children, Too. Creative Journeys of DAWN's Japanese-Filipino Children Members*. Manila: Development Action for Women Network.

De Dios, J. R. (2012). *An Ambivalent Homecoming: Case Studies of Japanese-Filipino Youth in Japan*. Proceedings of the JSA–ASEAN 3rd International Conference, Hotel Armada, Petaling Jaya, Kuala Lumpur, 22–23 February, pp. 22–35.

Erikson, E. (1968). *Identity: Youth and Crisis*. New York: Norton.

Goffman, E. (1963). *Stigma. Notes on Management of Spoiled Identity*. New York: Simon & Schuster Inc.

Hau, C. S. (2014). *The Chinese Question: Ethnicity, Nation, and Region in and Beyond the Philippines*. Kyoto: Kyoto CSEAS Series on Asian Studies 12.

Jabar, M. A. (2013). 'The Identity of Children of Japanese-Filipino Marriages in Oita, Japan'. *Japan Journal of Multilingualism and Multiculturalism* 19(1), pp. 28–39.

Jenkins, R. (2008). *Rethinking Ethnicity*. 2nd edn. London: SAGE Publications Ltd.

Kachtan, D. G. (2015). '"Acting Ethnic" – Performance of Ethnicity and the Process of Ethnicization'. *Ethnicities*, pp. 1–20.

Lorenzana, J. A. (2013). 'Being Indian in Post-colonial Metro Manila. Identities, Boundaries and the Media'. In *Migration and Diversity in Asian Contexts*. Singapore: ISEAS, pp. 182–206.
Matsunaga, M. (2007). 'Shaping, Masking, and Unmasking of a Stigmatized Identity: The Case of Japan-residing Koreans'. *The Howard Journal of Communications*, pp. 221–238.
Ministry of Health Labour and Welfare, Japan (2015). 'Table 1-37 Number of Marriages by Nationality of Husband and Wife , by Year'. In *Handbook of Health and Welfare Statistics 2015, Part 1 Population and Households*. Available at: www.mhlw.go.jp/english/database/db-hh/1–2.html (accessed: 17 March 2017).
Morris-Suzuki, T. (2000). 辺境から眺める―アイヌが経験する近代 *[Seen from the Frontier – the Ainu Experience Modernity]*. Tokyo: みすず書房 (Misuzu Shobo).
Park, R. (1928). 'Human Migration and the Marginal Man'. *The American Journal of Sociology* 33(6), pp. 881–893.
Poole, R. (1999). *Nation and Identity*. New York: Routledge.
Rafael, V. L. (2000). *White Love and Other Events in Filipino History*. Durham: Duke University Press.
Rafael, V. L. (2015). *Racism in the Philippines: Does it Matter?* Available at: www.rappler.com/thought-leaders/97514-racism-philippines (accessed: 14 March 2017).
Rappler (2012). *[VIRAL] Bayo's 'What's your Mix' Campaign Earns Ire of Netizens*. Available at: www.rappler.com/life-and-style/technology/136-viral/6559-viral-what-s-your-mix-campaign-earns-ire-of-netizens (accessed: 14 March 2017).
Rocha, Z. L. (2013). *Betwixt, Between, and Beyond: Racial Formation and "Mixed Race" Identities in Singapore and New Zealand*. PhD thesis, Singapore: National University of Singapore.
Satake, M., and Da-anoy, M. A. (2006). フィリピン―日本国際結婚―移住と多文化共生*ge (International Marriage Between the Philippines and Japan: Migration and Multiculturalism)*. Tokyo: めこん (Mekon).
Seiger, F.-K. (2014). *Claiming Birthright: Japanese-Filipino Children and the Mobilization of Descent*. PhD thesis, Singapore: National University of Singapore.
Song, M. (2003). *Choosing Ethnic Identity*. Cambridge: Polity Press.
Stonequist, E. V. (1937). *The Marginal Man*. New York: Russel & Russel.
Ubalde, Marianne. (2013). 'Diverging Narratives: Lives and Identities of Japanese-Filipino Children in the Philippines'. *Asian Studies: Journal of Critical Perspectives on Asia* 49(2), pp. 76–114.
United Japanese Filipino Children. (2009). 'Japanese-Filipino Children Joint Statement'. JFC Multisectoral Networking Project National Conference, Saitama, Japan. Available at: www.jfcmultisectoralnetworkingproject.org/index.php/en/joint-statement-jfcs (accessed: 14 March 2017).
Waters, M. C. (1990). *Ethnic Options: Choosing Identities in America*. California: University of California Press.
Yasuo – a Geography of memory. (2012). [Film] Regie: Fiona Seiger. Singapore.
Yuusuke, S. (2009). Diary of a Maligaya Intern. *Maligaya* March, Issue 58.

Part III
Malaysia and Singapore

7 Being 'mixed' in Malaysia

Negotiating ethnic identity in a racialized context

Caryn Lim

Introduction

Popular representations of Malaysia often depict the country as a multicultural paradise and home to four distinct 'races': Malays, Chinese, Indians, and the Indigenous people or 'others'.[1] Perhaps the most ubiquitous of these representations emerged out of state-led campaigns, including the former Prime Minister Mahathir Mohammad's call for *Bangsa Malaysia* (Malaysian Race or Malaysian Nation) and the current Prime Minister, Najib Razak's *1Malaysia* campaign which sought to conceptualize a civic Malaysian identity. However, neither has resulted in the emergence of a salient supra-ethnic identity. Instead, what has resulted is the suppression of instances of cultural boundary crossing and hybridity in favour of narratives of rigidly-defined groups coexisting under the umbrella of a Malaysian national identity (Khoo, 2010; Mandal, 2003). As such, official discourses of what it means to be Malaysian are inextricably tied with being Malay, Chinese or Indian.[2]

The British colonial administration is often credited as having laid the groundwork for what might be referred to as a 'plural society' (Furnivall, 1948) in the Malay peninsula by introducing Western notions of race and actively segregating the population economically as well as geographically according to racial categories (Shamsul, 2001, p. 360; Shamsul, 1996; Reid, 2001; Hirschman, 1987; Freedman, 1960). What began as relatively fluid identities based on common language, religion and geographical origin became discreet racial categories based on biological difference. Over time, the racial categories 'Malay', 'Chinese' and 'Indian' became widely used and internalized (Tan, 2000; Shamsul, 2001, Reid, 2001).[3] In post-independence Malaysia, race gained further political and social salience. It is said that a 'social bargain' was struck during the constitutional negotiations, where the non-Malays agreed to recognize the special position of the Malays in return for citizenship rights (Lee, 2002, p. 179). The Malays came to be known as *Bumiputera*, meaning 'sons of the soil' or indigenous people, and were accorded a 'special position' enshrined in the constitution (Art. 153) which provided for various socio-economic and political privileges. The constitution also defined the Malays as (among other things) Muslim (Art. 160), perpetuating a link between race and religion that would also see the Chinese linked with Buddhism, and Indians linked with Hinduism. Considering the politicized and institutionalized status of race, to be 'mixed' in Malaysia is a peculiarly awkward position to inhabit. This chapter thus explores the ways in which ostensibly mixed individuals negotiate racial identities and their place within a racialized society.

The discussion of 'mixed' identities is explored through an examination of the ways in which 'mixed' individuals deal with various interpellations of ethnic identity and how (if at all) this informs their own experience of identity. Louis Althusser's (1971) notion of interpellation is particularly useful in conceiving the way in which individuals may acquire identities through various Ideological State Apparatuses (ISAs). However, I seek to add nuance to this analysis by bearing in mind Stuart Hall's (2000) interpretation of Althusser's naming process, which offers the opportunity to reconcile the conflict between ideological structures and individual subjectivities. For Hall, interpellation is only successful when the subject is hailed, accepts the position offered and takes steps to assume that position. How one might do this can be better understood through an adaptation of Judith Butler's (1990) theory of gender performativity, in which she posits that identities such as 'Man' or 'Woman', rather than being immutable categories, can be shown to be identities sustained through acts of great will and which often require significant skill. Performances, Butler (1993, p. 2) contends, 'must be understood not as a singular or deliberate act, but rather, as the reiterative and citational practice by which discourse produces the effects that it names'. By citation, Butler refers to the reproduction of known and accepted symbols or codes. It may be said that Malaysians 'cite' from a plethora of existing norms and discursive practices such as actions, gestures and language, and in doing so construct or portray themselves as racialized subjects. For the 'mixed' Malaysians whose voices will be heard here, these performances require all the more will and skill, as they are perpetually torn in diverging directions, compelled by a larger social order to 'fit in' by embodying one of the few officialized identities.

This research was conducted in 2011 amongst nine Malaysian youth between the ages of 21 and 30. Participants either answered a call published on a dedicated Facebook page or were recruited through a snowballing process. The call specifically asked for participants who self-identified as 'mixed Malaysians'. I then conducted semi-structured interviews with the participants and qualitative analysis of those interviews. The research sought to understand the ways in which mixed Malaysians viewed their ethnicity and negotiated between various interpellations. Based on the analysis, I distinguish between three methods by which 'mixed' Malaysians have negotiated their ethnic identities: 'situational or unstable ethnic identities', 'stable ethnic identities' and 'trans-ethnic identities'. First, I will illustrate the fluid and instrumental use of ethnic identity by these participants. Second, I will argue that under the interpellative force of institutions, some 'mixed' Malaysians choose to identify with a stable ethnic identity and are able to reconcile this with their 'mixed' ancestry through a valuation of various signifiers that allows an understanding of themselves as, for example, 'more Malay' or 'more Indian'. Third, I will explore the emergence of trans-ethnic identities amongst 'mixed' individuals who, rather than choosing to work within the normative framework, rebel against it by creating for themselves alternative identities that they feel are better representations of themselves.

Situational or unstable ethnic identities

Paden (1967, cited in Okamura, 1981), first used the term 'situational ethnicity' in relation to 'the observation that particular contexts may determine which of a person's communal identities or loyalties are appropriate at a point in time' (Paden, 1970, p. 268). As many participants demonstrated, ethnic identity is often circumstantial and dependent upon a variety of factors including external expectations, their own perceptions of others and the potential risks or benefits of being perceived as one or another ethnicity. Some interviewees such as N[4] whose background includes Iranian and Sri Lankan heritage, tended to identify with an officially recognized ethnic identity out of convenience, because trying to explain their ethnicity would take too much time or because they thought it was too personal to relay to an acquaintance. Others chose their identities based on which would be of greatest advantage to them in a given circumstance. G, whose background includes a mixture of English, Malay and Chinese heritage, illustrates this instrumental aspect of ethnic identity:

C: What do you usually tick on forms and stuff?
G: Um, I always try to put others or mixed or something like that, but ... but they don't let me.
C: What do you mean?
G: I tried to put mixed when I reapplied for my degree ... and I tried to put mixed ... and I asked, 'Can I put mixed? Because I don't know what I am', and ... she said, 'You can't', and I asked, 'Why not?' [and she said] 'Because I have to take this form to the government and I have to tick a box and there are only three boxes'. There's not even 'Others'!
C: There's not even 'Others'?
G: There's not even 'Others'! I couldn't put 'Others'! So, I had to put Malay, Chinese or Indian. Because otherwise this person was panicking, she didn't know what to do ... it's not her fault she had to tick it on the government form. So, I had to pick one.
C: What did you pick?
G: Uh, I typically pick Malay. Usually to fill a quota, because at [the college that I go to] it's mainly Chinese. I tick the minority.

Though G is unsure about his own ethnic identity particularly in relation to those standardized in the discourse of ethnicity in Malaysia, he does choose to identify with one over others in circumstances where it becomes necessary, such as in official forms and documents. His decision is interesting, however, because it takes into consideration not only what would be beneficial to him at the time but also, as in the case he describes, the image of the institution. In her exploration of the situational selection of identity amongst 'Malays', Nagata (1974, p. 340) suggests that the three main considerations made by individuals when selecting ethnic identities are 'the desire to express social distance or solidarity', 'expediency, or the immediate advantages to be gained by a particular reference group selection on a particular occasion' and the 'consideration of social status and upward or downward social mobility'. However, G's decision, which, for the most part, appears not to be affected by any one of these factors, illustrates the complexity and individual subjectivity involved in selecting an ethnic identity (let alone embodying one).

In addition, as G's experience demonstrates, the extent to which one is able to choose an identity is, in any case, restricted by various factors, including the expectations of others. B, who is of Punjabi and Swiss descent, experiences a similar situation, which demonstrates the limits of situational ethnicity:

C: So, what do you usually tick on official forms and documents?
B: Umm well I could ... I'm ... see in school they used to always tick me as Others because they don't classify Punjabis or mixed as Indians so I'm usually under 'Others'.[5]
C: So, what about ... unusually?
B: So, like for SPM I tried to put myself under Indian.
C: And what happened?
B: The school was like no you're *lain-lain* [Others] so, okay ...
C: Can I ask why?
B: I don't know actually because they say, um, my mom has origins from Switzerland, so we're not actually fully Indians.
C: Okay, but why did you try to put yourself down as Indian?
B: Because I'm sitting for a government exam in a private government-based school. And you know how there's always racial discrimination in this country right ... if I could [I would] have put myself as Malay....

Again, ethnic identity is used as a tool to avoid discrimination and/or for the potential benefits. However, B's decision to identify as Indian for the potential benefits or to avoid perceived discrimination in this case was not accepted because others around her interpellated her as mixed and she quickly accepted the role. In this way, ethnic identities reveal themselves to be both instrumental at times, as well as quite constrained by dominant structural forces at others.

Whilst interviewees such as G and B have found themselves forced to conform to being interpellated in a manner they would not have chosen, others such as P described how they had positively taken advantage of their ambiguous identity, and that they do so regularly. For P, her ability to 'act' or 'adapt' in different circumstances allows her to conform strategically to a variety of expectations of officialized identities. Her self-ascribed identity, 'Chinese Bumiputera', can be difficult to understand in the context of Malaysia where 'Bumiputera' and 'Chinese' are understood to be mutually exclusive. However, her ability and willingness to acquiesce to the ethnic categorization of those around her, according to P, contributed to her 'popularity' with peers.

P: When I was in primary school, I had a much more balanced make up of friends and I never saw it as a problem and because of how I grew up I never had a problem. Like when I'm speaking to you, I know you are very well-versed in English so I speak fine in English. Maybe it's a mixed thing ... I noticed a lot of people do this, but if I'm talking to a Malay, then I speak Malay like any other Malay person, like my *Melayu* [Malay] will be like super *gila babeng* [Malay slang for extremely good]. So, it's like, to the extent that my English words will sound Malay. So, that's when you know my Malay is good, because my *bahasa kuasa* [language is powerful]. But I have, like, this on and off switch. Like when I'm speaking to Chinese people, I will speak English but with a slightly more Chinese ... slang.

The above excerpt demonstrates two things; first, the complex channels through which interpellation of ethnic identities occurs and second, the citationality that accompanies the assumption of an ethnic identity. Okamura (1981, p. 455) notes that what is important to the situational selection process as the external perception of the individual's ethnic identity is the reverse, i.e. the individual in question's perception of the ethnic identity of others. Indeed, interpellation not only refers to the process in which individuals are hailed by a dominant power structure, but also to the hailing of individuals by others who are similarly within the constraints of the dominant ideology. Thus, in deliberating which identity to portray, P's choice between Malay and Chinese is as much determined by the ethnic categories assigned to her as the ethnic categories she assigns to the individuals she encounters. To those she regards as 'Malay', P cites from a 'library' of 'Malay' signifiers and mimics various 'Malay' characteristics such as speaking the Malay language, complete with colloquial phrases and, as a display of true mastery, the Malay accent even in English conversations.

In her actions, her performance of 'the Malay' or 'the Chinese' role, P produces the Malay/Chinese subject if only for a moment. In this way, 'mixed' Malaysians may at once subvert and reify the ethnic identities that render them ambiguous; by traversing purportedly rigid boundaries in their practiced embodiment of various ethnic identities on the one hand, and by reproducing those very boundaries in their complicit interpellation of officialized identity on the other. What this contributes to our understanding of 'mixed' identities and their relationship to ethnicity can, *mutatis mutandis*, be understood in terms of Butler's (1993, p. 232) assertion that gender performativity is in fact not a 'product of choice', but a compulsory 'doing' that is necessitated from the very first instance that an individual is named a 'girl'. Furthermore, she suggests that rather than understanding performativity as a conscious act perpetrated by an actor, whose true 'self' or identity is concealed in the act, it should instead be understood as an act which constitutes the actor as a 'self' that is able to assume a gendered identity. When applied to the context of ethnicity and 'race', this idea of ethnicity as a product of choice seems much more viable. Such an understanding of performativity is nevertheless useful in conceiving those choices less as conscious and intentional acts and more as unconscious mechanisms of survival made necessary by a hegemonic social order. It suggests also that *being* an ethnicity or 'race' is impossible, and whereas P may perform Malay or Chinese identities, this does not imply that a true 'mixed' ethnic identity resides beneath those performances. These performances are, however, required for acceptance into (Malaysian) society.

Stable ethnic identities

Stable ethnic identity is a phrase I use to refer to instances when 'mixed' Malaysians choose to identify consistently with one ethnic group over others. In the course of my interviews, two interviewees in particular, Z and S, said that although they were aware of their mixed ancestry, they did not usually identify as 'mixed' and preferred to identify as 'Malay'. Though many studies on 'mixed' identities show that most individuals of 'mixed-heritage' or 'mixed-parentage' tend towards multiple identities, with few choosing to identify with just one ethnic identity (see Tizard and Phoenix, 1995; Stephan and Stephan, 1989; Stephan, 1991), the socio-political conditions of Malaysian society are such that there is a much greater pressure for individuals to take up either the position of 'the Malay', 'the Chinese' or 'the Indian' or risk rejection by the social order.

What is most interesting about participants who engaged in selected ethnic identification was that they understood themselves as both mixed and yet 'more' one 'race' than the other(s). During the interview, the participants were asked to identify their ethnic background in as much detail and as far back as they could remember. Most interviewees described only their parents' ethnicities as differing, with some relaying more information about their grandparents and even fewer referring to ancestral lines going further back. S, for example, replied simply, 'My paternal granddad is Indian and my maternal grandmum is Chinese'. However, when asked later what he identifies as most, he answered emphatically, 'Malay ... more than anything'. To a slightly differently worded question, S again explained that he identifies more with Malay culture, and he reasons that this is because he participates more in 'Malay culture' than other 'cultures'.

s: That's why when people ask me about my background, why I say Malay, is because in terms of language I speak B.M. [*Bahasa Malaysia*] not Mandarin and dressing ... it's like when people say they're mixed but then when you ask them do they speak [the languages]? 'No I don't'. Okay, it's a good thing that you're familiar with your heritage background but if you do not speak, if you do not follow, [then] do you really consider [yourself mixed]? That's why when people ask, I won't really say I'm mixed.

S's admission that he doesn't usually identify himself as 'mixed' because he does not speak any language other than *Bahasa Melayu* (and English) suggests that for him, not being able to speak Mandarin denied him the possibility of identifying with that ethnic category and by extension that of 'mixed' ethnicity. On the other hand, S assesses his ability to speak and understand B.M. as automatically qualifying him as Malay. For S, to be 'mixed' requires doing a 'mixed' identity that includes adhering to the so-called cultural norms of two or more apparently different ethnicities. If, on the other hand, these pre-requisites are not met, then a 'true' ethnic identity can be easily determined based on those ethnic signifiers they exhibit. It may be the case that 'mixed' Malaysians in particular, for whom references to one's descent or cultural 'roots' may not be useful in according them a definitive ethnic identity, turn to other means to establish a stable ethnic identity.

Moreover, while it is difficult to generalize from such a small sample, the fact that the two participants who exhibited tendencies towards stable ethnic identities identified as Malay suggests that this ethnic category encourages such behaviour, perhaps because the Malay identity itself has historically been 'exceptionally open to new recruits' (Reid, 2001, p. 301), because of the politically and economically privileged position that the Malay identity holds in Malaysia, and because of its strong and salient links with religious identity (see Sakai, 2009; Martinez, 2001, p. 488) . In the excerpt below, Z, who described herself at first as 'Machindian'[6] but, like S, regards herself as 'more Malay', demonstrates that Malay identity is often intricately linked with Muslim identity and these connections are quite visible. Z begins by explaining the ways in which she perceived herself as 'looking' Malay, an idea she inferred earlier in the conversation.

C: How do you think you look Malay?
Z: Uh because I wear the *tudung* [Muslim headscarf] and my skin colour ... is ... brownish ... (laughs).
C: I think I'm more tanned that you.... [As someone who is regularly interpellated as Chinese, I try here to highlight that my skin tone was comparatively darker than hers.]
Z: (Laughs) No, no ... no but I have Malay features, right? Even though I'm mixed. Like if you see my dad, he looks Chinese ... but ... um....
C: Can you be a little more specific?
Z: Uh I think my skin colour ... and the giveaway is the fact that I wear the *tudung* because, you know, the *tudung* is worn by Malay girls.
C: Muslim girls?
Z: Well, in this country Malay ... you see someone wearing a scarf [and] you think, oh, she's Malay ... that's just the stereotype ... uh I don't know, I don't think it's a stereotype ... it's just a label....

So, for Z, her ethnic identity is not only written on her body phenotypically, but also worn. The *tudung* or headscarf acts in this instance both as a symbol of her religiosity and – perhaps even more so – as a marker of her ethnicity. Thus, in Malaysia it is commonplace, as Z describes it, for those seen wearing a headscarf to be automatically assumed Malay, rather than Muslim, the ethnic label perhaps being more useful because it already includes the Islamic. Thus, Islamic and Malay symbols and traditions often become conflated. As S noted in the interview, there are very few exclusively 'Malay' cultural practices or celebrations and in fact, most, such as Hari Raya (also referred to as Eid elsewhere in the world, which marks the end of the fasting month), are related to Islam.

As mixed Malaysians attempt to understand their own identity through the framework of officialized ethnic identity, it is also interesting to note that some participants found that they encountered resistance from others around them who rejected their self-ascribed identity. Both S and Z describe similar instances where their 'Malay-ness' becomes questioned by others who themselves struggle to reconcile their chosen ethnic categories with visible 'non-normative' characteristics. For S, the experience causes her to question her 'Malay' identity:

z: ... I would definitely say in government school its very, very ... they [Malay students] kind of like to keep to themselves ... and they're very, very ... I'm not sure if its pride but you know if you're Malay then you will speak Malay and, like, real fluent Malay and like really, really thick, with the accent and all. And I was kinda made fun of because my Malay wasn't really Malay and I don't really know how you define that because you know, I can write a paper ... ok I'm not that great in my Malay paper, but I can get an A. But like when I speak it ... it's ... you know they will say, 'Ooh why do you sound funny – aren't you Malay?', and I'll say, 'Yeah, I am'. But like how do you define what's Malay and what's not? Like I do speak a lot of English ... is that why I sound funny in my Malay?

c: And how does that make you feel when people sort of question your ... 'Malay-ness'?

z: At first ... well in school it was kind of hard like ... not hard as in like I wasn't [depressed] but it was ... it was unnecessary like ... why do you have to point it out ... like what difference does it make? Like, so what, I say a few words funnier ... and it doesn't sound as good as what it is ... like I didn't see the whole point behind getting picked on because I sounded funny. And because of that I think they were kinda confused and ... and I don't know ... confused and just ... aggravated by the fact that they couldn't stereotype me, like I didn't fit into the stereotype ... like *to* them. Because you know like Malay ... what's the normal stereotype for Malay? There are certain like, 'they do this' and 'they do that', 'they speak like this' and 'they're lazy' and all that. It's a stereotype and people just assume that we're Malay people but like when I don't talk like a 'real' Malay people ... and if you don't talk like a real Malay people ... person, then what are you?

Z is conscious of the fact that her identity is confusing and frustrating for those around her and, though she often took it for granted, this situation causes her to rethink her identity, or rather the Malay identity, and some of the things one has to *do* – such as speak like a 'real Malay person' – that would qualify you as actually or authentically 'Malay'. Such a *doing* of race validates Butler's (1990, p. 142) assertion that 'there need not be a "doer behind the deed", but that the "doer" [i.e. the racial subject] is variably constructed in and through the deed'.

Transethnic identities

Whereas most of those interviewed are happy to work with or around the officialized identities that are regularly interpellated, some are less willing to do so and choose instead to seek out alternative ways of representing themselves. I refer to these identities as transethnic in the sense of both a horizontal interaction of ethnic identities, as well as the transcending of ethnicity as a salient source of identity. E. Douglas Lewis (1989, p. 176) argued that new ways of being outside the dominant structure can become viable as a result of the 'imagination' of even a single person and 'the joint acts of will' of others. Amongst Malaysians, individuals are everyday redefining ethnic boundaries and, in the case of some of the mixed Malaysians interviewed here, reinventing normative identities. For Q, who often identifies as 'Indian and Chinese mixed', acknowledging his mixed ancestry is important, yet the same mixed ancestry makes it difficult for him to consider ethnicity a salient part of his personal identity.

Q: ... ethnic identity as a whole is not very important to me but both sides are equally important. I don't like if either side is diminished. For example, if people identify me as simply Chinese because I speak Chinese and not Punjabi, or identify me as Indian but not Chinese because it says race and I have a Singh in my name, I feel like it diminishes the other part which is as much a part of me as the other.

When asked whether he found it easier to fit in with any one ethnic group, he explained that he felt different and preferred instead to surround himself with others who did not 'define themselves so much by race'. 'I wasn't brought up in a traditional culture', he said. 'I can speak Chinese and I know quite a few of their practices but that doesn't change the fact that I'm different from them'.

Similarly, N, whose ethnic identity fluctuates between Indian, Ceylonese and Iranian, ranked her ethnic identity last after her religious identity as Baha'i (first) and her national identity as Malaysian (second). In the extract below, she explains her reasons for doing so. What becomes apparent is the discontent she feels with the ethnic categories presented to her. Like Q, she identifies a sense of difference and an inability to relate to idealized ethnic identities that are often taken for granted.

N: ... I don't feel ... uh ... conformed to one particular race or one particular culture. For me, it would be like religion, nationality and then race ... because I can't really know I'm Persian to a lot of ... on many levels I'm really not and then if you really look at the Ceylonese ... I'm really not also ... I find it really hard to relate to. I can, but it doesn't ... it doesn't feel natural?

C: [Uh-huh]
N: Yeah, it really doesn't feel natural. Yeah. Because I know that I don't really feel … because I don't feel Persian very well … so there's a lot of things I don't know … so it's really hard to relate-lah.
C: But you say that the *T'aarof* [Persian custom] thing is in you?
N: Yeah that's just that one small … there are some but it's just not strong enough for me.

Earlier, N had described to me in great detail the Persian custom of self-deference called *T'aarof*, which she felt she learned from her mother and which she found herself enacting as part of daily interactions with others. However, as both her narrative and, likewise, Q's, indicates, some of these questions, which they may have been facing for the first time in my interview with them, are not easy to answer and the result is significant hesitation and even contradiction. Whilst they were able to discuss quite easily the ways in which they participated in particular ethnic heritages, describing identity unambiguously proved more problematic. N and Q both express this idea that it is not enough to simply perform various aspects of 'Persian-ness' or 'Chinese-ness' to be Persian or to be Chinese. Instead, both Q and N look to alternative identities such as, for Q, a hybridized 'Chindian' identity, and, for N, a Baha'i or Malaysian identity.

In both cases, the interviewees sought alternative identities that better matched how they perceived themselves and that were ethnically neutral. For Q, his Chindian identity resembles partly a 'mash up' of Chinese and Indian identities but also something that is separate, neither distinguishably Indian nor Chinese. In a particularly intriguing moment, he says, 'I'm half Indian and I'm half Chinese so either I'm both or I'm neither, and if I'm neither then I don't exist'. On the one hand, the idea that without identifying as Chinese and Indian, he does not exist speaks to the strength of officialized conceptions of Malaysian identity which recognizes only Malay, Indian and Chinese subjects. On the other hand, the conviction with which he asserts his all-or-nothing identity speaks of a conscious effort to define an identity that is regularly negotiated and as yet unnamed and unrecognized. Instead, he creates for himself a hybrid identity reminiscent of Khoo's (2009) cosmopolitan space, where two or more identities exist simultaneously without necessarily challenging one another. Such an understanding of cosmopolitanism as ethnically and politically neutral spaces in which individuals of various cultural backgrounds may 'converge and mingle' (Khoo, 2009, 90), may be useful in imagining mixed-ness as a cosmopolitan space or mixed individuals as cosmopolitan bodies.

In a similar all-or-nothing fashion, N's inability to identify completely with either her mother's Persian identity or her father's Ceylonese identity results in a disavowal of ethnic identity altogether. She prefers instead to answer the interpellative call for Baha'i subjects and for Malaysian subjects.

C: What is the first thing that comes to mind when asked 'what are you?' or 'who are you?' and you'd say….

N: Actually, I'd say I'm Malaysian.
C: Malaysian.
N: Yeah. Because when I think about the Persian culture, there's a lot – a lot of Persian culture which I'm not really ... into? That I don't really ... follow. There are some but ... like no. I – I wouldn't consider myself very Persian at all. And then let's just say the ... maybe the – I don't really know much of the Ceylonese culture. I don't.

A Malaysian identity in particular allows for the formation of what Mandal (2003) terms 'transethnic solidarities'. In a challenge to primordialist notions of race in Malaysia, Mandal argues that in fact cultural hybridity is entrenched in the historical development of the Malay Peninsula and, though suppressed or suffering from state erasure, does continue today. People and spaces that recognize these and allow for their visibility constitute important transethnic solidarities that poignantly dispute the place of racialized politics and social policy. N's identification with the label Malaysian is, thus, just that; it suggests more than identification with being Malaysian and should instead be read as a signal of growing discontent with the over-generalized, ill-fitting categories that apparently define them. In substituting an officialized ethnic identity for a Malaysian identity, N is not only recruited as a Malaysian, but the notion of Malaysian is redefined to mean more than simply an Indian, a Chinese or a Malay citizen of Malaysia. For N, being Malaysian infers a culture of its own that includes, but is not defined by, its ethnic diversity, or rather is transethnic. In the extract below, N elucidates her thoughts on *being* Malaysian and the distinct 'culture' that accompanies it.

C: What do you think it means to be Malaysian then?
N: (laughs) Good one! To be Malaysian ... what is it to be Malaysian ... [pauses]. One thing that comes to my mind is the fact that we don't really know um with regards to time ... like anything can happen anytime. You can certainly have meals at 12 o'clock at night ... and it's a very *lepak* [laid back] kind of lifestyle. There's no ... one of the things about being Malaysian to me is that there are hardly any rules ... because being Malaysian is very much about having all kinds of influences from other cultures, and so there's like ... you don't really know what you're following ... it's just ... because I'm just thinking with regards to Persian culture and Indian culture ... more or less a lot of things ... there are a lot of rules! Indian culture – there are certain days you can't eat meat and when the girl gets her period you can't leave the house ... it's all these things but when you really think about it ... in the Malaysian context ... there's nothing! If you ask me being Malaysian means there are no rules to follow ... you just do what you like! [Laughs.]

Throughout the interview, N used the term Malaysian and contrasted a Malaysian culture with others such as Persian and Indian unproblematically. However, when asked to describe Malaysian culture, she is caught off guard. Without an established idea of Malaysian-ness from which to cite, she imagines in the moment a Malaysian culture much like a mixture of disparate cultures that have in time melded into a new type of culture or identity that can be called uniquely Malaysian. Other participants including B, also speak about a Malaysian culture in the same way. Taken together, these calls for alternative trans-ethnic identities by real individuals who together reject ill-fitting collective categories and essentialist labels, perhaps represent those choices by creative individuals that may one day result in the realization of a true '*Bangsa Malaysia*'. Indeed, a recent attempt by Malaysian politician Hannah Yeoh and husband to register their newborn child's race as 'Anak Malaysia' (Chong, 2011) – meaning Malaysian or, literally, child of Malaysia – is evidence of a slow but sure paradigm shift.

Conclusion

This chapter has demonstrated the multiplicity of ways in which ethnic identity can be experienced and negotiated, indicating that for these individuals, the experience of their 'ambiguity' is varied and not always wholly embraced. As individuals, they regularly negotiate between authority-defined discourses and their own lived experiences, to make sense of themselves and their place within the larger social structures.

For some, ethnic identity is fluid and context-specific. As they are regularly interpellated with a number of identities, 'mixed' Malaysians find they are able to use their ethnic identity (or identities) instrumentally to achieve various desired outcomes. The extent to which they can 'switch' between identities is nevertheless limited as they continue to work within normative social structures where the successful performance of ethnic identity is an important determinant of one's acceptance into the social order.

Other 'mixed' Malaysians are able to find comfort in stable ethnic identities though this is not without its own challenges. Individuals are faced with the arduous task of reconciling their diverse heritage with one officialized ethnic identity, and this is commonly conducted through a consideration of various cultural and religious factors. Again, the performance reveals itself to be a vital piece when maintaining a coherent identity. These narratives show that while interpellations of officialized ethnic identity are easily accepted in official discourse, these ethnic labels become much more problematic in their everyday lives. Through their interactions with others and with institutions, 'mixed' Malaysians must continuously negotiate and confabulate a sense of belonging with one of a number of identities.

Finally, there are those who reject officialized ethnic labels altogether and choose instead to reinvent for themselves alternative identities that they find more fitting. These are individuals that refuse to be categorized and that reject simplistic notions of sameness and difference. These emerging transethnic identities hint at the possibility of a future where the current reified ethnic or cultural boundaries may become less important to the way in which Malaysians understand themselves and their relations to others.

On the one hand, this study demonstrates the way in which some 'mixed' Malaysians continue to work with officialized ethnic identities, and in the reproduction of Malay, Indian or Chinese identities, subjects may reinforce rather than challenge essentialist notions of ethnicity. On the other hand, I would suggest that in their conscious or unconscious traversal of ethnic boundaries, their rational take on belonging, and their active creation of alternative transethnic identities, 'mixed' Malaysians also reject such notions. The varied ways in which they negotiate their identities make visible the 'doing' (Butler, 1990, p. 25) of race and destabilize naturalized notions of ethnic identity and, certainly, race. In doing so, they confirm Jackson's (2002) argument that the reification of categorical identities only conceals the complex subjectivities and the real lived experiences of individuals. Rather, it is, as Jackson (2002, p. 125) articulates: 'the phenomenal interplay between persons and such categories – between the confusion and flux of immediate experience on the one hand, and finite forms and fixed ideas on the other – that constitutes the empirical reality of human life'. Indeed, that Malaysians recognize the label 'mixed' – even though understood as a mixture of 'pure' or 'authentic' 'races' – ultimately suggests an awareness of the increasing inadequacies of such concepts for describing their lived realities, and a desire for something more.

Notes

1 A number of groups, particularly populous in Sabah and Sarawak, are thought of as indigenous and classified as '*Dan Lain Lain*' or 'others'. Although they share *Bumiputera* status with the Malays (see below), they are distinct from Malays in culture.
2 I have discussed the ways in which 'mixed' Malaysians are interpellated into these categories by the state elsewhere (Lim, 2012).
3 A fourth category exists. In official census and most forms, *Dan Lain Lain* (Others) appears as an option. Identities outside of the three officially recognized identities are subsumed under this category.
4 Participants are identified by initials rather than pseudonyms in order to avoid the issue of deciding whether to give them names that match their ethnicities and inadvertently interpellating them myself. In Malaysia, where there is a strong relationship between ethnic identity, language and religion, names are also salient markers of ethnicity. For example, one participant noted the fact that having Singh in his name identifies him as Indian.
5 Some ambiguity regarding Punjabi identity exists. Though they may sometimes be interpellated as Indian, Punjabis usually self-identify as a separate ethnic group. Moreover, Indian in the Malaysian context is commonly imagined as Southern Indian, usually Tamil and Hindu.
6 Machindian is a portmanteau of the words 'Malay', 'Chinese' and 'Indian' used here to indicate her mixed heritage.

Bibliography

Althusser, L. (1971). *Lenin and Philosophy, and Other Essays*. Ben Brewster (trans.). London: New Left Books.
Butler, J. (1990). *Gender Trouble: Feminism and the Subversion of Identity*. New York: Routledge.

Butler, J. (1993). *Bodies That Matter: On the Discursive Limits of Sex*. New York: Routledge.

Chong, D. (2011). 'DAP backs couple's 'Anak Malaysia' bid'. *The Malaysian Insider*. Available at: www.themalaysianinsider.com/malaysia/article/dap-backs-couples-anak-malaysia-bid (accessed: 20 October 2011).

Freedman, M. (1960). 'The Growth of a Plural Society in Malaya'. *Pacific Affairs* 33(2), pp. 158–168.

Freeman, D. (1981). 'The Anthropology of Choice'. *Canberra Anthropology* 4(1), pp. 82–100.

Furnivall, J. S. (1948). *Colonial Practice and Policy*. Cambridge: Cambridge University Press.

Hall, S. (2000). 'Who Needs "Identity"?' In P. Du Gay, J. Evans, and P. Redman (eds), *Identity: A Reader*. London: SAGE Publications, pp. 15–30.

Hirschman, C. (1987). 'The Meaning and Measurement of Ethnicity in Malaysia: An Analysis of Census Classifications'. *The Journal of Asian Studies* 46(3), pp. 555–582.

Jackson, M. (2002). *The Politics of Storytelling: Violence, Transgression, and Intersubjectivity*. Denmark: Narayana Press.

Khoo, G. C. (2009). 'Kopitiam: Discursive Cosmopolitan Spaces and National Identity in Malaysia Culture and Media'. In A. Wise and S. Velayutham (eds), *Everyday Multiculturalism*. New York: Palgrave Macmillan, pp. 87–104.

Khoo, G. C. (2010). 'Listen to the Sound of the Azan: Independent Malaysian Films Undoing Racialisation'. In J. C. H. Lee (ed.), *The Malaysian Way of Life*. Shah Alam: Marshall Cavendish Editions, pp. 22–26.

Lee, H. G. (2002). 'Malay Dominance and Opposition Politics in Malaysia'. In D. Singh and A. L. Smith (eds), *Southeast Asian Affairs 2002* (29). Singapore: Institute of Southeast Asian Studies, pp. 177–195.

Lewis, D. E. (1989). 'Why did Sina Dance?' In P. Alexander (ed.), *Creating Indonesian Cultures*. Sydney: Oceania Publications.

Lim, C. (2012). 'Locating Mixed Identities in a Racialised Society'. In J. Hopkins and J. C. H. Lee (eds), *Thinking through Malaysia: Culture and Identity in the 21st Century*. Petaling Jaya: Strategic Information and Research Development Centre.

Mandal, S. (2003). 'Transethnic Solidarities in a Racialised Context'. *Journal of Contemporary Asia* 33(1), pp. 50–68.

Martinez, P. (2001). 'The Islamic State or the State of Islam in Malaysia'. *Contemporary South East Asia* 23(3), pp. 474–503.

Nagata, J. (1974). 'What is a Malay? Situational Selection of Ethnic Identity in a Plural Society'. *American Ethnologist* 1(2), pp. 331–350.

Okamura, J. (1981). 'Situational Ethnicity'. *Ethnic and Racial Studies* 4(4), pp. 452–465.

Paden, J. (1970). Urban Pluralism, Integration and Adaptation of Communal Identity in Kano, Nigeria'. In R. Cohen and J. Middleton (eds), *From Tribe to Nation in Africa: Studies in Incorporation Processes*. Scranton: Chandler Publishing, pp. 242–270.

Reid, A. (2001). 'Understanding Melayu (Malay) as a Source of Diverse Modern Identities'. *Journal of Southeast Asian Studies* 32(3), pp. 295–313.

Sakai, M. (2009). 'Reviving Malay Connections in Southeast Asia'. In H. Cao and E. Morrell (eds), *Regional Minorities and Development in Asia*. Oxon: Routledge.

Shamsul, A. B. (1996). 'Debating about Identity in Malaysia: A Discourse Analysis'. *Southeast Asian Studies* 43(3), pp. 476–499.

Shamsul A. B (2001). 'A History of an Identity, an Identity of a History: The Idea and Practice of "Malayness" in Malaysia Reconsidered'. *Journal of Southeast Asian Studies* 32(3), pp. 356–366.

Stephan, C. (1991). 'Ethnic Identity Among Mixed-Heritage People in Hawaii'. *Symbolic Interaction* 14(3), pp. 261–277.

Stephan, C., and Stephan, W. (1989). 'After Intermarriage: Ethnic Identity Among Mixed-Heritage Japanese-Americans and Hispanics'. *Journal of Marriage and Family* 51(2), pp. 507–519.

Tan C. B. (2000). 'Ethnic Identities and National Identities: Some Examples from Malaysia'. *Identities* 6(4), pp. 441–480.

Tizard, B., and Phoenix, A. (1995). 'The Identity of Mixed Parentage Adolescents'. *The Journal of Child Psychology and Psychiatry* 36(8), p. 1399–1410.

8 Chinese, Indians and the grey space in between

Strategies of identity work among Chindians in a plural society

Rona Chandran

Introduction

The ethnic diversity in Malaysia today is a direct result of its history as a British colony between 1786 and 1957 (Carstens, 2006; Jayum, 2007). Along with British colonization came the segregation of Malaysia's inhabitants on the basis of skin colour and phenotype, using the contested concept of 'race'. The contemporary Malaysian census continues to classify the population into race-based categories: in 2011 the census captured the population as 67.4 per cent *Bumiputera*[1] (Peninsular, Sabah and Sarawak), 24.7 per cent Chinese, 7.3 per cent Indians and 0.7 per cent Others (Department of Statistics, 2011). Syed (2008) describes Malaysia as a nation made up of 'several ethnic groups with diverse history, culture, religion, language and even economic roles. Ethnic differences exist, which often manifest in stereotypes, discriminations, tensions and conflicts that complicate the process of building national unity' (p. 1).

The term 'race' is often used interchangeably with the term 'ethnicity' in Malaysia (Ibrahim, 2011). Race is understood as human groupings which are seen as connected on a biological basis, through characteristics such as genes and phenotype association (Cheah, 2009; Kottak 2008; Nagai, 2010) resulting from interbreeding due to geographical proximity (Goldsby, 1977). Syed (2008) argues that the term ethnicity is more applicable to the Malaysian population than the term race, as the population is more distinguishable in terms of ethnic differences, based around culture and practice, than racial differences. He points out that Malays and Chinese belong to what was traditionally understood as the Mongoloid racial category, but that they differ in terms of ethnicity. Simplistic racial categorization has been significantly challenged, and a broad biological basis for race has been widely disproven (Banton, 1998; Lewontin 1972; UNESCO, 1951). This chapter discusses identity from an ethnic perspective while recognizing that aspects of race, in terms of visible difference, are salient in the social construction of mixed identities.

'Chindians', also known as Sino-Indians, are individuals of mixed Indian and Chinese parentage. The term 'Chindian', coined from the words 'Chinese' and 'Indian', is a socially accepted term in Malaysia and Singapore (David, 2008; Gopan, 2011). However, the category 'Chindian' or 'Sino-Indian' is not formally

Chindian identity: the grey space in between 133

recognized in Malaysia. The Chindian population is instead officially designated as either Chinese or Indian, along patrilineal classificatory lines. Socially, Chindian identity is also viewed rather simplistically, and along stereotypical lines by other ethnic groups.

The subject of mixed ethnic identities is becoming increasingly important around the world, and has received scholarly attention in countries such as Japan, the United Kingdom and the United States (see, for example, Chaudhari and Pizzolato, 2008; Moss and Davis, 2003; Oikawa and Yoshida, 2007; Rockquemore and Laszloffy, 2003; Root, 1996; Talbot, 2008; Wardle, 2000; Zack, 1993). In Malaysia, there is limited literature on mixedness, and a lack of in-depth research on the ethnic identities of Chindians. Much of the available literature instead focuses on specific aspects of the Chindian community, such as language preference (David, 2008). This chapter provides a different approach to understanding the ethnic identities of Malaysian Chindians, by analysing the outward manifestation of their identities through their use of strategies of identity work, which they utilize to gain the acceptance of their reference group members.

The chapter works to bridge the gap between theory and practice by investigating how biethnic Chindians negotiate and portray their ethnic identity in mainstream Malaysian society. This is achieved using two main research questions:

a   How are strategies of identity work used by Chindians to gain acceptance among Chinese and Indian reference groups in Malaysia?
b   What are the conditions for the acceptance of Chindians set by the reference groups?

The empirical findings of this chapter also contribute to the knowledge about the effects of macro-level structures on biethnic identity establishment and individual behaviour, due to the reciprocal relationship between formal and informal social structures and individual identity (Stets and Burke, 2005).

Official structures

Mixed marriages and relationships between Chinese and Indian individuals have led to a growing population of 'Chindians' in Malaysia (David, 2008). Between 2003 and 2010, according to unpublished data, a total of 6,509 Chindians were born in Malaysia (Department of Statistics, 2013). However, Chindians do not fit easily into the existing official ethnic categories of Malay, Chinese, Indians and Others.

Formal registration policies and ethnic/racial categories such as these serve as structures which influence the perception and acceptance of biethnic individuals in a society (Koshy, 2001). Recently, countries such as the United States and Singapore have altered their systems of ethnic/racial categorization, to better capture demographic complexity. In 2000, the US Census Bureau allowed its citizens to select more than one racial category to represent their racial identities.

This move was well accepted, as over 6.8 million individuals checked more than one box (Rockquemore and Brunsma, 2002; Rockquemore and Laszloffy, 2003). According to the 2011 birth registration policy in Singapore, interethnic married couples, or parents with two ethnic backgrounds, are now permitted to register their children with either singular or double-barrelled ethnic labels (Immigration Checkpoints Authority, 2011), allowing for acknowledgement of mixed parentage.

In Malaysia, Section 13A of the Births and Deaths Registration Act 299 dictates strict patriarchal ethnic categories for non-Malay couples. Chindians are thus either categorized as Indians or as Chinese, in accordance with the registered ethnicity of their fathers. Between 2003 and 2010, 2,710 Chindian individuals were officially categorized as Chinese, while 3,799 Chindian individuals were officially categorized as Indian. This practice predefines the ethnicity of a biethnic person, prescribes the individual's position in society and fails to capture the actual ethnic composition of the Malaysian population (Rona and Yahya, 2015). The official categorization of ethnicity has significant influence in everyday life, as Malaysia operates an ethnic/race based quota system in areas such as public tertiary education, scholarships, sale of government bonds, licensing and government jobs. Individuals of mixed descent, such as Chindians, are thus particularly affected by such restrictive categorization, which has practical consequences.

Biethnic identity dynamics within social structures

Identity construction is not an isolated process. Society plays a key role in the identity development of biethnic individuals (Taylor, 2004; Rocha, 2010). The Social Identity Theory of Tajfel and Turner (1986) highlights the importance of a strong sense of belonging and self-esteem based on group membership. The theory stresses the tendency amongst people to form social groups based on similar qualities and to demarcate others who do not belong to the group. Ethnic groups are one of the most common social groups in which people seek membership, and such membership can prove important to a person's sense of self (see Barth, 1969).

Reference groups are sociocultural groups against which people benchmark their culture and social behaviour (Heng, Lehman, Peng and Greenholtz, 2002). According to Park and Lessig (1977), 'a reference group is defined as an actual or imaginary individual or group conceived as having significant relevance upon an individual's evaluations, aspirations, or behaviour' (p. 102). Reference groups serve to validate feelings of belonging and identity, something which can be problematic for individuals of mixed descent, as members of society often insist in placing people into compartmentalized ethnic categories (Khanna and Johnson, 2010; Kich, 1992; Rockquemore, 1998; Talbot, 2008). In this chapter, reference groups refer to the ethnic groups of the parents of the Chindian individuals.

Besides Chindians, other biethnic groups in Malaysia include the Baba Nyonyas, Malacca Chitty and the Peranakan Punjabi. In terms of social acceptance in Malaysia, biethnic communities often find themselves in a marginal position. Due to differences in their daily spoken language, customs, physical appearance and skin colour, their efforts to gain acceptance from their reference group members can be futile (Khoo, 1996; Teo, 2003). Such experiences play a prominent role in the identity construction process, and in promoting feelings of belonging or exclusion for individuals of mixed descent.

Theoretical discussions on mixed ethnic identity have shifted over time. The Marginal Man Theory (Stonequist, 1935), discussed further by Clark in 1966, suggested that biethnic individuals occupy a marginal situation: they are culturally similar to their reference groups, yet they are not accepted socially as in-group members. A few decades later, Poston's (1990) model suggested that biethnic individuals move through five stages of identity development before they arrive at the final stage of an integrated form of ethnic identity. Both these theories suggest that ethnic identity development for individuals of mixed parentage is a linear process. Other studies postulate that biethnic individuals deal with their ethnic identity development in different, more complex, ways and claim to belong to different categories of ethnic identity. Padilla (2006) suggests that individuals of mixed parentage might accept a socially prescribed identity, identify with both ethnic groups, chose one ethnic group over the other or even identify as an entirely new ethnic group.

Although certain predefined ethnic categories exist in society, these categories are neither fixed nor permanent. Instead, ethnic categories are susceptible to change and are able to accommodate social changes. Qian and Litcher (2007) suggest that ethnic categories can be dealt with in three ways: crossed, blurred and shifted. Crossing an ethnic boundary refers to moving over the boundary to another group without any real effect or alterations to the boundary. The blurring of ethnic boundaries refers to a situation where the ethnic boundaries are no longer easily distinguished due to the prevalence of biethnic individuals in society. Shifting ethnic boundaries refers to the acceptance of outsiders as in-group members. This suggests that ethnic boundaries are not static, and that ethnic identity is a fluid concept. Ethnic identity is thus derived through negotiation between the individual, members of society and official structures.

Two important variables which affect ethnic identity development are the comprehensiveness of ethnic identity and the degree to which it is asserted or assigned. According to Cornell and Hartmann (1998), ethnic identity formation takes place between these variables. The comprehensiveness of ethnic identity refers to the influence that ethnic identity has over the various spheres of a person's social life and collective action – significant influence, in the case of Malaysia. The comprehensiveness of ethnic identity can change according to situation and time and allows for heterogeneity within the group.

Furthermore, there are three factors that determine how ethnic identity is asserted and/or assigned: boundaries, perceived position and meaning (Cornell and Hartmann, 1998). Boundaries function to include people who meet certain criteria as 'in-group members'. They also exclude others who do not meet the criteria of the group, as 'out-group members'. Factors such as shared culture, phenotype and common origin can play prominent roles in the construction of these boundaries. Perceived position refers to the notion of placing a group in a hierarchy on the socio-economic ladder. This determines the relationship of the group to other groups that coexist in society. Meaning refers to the values and stereotypes (positive or negative) attached to the members of a certain group. Positive values and stereotypes might attract people to a certain group, while negative stereotypes and values may cause people to disassociate themselves from that particular group.

Chaudhari and Pizzolato (2008) found that, besides seeking the acceptance of reference group members, biethnic individuals developed their own perceptions about these reference groups. Some felt comfortable and had a sense of belonging to one or both groups, whereas others did not feel like they belonged to either group. Such feelings of not belonging are usually caused by negative reflected appraisals (Khanna and Johnson, 2010), or due to the rejection that these biethnic individuals received from their reference group members. The perception that biethnic individuals have about their reference groups strongly influences their own ethnic identity development (Khanna and Johnson, 2010; Taylor, 2004). Based on these perceptions, biethnic individuals apply strategies of identity work in order to be accepted by members of the identified reference group or to disassociate themselves from a particular group (Khanna and Johnson, 2010).

Research approach

The conceptual framework for this research is based on the understanding that ethnic identity is a fluid concept, with varying degrees of comprehensiveness, influenced by the forces of assignment and assertion (Cornell and Hartmann, 1998). Reference groups play a vital role in influencing identity, and biethnic individuals apply strategies of identity work in relation to their reference groups (Khanna and Johnson, 2010). This chapter explores how Chindians apply verbal identification or disidentification, highlighting or downplaying cultural symbols, and how they perceive themselves 'to be me', using specific strategies of identity work in order to be accepted by, or disassociated from, a particular reference group.

The research adopted a qualitative, ethnographic research design. The analysis is based on semi-structured interview data collected from 31 individuals with one Indian and one Chinese parent, some of whom self-identified as Chindian, as well as 20 Chinese individuals and 20 Indian individuals.[2] Observation and field visits were also used to gather detailed descriptive data. This triangulation of data sources enabled the researcher to verify the data collected (Merriam, 2002).

The Chindian journey: acceptance by reference group members

Acceptance by the Indian community

The acceptance of Chindians by the Indian community fell into two main categories: acceptance without conditions, and acceptance with conditions. Half of the Indians interviewed said that they would accept Chindians as part of the Indian community without any preset conditions around language or cultural practice. Some framed this as biological fact: they had 'Indian blood', and were persons of Indian origin, therefore they should be accepted as part of the Indian community. Some felt it would be unfair to deny Chindians their place in Indian society due to their inability to speak Tamil, as there were many 'pure' Indian people who could not converse in Tamil. Tamil is the language spoken by majority of the South Indian population in Malaysia and it serves as an important solidarity marker. Others viewed having Chindians as part of the Indian community as beneficial, as they could offer new ideas, approaches and world views. The ability of some Chindians to speak Chinese was seen as a link between the Indian and Chinese communities.

Ten Indian participants said that they would accept Chindian individuals as part of the Indian community only if they fulfilled certain cultural conditions. Some respondents cited religious obligation as a condition for acceptance: Indian culture is highly influenced by Hinduism, and to be part of the Indian community, some thought that an individual should understand, respect and embrace Hinduism. Other respondents used the justification that Chindians with Indian fathers were registered as Indians by law; therefore, it was important for them to embrace Hinduism and thus be part of the community. This clearly demonstrates the influence of official structures on perceptions of the acceptance of biethnic individuals.

Other respondents cited the manipulation of cultural symbols or behaviours as a condition for acceptance. They judged whether someone wanted to be seen as a Chinese or Indian by the way they dressed and spoke. This demonstrates that some reference group members are aware that Chindians actively code-switch and use cultural symbols to associate with a preferred identity. Some respondents mentioned that being able to understand the Tamil language was important for a person to be part of the Indian community, as it played such a dominant role. Overall, cultural factors such as language, religion and customs were important for gaining acceptance and validating ethnic identity for a large part of the Indian community.

Acceptance by the Chinese community

Acceptance of Chindians by the Chinese community was similar to the Indian community. Out of the 20 Chinese participants, ten would accept Chindians only if they met certain conditions. Several respondents accepted Chindians as part of the Chinese community based solely on the fact that they had a Chinese parent. Others said that they would accept Chindians as part of their community on wider moral grounds: as human beings they had an obligation to embrace humanity and to be welcoming to one another. Thus, most participants who did not set any preconditions for acceptance justified their views based on biological and humanitarian grounds.

As with the Indian community, ten Chinese respondents said that they would accept Chindians based on conditions that were closely related to language and culture. Adherence to the food, lifestyle and clothing choices of the ethnic Chinese community was a requirement for one participant. Several others specifically mentioned language in addition to culture as an important prerequisite for acceptance. They stressed that Chinese language and education were particularly important to the Chinese community. Therefore, in addition to practicing Chinese culture, a Chindian should be able to converse in Chinese (Mandarin or another Chinese dialect) in order to gain acceptance. Unlike the Indian respondents, none of the Chinese participants mentioned religion as a prerequisite for acceptance.

Harnessing strategies of ethnic identity work

The empirical data revealed that the degree of acceptance from reference group members and their own perceptions of reference groups were interpreted in different ways by Chindians. These interpretations were then translated into different strategies of identity work (Khanna and Johnson, 2010). This section deals with two strategies of identity work: the use of cultural symbols and verbal identification, as well as looking at a third form of identification, 'to be me'.

Cultural symbols

Cultural symbols are important ethnic identity markers (Teo, 2003; Janzen, 2000). These verbal and non-verbal symbols are connected to the elements that they signify, such as traditions, customs and beliefs (Kottak, 2008). The majority of Chindian respondents said that they highlighted Indian cultural symbols irrespective of their father's ethnicity, because they were familiar with and proud of their rich Indian cultures. One of the participants said: 'I love the Indian culture. It is very rich and unique. It makes me proud to be Indian'. A small number of respondents said that they intentionally downplayed Indian cultural symbols, because they felt that the Indian community was sometimes seen as inferior, and they did not want to expose themselves to judgment. A participant shared 'I intentionally remove the holy prayer ash from my forehead before I enter the school compound to avoid being criticized'. Other participants said that they downplayed both Chinese and Indian cultural symbols, although interestingly, none of the participants said that they only downplayed Chinese cultural symbols. This may be because they felt that belonging to the Chinese community associated them with the higher economic status of the Chinese in Malaysia.

The Chindian participants who downplayed their Indian cultural symbols gave various reasons. Some respondents admitted to intentionally not adopting cultural symbols such as the Hindu prayer string, holy ash and *pottu* (a small mark placed on the forehead between eyebrows) especially when in public among other ethnic groups, because they either wanted to disassociate themselves from the Indian community or because they feared that they would be ostracized by Chinese friends if they displayed these symbols.

Several participants deliberately downplayed both Indian and Chinese cultural symbols, such as wearing traditional costumes, (saree or cheong sam), wearing *pottu*, and speaking Chinese or Tamil. They indicated that previous negative encounters with reference group members caused them to desire to remain ambiguous in terms of ethnic identity, and to refrain from highlighting any ethnic identity markers. One respondent felt that 'it was much easier to remain vague in terms of ethnic identity as it avoided unwanted judgments'. Another respondent said that 'people could be very quick at passing obnoxious remarks that sometimes were very hurtful, such as questioning why my parents chose to marry each other'. Some Chindians sought to hide their biethnic identity in public to avoid stereotypes around ethnicity and phenotype. These individuals felt compelled to project an identity that satisfied societal expectations.

Other participants did not see a need to downplay cultural symbols. Some deliberately highlighted Indian cultural symbols through traditional dress, prayer strings and language, as they felt proud of and were comfortable with their Indian heritage. Some did so to their advantage, in order to attract Indian girls, or to avoid being mistaken for Malays due to their phenotype features and skin colour. Being mistaken for a Malay would be problematic due to the Islamic laws practiced in Malaysia; for example, it would be an offence for a Malay (assumed to be Muslim) to eat in public during the Muslim fasting period of *Ramadhan*. Thus, many Chindian participants were proud of their Indian culture and chose to highlight Indian cultural symbols, while some participants only highlighted these cultural symbols when it was to their advantage.

Five participants highlighted both Indian and Chinese cultural symbols, by speaking both languages. One respondent was comfortable in manipulating cultural symbols from both sides, such as dressing in traditional Indian and Chinese clothing, speaking both heritage languages and practicing both sets of customs. However, on several occasions he was selective in his use of these symbols, for example in hiding his Indian ethnicity to secure a lease, as the landlords refused to rent the room to non-Chinese. Some respondents spoke Mandarin to gain acceptance into the Chinese community, as being able to speak Mandarin or another Chinese dialect was an important prerequisite for acceptance into the Chinese community.

A number of respondents felt a strong sense of pride in speaking Mandarin as their heritage language, irrespective of whether it was the heritage language of their mother or their father. To the others who were more proficient in English, Tamil or Malay, it was a constant effort and struggle to speak Mandarin, mostly because the language was not a common language in the household and they did not receive any formal education in Mandarin, a notoriously difficult language. Therefore, gaining acceptance from the Chinese community was a difficult task, linguistically.

Thus, Chindians were aware of the advantages and disadvantages of their ethnicities in the Malaysian social context, due to the hierarchy and perceived position of ethnic groups in Malaysia. They chose to highlight or downplay their cultural symbols according to the demands of a particular situation, based on their judgment and past experiences.

Verbal identification

Over half the participants verbally identified themselves as both Indian and Chinese. One respondent claimed to be alternately Chinese or Indian, at opportune moments, to escape stereotypical expectations. When he was unable to meet the expectations associated with the Indian community, he would claim to be Chinese; and when unable to meet the expectations attached to the Chinese, he would claim to be Indian. Being Chindian gave him the prerogative to claim belonging to both ethnicities, but not to have to conform to one ethnicity in totality. Another respondent said that she was not ashamed of either side of her lineage, and that there was no reason for her to be in denial. She stated: 'I am Chinese and I am Indian. I accept the good and bad of both ethnic groups as part of who I am'.

One respondent said that people often assumed she did not care much about either community because she was a Chindian. At times, she found herself in situations where her Malay friends would verbally insult or condemn her Chinese or Indian friends or community, with the assumption that being only 'half' of each ethnic group, she would not associate herself with either.

Seven participants said that they neither verbally identified as Chinese nor as Indian because they wished to remain neutral, in order to avoid being pressured into meeting stereotypical expectations. Therefore, they resorted to the non-disclosure of their ethnic identity, which was achievable due to their phenotypical features, and they spoke English instead.

One respondent regularly identified herself as Chinese, a claim she was comfortable with. She said that she associated a lot with her Chinese family, friends and the Chinese community. Her ability to speak Mandarin also facilitated good relationships with members of the Chinese community. She has never verbally identified herself as Indian, as she felt detached from the Indian community and culture.

Interestingly, only two participants said that they verbally identified themselves as Indian. One explained that when his Chinese friends made nasty remarks about his Indian friends behind their backs, he would ask them to stop doing so, admitting that he was half-Indian. He did not identify himself as Indian, but was explicit about the fact that he was half-Indian, which is a direct indication of his emic perspective about his identity – neither purely Chinese nor Indian, but rather half of both. Another respondent said that he had always

Chindian identity: the grey space in between

identified himself as Indian, because he had been constantly reminded of this by his Indian father. Interestingly, he also admitted that he had also claimed to be Chinese, especially when people tried to challenge his ethnicity and rights as a biethnic person.

Few Chindian participants identified themselves verbally as Indian, exclusively. This is interesting as more than 20 participants have Indian fathers and are officially registered as Indian. It indicates that the current practice of categorizing Chindians based on their father's ethnicity does not necessarily correlate with people's actual sense of ethnic identity. It is important to note that both Indian and Chinese cultures are patriarchal, so it could have been expected that Chindians would identify with whichever ethnic group their father is from. Their choices were thus influenced by the lower socio-economic status of the Indian community in Malaysia, in comparison to the dominant Malay and Chinese ethnic groups. In some cases, identifying verbally as Indian was irrelevant, as their heritage was obvious from their name or their phenotype.

Self reflection: 'to be me'

Chindian participants had different perceptions about what it meant to be Chindian in Malaysia. Figure 8.1 provides an overview.

The majority (77 per cent) of participants felt positive about being Chindian in Malaysia. Detailed analysis suggests that although participants occasionally

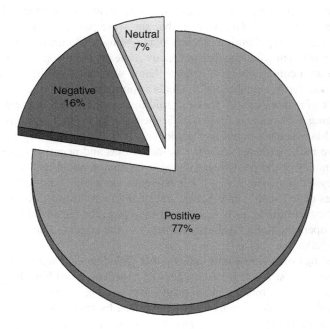

Figure 8.1 Perceptions of being a biethnic person in Malaysia.

faced some trials and encountered negative judgments, they managed to overcome such experiences by looking at their situation from a positive angle. On the whole, they thought that being biethnic helped them to develop a broader worldview. Their biethnic identity had helped them to develop respect and acceptance towards diversity of people.

Many respondents gave insightful reasons for this positive perspective. Some felt that they had 'the best of best of both worlds' by being able to pick and choose the best qualities from both ethnic groups. Some felt unique and special because of 'having parents of different ethnicities which most people will not experience', and having access to a range of cultural knowledge and practices. Some felt that the ability to speak several languages/dialects provided an added advantage, enabling Chindians to join a wider range of conversations among ethnically diverse Malaysians. Some felt excited when meeting other Chindians, because they understood each other and had many things in common. One person responded that being biethnic made her 'feel proud because people were always curious about me'. Another respondent felt that being Chindian made them 'a true Malaysian with added advantages': Malaysia is well known for its ethnic diversity, hence being biethnic was representative of the nation.

Other respondents (16 per cent) said they had negative perceptions about being a Chindian, as a result of the compartmentalized context in which they lived. Frequent negative encounters and a lack of acceptance by reference communities contributed to this negative perspective. One respondent felt that being biethnic was far more complicated than being monoethnic. Another respondent echoed this, saying that a 'demarcation based on ethnic divide was a source for most complications and issues'. One wished that she were pure Chinese, as it would resolve all her issues, claiming 'society made being a Chindian complicated'. Another respondent said that being Chindian meant living up to many expectations from both communities. A general theme was that both the Indian and Chinese communities treated these individuals as out-group members.

A small number of respondents (7 per cent) said they neither felt positive nor negative about being Chindian in Malaysia. Some said they felt like normal human beings or Malaysians without any particular ethnic label, and they tried their best to ignore racist attitudes such as race-based bias and negative stereotypes. A small minority of the participants chose to be neutral about their biethnic identity, as they did not wish to view their existence along ethnic lines. Their view of themselves defied such demarcations and therefore contributed towards feeling neutral. They admitted that it was not an easy task, for the social structures in Malaysia operated along rigid ethnic lines, and the ethnicity/race-based quota system was pervasive.

The overall findings of this research indicate that Chindians engage in identity work to deal with the structures, stereotypes and expectations within Malaysian society. Most of the Chindian participants expressed a strong sense of nationalism and articulated their desire to be recognized by their nationality as Malaysians, instead of being forced into ethnic groups. This finding supports the notion of nationality as a potential unifier in multi-ethnic countries. They strongly felt that the patrilineal ethnic categorization under Malaysian law was obsolete in the current social setting, locally and globally. Ethnic classification made them feel colonized in a now-independent nation.

Conclusion: from purity to plurality

This chapter explored the conditions for the acceptance of biethnic Chindians by the Chinese and Indian communities, and how strategies of identity work are used by Chindians to gain acceptance in Malaysia, where ethnic identity is a pervasive aspect of a person's life. The findings highlight the subtle variations in these strategies of identity work. The research also demonstrates that institutionalized macro-level structures that limit ethnic-based demarcation to singular ethnic categories restricts the perceptions and acceptance of Chindians in Malaysia.

The research found that half of the Chinese and Indian respondents accepted Chindians as in-group members, as long as they met certain prerequisites. On the other hand, the other half accepted Chindians without any preset conditions. Further analysis showed that the prerequisites set by the Indian community focused mainly on culture, religion and language, while the Chinese respondents identified language followed by culture as priorities. The ethnicity of a Chindian individual's father did not facilitate immediate acceptance by the reference group members, despite the patrilineal tendencies of Malaysian society. Rather, reference group members placed more importance on shared culture, religion and language, in comparison to primordial moorings.

In the process of Chindians' ethnic identity development, patriarchy becomes complex, as mothers play an important role in the nurturing of their children and therefore have a considerable influence over their identity development. Hence, it is not enough to allow Chindians to choose one ethnic identity over another, because in reality their ethnic identities are the result of an amalgamation of ethnicities and experiences. Thus, the participants strongly felt that the term Chindian best described them, although they verbally identified in different ways in different situations. Most participants felt it was necessary to associate themselves with the ethnic group with higher socioeconomic status for benefits, such as job opportunities and social status. This perceived position, and the meaning attached to the reference groups, determined the direction of strategies of identity work deployed by Chindians in Malaysia.

The governing structures, rejection and acceptance by reference groups, stereotype perceptions and challenges faced by biethnic individuals in their daily life contributed towards their ethnic identity development, as Chindians sought to deploy strategies of identity work to assert their ethnic identity. Ethnic identity is a fluid concept among Malaysian Chindians, which is constantly being altered and reconstructed, and does not fit into the rigidly compartmentalized ethnic categories currently practiced in Malaysia.

Notes

1 'Sons of the soil' or indigenous people.
2 More methodological details are available upon request from the author.

Bibliography

Banton, M. (1998) *Racial Theories*. Cambridge: Cambridge University Press.
Barth, F. (1969). *Ethnic Groups and Boundaries*. Boston: Little Brown.
Carstens, S. (2006). *Histories, Cultures, Identities: Studies in Malaysian Chinese Worlds*. Singapore: Singapore University Press.
Chaudhari, P., and Pizzolato, J. (2008). 'Understanding the Epistemology of Ethnic Identity Development in Multiethnic College Students'. *Journal of College Students Development* (49), pp. 443–458.
Cheah, B. (2009). 'Race and Ethnic Relations in Colonial Malaya During the 1920's and 1930's'. In T. Lim, A. Gomez, and A. Rahman (eds), *Multiethnic Malaysia-Past, Present and Future*. Selangor: Strategic Information and Research Development Centre, pp. 33–57.
Clark, H. (1966). *The Marginal Situation – A Sociological Study of a Coloured Group*. London: Routledge and Kegan Paul Limited.
Cooley, C. (1902). *Human Nature and the Social Order*. New York: Scribner's.
Cornell, S., and Hartmann, D. (1998). *Ethnicity and Race, Making Identities in a Changing World*. California: Pine Forge Press.
David, M. (2008). *Language Choice of Urban Sino-Indians in Kuala Lumpur, Malaysia*. Unpublished manuscript. University of Malaya.
Department of Statistics Malaysia. (2011). *Population Distribution and Basic Demographic Characteristic Report 2010 (Updated: 05/08/2011)*. Available at: www.statistics.gov.my/index.php?r=column/ctheme&menu_id=L0pheU43NWJwRWVSZklWdzQ4TlhUUT09&bul_id=MDMxdHZjWTk1SjFzTzNkRXYzcVZjdz09 (accessed: 13 October 2014).
Department of Statistics Malaysia. (2013). *Birth Rate of Sino-Indians 2003–2010*. Unpublished raw data. Putrajaya: Malaysia Government.
Goldsby, R. (1977). *Race and Races*. New York: Macmillan Publications.
Gopan, T. (2011). *Being Chindian*. Malaysia Kini. Available at: www.malaysiakini.com/news/167760 (accessed: 1 May 2011).
Heng, S., Lehman, D., Peng, K., and Greenholtz, J. (2002). 'What's Wrong With Cross-Cultural Comparisons of Subjective Likert Scales?: The Reference-Group Effect'. *Journal of Personality and Social Psychology* 82(6), pp. 903–918.
Ibrahim, V. (2011). 'Ethnicity'. In S. Caliendo and C. McIlwain (eds), *The Routledge Companion to Race and Ethnicity*. London: Routledge, pp. 12–19.
Immigration Checkpoints Authority. (2011). *Birth and Death Registration*. Available at: www.ifaq.gov.sg/ica/apps/ (accessed: 12 May 2011).
Janzen, M. (2000). 'You are Not Enough: The "Faceless" Lives of Biethnic and Biracial Americans a Challenge for Truly Inclusive Multicultural Education'. *Multicultural Perspectives* 4, pp. 3–8.
Jayum, J. (2007). *Malaysian Politics and Government*. Malaysia: Karisma Publications.
Khanna, N., and Johnson, C. (2010). 'Passing as Black: Racial Identity Work Among Biracial Americans'. *Social Psychology Quarterly* 73(4), pp. 380–397.
Khoo J. (1996). *The Straits Chinese – A Cultural History*. Amsterdam: The People Press.

Kich, G. (1992). 'The Developmental Process of Asserting a Biracial, Bicultural Identity'. In M. Root (ed.), *Racially Mixed People in America*. Newburry Park: SAGE Publications, pp. 304–317.

Koshy, S. (2001). 'Morphing Race into Ethnicity: Asian Americans and Critical Transformation of Whiteness'. *Project Muse* 28, pp. 153–194.

Kottak, C. (2008). *Cultural Anthropology*. New York: Mc Graw-Hill.

Lee S. (2011). 'The Peranakan Chinese: Another Kind of "Chineseness"'. In Centre for Malaysian Chinese studies (ed.), *Malaysian Chinese: An Inclusive Society*. Kuala Lumpur: Centre for Malaysian Chinese Studies, pp. 145–156.

Lewontin, R. C. (1972) 'The Apportionment of Human Diversity'. *Evolutionary Biology* 6, pp. 381–398.

Merriam, S. (2002). *Qualitative Research in Practice*. San Francisco: Jossey Bass.

Moss, R., and Davis, D. (2003). 'Counselling Biracial Students: A Review of Issues and Interventions'. *Journal of Multicultural Counselling and Development* 36, pp. 219–230.

Nagai, T. (2010). *Multiracial Identity and the U.S. Census*. Available at: www.csa.com/discoveryguides/census/review2.php (accessed: 31 May 2010).

Nakamura. R. (2015). 'Race or Ethnic Group: Politics of Race in Malaysia'. *Sociology and Anthropology* 3(8), pp. 389–398.

Oikawa, S., and Yoshida, T. (2007). 'An Identity Based on Being Different: A Focus on Biethnic Individuals in Japan'. *International Journal of Intercultural Relations* 31, pp. 633–653.

Padilla, A. (2006). 'Bicultural Social Development'. *Hispanic Journal of Behavioral Science* 28(4), pp. 467–497.

Park, C., and Lessig, V. (1977). 'Students and Housewives: Differences in Susceptibility to Reference Group Influences'. *Journal of Consumer Research* 4, pp. 102–110.

Poston, W. (1990). 'The Biracial Identity Development Model: A Needed Addition'. *Journal of Counselling and Development* 69(1), pp. 152–155.

Qian, Z., and Litcher, D. (2007). 'Social Boundaries and Marital Assimilation: Interpreting Trends in Racial and Ethnic Intermarriage'. *American Sociological Review* 72(1), p. 68–95.

Renn, K. (2000). 'Patterns of Situational Identity Among Biracial and Multiracial College Students'. *The Review of Higher Education* 23(4), pp. 399–420.

Rocha, Z. (2010). 'Mixed Messages, Mixed Memories, Mixed Ethnicity: Mnemonic Heritage and Constructing Identity Through Mixed Parentage'. *New Zealand Sociology* 25(1), p. 75–99.

Rockquemore, K. (1998). 'Between Black and White: Exploring the "Biracial" Experience'. *Race and Society* 1(2), pp. 197–212.

Rockquemore, K., and Brunsma, D. (2002). 'Socially Embedded Identities, Theories, Typologies and Processes of Racial Identity Among Biracial'. *The Sociological Quarterly* 43, pp. 335–356.

Rockquemore, K., and Laszloffy T. (2003). 'A Relational Narrative Approach in Therapy with Black-white Mixed Race Clients'. *Family Relations* 52(2), pp. 119–128.

Rona, C. (2016). *Blurring Boundaries: The Chindian Identity Quest*. Kuala Lumpur: University of Malaya Press.

Rona, C., and Yahya M. (2015). 'Beyond Arbitrary Labels: Understanding Ethnic Identity Development Among Chindians'. *SEARCH: The Journal of South East Asia Research Centre for Communication and Humanities* 7(2), pp. 1–17.

Root, M. (1996). 'A Bill of Rights for Racially Mixed People'. In M. Root (ed.), *The Multiracial Experience: Racial Borders as the New Frontier*. California: Sage Publications, pp. 3–14.

Snow, D., and Anderson, L. (1987). 'Identity Work Among the Homeless: The Verbal Construction and Avowal of Personal Identities'. *American Journal of Sociology* 92(6), p. 1336–1371.

Stets, J., and Burke, P. (2005). 'A Sociological Approach to Self-identity'. In M. Leary and J. Tangney (eds), *Handbook of Self and Identity*, 1st edition. New York: Guilford Press, pp. 128–152.

Stonequist, E. (1935). 'The Problem of the Marginal Man'. *American Journal of Sociology* 41(1), pp. 1–12.

Syed, H. (2008). *Ethnic Relations in Malaysia: Harmony and Conflict*. Malaysia: Strategic Information and Research Development.

Tajfel, H., and Turner, J. C. (1986). 'The Social Identity Theory of Intergroup Behaviour'. In S. Worchel and W. G. Austin (eds), *Psychology of Intergroup Relations*, 2nd edition. Chicago: Nelson-Hall, pp. 7–24.

Talbot, D. (2008). 'Exploring the Experiences and Self-labeling of Mixed-race Individuals with Two Minority Parents'. *New Directions for Student Services* 123, pp. 23–31.

Taylor, M. J. (2004). 'Sociohistorical Constructions of Race and Language: Impacting Biracial Identity'. In J. L. Chin (ed.), *The Psychology of Prejudice and Discrimination: Vol. 2. Ethnicity and Multiracial Identity*. Alameda, CA: Prageas Press, pp. 87–108.

Teo, K. (2003). *The Peranakan Chinese of Kelantan: A Study of the Culture, Language and Communication of an Assimilated Group in Malaysia*. London: ASEAN Academic Press.

UNESCO. (1951). 'Statement on Race'. Paris: United Nations Educational, Scientific and Cultural Organization.

Walton, F., and Caliendo, M. (2010). 'Origins of the Concept of Race'. In S. Caliendo and C. McIlwain (eds), *The Routledge Companion to Race and Ethnicity*. London: Routledge, pp. 3–11.

Wardle, F. (2000). 'Multiracial and Multiethnic Students: How they Must Belong'. *Multiracial Perspectives* 2(4), pp. 11–16.

Zack, N. (1993). *Race and Mixed Race*. Philadelphia: Temple University Press.

9 'Our Chinese'

The mixedness of Peranakan Chinese identities in Kelantan, Malaysia[1]

Pue Giok Hun

Introduction

The issue of ethnicity, that of 'descent and culture' (Fenton, 2003), remains a salient feature and is pivotal in the lives of Malaysians. The practice of organizing social differences according to a categorization system that recognizes only three racial categories: Malay, Chinese and Indian, means that the existence of various groups of mixed heritage is obscured, despite their long and ubiquitous presence. Along with others, they are collapsed into a miscellaneous category, labelled Others. The introduction of policy-oriented social categories during the British colonial era saw the beginning of racial identities in Malaysia (Shamsul, 2000, p. 196; Hirschman, 1986; Kessler, 2012). The categorization system was adopted by the newly formed Malaysia in 1957 with few changes, and has remained in place for almost six decades. As a result, racial identities that build on this silo approach have become crucial at the level of the state, effectively influencing many aspects of social life, including the predominance of race-based political parties and parallel judicial systems of civic and sharia laws. More importantly, racial identification influences people's life chances and choices at the individual level, via the implementation of various socio-economic policies that advocate affirmative action along racial lines, such as in education, finance and property (Holst, 2012; Milner et al., 2014).

The dominance of the race[2] factor can be observed in Malaysia where the issues of race and ethnicity are debated as one of the nine 'contradictories'[3] that urgently need to be resolved before national unity can be achieved (Shamsul, 2014). In the context of ethnicity, Malaysian society is described as being in constant 'stable tension' with fault lines along the thick racial borders (Noor, 2012; Shamsul, 2006a). Chin et al. (2015) find that while Malaysians are seen to possess high ethnic consciousness of their own ethnic group, they have little or no consciousness about others, especially minority groups. Instead, the society focuses on stereotypes, including racial markers in social media and public discourse around Malayness, Chineseness, and Indianness, that stresses their distinct differences (Fong and Ishak, 2014; Tong, 2006). As a result, racial groups are seen as having few similarities; and even see each other as a threat in the competition for survival (Holst, 2012; Milner and Ting, 2014; Shamsul, 2006b).

Discussions of mixed race in Malaysia have yet to begin in earnest, despite the topic being relevant to every ethnic group in the country. Lack of discourse on mixed race continues regardless of increased numbers, in tandem with the upward trend of interethnic marriages (Osman, 1981) from less than 1 per cent in the 1970s (P. C. Tan, 1989) to just under 5 per cent of marriages in the 2000s (Nagaraj, 2009; Chong, 2009). The majority of interethnic marriages are also inter-religious, particularly between Muslim and non-Muslim couples (J. P. Tan et al., 2008). Such couples are the main focus of intermarriage research in Peninsular Malaysia, primarily due to the notoriety of political and legal contestations between civic and sharia judicial law and its effects on family relationships (Lindenberg, 2009; Hak, 2012).

The strength of what Shamsul (1996) refers to as 'authority-defined' social reality, which is based on the perspective of powerful players such as the state and influential agencies in the discourse of race relations in Malaysia, has created 'authoritatively-applied identities' that significantly influence individual experiences in everyday life (Jenkins, 2000, p. 9). As a result, minority groups that exist in the 'in-between' space of social categorisation, often find themselves excluded from the mainstream discourse of race relations and identity. Today, the presence of the mixed-race groups whose members consist of descendants of mixed heritage in both lineage and culture, is seen as at odds with the mainstream for not conforming to the stereotypes of particular racial identities (Pillai, 2015; Pue and Kaur, 2014; Pue and Sulaiman, 2013).

Yet the phenomenon of mixed race has been an integral part of ethnically diverse societies through the practice of intermarriage, one of many dimensions of social amalgamation, also known as 'marital assimilation' (Gordon, 1964). Gordon's theory proposes that the process of assimilation occurs in at least one of seven dimensions[4] at any given time, with marital assimilation the only dimension that involves biological intermixing on a large scale. This dimension is an 'inevitable by-product of structural assimilation' whereby the minority group integrates into the majority-dominated social institutions in the society (Gordon, 1964, p. 80). The assimilation process may not end with the absorption of the minority ethnic group into the majority. Instead, they may remain as separate entities with increased similarities and stronger ties; the extrinsic elements of their ethnicity often display higher similarities than the intrinsic elements.

Such large-scale intermarriage has occurred in Malaysian society for centuries. In Peninsular Malaysia, in particular, the phenomenon of mixed race is synonymous with a type of mixed race known as the Peranakan groups, formed predominantly through the practice of intermarriage of non-native men from other regions including Arab countries, India, Europe, and China, with local women.

Despite their long history in the Southeast Asian region, the discourse on Peranakans is largely absent in the academic literature on 'mixed race' peoples. This chapter seeks to address this gap: what can we learn about Peranakan as a mixed race? This chapter explores the idea of Peranakan as mixed race by highlighting how the Peranakan Chinese community in Kelantan constructs and negotiates 'mixedness' in their everyday lives and practices. By drawing on Milton Gordon's description of social amalgamation, the paper argues that the Peranakan Chinese community in Kelantan may be seen as an example of a mixed group successfully integrating into a host society, by identifying with the locals without losing their elements of their cultures of origin. The extrinsic elements of their ethnic identity are highly localized while intrinsic elements remain distinctly Chinese. Furthermore, it is the mixedness of Kelantan Peranakan Chinese identity that contributes to the blurring of racial divisions in the society in practice, if not officially.

The Peranakan phenomenon in Peninsular Malaysia

Historically, the phenomenon of mixed race has long been an integral part of societies in Southeast Asian (Salleh, 2006, p. 8). Peninsular Malaysia, in particular, is the centre for mixed race in the Malay Archipelago, with the Peranakan groups. The term 'Peranakan' is a Malay/Indonesian term derived from the root word '*anak*' which means child (offspring). When circumfixed with '*per-* ... *-an*', Peranakan originally referred to the womb, but eventually evolved into a metaphor that refers to local-born of non-indigenous descent.

Although the term Peranakan is used to refer to mixed race in Malay-speaking regions in Southeast Asia such as Indonesia, southern Thailand, southern Philippines and Malaysia, the term Peranakan has different meanings in different societies (Pue, 2016, p. 74). In Peninsular Malaysia, it initially referred to local-born progeny of intermarriage, but subsequently denoted sociocultural aspects as well, including the practice of highly localized non-indigenous culture (C. B. Tan, 1988; Teo, 2003). The use of the term Peranakan signifies acceptance of mixed race individuals as part of their own 'flesh and blood' by the host society, instead of treating them as 'half-breed' foreigners or strangers (Pue and Shamsul, 2012). Such positive reception is unusual, as mixed race offspring in racially differentiated societies are often referred to in a negative manner, using derogatory terms such as 'mulatto' and 'mestizo' (Forbes, 1993; Thompson, 2012).[5]

Interestingly, while the Peranakans in other Southeast Asian countries are often synonymous with mixed race of Chinese descent, Peninsular Malaysia is home to Peranakan groups of the progeny of intermarriage between the native and various non-native descents, including the Peranakan Arab, Peranakan Hindu (Chetti), Peranakan Jawi, Peranakan Serani (Kristang) and Peranakan Chinese (Pue, 2016). However, Peranakan Chinese communities in the west coast of Peninsular Malaysia, such as the Straits Chinese in Penang and the Baba-Nyonya in Melaka, receive the lion's share of attention, both in the tourism and academic sectors. This can be observed in the definition of the term 'Peranakan' that was based on the Peranakan Chinese communities on the west coast of the Peninsula (Lim, 2005, p. 1; Aw, 1994, p. 21).[6]

Due to the intense assimilation process during the formative period, their Peranakan identity is visibly distinct from the non-Peranakan. Mixed marriage which was practiced *en masse*, particularly in the early years, has produced offspring believed to possess different phenotypical traits compared to the non-Peranakan mainstream. Their Peranakan cultures include elements of native culture while still retaining the original ethnic 'mould', generating unique Peranakan identity markers such as language, clothes, food, leisure and entertainment activities (Pillai, 2015; Teo, 2003).

Nevertheless, scholars believe Peranakan communities are doomed to 'extinction' due to intermarriage, modernization, globalization and the bureaucratic rigidity in the implementation of the ethnic categorization system. In terms of ethnic Chinese, the term 'resinicization' is used to refer to the process of abandoning elements of local culture(s) in Peranakan identity in order to increase their 'visibility, acceptability and self-assertiveness' as ethnic Chinese (Hau, 2014, p. 283). Peranakan identity among the Peranakan Chinese communities on the west coast of Peninsular Malaysia has diminished, insofar as only its essence is preserved and the identity is practiced infrequently during special events, and re-enacted for tourism and nostalgic purposes (Lee, 2008).

In comparison, Peranakan Chinese communities in Kelantan and Terengganu on the east coast of the Peninsula, retain the mixed cultures, yet remain understudied. In particular, the Peranakan Chinese community in Kelantan offers an interesting case study to help understand the interplay of mixedness in ethnic identities, for two reasons. First, the formation of the community stemmed from interethnic interaction with not one, but two local ethnic groups: Kelantanese Malay and local Siamese. Second, 'Peranakan-ness' continues to be a reality in their daily life. Many still live in traditional settlements and maintain the practice of Kelantan Peranakan Chinese culture (discussed shortly) despite the potent pressure of resinicization in the form of vernacular schooling, popular culture, increased interpersonal contact with mainstream Chinese, and even outward migration from their community for education and work.

Case study: the Peranakan Chinese community of Kelantan

The empirical data discussed in this chapter was obtained from an ethnographic study conducted from January 2009 to February 2010 in a Peranakan Chinese community in Wakaf Bharu, Kelantan. Sixty-three members of six extended families, whose matriarch or patriarch and the majority of family members resided in the community, participated in the research.

Background

From as early as the thirteenth century until the beginning of nineteenth century, Chinese men from the southern region of China arrived in small groups with their kinsmen to Kelantan (C. B. Tan, 1982; Wee, 1987; Teo, 2003). Unlike the forefathers of the Baba-Nyonya community in Malacca who were merchants, the Hokkiens who came to Kelantan were mostly peasants. Travelling along the path of Sungai Kelantan, they settled in the northern area of the Kelantan delta, particularly along the river banks, among local ethnic groups such as the Malay and

Thai, and became mainly involved in business and agricultural activities (Tweedie, 1953). The practice of intermarriage was widespread among the three ethnic groups, but gradually the axis shifted to Chinese-Thai marriage after the Islamization of the Malays following the conversion to the religion by the ruler of the day, Maharaja Kumara (Sultan Iskandar Shah) in the fifteenth century (Graham, 1908; Rentse, 1934).

This practice of interethnic marriage marked the beginning of the formation of the Peranakan Chinese community in Kelantan (Teo, 2008, p. 214). Arguably, it is the result of three main challenges that the Chinese faced in order to settle in Kelantan at the time: incompatibility of religion, cultural difference and lack of Chinese women. Chinese men addressed these by choosing local Thai women as wives. The offspring of Chinese-Thai couples often had distinct phenotypical traits and cultural characteristics. Their socialization process was highly influenced by their Thai mothers and relatives, as well as the Malay-dominated local settings. Nevertheless, they were considered Chinese and continued to practice Chinese culture according to the patrilineal system.

Gradually, the localization process, combined with social amalgamation, generated a distinct local Chinese community with its own unique ethnicity that was not 'fully' Chinese, Thai or Malay. At the community level, the Peranakan Chinese of Kelantan are referred to by local Malays with terms such as *Cina kita* (our Chinese), *Cina sini* (Chinese [from] here), *Cina tempatan* (local Chinese) and *Cina kampung* (rural Chinese) (C. B. Tan, 1982; Teo, 2003; Winzeler, 1981, 1983). Even today, the Peranakan Chinese of Kelantan are distinguished from other Chinese with the term *Cina Kelantan* (Kelantan Chinese). Similarly, local Thais also use the terms, albeit spoken in local Thai dialect. These terms, that imply closeness, togetherness, acceptance and warmth of the Kelantan Malay and Thai communities towards Peranakan Chinese as fellow members of the society, are not used to refer to mainstream Chinese.

The synergy of Chinese–Malay–Thai ethnic elements that is particular to the identities of Peranakan Chinese of Kelantan, is distinctly seen in Peranakan Chinese who hail from Tumpat, Pasir Mas and Tanah Merah districts in the vicinity of the Malaysia–Thailand border (Teo, 2003). This also applies to the Peranakan Chinese community in Wakaf Bharu which is situated in the Tumpat district. Wakaf Bharu was selected as the location for the fieldwork for two reasons. First, the highest number of ethnic Chinese in the Tumpat district is found in Wakaf Bharu. In 2010, Chinese made up 10.7 per cent of the population (Malaysia, 2011, p. 271). Second, Wakaf Bharu has bloomed into an important contact point. Its strategic location means it has become a major transit hub for train and land transportation that serves to connect people and goods from the northern-most area in the Tumpat district to the capital city of Kota Bharu, as well as the rest of the state. Wakaf Bharu town is the focus for people from surrounding rural areas, for getting access to basic public utilities such as a post office, schools, a government clinic, police station, district officer's office, and the market. As such, Wakaf Bharu serves as an ideal location to study the Peranakan Chinese community in their natural setting.

Based on the informants' profiles, the Peranakan Chinese community in Wakaf Bharu can be divided into two distinct generation-based groups:

The 'Older Generation'

The Older Generation consisted of community members born in the 1950s or earlier, in Kelantan. This generation grew up predominantly in a time when access to formal education was considered a luxury, thus, many had little or no formal education. Those who had, went to a Malay school that was often the only school available in the vicinity. This limited their employability and they often resorted to various odd jobs[7] or ran small family-based businesses. With the community and its immediate surroundings as the axis of their world, every informant in this generation speaks fluent Kelantanese Malay, their own version of Hokkien, as well as the local Thai dialect. They are also more commonly known among local folks by their Malay nicknames such as Awang, Ali, Hasan, Mek Bunga and Mek Yam, instead of their Chinese birth names. This generation is also unable to converse in Mandarin. However, due to having little or no interaction with non-Peranakan Chinese during their heyday, this is not seen as an issue, except perhaps when their grandchildren and other relatives who reside outside Kelantan pay occasional visits.

The 'Younger Generation'

This group consists of members born in the Tumpat district from the 1960s to 1990s. Generally, this group have had formal education, at least to a high school level. This level of education facilitated their upward social mobility whereby they could obtain blue- or white-collar jobs in private and government sectors. Some opted to establish their own business instead of taking over the family business. Relative to the Older Generation, the Younger Generation began to be more exposed to mainstream Chinese through the education system or working environments. This generation began to learn Mandarin, often during informal interpersonal communication with non-Peranakan Chinese, known locally as *Cina bandar* (urban Chinese). The Younger Generation's children, the 'Millennium Generation', were born in Kelantan from the year 2000 onwards. They are generally able to converse in Mandarin, along with Hokkien and some English. Their main language may be Mandarin or Hokkien, depending on parental influence and residential locations.[8] They have been exposed to the Mandarin language at school as early as at kindergarten level. Older children were sent to a Chinese school either in Tumpat town or in Kota Bharu; both about eight kilometres from Wakaf Bharu. According to their parents, the main reason for sending the children there was to ensure that they would be able to learn Mandarin, at least at the conversational level, and not because of cultural differences between Peranakan Chinese and non-Peranakan Chinese. For the purpose of the present paper, the Millennium Generation is excluded from the current analysis.

Changes in Kelantan Peranakan Chinese identity markers

Findings from the fieldwork suggest that Kelantan Peranakan Chinese identity consists of five key markers: phenotypical traits, language, clothes, food and leisure activity. However, characteristics of the identity markers are distinctly different for each generation as follows:

Phenotypical traits

While the credibility of the term 'race' as categorizations of human 'subspecies' has been effectively debunked and rejected (Hirschman, 1986, p. 340), race in the context of socially constructed phenotypical differences remains a significant dimension of social identification (Jenkins, 2000). Thus, perceived 'racial' characteristics which are believed to be inherited may be used as an identity marker to enhance differences between ethnic groups (Fenton, 2003). The three main races in Malaysia have been represented on the basis of certain phenotypical characteristics, often distinctly different from one another (Pue, 2009). Both mainstream Chinese and Peranakan Chinese communities in the west coast of Peninsular Malaysia have what is widely perceived as a 'Chinese appearance' (C. B. Tan, 1979, p. 98; Teo, 2003, p. 59), such as 'yellowish hue' skin tone, thick, straight, black hair, and a distinct eye shape. In comparison, the general consensus among the Peranakan Chinese of Kelantan is that their own phenotypical traits resemble those of the Malays and Thais, including relatively darker brownish skin tone (*sawo matang*), slightly wavy hair and 'wider' eyes. In particular, darker skin tone is more observable among the Older Generation than the Younger Generation. The similarities with the local ethnic groups are so striking that the Kelantan Peranakan Chinese's physical appearance can easily be mistaken for that of Malays or Thais. The Peranakan Chinese of Kelantan believed that these phenotypical traits are inherited from the mixed parentage in their lineage, but to some degree, the darker complexion could also result from long hours working under the sun as peasants and odd job workers.

Language

A prominent identity marker for the Peranakan Chinese of Kelantan is language. Unlike the Peranakan Chinese in Melaka whose lingua franca is Baba Malay, both the Older and Younger Generations of the Peranakan Chinese of Kelantan are bilingual, namely in Kelantanese Malay and their own version of Peranakan Hokkien (Teo, 2003, 2008). It is also not uncommon to find many trilingual members, with the inclusion of a local Thai dialect, especially among those who live in the northern parts of the state such as Tumpat, Pasir Mas and Tanah Merah districts. In terms of Kelantanese Malay, both generations were fluent in the language to the point that they were often mistaken for Malay, especially in telephone conversations. Some of the Older Generation could also read and write the language in Jawi script as this was a skill taught as part of the syllabus of formal education they received in Malay schools prior to the 1930s. The Kelantanese Malay dialect was not only used to communicate with members of other local ethnic groups, but also as an alternative to Hokkien when communicating among themselves, especially between male speakers.

As for the Younger Generation, particularly those in their late 20s or younger, their grasp of Kelantanese Malay was 'less rich' in terms of vocabulary. This may be due to the increasing use of the standard Malay language in the education system and mass media, less interpersonal interaction with local Malay neighbours, as well as declining exposure to linguistically rich traditional Malay entertainment and arts such as *wayang kulit* (shadow play), *mak yong* (dance-drama) and *dikir barat* (group singing). Nevertheless, the fluidity in everyday interethnic communication with the Malays remained unaffected, and the Younger Generation's Kelantanese Malay dialect, and Malay language in general, was still distinctly different from that of non-Peranakan Chinese.

Albeit proficient in Kelantanese Malay, it was their own version of a localized Hokkien dialect that distinguished the Kelantan Peranakan Chinese community from the other local ethnic groups in Kelantan, or other Peranakan Chinese communities elsewhere. Its formation stemmed from acculturation between the Hokkien dialect with both Kelantanese Malay and local Thai dialects in terms of vocabulary, grammar and phonetics. The fusion has rendered the Kelantan Peranakan Chinese's Hokkien dialect a notoriously challenging language even by the standards of Hokkien speakers elsewhere (C. B. Tan, 1982, p. 26). When juxtaposed with the Older Generation's Hokkien dialect, the Younger Generation's was found to be 'more Chinese', especially among those who interacted more often with the mainstream Chinese, whether at work or school. For example, Malay-infused terms such as *natu (menantu) ca po* (son-in-law) and Malay-influenced grammar such as *pui char* (fried rice), have been replaced with proper Hokkien words and grammar: *kiasai* and *char pui* respectively.

Kelantan Peranakan Chinese in Wakaf Bharu are generally trilingual with the inclusion of the local Thai dialect. Often, they inadvertently picked up the language through at least three informal sources: participation in Thai Buddhist religious activities and Thai cultural events, consumption of Thai media products including television and radio programmes which were aired directly from Thailand, and interaction with the Thai community whose settlement was the highest in the Tumpat district, including in the form of intermarriages. In comparison to the Older Generation, the Younger Generation were less fluent in conversing in the local Thai dialect due to the differences in linguistic styles between the dialect and the standard Thai language. As a result, they could understand conversations, but not speak in the dialect. The Older Generation were fluent in the local Thai dialect and used it in conversations with the Thai community, Buddhist monks, and even as an alternative to Hokkien when speaking among themselves.

Clothes

The classic image of Kelantan Peranakan Chinese clothing is a fitted, long-sleeved local blouse called *kebaya*, worn with the long, tube-like *sarung* for the females; and the males wearing only a *sarung* from the waist down, while shirtless with head gear made of a long cloth called *semutar*. Among the Older Generation, such costume was still common among the men, except for the *semutar*, which had been replaced by a more convenient modern cap. Many women, however, no longer wore the *kebaya*; those who did wore it only for special occasions. Overall, the women opted for either short-sleeved blouses locally referred to as *sa lau lang* which literally means 'elder's shirt', or loose-sized T-shirts, and both were paired with either a *sarung* or a pair of long trousers. The Younger Generation from both genders preferred westernized fashions such as T-shirt and jeans, or Bermuda pants, not unlike young people from other ethnic groups including the Malay and local Thais. Nevertheless, they conformed to the local norm in terms of sensitivity and modesty in their attire. Compared to the mainstream Chinese in Kelantan, the Younger Generation of Peranakan Chinese were seldom seen wearing clothes that might be considered offensive or revealing by local standards, such as plunging necklines or sleeveless shirts, or short skirts/pants (above the knees) for women except in private.

Food

On the one hand, both generations fondly identified local dishes as part of their Peranakan Chinese identity. They were ardent consumers, as well as being skilled in the preparation of local Malay and Thai dishes such as *nasi kerabu*,[9] *nasi lemak*[10] and *kaeng khi lek*.[11] However, the skill and practice of making the favourite local condiment, *budu*, was no longer widespread among the community. Local dishes were considered popular delicacies during Chinese celebrations such as Chinese New Year, weddings and newborn babies' full moon ceremonies; or, as a gift in the form of *pulut kuning*.[12] On the other hand, the Peranakan Chinese of Kelantan have developed their own unique Peranakan Chinese signature dishes that incorporate locally available ingredients such as *bak hong*[13] and *kaeng hae bokji*.[14] Aspects that stood out as different between the Younger Generation and the Older Generation were the customs of consumption. The Older Generation still favoured rice for every meal with typical *kampung* cuisine including *ulam-ulaman* (fresh vegetables). The Younger Generation consumed a wider range of cuisines, ranging from local and Chinese cuisine to Western and Asian food. The use of modern utensils such as spoons and forks is favoured by both generations over the traditional custom of eating with the hands, as it was perceived as more convenient, particularly when attending a social event such as a wedding.

Leisure activities

Like other identity markers, leisure activities have undergone distinct changes. During their youth, the Older Generation actively participated in the traditional local leisure activities such as collecting *ikan laga* (fighting fish; *Betta splendens*), gamecocks and birds (for aesthetic and/or competition purposes), top-spinning, kite-flying, as well as folk drama such as *wayang kulit* and *mak yong*. However, factors such as modernization, urbanization and the severe restrictions imposed upon seemingly 'un-Islamic' local cultural activities by the conservative state government's policies have resulted in many traditional leisure activities been replaced by modern leisure activities, such as watching television and listening to the radio. While many activities were shared with the Older Generation, the Younger Generation also enjoyed other activities such as participating in indoor sports including basketball or badminton, video games or internet surfing. Although not uncommon in other ethnic groups, leisure activities could still be considered one of the Kelantan Peranakan Chinese identity markers due to their preference for programmes from Thai television and radio stations rather than local programmes that were seen as boring and too Malay-oriented.

Adherence to age-old customs and rites

In contrast to the extrinsic cultural traits that shared many similarities with Kelantanese Malay and local Thai cultures as described above, mixedness in the intrinsic aspects of Kelantan Peranakan Chinese identity was minimal. Those that were, were adapted in order to conform to the Chinese customs or rites. In this context, both Older and Younger Generations were seen to adhere to the same age-old customs and rites. Institutions such as family, kinship and religion, as well as the practices of customs and rituals associated with weddings, funerals and births, remained structurally unchanged. For example, at a wedding, the selection of food provided to the newlyweds and guests during a wedding banquet might consist of local cuisine to suit the 'localized' food preferences. However, foods with symbolic meanings during Chinese rituals such as consumption of *ee*[15] and tea in wedding rituals were retained. As for a token of appreciation for wedding guests, Kelantan Peranakan Chinese distribute small cakes instead of the traditional wedding biscuits, simply because they were not available at local bakery shops. Nevertheless, they believe that cakes also fulfil the symbolism behind the practice, that a wedding is a sweet and happy occasion (I-Ling, 1991).

Generational changes were also detected in terms of simplifying certain parts of a ritual. In wedding customs for example, the tea ceremony may be conducted for the bride's side of the family first rather than the groom's. Certain symbolic gestures such as kneeling and bowing to the family members whose statuses were higher than that of the groom or the bride might be omitted, with the exception of their parents and most senior family members. However, some traditional customs and rites were still followed by the Younger Generation, despite their

Peranakan Chinese identities in Malaysia 157

use of modern technologies, higher education levels and scientific knowledge, when the issue of mortality is directly involved, such as care practices for newborns and mothers, post-partum. For example, during post-partum confinement, Kelantan Peranakan Chinese new mothers continue to practice physical recuperation by undergoing traditional massages (*mengurut*) and applying heat therapy (*bertungku*) as practiced in the Kelantan Malay culture. Yet at the same time, they also consult alternative health providers such as Buddhist abbots, Taoist mediums or Malay or Thai healers (*bomoh*) in order to protect themselves and their newborns from unwanted supernatural interferences.

Conclusion

Despite the increasing visibility of mixed race in Malaysian society, there have been few studies on the phenomenon. This is in part because mixedness is eclipsed by the dominance of the political authorities' narrow conception of racial homogeneity. The Peranakan Chinese community in Kelantan demonstrates the ubiquity and intersectionality of the phenomenon of mixed race. As with other social phenomena, Peranakan identity is socially constructed, thus naturally dynamic, fluid and heterogeneous – in this case it is formed from a mixture of Chinese, Kelantan Malay and local Thai heritages, and is thus distinct from the typical Chineseness found in the mainstream Chinese society.

The community's Chineseness and 'nativeness' are intertwined and displayed simultaneously in everyday life. Nevertheless, there is an interplay between the extrinsic and intrinsic elements of their ethnic identity. The findings of the study show that on the one hand, Chinese elements were underplayed in the extrinsic part of their ethnic identity, or removed, in order to make way for elements adapted from the local cultures. On the other hand, priority was given to Chinese elements in the intrinsic part of their ethnic identity, with minimum inclusion of local elements. The selected local elements were instead adapted into the Chinese setting, remaining distinctly Chinese. Overall, the findings conform to Gordon's (1964) explanation of social amalgamation.

Despite changes which have occurred across both generations due to modernization, globalization and even Islamization, the core of being (Peranakan) Chinese remains intact among the Peranakan Chinese of Kelantan: the practice of highly localized Chinese culture, identification with all that is Kelantan, and a close interethnic relationship with the local ethnic groups. In other words, the mixedness within the Kelantan Peranakan Chinese identity succeeds in blurring the racial divisions in Kelantan society, paving the way towards unity in diversity, acknowledged and celebrated in the spirit of '*anak Kelantan*' (children of Kelantan), irrespective of race.

This chapter has argued that Peranakan identity should be considered part of the mixed-race phenomenon. In addition, the study of the Peranakans may offer a new perspective in the discourse of mixed race, which is all too often Western-centric and perceived negatively. The term Peranakan itself opens up the possibility for mixed race to be referred to in a positive light, without the negative sentiment of racial or cultural inequality contained in other terms such as mulatos and mestizos. In short, Peranakan is a social concept that does not connote racial contestation but instead, celebrates diversity. As such, the term Peranakan could be a significant contribution from the Southeast Asian region to the study of mixed race as a useful social concept to explain mixed race harmoniously.

Notes

1 The present paper is based on the author's doctoral thesis (Pue, 2012). An earlier version was delivered at the International Conference on Humanity, Society and Culture, held in Kuala Lumpur, Malaysia on 5–7 November 2011 and subsequently published in the proceedings (Pue and Shamsul, 2011).
2 Today, despite the fact that the scientific credibility of 'race' has been debunked, it remains strong in the social discourse about human diversity. The increase in fluidity between race and ethnicity in terms of theoretical and conceptual development also results in the concepts being used interchangeably to denote 'groupness' (Morning, 2015). This chapter draws on both socially constructed concepts; race is used primarily as a preamble to the connotation of racism (the sentiment that one racial group is superior to the other) which underlies the condition that Shamsul (2014) refers to as the 'stable tension' in Malaysian society.
3 Eight other contradictories identified by Shamsul (2014) are religion, social class, education, language, generation (old–young), gender, federalism politics and space (urban–rural).
4 The seven dimensions of assimilation are cultural (acculturation), structural, marital (intermarriage), identification, attitude-receptional (absence of prejudice), behaviour-receptional (absence of discrimination), and civic (absence of power conflicts).
5 Pue and Shamsul (2012) show that the origin of terminologies used for referring to mixed race peoples, often can be traced back to racism. For example, the term '*mulatto*' for progeny of white-black descent, originally means 'crossbreed of different species', i.e. between human (white) and 'sub-human' (black), whereas '*mestizo*' which means 'mixed', are used to refer to progeny of European and the native inhabitants of their colonies. In the colonial racial hierarchy, although mestizo is placed superior to the 'pure' native, they remain inferior to Europeans themselves.
6 Lim's book entitled *Gateway to Peranakan Culture* begins with a question about what Peranakan is. As a way to answer the question, he lists out other terminologies that are exclusively found in the Peranakan Chinese community in the Straits Settlement: '… Babas, Nyonyas, Bibiks, Strait Chinese, Strait-born Chinese …' (2005, p. 1).
7 Locally known as *kerja kampung* which refers to miscellaneous small-scale jobs found within the locality and done on a one-off, short-term, temporary or seasonal basis. This included working as handymen, construction workers or fruit pickers for men, and traditional *kueh* makers and house cleaners for women.
8 The children who live in rural areas with close-knit Peranakan Chinese relatives, tend to be fluent in the Hokkien dialect, whereas children who live in the cities are often able to converse in Mandarin.
9 Green-coloured steamed rice mixed with fried grated coconut, steamed fish flakes, various locally available fresh vegetables (*ulam*) and *budu* (fermented fish sauce) for flavour.
10 Steamed coconut milk rice with anchovies, *sambal* (traditional chilli and spice paste), cucumber slices, hard-boiled eggs and fried peanuts.
11 Thai *khi-lek* (Siamese cassia) leaves curry stew.
12 Yellow glutinous rice, often prepared and ritually presented as a symbol of gratitude in Malay society.

13 Literally means 'fragrant meat'.
14 Prawn and black fungus gravy.
15 A type of dessert consists of a glutinous rice ball with syrup.

Bibliography

Aw, A. J. (1994). *The Peranakan Identity: To Be or Not To Be*. PhD. University of Oklahoma.
Chin, Y. M., Lee, Y. F., Jawan, J., and Darshan, S. S. (2015). 'From Individual Choice to Collective Actions: Ethnic Consciousness in Malaysia Reconsidered'. *Ethnic and Racial Studies* 38(2), pp. 259–294.
Chong, B. S. (2009). 'A Note on Malaysians of Mixed Parentage'. *Malaysian Journal of Economic Studies* 46(1), pp. 93–95.
Fenton, S. (2003). *Ethnicity*. Cambridge: Polity Press.
Fong, Y. L., and Ishak, M. S. (2014). 'Framing Interethnic Conflict in Malaysia: A Comparative Analysis of Newspapers Coverage on the Keris Polemics'. *Ethnicities* 14(2), pp. 252–278.
Forbes, J. D. (1993). *Africans and Native Americans: The Language of Race and the Evolution of Red-Black People*. 2nd edition. Urbana: University of Illinois Press.
Gordon, M. M. (1964). *Assimilation in American Life: The Role of Race, Religion and National Origins*. New York: Oxford University Press.
Graham, W. A. (1908). *Kelantan: A State of the Malay Peninsula – A Handbook of Information*. Glasgow: Glasgow University Press.
Hak, N. A. (2012). 'Rights of a Wife in the Case of Conversion to Islam Under Family Law in Malaysia'. *Arab Law Quarterly* 26(2), pp. 227–239.
Hau, C. S. (2014). *The Chinese Question: Ethnicity, Nation, and Region in and Beyond the Philippines*. Singapore: NUS Press.
Hirschman, C. (1986). 'The Making of Race in Colonial Malaya: Political Economy and Racial Ideology'. *Sociological Forum* 1(2), pp. 330–361.
Holst, F. (2012). *Ethnicization and Identity Construction in Malaysia*. London: Routledge.
I-Ling, K.-H. (1991). *Symbolism in Chinese Food*. Singapore: Graham Brash.
Jenkins, R. (2000). 'Categorization: Identity, Social Process and Epistemology'. *Current Sociology* 48(3), pp. 7–25.
Kessler, C. S. (2012). *What Every Malaysian Needs to Know About 'Race'*. Bangi: Institute of Ethnic Studies (KITA).
Lee, S. K. (2008). 'The Peranakan Baba Nyonya Culture: Resurgence or Disappearance?' *SARI* 26, pp. 161–170.
Lim, G. S. (2005). *Gateway to Peranakan Culture*. 5th edition. Singapore: Asiapac Books.
Lindenberg, J. (2009). 'Interethnic Marriages and Conversion to Islam in Kota Bharu'. In G. W. Jones, H. L. Chee, and M. Mohamad (eds), *Muslim-non-Muslim Marriage: Political and Cultural Contestations in Southeast Asia*. Singapore: Institute of Southeast Asian Studies, pp. 219–254.
Malaysia. (2011). *Population Distribution by Local Authority Areas and Mukims*. Putrajaya: Jabatan Perangkaan Malaysia.
Milner, A., and Ting, H. (2014). 'Race and its Competing Paradigms: A Historical Review'. In A. Milner, A. R. Embong, and S. Y. Tham (eds), *Transforming Malaysia: Dominant and Competing Paradigms*. Singapore: ISEAS Publishing, pp. 18–58.

Milner, A., Embong, A. R., and Tham, S. Y. (eds) (2014). *Transforming Malaysia: Dominant and Competing Paradigms*. Singapore: ISEAS Publishing.

Mohamad, M., Aziz, Z., and Chin, O. S. (2009). 'Private Lives, Public Contention: Muslim-non-Muslim Family Disputes in Malaysia'. In G. W. Jones, H. L. Chee, and M. Mohamad (eds), *Muslim-non-Muslim Marriage: Political and Cultural Contestations in Southeast Asia*. Singapore: Institute of Southeast Asia Studies, pp. 59–101.

Morning, A. (2015). 'Ethnic Classification in Global Perspective: A Cross-national Survey of the 2000 Census Round'. In P. Simon, V. Piché, and A. A. Gagnon (eds), *Social Statistics and Ethnic Diversity: Cross-national Perspectives in Classifications and Identity Politics*. Cham: Springer International Publishing, pp. 17–37.

Nagaraj, S. (2009). 'Intermarriage in Malaysia'. *Malaysian Journal of Economic Studies* 46(1), pp. 75–92.

Noor, M. M. (2012). *Kerencaman Sosial dan Penipisan Batas Etnik: Kepelbagaian Etnik dan Perkongsian Hidup Bersama di Malaysia*. Bangi: Penerbit Universiti Kebangsaan Malaysia.

Osman, S. (1981). 'Perkahwinan Antara Etnik: Satu Kajian di Bandar Melaka'. *Akademika* 19, pp. 29–38.

Pillai, P. (2015). *Yearning to Belong: Malaysia's Indian Muslims, Chitties, Portuguese Eurasians, Peranakan Chinese and Baweanese*. Singapore: ISEAS-Yusof Ishak Institute.

Pue, G. H. (2009). *On Being Peranakan Chinese of Kelantan: Embodiment and Mistaken Ethnic Identity*. Southeast Asia Psychology Conference, Kota Kinabalu, Sabah, 10 July.

Pue, G. H. (2012). *Peranakan Sebagai Fenomena Sosial Dengan Tumpuan Kepada Komuniti Cina Peranakan di Kelantan*. PhD. Universiti Kebangsaan Malaysia.

Pue, G. H. (2016). 'Peranakan as Plural Identity: Cases from Peninsular Malaysia'. *Regional Journal of Southeast Asian Studies (RJSEAS)* 1(1), pp. 67–93.

Pue, G. H., and Kaur, C. (2014). 'Identiti Etnik Minoriti di Malaysia: Antara Realiti Sosial Tafsiran Autoriti dan Tafsiran Harian' (Ethnic Minority Identity in Malaysia: Between Authority-defined and Everyday-defined Social Reality). *Akademika* 84(1–2), pp. 57–70.

Pue, G. H., and Shamsul, A. B. (2011). 'Discourse on "Peranakanness" With Focus on the Peranakan Chinese Community in Contemporary Kelantan, Malaysia'. In *International Proceedings of Economics Development and Research* 20. Singapore: IACSIT Press, pp. 241–245.

Pue, G. H., and Shamsul, A. B. (2012). *Peranakan as a Social Concept*. Bangi: Institute of Ethnic Studies.

Pue, G. H., and Sulaiman, N. (2013). '"Choose One!": Challenges of Inter-ethnic Marriages in Malaysia'. *Asian Social Science* 9(17), pp. 269–278.

Rentse, A. (1934). 'History of Kelantan'. *JMBRAS* 12, pp. 44–62.

Salleh, H. (2006). 'Peoples and Traditions'. *The Encyclopedia of Malaysia* 12. Singapore: Archipelago Press.

Shamsul, A. B. (1996). 'Debating about Identity in Malaysia: A Discourse Analysis'. *Southeast Asian Studies* 34(3), pp. 476–499.

Shamsul, A. B. (2000). '"Ilmu kolonial" dan Pembinaan "Fakta" Mengenai Malaysia'. In R. A. Aziz and M. Y. Ismail (eds), *Masyarakat, Budaya dan Perubahan*. Bangi: Penerbit Universiti Kebangsaan Malaysia, pp. 189–201.

Shamsul, A. B. (2006a). 'The Constructions and Management of Ethnic Relations in Plural Malaysia'. In J. A. Jawan and Z. Ahmad (eds), *Inter-ethnic Relations in Malaysia*. Serdang: UPM Press, pp. 158–171.

Shamsul, A. B. (2006b). 'Identity Contestation in Malaysia: A Comparative Commentary on "Malayness" and "Chineseness"'. In J. A. Jawan and Z. Ahmad (eds), *Inter-ethnic Relations in Malaysia: Selected Readings*. Serdang: UPM Press, pp. 118–139.

Shamsul, A. B. (2014). *Perpaduan, Kesepaduan dan Penyatupaduan: Satu Negara, Satu Kata Akar, Tiga Konsep Keramat*. In Persidangan Pemantapan Citra Kenegaraan: Perkongsian Pengalaman, Bangi, 19–21 January.

Tan, C. B. (1979). *Baba and Nyonya: A Study of the Ethnic Identity of the Chinese Peranakan in Malacca*. PhD. Cornell University.

Tan, C. B. (1982). 'Peranakan Chinese in Northeast Kelantan with Special Reference to Chinese Religion'. *JMBRAS* 55, pp. 26–52.

Tan, C. B. (1988). *The Baba of Melaka: Culture and Identity of a Chinese Peranakan Community in Malaysia*. Petaling Jaya: Pelanduk Publications.

Tan, J.-P., Baharuddin, R., Juhari, R., and Krauss, S. E. (2008). 'Socio-demographic Characteristics of Intercultural Marriage: A Study of a Multi-ethnic Community in Malaysia'. *European Journal of Social Sciences* 5(4), pp. 30–44.

Tan, P. C. (1989). 'Perkahwinan Campur Etnik di Semenanjung Malaysia'. In A. S. Cheek (ed.), *Cabaran Malaysia Tahun Lapan Puluhan*. Kuala Lumpur: PSSM, pp. 235–243.

Teo, K. S. (2003). *The Peranakan Chinese of Kelantan: A Study of the Culture, Language and Communication of an Assimilated Group in Malaysia*. London: Asean Academic Press.

Teo, K. S. (2008). 'Chinese-Malay-Thai Interactions and the Making of Kelantan Peranakan Chinese Ethnicity'. In M. J. Montesano and P. Jory (eds), *Thai South and Malay North: Ethnic Interactions on a Plural Peninsular*. Singapore: NUS Press, pp. 214–230.

Thompson, D. (2012). 'Making (Mixed-)Race: Census Politics and the Emergence of Multiracial Multiculturalism in the United States, Great Britain and Canada'. *Ethnic and Racial Studies* 35(8), p. 1409–1426.

Tong, C. K. (2006). 'The Chinese in Contemporary Malaysia'. In K. F. Lian (ed.), *Race, Ethnicity and the State in Malaysia and Singapore*. Leiden: Koninklijke Brill NV, pp. 95–119.

Tweedie, M. W. F. (1953). 'An Early Chinese Account of Kelantan'. *JMBRAS* 26(1), pp. 216–219.

Wee, K. H. (1987). 'Kelantan and the Chinese Kelantanese'. In N. K. Rahman (ed.), *Kelantan Zaman Awal: Kajian Arkeologi dan Sejarah*. Kota Bharu: Perbadanan Muzium Negeri Kelantan, pp. 216–228.

Winzeler, R. L. (1981). 'The Rural Chinese of the Kelantan Plain'. *Journal of Malaysian Branch of the Royal Asiatic Society* 54, pp. 1–23.

Winzeler, R. L. (1983). 'The Ethnic Status of the Rural Chinese of the Kelantan Plain'. In P. Gosling and L. Y. C. Lim (eds), *The Chinese in Southeast Asia: Identity, Culture and Politics*. Singapura: Maruzen Asia, pp. 34–55.

10 Eurasian as multiracial

Mixed race, gendered categories and identity in Singapore

Zarine L. Rocha

Introduction

Mixed race is a concept with a complex history, and mixed race in Singapore is no exception. Singapore is a multicultural, post-colonial city-state, with a past influenced by issues of race, ethnicity, diversity and mixedness. As in other contexts, contemporary understandings of mixed race are key to wider racial/ethnic relations, and have shifted over time. In this context, race and mixed race bring power dynamics to the fore, highlighting racialized gender roles and post-colonial hierarchies. Singapore presents an important case study in exploring mixed race, as significant diversity exists against a backdrop of singular racial categorization, with extensive symbolic and practical outcomes.

This chapter explores the history of mixed race in Singapore, as related to the category of 'Eurasian'. Drawing on 20 narrative interviews with individuals of mixed Chinese and European[1] descent, it looks at race, gender and belonging in the Singaporean context, and particularly how 'Eurasian' both includes and excludes individuals as a way to belong. 'Eurasian' highlights the potential and the limitations of a 'multiracial' categorization, and individual experiences illustrate the ways that the institutionalization of race (and mixed race) frame personal identities in everyday life.

Researching and classifying mixed race

Literature around mixedness has a long history, ranging from early studies on pathology and marginality, to contemporary approaches to mixed race and 'multiracial identity'. Mixed race research has increased dramatically over the past two decades, particularly in the contexts of the United States and Britain[2] (see Ifekwunigwe, 2004; Parker and Song, 2001; Root, 1996). Most recently, research seeks to highlight experiences of exclusion as well as new forms of belonging; working to understand both personal identity and the far-reaching impacts of social context and racial categorization (Rockquemore et al., 2009).

Theoretical understandings of mixed race, particularly as marginal or exotic, are closely tied to questions of gender, sexuality and power. Furedi (2001) suggests that the shift from looking at mixed race as biological to social discourses of marginality highlights the discomfort around the 'mixing' of 'races'. Group boundaries – national, racial or ethnic – are highly gendered, and mixed race has often historically been perceived as a boundary transgression, particularly in colonial contexts (Kitch, 2009; Stoler, 1992). Pathological discourses of mixed race often relate to the (gendered) body. Seen in visible qualities of skin colour and appearance, and linked to assumed biological truths of mixed blood, the embodiment of mixed race presents itself at the intersection of race and gender, something reflected in the words used to describe mixed race, which relate directly to implications of sexual relations, the mingling of blood, and gendered power dynamics.

Thus, words are particularly important. Historically, there have been multiple descriptive terms used, and within academic circles there is no consensus on which term is most appropriate (Aspinall, 2009). Mixed race, 'multiracial' and 'biracial' tend to be favoured in North American research, 'mixed ethnicity' or 'mixed heritage' are more common in Britain, while a number of gendered and derogatory terms exist in both contexts (Aspinall, 2003). For the purposes of this chapter, mixed race or 'mixed' will be used, to indicate individuals descended from two different groups as defined by popular conceptions of race and difference, and as a way to highlight the intersections and divergences from the category of 'Eurasian'.

Moving towards issues of classification, definitions of 'race' and mixed race are contextual and changing, as classification systems shift: race and ethnicity are classified by different states in different ways. Such classification is important for individuals of mixed descent, due to the frequent dissonance between the available racial categories and lived identities around mixedness. Regardless of the flexibility of the categories, individuals experience their identities as more complex, less fixed and ever changing (Aspinall, 2012, Rocha, 2012a). However, official categories remain salient in everyday life, and individuals of mixed heritage must locate themselves within the existing structures in order to be counted (Perlmann and Waters, 2002). Mixed race then highlights the difficulties inherent in categorization: should mixed race be a form of categorization in itself, as a multiracial category? (Goldberg, 1997; Rockquemore et al., 2009).

Prior to the change to the US census in 2000, which allowed for the selection of more than one racial group, there was a push to include a 'multiracial' category on the census itself. In the lead up to the census change, a number of advocacy groups suggested that due to a shared history of discrimination, and a common mixed heritage, the mixed population could be identified as a coherent group – as 'multiracial' (Spencer, 1997; DaCosta, 2007). This movement was subject to much criticism, with research finding that this coherence was not substantiated (Nash, 1997/2004). The mixed population was found instead to be particularly heterogeneous (Harris, 2001) and creating a multiracial category was perceived as both pushing against race as a category and arguing for a new form of racialized categorization (Rockquemore et al.,

2009). Although the push for a multiracial category was not successful, the idea of a multiracial identity still has some support. Does the case of Singapore shed light on whether such a categorization could be useful in understanding mixed race?

Mixed race in Singapore

The categorization of race and mixed race has a long legacy in Singapore. A national narrative based around multiracialism and the management of race has been key in shaping Singapore's national identity (Benjamin, 1976). Racial categories were initially put in place under British colonial rule and then carried over by the independent Singaporean government from 1965. These divisions became the well-known framework of Chinese, Malay, Indian and Other (CMIO) shifting the same colonial classifications, with the accompanying gendered and racialized assumptions, into the new state framework (Hirschman, 1987; Pereira, 2006).

The term 'Eurasian' has a very specific and contextual history, with embodied meanings around space, race and gender (particularly the gendered power dynamics of relationships between the colonized and the colonizer), which differ across colonized countries such as India, Singapore and Malaysia (Matthews, 2007). 'Eurasian' was first utilized in Singapore by the colonial government, acknowleging mixed race and seeking to manage racial boundary crossings. The classification originally described those with European fathers and Asian mothers, highlighting a patrilineal transmission of race. Eurasian became a category for most European/Asian mixes:[3] an official label for mixedness (Puru-Shotam, 1998). Pre-1965, Eurasian identity was situated somewhere between the colonizers and the colonized, yet it was often rejected by both the Chinese and the European communities on the grounds of authenticity (Jayawardena, 2007). In response to such exclusion, Eurasian individuals sought a more coherent community, forming the Eurasian Association (EA) in 1919 (Braga-Blake, 1992). This community consolidated key features of Eurasian identity: mixed European/Asian descent (along patrilineal lines), Christianity, and speaking English (Pereira, 1997).

Post-1965, Eurasian identity lost much of its privileged status. This brought about a key shift for the community, which did not fit easily into the CMIO multiracial model. Each administrative group worked to link descent, language, religion and custom, creating idealized versions of 'separate but equal' racial groups (Chua, 1998; Siddique, 1989). Therefore, according to the multiracial model, the Chinese speak Mandarin, practice Buddhism and wear the *Cheongsam*, the Malays speak Malay, practice Islam and wear the *Sarong Kebaya*, and the Indians speak Tamil, practice Hinduism and wear the *Sari* (Benjamin, 1976; Pereira, 2006).

Individuals of mixed parentage were generally categorized according to the ethnic group of the father (Leow, 2000), continuing the patrilineal bias. Eurasians, however, were classified as a group under 'Other', as

Eurasian as multiracial 165

... persons primarily of mixed European and Asian descent ... *do not belong to any specific ethnic grouping.* However, it has been the practice ... to treat them as a specific community and this practice has also been continued in the current census.

(Arumainathan, 1973, 247, emphasis added)

Being 'othered' at such a macro level by the multiracial model significantly affected the Eurasian community, and defining the boundaries of 'Eurasian' became more difficult. Classification shifted away from mixed European and Asian, towards a definition based around heritage, such as those who had two Eurasian parents or a Eurasian father (Pereira, 1997). 'Eurasian' then became less a mixed group in and of itself, and instead a small ethnic group with a history of mixedness. To combat marginalization, the Eurasian community worked to highlight its distinctiveness as a defined community. The state supported these efforts, acknowledging the Eurasians as a distinct group (Pereira, 2006; Pereira, 1997). However, despite such simplification, much like other racialized groups, the day-to-day reality of Eurasian identity remained more complicated.

Contemporary Singapore officially recognizes more than 90 racial/ethnic groups, and these are then categorized into four main groupings: Chinese, Malay, Indian and Other. Of the population, 74.1 per cent are recorded as Chinese, 13.4 per cent as Malay, 9.2 per cent as Indian and 3.3 per cent are in the category 'Other' (Singapore Department of Statistics, 2010a). These categories play a key role in everyday life, affecting both state policy and individual choices (Barr and Skrbis, 2008). Public housing estates, in which the majority of the population reside, are built to be multiracial. Racial quotas within each building are carefully maintained, to ensure that no racial group is over-represented (Loh, 2009b; Loh, 2009a; Chua, 1995). Race also touches issues of social welfare. In the absence of a state welfare system, 'self-help' groups are organized around racial and religious lines, based on the idea that each group is itself best equipped to take care of itself. Assistance is provided by MENDAKI for the Malay population, SINDA for the Indian population and CDAC for the Chinese population, and more recently, the Eurasian Association for some of the 'others' (Chua, 1998; Lai, 1995).

Education and language policy have also been shaped by race. The second language policy mandates the learning of a 'mother tongue' for all students. 'Mother tongue' has been defined as the 'natural' second language based on the race of the father. This highlights an interesting and gendered contradiction – 'mother tongue' in fact has nothing to do with the mother, nor with the language spoken at home: it is determined instead by the patrilineal racial framework, and the idea of a 'true' racial essence. For those from Eurasian and mixed backgrounds, the situation is more complex. Even though English is frequently the language spoken at home, it cannot be officially recognized as a mother tongue, as it is seen as a neutral language. Individuals are frequently assigned to the 'mother tongues' of their fathers' racial grouping, or assigned to a separate second language in order to fit within the bilingual framework (Chua, 2005; Wee, 2002).

Thus, racial categories have a significant impact on the day-to-day lives of individuals. These categories are reinforced further through constant recording on official forms, questionnaires and national identity cards (ICs), as well as through symbolic representation in national events (PuruShotam, 1998). Narratives of everyone 'having a single race' are very visible at both state and individual levels, reinforcing racial boundaries, and, until recently, curtailing options for multiplicity (Rocha, 2012b).

Despite this history of singular categorization, the population of Singapore continues to cross boundaries in everyday life. Levels of intermarriage have been steadily increasing over the past decades: in 1988, 4.3 per cent of marriages under the Women's Charter and 16.4 per cent under the Muslim Law Act[4] were registered as interethnic[5] (Siddique, 1990), but by 2009, 15.7 per cent Women's Charter and 32.8 per cent Muslim Law Act marriages were classified as interethnic. Of all marriages in Singapore, 18.4 per cent – almost one in five[6] – are interethnic (Singapore Department of Statistics, 2010b).

Reflecting the changing demography, classifications have shifted to allow for children to be classified as the race of either parent, as Eurasian (Singapore Department of Statistics, 2010b), or as having a 'double-barrelled race' (Immigration and Checkpoints Authority, 2010). This move was controversial, leading to the caveat that individuals with 'double-barrelled' classifications must also select a *primary race* – the race before the hyphen (Rocha, 2016). The change was largely symbolic: a state-sanctioned way to recognize mixedness, with minimum disruption. It allows for official recognition of mixed race, while at the same time reinforcing the CMIO system at institutional and societal levels, maintaining quotas and structure around housing, social welfare and education.

The category of Eurasian has been affected by the changes over the past years. Its meaning has developed, and it currently ostensibly provides an official space for individuals of mixed descent, akin to a 'multiracial' option for classification. However, there remains an important distinction between 'new' Eurasians (those with one European and one Asian parent) and individuals of Eurasian heritage (with one or two Eurasian parents). 'New' Eurasians are less likely to identify with the carefully structured heritage of the traditional Eurasian identity, while in the latter case, Eurasian ethnic/racial identity is passed down through generations as a distinct and separate ethnic group.

Being, and not being, Eurasian

Against this complex background, the label of Eurasian has come to mean many different things. Instead of a general 'mixed' category, the reality of this label is much more nuanced. Eurasian identity occupies an in-between space, reinforcing gendered and racial boundaries, and crystallized around historical notions of authenticity. This chapter draws on 20 narrative interviews with individuals of mixed Chinese and European descent. Thirteen women and seven men were interviewed, ranging from 19 to 64 years old, and encompassing a wide range of backgrounds and occupations. Rather than seeking to generalize about mixed race for the entire Chinese-European population(s) of Singapore, these interviews sought to illuminate key experiences and narrative themes, looking at the simultaneous undermining and reinforcement of racial categories.

Defining Eurasian

The term Eurasian provided a label which was equally inclusive and exclusionary for participants, as a racial category that encompasses a multitude of backgrounds. Participants used the word in both the casual sense of 'mixed', and in a more precise way, highlighting its position within the multiracial framework. Several spoke of the difficulties around definition:

> I mean, are you Eurasian? Eurasian, I mean, even up till today there's a debate in the Eurasian community, what is a Eurasian? I mean, do you, do you define Eurasians as of Dutch and Portuguese descent? Do you define Eurasian as being anyone with European heritage plus an Asian heritage?
>
> I mean, all that, and do, you know, only paternal lines count, or do you count the maternal lines as well? I mean, it was all debated in the community that I grew up within, so, messy to say the least.
>
> (35, female, Chinese/Eurasian)[7]

A smaller number of people felt that Eurasian should be very strictly defined, re-racializing the hybridity of the category into a defined group. This young woman felt strongly that these boundaries should be monitored:

> And I kind of feel like ... Eurasian, sort of like, you can't mix other stuff with it. Like with Asian and white, because then it becomes something else. 'Cause I feel like, um, like the whole point of like recognizing Eurasians is recognizing a unique mix. So then when you have like another unique mix, which is like Eurasian and something else, then I think that should be given its own name as well, like, acknowledged for itself.
>
> (19, female, Chinese/Australian)

For her, Eurasian meant only a European/Asian mix, at odds with the wider Singaporean definition, which encompasses a significant historical dimension. Other participants were very aware of this historical meaning in Singapore, and the essentialization of a distinct Eurasian identity, to the exclusion of 'new Eurasian' identities.

> Like I said, on my IC it's written Chinese. I can't say I'm Eurasian because ... (although I am Eurasian) because the term Eurasian defines the person half/half, Europe and Asian, right? But in Singapore if you're Eurasian, it's not even what I am. Because that group of people, that doesn't describe the kind of mix that I am. So, I can't really, that doesn't apply to me as well.

I'm not pure Chinese. But it's written Chinese because I have a Chinese name after my father.

(30, female, French/Singaporean Chinese)

For this woman, Eurasian was a category into which she couldn't fit, given its historical connotations. The race of her father simplified her official categorization, but left her personal identity at odds with her official label.

Another young man learned of these historical implications when he undertook National Service, discovering that Eurasians were widely considered to have particular unique customs.

I only realized that they had a really strong Eurasian community in national service when they started like teaching everybody about, like cultures in Singapore. And apparently, we have, Eurasians have, special food [laughs], special games and all this kind of stuff. I was just kind of like, 'I've never experienced that', and everyone starts looking at me like 'really?'. I don't think so [laughs]. I don't recall this *ever* growing up.

(21, male, Chinese/Caucasian)

His education about different cultures in Singapore presented the Eurasian community as a homogenous group, in much the same way as the Chinese, Malays and Indians are presented as coherent communities despite significant diversity (Chua, 2003). This highlights the gap between the historical understanding of Eurasian, and the idea of 'new' Eurasians. He considered himself as Eurasian, yet couldn't place himself within the framework. However, two participants commented particularly on the fact that the definition of Eurasian was becoming broader and more inclusive, relating this to power dynamics within the multi-racial state framework.

Originally the Eurasians meant that the two parents were mixed, it was a flat case. Now they've changed the constitution to stretch it a little bit more so that anyone who's got a connection will be called Eurasian for the sake of this identity.... It's a bit ... something you've got to get used to. Otherwise we'll be dwindling right down to about 7,000 of us or, you know, so we need to grow a little bit.

(64, male, Chinese/British)

'Cause I mean, Eurasian is a very broad term. So ... I guess it's a very broad term. And it's only recently that they, I think, made it more encompassing, ah. I think, it's more like, it's not like a specific domain or definition of people, it's more like an umbrella grouping now. Like, anyone ... when you think about it, anyone can be Eurasian, ah. Most, I think ... most racial groups in Singapore, like, SINDA, MENDAKI, I think the tendency now is for them to become more inclusive. 'Cause, they like, if you don't become inclusive, you never grow, lah. If you grow means, if you grow means government gives you more money, lah. Gives you, cause you're addressing more, a larger group, ah.

(26, male, Filipino-Chinese/Australian)

The first excerpt describes how inclusion boosts the Eurasian community's profile and numbers, going beyond the historical understanding of identity. The second takes this even further, highlighting how this inclusion allows for increased allocation of resources, allowing the Eurasian community to turn this dilution of historical culture to their advantage.

For a number of people, however, being Eurasian was a source of pride – whether it was defined as historical or new. One woman, who saw herself as historically Eurasian, felt that her identity as Eurasian was both important and unique:

For me ... I've always felt that I will be a Eurasian no matter what. And ... that is very important to me. My race is that I'm a Eurasian. And um ... it's just, I feel very proud now, you know. To have a grandfather who is Indian, a grandmother who is Chinese. And um, also because I married a Eurasian.... But I personally feel that being a Eurasian is Eurasian. You will always be a little bit different from anyone else.

(37, female, Sikh-Chinese/Eurasian)

Her sense of difference was thus linked to her heritage and her links to the Eurasian community. A second participant also felt this difference keenly, but for him it translated to feelings of isolation and not always feeling included by the Eurasian community, nor by any other community. His identity as Eurasian made him feel out of step with other groups in the population.

It's different, being Eurasian. We find that the Chinese Singaporeans have a sense of humour that we can't identify with. So, when we, we have the banter or being witty or telling jokes, it falls on deaf ears to Chinese Singaporeans. Eurasians understand us completely. There's this gulf really, that's hard to fill. Really hard to fill. Um ... so we think maybe we should try making friends with the Eurasian community. Finding therein also lies a different set of problems.

(36, male, English and German/Eurasian)

For him, Eurasian identity was about more than race and history, it implied a commonality and sense of belonging. He used this categorization in his everyday life, assigning characteristics to an individual's race.

For other participants, the category of Eurasian provided a way to subvert static racial categories, and a way of recognizing mixedness. One man used the categorization to acknowledge both sides of his heritage, pushing for a Eurasian label on his identity card. Another woman felt that her racial classification was separate from, and perhaps less important than the reality of her mixedness.

> I mean, it's fine to be classified under mixed.... And um ... I think being Eurasian is fine. Listing that category or the Others category. Yeah. But I mean, when filling out forms and stuff, I just instinctively tick Chinese, because it's stated Chinese on my IC. Yeah, because, back then Singapore hasn't had the rule that you can state Eurasian. But now they have that rule. So, if both parents are agreeable, it's fine. So, my friends have told me 'why don't you just go and change it' and I said 'I don't want to spend the money changing my IC!' Yeah, so I say it's all right. It's not important what is stated on a form, as long as you know inside of you, where you are and what you are.
>
> (23, female, Eurasian/Singaporean Chinese)

Although she had the option to change her classification, she was content with the patrilineal classification of Chinese. In her case, external labels didn't need to match her internal sense of who (and *what*) she was.

The category of Eurasian thus highlighted a number of definitions, providing a broad space in which participants could manoeuvre. For some people, a historically and culturally specific community represented another form of exclusion from a racialized framework. For others, the meaning of Eurasian could be re-purposed, bringing in 'new Eurasians' and different understandings of mixed heritage, even without identifying with the Eurasian community as a whole.

Eurasian identity, belonging and the body

An everyday aspect of being mixed in Singapore was related to the body. The social reality of mixed identities comes to the fore when discussing physical appearance and external reactions to different appearances. Skin colour and appearance remain key signifiers of difference, serving as physical reminders of social boundaries. Historically, judgments of physical appearance based on racial/ethnic hierarchies were distinctly gendered, with differing standards applied to men and women. This imbalance continues today, through the disproportionate focus on the bodies of women, particularly the racial characteristics of their appearance (Rockquemore, 2002).

In Singapore, many participants spoke of being judged on the basis of their physical appearance. They often found such external judgment destabilizing or even insulting, as it could contradict how they saw themselves. They described being constantly 'raced': having their identities reduced to their physical features (see Perkins, 2007). Many described experiences where people guessed at their ethnic backgrounds. One woman was often categorized by others as 'Malay', and had an interesting interpretation of this guess:

> But also at times people just get confused as to what race I am. Because on my IC it says Chinese. Yeah, but then when you look at me ... when I was younger, I was very dark.

Eurasian as multiracial 171

So, people used to think that I was a Malay.... So, after that, then I was talking to my other Eurasian friends, and they say yeah, they get the same thing too.

So, we came up with a logic as to why they thought we were Malay: 'cause I mean, we don't look Chinese, and we are too fair to be Indians, so, naturally they think that we are Malays.

(23, female, Eurasian/Chinese)

She suggested that others would attempt to categorize her according to the CMIO framework, through a process of elimination: not Chinese, not Indian, must be Malay. For her and others, such judgments left them constantly reiterating their backgrounds, and justifying how they belonged in Singapore.

Ambiguous physical appearance was also related to stereotypes around Eurasian identity, for both men and women. Several people commented that these stereotypes did not match the reality of their lives, being based on historical prejudices. As in other countries, one of the most common stereotypes was that people of mixed descent were promiscuous and immoral. One woman mentioned that her classmates had spoken to her about how they thought Eurasians would be arrogant and promiscuous. Another man went into more detail about the stereotyping that he had encountered:

The old expression for Eurasians used to be 'Happy Charlie'. I don't know where that comes from, but they'd say the 'Happy Charlie', the Eurasians are ... the British colonizers would call them party-goers, bossing people round, holding high positions. Really just the leisure class they used to be. And we still have that today.

I always get that from ... I got that from a taxi driver, he just said, 'you look like a player to me'. I said 'excuse me, you don't know me. How can you say I'm a player? What do you mean by a player?' 'You know, all Eurasians, always chasing women, chasing skirts...'.

(36, male, English and German/Eurasian)

For him, such gendered stereotypes were difficult to deal with, seeing male Eurasians as immoral and unfaithful. His identity placed him outside of the familiar, singular racial categories, and also subjected him to assumptions about his character and morality. He found this tiresome, seeking to separate ascribed notions of group identity from his own individual characteristics and experiences.

Physical appearance was also powerful for women of mixed descent, with several mentioning the idea that mixed women were supposed to be beautiful and exotic. One woman found that her atypical body-type led to a great deal of exclusion in her childhood.

You know, when I was here in school, I had to join like the trim and fit club.[8] And, um, you know they were always, 'oh you're fat, you're fat, you're fat' and when I was a kid, I wasn't fat. You know, and I was a very

active child. And, but I have very big bones. And, they don't get that here....
And um, and I had, it has gotten to the point where I'm like 'you know
what, fuck you' like, I don't care what you think. But then that has never
allowed me to feel like I belong here.

(27, female, Singaporean Chinese/British)

A second woman fit into this stereotype of attractiveness more easily, and even expressed a belief in this inherent appeal of mixedness.

It seems like, um, they [mixed models] seem to be in demand. The pan-Asian look. In Singapore. Because it's better than having ah, someone completely white, um … to do an ad, that you know, the locals, the Asians, cannot really relate to the face. So as long as there is kind of an Asian look, it looks more classy and also I can relate to the face....

I read a book about how when you're beautiful, you get more advantages, like people treat you better. And I think that's true. You get more attention. It's harder to hide.

(33, female, Hainanese/Welsh)

This excerpt illustrates an internalization of beliefs around exoticism, as she describes her experiences of being beautiful, and the relatability of a 'mixed' Asian face. Mixedness can thus be made visible on the body, and such difference is then interpreted in highly gendered ways (Alcoff, 2006; Perkins, 2005). This is illustrated in popular understandings of mixed race as either marginal or exotic in different contexts, as in the examples above, and in individual experiences of hierarchies of gender and race: where female gender roles are often placed at the centre of how racial identity is understood (Yuval-Davis, 1997). In the case of Eurasian identity and gender, women are commonly seen as exotic, beautiful and inherently cosmopolitan, and this 'is achieved by virtue of being differently sexualised and racialised' (Matthews, 2007, 49). For women and men in Singapore, the body was thus a powerful site of racialization and beliefs around identity for individuals of mixed descent.

Conclusion

Eurasian is a complicated and often conflicted racial label in Singapore, set against a background of pervasive multiracialism. Wider understandings of racial belonging as key to national identity continue to frame the identifications of those with multiple affiliations. However, in spite of strict racial categorization, individuals of mixed descent negotiated different ways of understanding their identities and addressing what they saw as a public/private divide. Belonging proved complex for participants, both symbolically and practically, as they sought ways to reconcile the administrative and felt aspects of national identity.

The category of Eurasian then provided a way to belong for individuals of mixed descent, but in practice was neither defined nor broad enough for participants to feel fully included. The historical aspects of definition meant that many markers of traditional Eurasian culture were not relevant in contemporary life, and the divisions between 'old' and 'new' Eurasians highlighted the difficulties inherent in trying to force coherence from significant diversity. While it provided a multiracial label of sorts, in that it attempted to include all forms of mixedness, it did not guarantee feelings of belonging, and in some cases, reinforced negative external perceptions of what it means to be mixed. Thus, the classification of Eurasian is an important example of the ways in which a label of multiplicity can serve to exclude, and even re-racialize, identities within a strictly regulated multiracial society. Even complex categories, such as this, thus struggle to adequately encompass the fluidity and complexity of identity.

Race and gender also proved closely intertwined when looking at mixed race. From initial understandings of appropriate racial boundary crossings, racial mixing has always been tinged by cultural understandings of gender-appropriate behaviour. This continues today, through older views of patrilineal racial descent, and the peculiar definition of 'mother tongue' in the Singaporean context. In stories of everyday life negotiations, the gendering of race is equally evident, with particular stereotypes of how Eurasians should look and behave; and with young women being viewed as exotic and young men as players, with mixedness marked on their bodies.

Exploring these labels and frameworks, this chapter has shown the considerable complications experienced by individuals of mixed heritage around issues of race, gender and national belonging. Participants spoke of how their identities could require much thought and negotiation in different situations, as well as how they sought a balance between internal and external understandings of belonging. While categorization remained simplistic and rigid, the complexity of everyday life identities provided an important thread across stories. Personal feelings of being mixed were complicated by social expectations, and individuals brought together various personal and social narratives to create their own unique sense of belonging: as situational, shifting and non-traditional, both including and excluding aspects of heritage, ethnicity, racial categories and national identity.

Notes

1 The terms 'Chinese' and 'European' were used in this research, to reflect popular meanings and salience in the Singapore context. These terms certainly have racial, ethnic, cultural and national connotations, many of which are not always relevant to each individual. Parents of participants were often neither from Europe nor China, yet these were the labels which they most often used to describe their origins. Thus, it is important to acknowledge that social classification is often based on phenotype (regardless of the biologically baseless nature of 'race'), and related to an individual's perception of their appearance, their self-definition and the generalizations of others.
2 More research is emerging in other parts of the world, moving the focus to encompass a wider variety of national contexts. See Edwards *et al.* (2012) and King-O'Riain *et al.* (2014), as well as this volume.

3 Other forms of intermixing (particularly inter-Asian intermixing) were often unrecorded.
4 Marriages in Singapore can be formalized either under the 1961 Women's Charter, or the Muslim Law Act of 1966.
5 Interestingly, interethnic is the term used by the state, while in practice this refers back to the groups which are very much delineated along racial lines: the CMIO groupings.
6 These numbers may be lower than reality, given the practice of classifying children as the race of their father, and making it impossible to know how many marriages involved individuals of mixed descent.
7 Biographical details are provided in the following format, as described by the participant: (age, gender, mother's race or ethnicity/father's race or ethnicity).
8 The trim and fit programme (TAF) was a targeted institutional programme in Singapore schools in the 1990s and early 2000s, aimed at helping students deemed overweight to have a healthier lifestyle. With its unfortunate acronym and targeted approach, it was controversial, and has since been replaced.

Bibliography

Alcoff, L. M. (2006). *Visible Identities: Race, Gender and the Self*. Oxford: Oxford University Press.

Arumainathan, P. (1973). *Report on the Census of Population 1970 Singapore*. Singapore: Department of Statistics.

Aspinall, P. (2003). 'The Conceptualisation and Categorisation of Mixed Race/Ethnicity in Britain and North America: Identity Options and the Role of the State'. *International Journal of Intercultural Relations* 27, pp. 269–296.

Aspinall, P. (2009). '"Mixed Race", "Mixed Origins" or What?: Generic Terminology for the Multiple Racial/Ethnic Group Population'. *Anthropology Today* 25(2), pp. 3–8.

Aspinall, P. (2012). 'Answer Formats in British Census and Survey Ethnicity Questions: Does Open Response Better Capture "Superdiversity"?' *Sociology* Online before print: 2 February 2012, pp. 1–11.

Barr, M. D., and Skrbis, Z. (2008). *Constructing Singapore: Elitism, Ethnicity and the Nation-Building Project*. Copenhagen, NIAS Press.

Benjamin, G. (1976). 'The Cultural Logic of Singapore's "Multiracialism"'. In R. Hassan (ed.), *Singapore: Society in Transition*. Kuala Lumpur: Oxford University Press, pp. 115–133.

Braga-Blake, M. (1992). 'Eurasians in Singapore: An Overview'. In M. Braga-Blake (ed.), *Singapore Eurasians: Memories and Hopes*. Singapore: Times Editions, pp. 11–23.

Chua, B. H. (1995). *Communitarian Ideology and Democracy in Singapore*. London, Routledge.

Chua, B. H. (1998). 'Racial-Singaporeans: Absence after the Hyphen'. In J. S. Kahn (ed.), *Southeast Asian Identities: Culture and the Politics of Representation in Indonesia, Malaysia, Singapore, and Thailand*. Singapore: Institute of Southeast Asian Studies, pp. 28–50.

Chua, B. H. (2003). 'Multiculturalism in Singapore: An Instrument of Social Control'. *Race and Class* 44(3), pp. 58–77.

Chua, B. H. (2005). 'The Cost of Membership in Ascribed Community'. In W. Kymlicka and B. He (eds), *Multiculturalism in Asia*. Oxford: Oxford University Press, pp. 170–195.

DaCosta, K. M. (2007). *Making Multiracials: State, Family and Market in the Redrawing of the Color Line*. Stanford: Stanford University Press.

Edwards, R., Ali, S., Caballero, C., and Song, M. (eds) (2012). *International Perspectives on Racial and Ethnic Mixedness and Mixing*. London: Routledge.
Furedi, F. (2001). 'How Sociology Imagined "Mixed Race"'. In D. Parker and M. Song (eds), *Rethinking 'Mixed Race'*. London: Pluto Press, pp. 23–41.
Goldberg, D. T. (1997). *Racial Subjects: Writing on Race in America*. New York: Routledge.
Harris, D. R. (2001). *Does It Matter How We Measure? Racial Classification and the Characteristics of Multiracial Youth*. Ann Arbor: Department of Sociology and Institute for Social Research, University of Michigan.
Hirschman, C. (1987). 'The Meaning and Measurement of Ethnicity in Malaysia: An Analysis of Census Classifications'. *The Journal of Asian Studies* 46(3), pp. 555–582.
Ifekwunigwe, J. O. (ed.) (2004). *'Mixed Race' Studies: A Reader*. London: Routledge.
Immigration and Checkpoints Authority. (2010). *Greater Flexibility With Implementation Of Double-Barrelled Race Option From 1 January 2011*. Singapore. Available at: www.ica.gov.sg/news_details.aspx?nid=12443 (accessed: 30 December 2010).
Jayawardena, K. (2007). *Erasure of the Euro-Asian: Recovering Early Radicalism and Feminism in South Asia*. Colombo, Social Scientists' Association.
King-O'Riain, R. C., Small, S., Mahtani, M., Song, M., and Spickard, P. (eds) (2014). *Global Mixed Race*. New York: NYU Press.
Kitch, S. L. (2009). *The Specter of Sex: Gendered Foundations of Racial Formation in the United States*. Albany: State University of New York Press.
Lai, A. E. (1995). *Meanings of Multiethnicity: A Case-study of Ethnicity and Ethnic Relations in Singapore*. Kuala Lumpur: Oxford University Press.
Leow, B. G. (2000). *Census of Population 2000: Demographic Characteristics*. Singapore: Singapore Department of Statistics.
Loh, K. S. (2009a). 'Conflict and Change at the Margins: Emergency Kampong Clearance and the Making of Modern Singapore'. *Asian Studies Review* 33(2), pp. 139–159.
Loh, K. S. (2009b). 'History, Memory, and Identity in Modern Singapore: Testimonies from the Urban Margins'. *The Oral History Review* 36(1), pp. 1–24.
Matthews, J. (2007). 'Eurasian Persuasions: Mixed Race, Performativity and Cosmopolitanism'. *Journal of Intercultural Studies* 28(1), pp. 41–54.
Nash, P. T. (1997/2004). 'Will the Census Go Multiracial?' In J. O. Ifekwunigwe (ed.) *'Mixed Race' Studies: A Reader*. London: Routledge, pp. 214–218.
Parker, D., and Song, M. (eds) (2001). *Rethinking 'Mixed Race'*. London: Pluto Press.
Pereira, A. (1997). 'The Revitalization of Eurasian Identity in Singapore'. *Southeast Asian Journal of Social Science* 25(2), pp. 7–24.
Pereira, A. (2006). 'No Longer "Other": The Emergence of the Eurasian Community in Singapore'. In K. F. Lian (ed.), *Race, Ethnicity and The State in Malaysia and Singapore*. Leiden: Brill, pp. 5–32.
Perkins, M. (2005). 'Thoroughly Modern Mulatta: Rethinking "Old World" Stereotypes in a "New World" Setting'. *Biography* 28(1), pp. 104–116.
Perkins, M. (ed.) (2007). *Visibly Different: Face, Place and Race in Australia*. Bern: Peter Lang.
Perlmann, J., and Waters, M. C. (2002). 'Introduction'. In J. Perlmann and M. C. Waters (eds), *The New Race Question: How the Census Counts Multiracial Individuals*. New York: Russell Sage Foundation, pp. 1–30.
PuruShotam, N. (1998). 'Disciplining Difference: Race in Singapore'. In J. S. Kahn (ed.), *Southeast Asian Identities: Culture and the Politics of Representation in Indonesia, Malaysia, Singapore, and Thailand*. Singapore: Institute of Southeast Asian Studies, pp. 51–93.

Rocha, Z. (2012a). 'Identity, Dislocation and Belonging: Chinese/European Narratives of "Mixed" Identity in Aotearoa/New Zealand'. *Identities: Global Studies in Culture and Power* 19(6), pp. 673–690.

Rocha, Z. (2012b). 'Multiplicity within Singularity: Racial Categorization and Recognizing "Mixed Race" in Singapore'. *Journal of Current Southeast Asian Affairs* 30(3), pp. 95–131.

Rocha, Z. (2016). *"Mixed Race" Identities in Asia and the Pacific: Experiences from Singapore and New Zealand*. London: Routledge.

Rockquemore, K. A. (2002). 'Negotiating the Color Line: The Gendered Process of Racial Identity Construction Among Black/White Biracial Women'. *Gender & Society* 16(4), pp. 485–503.

Rockquemore, K. A., Brunsma, D. L., and Delgado, D. J. (2009). 'Racing to Theory or Retheorizing Race? Understanding the Struggle to Build a Multiracial Identity Theory'. *Journal of Social Issues* 65(1), pp. 13–34.

Root, M. P. P. (ed.) (1996). *The Multiracial Experience: Racial Borders as the New Frontier*. London: Sage.

Siddique, S. (1989). 'Singaporean Identity'. In K. S. Sandhu and P. Wheatley (eds), *Management of Success: The Moulding of Modern Singapore*. Singapore: Institute of Southeast Asian Studies, pp. 563–577.

Siddique, S. (1990). 'The Phenomenology of Ethnicity: A Singapore Case Study'. *Sojourn* 5(1), pp. 35–62.

Singapore Department of Statistics. (2010a). 'Census of the Population 2010: Statistical Release 1 (Demographic Characteristics, Education, Language and Religion)'. Singapore: Singapore Department of Statistics.

Singapore Department of Statistics (2010b). 'Yearbook of Statistics Singapore'. Singapore: Singapore Department of Statistics.

Spencer, J. M. (1997). *The New Colored People*. New York: New York University Press.

Stoler, A. L. (1992). 'Sexual Affronts and Racial Frontiers: European Identities and the Cultural Politics of Exclusion in Colonial Southeast Asia'. *Comparative Studies in Society and History* 34(3), pp. 514–551.

Wee, L. (2002). 'When English is Not a Mother Tongue: Linguistic Ownership and the Eurasian Community in Singapore'. *Journal of Multilingual and Multicultural Development* 23(4), pp. 282–295.

Yuval-Davis, N. (1997). *Gender and Nation*. London: Sage Publications.

Part IV
India and Indonesia

11 Is the Anglo-Indian 'identity crisis' a myth?

Robyn Andrews

Introduction

Debashis Bandapydyoyay writes, in his publication on the works of Anglo-Indian author, Ruskin Bond:

> It is important for the reader to know, that on the eve of India's Independence, the identity crisis of Anglo-Indians turned into a nightmare as they were jettisoned by the British Government as flotsam of the Empire, and spurned by nationalist Indians for their English bearing and alleged truck with the colonists.
>
> (2011, p. 117)

The idea of Anglo-Indians experiencing an identity crisis, as reported rather melodramatically in this instance, is an increasingly common, yet unexamined claim. The taken-for-grantedness of this idea is the starting point for this chapter, which seeks to problematize the notion of identity crisis and address questions around Anglo-Indian identity in India.

The chapter begins by briefly defining the concept of identity: both ethnic identity and identity formation for 'mixed race' groups.[1] This sets the scene to discuss what it might mean for such an identity to be in crisis. It then looks at the Anglo-Indian situation by first discussing Anglo-Indian origins and cultural characteristics, then arguing that although they have mixed descent origins, they may be considered a distinct ethnic group with an enduring identity. If this is the case, where do ideas of an identity crisis come from, and are they well-founded? Anglo-Indian identity issues are complex and heterogeneous, making this a challenging topic to explore, but the idea of an identity crisis is overdue for examination.

Before discussing the identity context, I take a few lines to outline my position vis-à-vis the community. I am a New Zealand anthropologist with a long standing and continuous research interest in the community, drawing from data and experiences from a range of projects including an ethnographically researched PhD (2005), *Being Anglo-Indian: Practices and Stories from Calcutta*, a collection of India-resident life stories and essays (see 2014), research with Anglo-Indians in 'small towns' of India, a project looking at the place of religion in Anglo-Indian lives, as well as a project on Anglo-Indian ageing in India and abroad. This body of work suggests that while Anglo-Indian identity is fluid, variable and changing, it is not in a state of crisis.

Identity

The study of ethnicity and ethnic groups has experienced paradigmatic shifts over time, with the pioneering work of social constructionist Frederik Barth (1969) on ethnic groups and ethnic boundaries representing a significant shift in the field. According to Barth (1969) an ethnic group is one in which the population:

1 is largely biologically self-perpetuating
2 shares fundamental cultural values, realized in overt unity in cultural forms
3 makes up a field of communication and interaction
4 has membership which identifies itself, and is identified by others, as constituting a category distinguishable from other categories of the same order.

Contemporary anthropology builds on these ideas, emphasizing that ethnic identity is fluid and dynamic, and is constantly moving and changing (Sökefeld, 1999). Identity is socially constructed, negotiated, defined and produced through interactions between members of a group (Nagel, 1994). According to Barth's theoretical emphasis on boundary formation and maintenance, members of other groups are also involved in determining membership of ethnic groups, at times through exclusionary practices.

Nagel (1994) writes about 'nested identities' indicating that a person may have many different identities, personal and social, depending on their context and situation. In the case of Anglo-Indians, their national identity is also a significant part of their nest of identities. National identity in its ideal and most simple form requires that ethnic boundaries do not cut across political boundaries (Gellner, 1983). However, this ideal is less and less likely anywhere in the contemporary globalizing context. In India, which has significant ethnic and communal diversity, a singular national identity is unrealistic. Importantly then, according to political scientist, Subrata Mitra, the main articles of the Indian Constitution 'abjured racial purity in favour of birth and residence on the soil of India' (Mitra, 2010, p. 46) with the Constitution recognizing as Indian citizens, those who are born in India.[2] The 5th Article of the Constitution states that:

5 At the commencement of this Constitution, every person who has his domicile in the territory of India and –

    a who was born in the territory of India; or
    b either of whose parents was born in the territory of India; or
    c who has been ordinarily resident in the territory of India for not less than five years immediately preceding such commencement, shall be a citizen of India.

Anglo-Indians in India meet the criteria of citizens of India, but do Anglo-Indians *feel* 'Indian' (even bearing in mind the multiplicity of what such a term means)? And do non-Anglo-Indians recognize them as 'Indian'?

Turning now to the idea of identity crisis: Erik Erikson, who introduced the concept, wrote of an individual or group identity crisis stating:

> Identity formation normatively has its negative side which throughout life can remain an unruly part of the total identity. The negative identity is the sum of all those identifications and identity fragments which the individual had to submerge in himself as undesirable or irreconcilable or by which atypical individuals and marked minorities are made to feel 'different'. In the event of aggravated crises, an individual (or, indeed, a group) may despair of the ability to contain these negative elements in a positive identity.
>
> (Erikson, 1970, p. 733)

In his work Erikson refers to groups, not just individuals, and draws from anthropological observations, rather than only from his clinically based data. In the quote above he asserts that despair about containing negative elements is a characteristic of an identity in crisis, whereas a positive identity would preclude such a crisis. He also talks about versions of identity crises. For example, in writing about native Americans, he states:

> A different version of such a crisis could be seen in the American Indians, whose expensive 're-education' only made them fatalistically aware of the fact that they were denied both the right to remain themselves or to join America.
>
> (Erikson, 1970, pp. 748–749)

This was written at a particular period of history when the prevailing view was that assimilation into the mainstream majority was the desirable outcome for minority groups.[3] This is now rarely an overt aim, but this 'different version' of an identity crisis may have resonance with the Anglo-Indian situation in terms of how they felt about being encouraged to 'be Indian' especially at the time of Independence. Native Americans, perhaps in a similar manner to Anglo-Indians, may themselves not have aspired to be thought of as anything other than what they were, in this case, the indigenous peoples of a particular geographical location. Is this a situation of members of the majority population imposing their acculturation ideals on members of a minority group, inferring an identity crisis that is not felt by members of the minority group if full acculturation is not achieved? Over the last four decades, social groups such as the native peoples of America have had a strong agenda of reclaiming and strengthening their identities. While this may have been in the face of a prognosis of decline and demise as an ethnic group (a fear shared by other indigenous groups, such as New Zealand Maori), the anxiety was tied to their socio-cultural longevity, rather than not knowing who they are. The idea of their identities being in crisis is therefore not convincing, rather it is a sense of crisis about their on-going existence, which is now being addressed.

Others offer psychological interpretations of Erikson's concept to imply that 'an identity is in crisis if an individual exhibits or expresses indeterminacy' (Lahiri, 2000, p. xiii).[4] This idea has been a familiar trope in mixed-race literature (and other mixed-identity situations, such as indeterminate or multi sexual and/or gender identity) with mixed-race individuals understood to have to choose their identity from one or other of their heritages. The next section reviews selected mixed-race literature, setting the scene to argue that Anglo-Indians are a particular type of 'mixed race', with a strong and enduring identity, for all it may not be homogenous.

Rockquemore *et al*. (2009) in the opening sentence of their article state: 'In the United States, the debate over how individuals with parents of different races (i.e. mixed-race people) would be racially categorized …' makes clear their understanding of what or who a mixed race person is. They are *individuals* with mixed parentage. Mixed race scholar, Gilbert (2005), when writing of this 'group' identify them as being 'from dual ethnic or racial groups' (2005, p. 58) but also makes it clear that he is looking at individuals and their experiences of being mixed race. The authors of both articles are at pains to move away from theories depicting the mixed race experiences as being entirely negative.

The strength of Rockquemore *et al*.'s (2009) article is the theoretical identity framework they propose which offers a nuanced range of ways identity (which they differentiate from identification) may be claimed. They propose the following theoretical approaches to identity: the problem, the equivalent, the variant approach, and the ecological approach. The problem approach sees the individual as being 'in a problematic social position that is inevitably marked by tragedy' (2009, p. 16). This approach emerged at a particular historical juncture based on a 'racist and eugenic epistemology' (2009, p. 16) in which the 'focus on deficits, dilemmas, and negative experiences' due to being mixed race was prevalent (2009, p. 16). Identity work required an individual to adjust and assimilate to one of their parent's identities, usually to the dominant group. Such individuals were understood to be 'doomed to a permanent state of crisis' (2009, p. 16) due to not being able to achieve this. This theoretical approach sees mixed identity in terms of a binary, which appears to be the way in which Anglo-Indians are viewed by those who assert they are in crisis.

The equivalent approach drew on Erickson's ego development model and saw, in the United States' situation, both phenotypically based, and 'one-drop' understandings of identity, which resulted in mixed race people being identified as, and treated as, equivalent to 'black'. The authors make the point that this approach also reflects a particular historical moment in the United States (2009, pp. 17–18).

The variant approach which emerged in the 1980s and 90s, shifted the focus from the problematics of the experience of mixedness, to viewing people of mixed parentage as potentially having an identity distinct from either of the parent groups, that of bi- or multi-racial identity. In addition, mixed-race was seen as a group in and of itself – for analytical purposes at least. It comprised people who potentially still faced challenges, yet those would be 'located in the process of developing a multiracial identity, not essential to the multiracial location itself' (2009, p. 18). This and the next approach are particularly opposed to the idea that identity must be based on parental identity, and that it must be problematic.

The ecological approach, the most recent approach, allows for the most variation in identity outcomes, seeing identity as being determined by context, including that of time and stage of life, and socio-political setting. It allows for single, bi, multi-'racial' positioning, or the rejection of identity categorization altogether (2009, p. 19).

Gilbert's (2005) discussion of identity also critiques early eugenics-based models which focus on the mostly negative experiences of people of 'mixed race' which draw on a 'deficit-model' (2005, p. 60). He tenders his surprise that such a model has endured, and is concerned about the social, educational and psychological impacts of this (2005, p. 60). He seeks and offers more nuanced accounts, some of which fit into or overlap those discussed above. Drawing on empirical material he addresses 'the question of belonging' (2005, pp. 67–68) at an individual level. This issue is of concern to Anglo-Indians too, but at the group level.

As will be seen, while the identity experiences of the earliest Anglo-Indians may fit Rockquemore, Brunsma and Delgado's (2009) earlier models of individual identity formation above, for some centuries they have been regarded as a distinct social group in the Indian context. Aspects of the 'problem' and 'equivalent' approach models are drawn on by people who describe Anglo-Indians as being in crisis vis-à-vis their identity, but this is not only erroneous, but simplistic and outdated – both in terms of contemporary ways of thinking about and understanding mixed race, and about this group who mostly are not the progeny of 'racially' distinct parents.

Singapore's Eurasians can provide an interesting comparison to Anglo-Indians. Alexius Pereira, a member of the 'group', who he defines as descendants of Europeans and Asians (1997, p. 7), describes the 'instrumental' revitalisation of their ethnicity. He explains that their revitalization and claim to a distinct ethnicity was a deliberate exercise carried out in order to gain social, economic and political benefits in the face of increasing marginalisation in Singapore's multi-ethnic social space. He claims that their 'shared ethnicity' did not arise from an existing sense of themselves as a community but rather their 'new identity is being constituted from various cultural aspects, some of which were not even practised in Singapore in the past' (1997, p. 21). The effect was that through essentializing their ethnic identity, 'Eurasian' became another bounded ethnic group in Singapore.

Looking at other mixed-descent groups, he also makes the point that Anglo-Indians have a history of identifying as a distinct group:

Anglo-Indian Eurasians in India in the 18th and 19th centuries were heavily discriminated against both by the British and the Indians because their hybridity was perceived to be a 'moral flaw' or 'dilution of the strong blood' (Gist and Wright, 1973) by both the parent groups. As a result, the Anglo-Indians were forced to become self-reliant, and eventually formed a tight-knit social group of their own.

(Pereira, 1997, p. 9)

The sense of identity crisis which seems closest to how it is used in reference to Anglo-Indians in India is that of being indeterminate about their identity. As the identity crisis refers to the social group of Anglo-Indians, rather than to individuals, the inference is that it is the group that is not firm or clear about their collective identity. That is the central idea that this chapter will explore and challenge.

To be able to assess whether Anglo-Indians are experiencing an identity crisis the chapter begins by describing their origins and cultural characteristics. It then looks at some of the challenges they face as a tiny minority, with origins in colonialism, within the population-dense milieu of Hinduism. It also considers an emic concern: whether it is necessary for a group to have a homeland. Does the urge to have a homeland demonstrate that Anglo-Indians recognize each other as a distinct minority ethnic community? Based on research within the community, the chapter shows that while there may have been obstacles and challenges for the community in India, Anglo-Indians are quite assured about who they are and how they are different from the majority population groups.

Origins: from colonized to globalized

Anglo-Indians are a product of colonization. It is through Western expansion of trade and rule from the very late fifteenth century that Europeans arrived in India: first the Portuguese, then the French. But it was the British who had the most significant and enduring impact until the middle of the twentieth century. Trade and colonialism were almost exclusively masculine endeavours and in the case of the British in India, tens of thousands of single males found themselves in India for years at a time, during which time many formed alliances with and married local women (Hawes, 1993, 1996). It is from these relationships that the first Anglo-Indians were produced.

In the earliest days of their existence these offspring, particularly those of British men (as opposed to Portuguese or other European men) and Indian women, were most often treated as if they were British. However, after some time, in response to eugenics, and racism combined with anti-miscegenation sentiments, the British began to distance themselves from Anglo-Indians (Pereira, 1997, p. 9). One result of this is that Anglo-Indians came to form a socio-culturally distinct community. Arguably, another factor in the formation of a discrete community was their exclusion from the caste-conscious Hindu society, which valued purity and regarded mixed-descent as a form of impurity or pollution.

Anglo-Indian 'identity crisis': a myth?

As both Christopher Hawes (1993, 1996) and Megan Mills (1998), amongst others, have documented, the British varied in their treatment of and attitude towards Anglo-Indians at different times, barring them from some positions but generally giving them preferential employment in subordinate roles in maintaining the infrastructure of British India. They worked in the railways, post and telegraph, customs, nursing and teaching, and in the armed forces. It is a point of pride for many (particularly older) Anglo-Indians that they have a history of unfailing support for the British in any altercation they entered into. In the first War of Independence (also known as 'the Mutiny'), for example, Anglo-Indians fought alongside the British, rather than Indian groups (Hawes, 1996).

Given Anglo-Indians' background of attachment to Britain it is understandable that Indian Independence in 1947 posed a potentially serious threat to them: Anglo-Indians were fearful of reprisals once India gained independence. These did not, in fact, eventuate; rather they were able to claim a number of benefits which were written into the Constitution of the newly elected government. The benefits included representation in State Legislative Assemblies where their population warranted it (Article 333), provision of two seats in the Lok Sabha – also known as The House of the People (Article 331), employment reservations (referred to by Anglo-Indians as 'quotas') in the railway, customs, postal and telegraph services (Article 336) and an allocation of grants for Anglo-Indian schools (Article 337) on the condition that the schools accept at least 40 per cent of non-Anglo-Indian students. These benefits, with the exception of State and National representation, were set up with a formula for their gradual disbandment. Even so, in 2016 schools still continue to be protected by a 'dearness allowance' scheme which subsidizes teachers' salaries, and other grants which enable Anglo-Indian students' preferential access to the schools. While other benefits have now gone, Anglo-Indians still have political representation at the national level and at state level in a number of states.

Even though there were benefits, rather than reprisals, with the first post-Independence Congress-led government, this did not ameliorate Anglo-Indians' sense of insecurity about their future in India. As the British left India, Anglo-Indians began to do the same, resulting in three major waves of migration (Blunt, 2005; Caplan, 2001; Mahar, 1962). Immediately after 1947, tens of thousands left for England, which they had always considered as some sort of a homeland (Blunt, 2002; Stark, 1926). The second major migratory wave was in the early 1960s coinciding with a move in India to replace English as the national language. The prospect of Hindi replacing English as the national language was a concern to Anglo-Indians as most did not speak Hindi well enough for employment and other purposes. Another reason for the migration at this time can be attributed to the closure of large international companies in the main centres where many Anglo-Indians had employment.[5] The third wave, from the 1970s and continuing, is described as the 'family reunion' wave (President of the All India Anglo-Indian Association (AIAIA), personal communication, February 2002) and is referred to in migration literature as 'family reunification'[6] (Massey et al., 1998, p. 161; Moch, 2005, pp. 98–99). There are now believed to be more Anglo-Indians living outside of India than within.

In terms of nomenclature, Anglo-Indians were initially known as Eurasians, with other terms, such as, 'half-caste', also used occasionally (Blunt, 2005; Caplan, 2001).[7] It was not until 1911 when the first census was conducted in India that the name Anglo-Indian became widely accepted and associated with the modern definition. In 1935, the current definition was adopted into the Government of India Act, and it became embedded in the Indian Constitution post-Independence.[8] Some scholars, particularly post-colonial, refer to them as a 'hybrid' community. Their hyphenated name suggests this, but they can equally be seen as distinctive in and of themselves rather than being a 'mixed race and culturally composite community' (Caplan, 2001, p. 1).[9] Before exploring this idea further, the next section discusses what it means, socially and culturally, to be Anglo-Indian in India.[10]

Anglo-Indian cultural characteristics

At the risk of simplifying and homogenizing a huge diversity of ways of being Anglo-Indian, I suggest a set of 'typical' cultural characteristics can be distilled. This may seem incongruous when I clearly value the richness and diversity provided by individual stories in research,[11] but it can serve a useful purpose, as a way to draw a rough sketch of the community by highlighting the ways they are differentiated from other Indian communities. The usual list (found in scholarly works such as Blunt, 2005; Caplan, 2001) of key characteristics differentiating Anglo-Indians from other communities in India are mostly associated with their practices: having English as their mother tongue (the AIAIA argues that this characteristic is crucial to their identification as Anglo-Indians), acknowledging their historical link to Europe, and being Christians. They frequently dress in Western clothing, especially in all Anglo-Indian company, enjoy their own unique cuisine, including vindaloo, ball curry, country captain, and employ Western eating practices such as using cutlery, and usually have European names.[12] In terms of appearance, Anglo-Indians range from being 'fair'[13] to swarthy. Some have 'coloured' (blue or green) eyes but most have brown. Some have what was described by Anglo-Indians as the 'pulled' eyes of north-eastern 'tribal' Indians. This phenotyping is not what provides their identity; rather it is adherence to the constitutional definition, for all its inherent gender bias.

Anglo-Indians themselves are quick to provide a list of their general characteristics, and to dispute others' portrayals of their characteristics. I was made aware of the latter aspect soon after the movie *Bow Barracks Forever* (Dutt, 2007) was released. This film was 'based on a true story', with that 'story' being about the proposal to demolish the former American army barracks in central Calcutta which became home to many Anglo-Indian families after the Americans left after World War II. There are still Anglo-Indians living there, with demolition of the buildings an ongoing possibility. The characters in the movie, mostly Anglo-Indians, are fictional, and generally negatively stereotyped.

Just after the movie was released, I was in Calcutta on a fieldwork trip and I managed to buy a copy to view. A few days later I attended an Anglo-Indian house party and took the opportunity to ask what other guests had thought of it. I was told in no uncertain terms that Anglo-Indians had been misrepresented by the movie, that 'even Bow Barracks Anglo-Indians' were not as bad as the director, Anjun Dutt, had portrayed. They were openly angry saying that Dutt has no idea about how Anglo-Indians live, and that his was a negative and quite inaccurate depiction.[14] His portrayal seems to draw on a 'deficit model' (Gilbert, 2005) focusing on negative characteristics purportedly attributable to mixed descent. They commented that the fighting, the womanizing, the 'wasters' who had been deserted by emigrating family, and who themselves longed to be in another land, were not Anglo-Indians as they knew them. They were particularly offended by the character of 'Aunty Lobo' as an Anglo-Indian woman selling homemade alcohol, saying that they don't even brew alcohol there. A little later in the evening my host told me that his guests were quintessential Anglo-Indians; that they get on with and look after each other, and have a good time together. I was told that *this* very convivial party was typical of Anglo-Indians, and was reminded by one of them, again, that they, not the Anglo-Indians in the film, were real Anglo-Indians.

The negative portrayal in India is something Anglo-Indians are aware of, and not surprisingly, are sensitive about. Their practices are quite different in many ways from most other Indian groups, particularly in their Western worldview and the way they socialize with those who are not of the same gender, or family.[15] Other groups in India are disparaging about these attributes of the community, judging them negatively in comparison with their own worldviews and practices.[16] Perhaps this 'othering' of Anglo-Indians as a particular social group results in a more coherent ethnic identity.

Ethnic identity

Given the history of Anglo-Indians and their shared socio-cultural characteristics, this section argues that Anglo-Indians are a particular type of 'mixed race' with a distinct and enduring identity, as opposed to an identity crisis. Laura Bear (2007), an historical anthropologist, has suggested that they are a railway 'caste', seeking to find a term that is meaningful to the majority of Hindus who frame groups by (usually symbolic) occupation, and in doing so, indicating that she also framed them as being distinct. Anjali Roy, in this volume, picks up this idea in her discussion of Anglo-Indians and explores it further drawing on occupations and recreation practices.

This section explores how the case of Anglo-Indians relates to Barth's ideas about ethnic groups and ethnic identity. First, ethnic groups are largely biologically self-perpetuating. Anglo-Indians have been generally endogamous until recently, so they *have* been biologically perpetuating. Up until the early 1960s Anglo-Indians very often lived together in colonies (for example, railway colonies) or in the same neighbourhoods. Now, with a reduced population of Anglo-Indians in India, combined with more social mixing in neighbourhoods, schools and universities, and in the workplace, there are more marriages outside of the community than was previously the case (Williams, 2002).

The second of Barth's criteria stipulates sharing fundamental cultural values. My research has involved spending time with members of the community from the hill stations in the north to railway towns through central India, to the Union Territory of Pondicherry, and the States of Kerala and Goa. Across this range of regions, Anglo-Indians appear to share fundamental cultural values as well as practices. These include being Christian, almost entirely English-speaking, with a Western world view, and socializing in particular ways which are distinguishable from other Indian communities' forms of socializing. While there are some points of difference between the groups in geographical locations, there is no question that they share significant characteristics.

Barth's third characteristic is that they need to make up a field of communication and interaction. Because the community is relatively small in India, Anglo-Indians often have links to each other, for example, shared family, friendships and school acquaintances.[17] It is not an uncommon occurrence in my research to meet people who have heard about me and my research beforehand, through these networks. Nationally, as well as internationally, the community is also linked through social media, community publications, and associations. Even when Anglo-Indians are not related or have people, schools, social media or membership of associations in common, Benedict Anderson's idea of an 'imagined community' seems to capture best how Anglo-Indians feel about their relationship to each other (Anderson, 1991), that is, that they feel connected even if they are not personally known to each other. The community's shared language and world view enables them to make up a field of communication and interaction, and importantly for Barth's theory which considers the effect of boundary maintenance, it differentiates it from others who do not.

Fourth, in terms of having a membership which identifies itself, and is identified by others, as distinguishable from others: they are identifiable both officially through the Constitutional definition of Anglo-Indians, and practically through cultural attributes which are recognized by both insiders and outsiders. In addition, as I have noted above, they form national associations, such as the AIAIA, with numerous local branches scattered throughout India, as well as other local but nationally recognized societies, clubs and organized groups.

Meeting Barth's criteria in the ways they do, Anglo-Indians can then be viewed as a distinct ethnic group. They are a community with a strong history and set of cultural practices that distinguish them from other groups. Counter to the idea of an identity crisis, despite all the changes since Indian independence, including large-scale Anglo-Indian migration to many parts of the world, their distinct identity has been retained.

While their identity is not 'in crisis', they do have concerns about belonging, specifically as part of the nation of India, in terms of inclusive citizenship: of belonging to the nation and identifying with the society. That this is seen as a common issue of community concern also confirms the strength of their identity as a community.

Concerns about belonging

India is a land of great diversity: it is home to different groups which generally have a link to a particular geographical location: the Bengalis (both Hindu and Muslim) to Bengal, Punjabis to the Punjab, for example. It is frequently pointed out that Anglo-Indians are the only people in India who have 'Indian' in their name, and, as is often added, are 'people of India', rather than of a particular region.

Lionel Caplan, who has carried out research with Anglo-Indians in Chennai, writes that post-Independence, Anglo-Indians face a paradox of belonging as they 'have for a considerable period constituted and recognized themselves as a separate collectivity with a distinctive character and agenda of their own' (Caplan, 2001, p. 106). Anglo-Indian politicians, such as Anthony and Gidney (the leaders of the AIAIA up to and around the time of Independence), have consistently been urging Anglo-Indians to stay, to consider themselves Indian, and make their home in India (Blunt, 2005, p. 59 and 124). They are, constitutionally, citizens of India but do Anglo-Indians *feel* they belong to the nation of 'India'?

One response to the question of whether Anglo-Indians feel they belong was demonstrated at a public discussion I witnessed in 2003 at a World Anglo-Indian day celebration in Calcutta. The theme for discussion was 'Tomorrow's People Speak Today'. The Anglo-Indian participants in the panel discussion included a high school student and three college students.[18] Two older Anglo-Indians, a social worker and an educationalist joined them.[19] The West Bengal MLA (Member of the Legislative Assembly) at the time facilitated the discussion on topics such as education, occupational opportunities, emigration, mixed marriages and contemporary Anglo-Indian lifestyles. He questioned the panellists about the ethnicity of their friends and, to the amusement of the good-natured audience, of their boyfriends and girlfriends. He asked them about their competence in a vernacular language. After they had unanimously agreed with him that knowledge of a vernacular was important they offered demonstrations, speaking in Hindi, Bengali or Nepali, with confident fluency. All but one of the student participants were dressed in traditional Indian clothing, reinforcing what emerged as one of the central themes of the morning's debate, that they were 'Indian'. One of the panellists, for example, ended his opening address with 'we are Indians, the Anglo-Indians'. As well as several of the young panellists articulating the desirability of integration of Anglo-Indians with 'the rest of India' (some going further, to say that Anglo-Indians were well along the road to integration), this sentiment was also evident in various forms of symbolism throughout the morning – for example, the opening celebration which involved the very Hindu lighting of oil wicks, and the reference to the discussion as an '*adda*' (a Bengali term for talking convivially amongst friends and associates).

The young panellists gave the impression that they were very much at home in India, except with one telling exception: the comment by one young woman that 'we don't have a country of our own' (which was quickly refuted by the chair who countered with 'all of India is our country'). The woman's comment seemed spontaneous; the others somewhat rehearsed, or scripted, in comparison.

A further example is this anecdote from my journal notes:

> On the morning of August the 2nd 2003, which is Anglo-Indian day, I asked a couple of young Anglo-Indian men (at the hostel I was living in) if they were going to the dance at the Rangers Club that night. Neither of them was but they knew about it. I asked if they were going to any other of the Anglo-Indian day events. One response was 'No but.... Oh, is that what the dance is for?' Why was the second of August chosen as Anglo-Indian day they wondered? One speculated that perhaps it was the date of Anglo-Indian independence. 'From what?' another asked, then ventured a reply: 'India? We'd love independence from India!'

This statement is revealing in terms of how these Anglo-Indians see themselves in relation to India – that they would prefer to be separated from it. This is behind the motivations of some in moves to establish their own space within India, for example, to form an Anglo-Indian homeland of McCluskiegung in Bihar (Blunt, 2003; Dutt, 1990), Woodfields near Bangalore (Blunt, 2003), and in the idea of settling in the Andaman Islands (Bear, 2007). At the Melbourne Reunion in 2003, this alleged opportunity was still being spoken about, with regret that it had not been achieved.

I have also come across alternative responses to the idea of belonging in India: for example, in this interview with an Anglo-Indian author who lives in a town in the north of India, he talks about his claim to be part of the soil of India, and what that means.

> In my case this little piece of land [on which his home is built], this is India to me. So how does it matter what I am, you know, what I call myself or what my ancestors were? These things are important; I'm not saying they are not.
>
> *But one can't say they're attached to 'India'?*
>
> That's right, well I talked about that in this book. You know, I said in there, any book that has the word India in its title is a fake because there is no such thing. You can't talk about it in an academic way.
>
> (December 2014 interview)

This interviewee makes the point that India is so vast and diverse geographically and politically that it does not make sense to refer to it as a homogenous unit. But that the part of India he lives on is home to him, and he is not alone in this view. As I found when carrying out research in the railway town of Asansol (see Andrews, forthcoming in 2017), other Anglo-Indians also indicated that owning a home gives them a sense of belonging, of being at home. It is a minority who do own their home though. For example, the results of a 2010/2011 survey carried out in West Bengal indicated that only 24 per cent lived in homes or apartments they owned, and in Calcutta that figure was at just 18 per cent (Andrews, 2015). So, while some Anglo-Indians may feel that they have a stake in the nation due to home ownership, that is, by owning a piece of land they symbolically own a piece of the nation, many more do not have this opportunity. For these Anglo-Indians, this may factor in their sense of still seeking to belong, or to migrate and belong somewhere else.

That they may not all feel 'at home' in the land of their citizenship does not take away from this identity. Rather, it is an indication of the strength of their identity that they would seek a convergence of their ethnic identity with a geographical locale by seeking a homeland within India.

Anglo-Indians represent something of an outlier or anomaly in that they fit none of Rockquemore *et al.*'s (2009) identity formation models, primarily due to the characteristics of their identity as a social group of long-standing, whose members identify and are identified by others as being socially and culturally distinct. Those who assert that Anglo-Indians have an identity crisis infer that they are indeterminate about who they are, as they seek to be something they are unable to be, that is, British. In Rockquemore *et al.*'s (2009) schema this would best be described through a 'problem' approach to understanding their 'mixed race' identity. This early model and attached ideas about the characteristics of people of 'mixed race' no doubt contributed to the Anglo-Indian experience of being negatively stereotyped.[20] Indian independence, which certainly caused anxiety for Anglo-Indians, may have added to the notion that they suffer an identity crisis, especially as so many initially migrated to Britain. So, while the genesis of the negative ideas about Anglo-Indians can be understood as a product of certain times and paradigms, it is hoped that the scholarship on mixed-race will bring about a more nuanced and accurate assessment of this 'mixed race' community.

Likewise, through an analysis of Anglo-Indians and their purported identity crisis, the scholarship regarding 'mixed race' groups is enriched, with further complications and extensions which may find resonance with the experience of other groups of mixed identity.

Conclusion

The identity of Anglo-Indians is complex and complicated, but on a day-to-day basis fails to indicate that they are in crisis about who they are individually or as a community. Due to their strong sense of being part of a distinct group that has existed for some centuries, many of the aspects usually associated with mixed communities are not relevant to them, such as being confused about their identity due to having to choose between one side or the other. Anglo-Indians do not, as some early scholars of 'mixed race' suggest, need to select from their heritages for their own identity: rather, they claim to be Anglo-Indian as a distinct ethnic identity. Those who write about an Anglo-Indian identity crisis, inferring that they are conflicted between being Indian or British, are operating out of a particular model of 'mixed race' identity that has been superseded by more complex and nuanced models. The binary of Indian versus British is not relevant in their everyday lives, and those who see their identity in this way have misunderstood their adherence to Western practices and characteristics. That they retain them does not mean they are aspiring to be something they are not, rather it is a sign that they are maintaining and augmenting their Anglo-Indianness in contemporary India.

Notes

1 I use inverted commas to indicate the highly contentious and contested nature of the term 'race' and the lack of foundation for claims based on biological essentialism.
2 Although Mitra uses the term 'race' rather than ethnicity, his argument is unaffected. In India, the term 'community' might also have been used to make the point that citizenship provides legitimate grounds for nationalism (that is, the feeling of being part of the nation).
3 American Vasundhara Mohan's publication (Mohan, 1987) focusing on Sri Lankan Muslims, also argues that an identity crisis can occur when the 'subordination of their separate identity' occurs through assimilation of a minority with the majority population, in this case the minority Sri Lankan Moors with Sri Lankan Tamils.
4 This is from her work on Anglicized Indians in Britain from 1880 to 1930, who are termed by her as Anglo-Indians.
5 This issue was highlighted to me by Anglo-Indians I interviewed (in Melbourne in 2007) about their reasons for coming to Australia, and is noted by Blunt (2005, p. 156).
6 The term 'chain migration' is also used to express the same idea.
7 Until 1911 the term Anglo-Indian was used to refer to Europeans who were domiciled in India, who after 1911 were called Domiciled Europeans.
8 The Indian Constitution states that:

> An Anglo-Indian means a person whose father or any of whose other male progenitors in the male line is or was of European descent but who is domiciled within the territory of India and is or was born within such territory of parents habitually resident therein and not established there for temporary purposes only.
> (Section 366 (2))

9 This situation is comparable with the Eurasians of Singapore, albeit with different foundations and claims to community.
10 Anglo-Indians' identities in the diaspora might be shaped differently again, due to the influences of different time and place contexts.
11 This preference is demonstrated in my work, *Christmas in Calcutta: Anglo-Indian Stories and Essays* (Andrews, 2014).
12 These characteristics may also be displayed by English-medium educated, middle class non-Anglo-Indians (with the exception of the names) but are characteristics of all Anglo-Indians, regardless of class and education.
13 To use their term which refers to skin tone, rather than hair colour – which is almost always dark.
14 I spoke to one of the real-life characters portrayed in Anjan Dutt's film. He said that Dutt had been hurt and saddened by the Anglo-Indian response to his film, claiming that Dutt had always had a 'soft corner' for Anglo-Indians and appreciated, envied, and perhaps even admired the fact they so obviously enjoyed life (personal communication, November 2007).
15 Interestingly, Parsis, another very small minority community in India, are also known for similar forms of sociability yet they are seen positively in India. I would conjecture

that it is a combination of two factors that contribute to that: they are known as being wealthy, and they are not 'mixed race'.
16 Ironically many Indians too have hankered after westernisation and Englishness, illustrated for example, by a number of their leaders being Oxbridge educated (See www.paveinternships.com/ten-distinguished-indian-personalities-studied-uk). So many students study in the West even now, so one can only wonder why the vitriol was reserved for Anglo-Indians who were accused of 'hankering for Englishness'.
17 The size of the community is unknown as it has not been enumerated in any type of census since 1951. Then, it was believed to be about 500,000, and while many have migrated the population has built up again (Anthony, 1969).
18 In India tertiary institutions are referred to as colleges.
19 In their introduction a distinction was made between them as 'people of today' and the students who were 'tomorrow's people'.
20 The film, *Bow Barracks Forever*, (2007) mentioned earlier is one example of an industry which portrays Anglo-Indians negatively, as do many examples of literature featuring Anglo-Indians. It is outside the scope of this chapter, however, to address this here.

Bibliography

Anderson, B. (1991). *Imagined Communities: Reflections on the Origin and Spread of Nationalism*. London: Verso.

Andrews, R. (2014). *Christmas in Calcutta: Anglo-Indian Stories and Essays*. New Delhi: Sage.

Andrews, R. A. (2015). 'Report on the 2010/2011 West Bengal Anglo-Indian Survey: "Anglo-Indians Count"'. *International Journal of Anglo-Indian Studies* 15(2), pp. 40–57.

Andrews, R. (Forthcoming in 2017). 'Asansol Anglo-Indians' Responses to a Changing India'. In Italo Pardo and Giuliana B. Prato (eds), *The Palgrave Handbook on Urban Ethnography*. London: Palgrave.

Anthony, F. (1969). *Britain's Betrayal in India*. Bombay: Allied Publishers.

Bandapydyoyay, D. (2011). *Locating the Anglo-Indian Self in Ruskin Bond: A Postcolonial Review*. Delhi: Anthem Press.

Barth, Fredrik. (1969). *Ethnic Groups and Ethnic Boundaries: The Social Organisation of Culture difference*. London: George Allen and Unwin.

Bear, L. (2007). *Lines of the Nation: Indian Railway Workers, Bureaucracy, and the Intimate Historical Self*. New York: Columbia University Press.

Blunt, A. (2002). '"Land of our Mothers": Home, Identity, and Nationality for Anglo-Indians in British India 1919–1947'. *History Workshop Journal* 54, pp. 49–72.

Blunt, A. (2003). 'Collective Memory and Productive Nostalgia: Anglo-Indian Homemaking at McCluskieganj'. *Environment and Planning D-Society and Space* 21(6), pp. 717–738.

Blunt, A. (2005). *Domicile and Diaspora: Anglo-Indian Women and the Spatial Politics of Home*. Oxford: Blackwell.

Caplan, L. (2001). *Children of Colonialism: Anglo-Indians in a Post-Colonial World*. Oxford: Berg.

Dutt, A. (2007). *Bow Barracks Forever*. Pritish Nandy Communications.

Dutt, K. L. (1990). *In Search of a Homeland: Anglo-Indians and McCluskiegunge*. Calcutta: Minerva.

Erikson, E. H. (1970). 'Notes on the Identity Crisis. The Making of Modern Science: Biographical Studies'. (Fall 1970) *Daedalus* 99(4), pp. 730–759.

Gellner, Ernest. (1983) *Nations and Nationalism*. Oxford: Blackwell Publishing Ltd.

Gilbert, D. (2005). 'Interrogating Mixed-Race: A Crisis of Ambiguity?' *Social Identities* 11(1), pp. 55–74.

Hawes, C. (1993). 'Eurasians in British India, 1773–1833: The Making of a Reluctant Community'. PhD thesis. University of London.

Hawes, C. (1996). *Poor Relations: The Making of a Eurasian Community in British India 1773–1833*. Surrey: Curzon Press.

Lahiri, S. (2000). *Indians in Britain: Anglo-Indian Encounters, Race and Identity 1880–1930*. London: Frank Cass.

Mahar, R. (1962). *These are the Anglo-Indians*. Calcutta: Sona Printers.

Massey, D. S., Arango, J., Hugo, G., Kouaouci, A., Pellegrino, A., and Taylor, J. E. (1998). *Worlds in Motion: Understanding International Migration at the End of the Millennium*. Oxford: Clarendon Press.

Mills, M. (1998). 'Ethnic Myth and Ethnic Survival: The Case of India's Anglo-Indian (Eurasian) Minority'. PhD thesis. York University.

Mitra, S. (2010). 'Citizenship in India: Some Preliminary Results of a National Survey'. *Economic and Political Weekly* 45(9), pp. 46–53.

Moch, L. (2005). 'Gender and Migration Research'. In Michael Bommes and Ewa T. Morawska (eds), *International Migration Research*. Hampshire: Ashgate, pp. 95–110.

Mohan, R. V. (1987). *Identity Crisis of Sri Lankan Muslims*. Delhi: Mittal Publications.

Nagel, J. (1994). 'Constructing Ethnicity: Creating and Recreating Ethnic Identity and Culture'. *Social Problems* 41(1), pp. 152–176, doi: 10.2307/3096847.

Pereira, Alexius. (1997) 'The Revitalization of Eurasian Identity in Singapore'. *Southeast Asian Journal of Social Science* 25(2), pp. 7–24.

Rockquemore, K. A., Brunsma, D. L., and Delgado, D. J. (2009). 'Racing to Theory or Retheorizing Race? Understanding the Struggle to Build a Multiracial Identity Theory'. *Journal of Social Issues* 65(1), pp. 13–34.

Sökefeld, M. (1999). 'Debating Self, Identity, and Culture in Anthropology'. *Current Anthropology* 40(4), pp. 417–448, doi: 10.1086/200042.

Stark, H. (1926). *Hostages in India: Or the Life Story of the Anglo-Indian Race*. Calcutta: Fine Arts Cottage Press.

Williams, B. R. (2002). *Anglo-Indians: Vanishing Remnants of a Bygone Era*. New Jersey: CTR Publishing.

12 Performing Britishness in a railway colony
Production of Anglo-Indians as a railway caste

Anjali Gera Roy

Introduction

Anglo-Indians are defined as persons born out of relationships between European men and indigenous women, in different waves of the Indian subcontinent's colonization dating back to the seventeenth and eighteenth centuries.[1] The colonial understanding of mixed race was framed within the eighteenth century discourse on miscegenation and racial degeneration theories, which posited that miscegenation could result in a mixed-race population that was mentally and physically weaker than 'the pure European race' (Hunt, 1863, p. 60).

Colonial anxieties about miscegenation were complemented in the Indian context by Indo-Aryan taboos against racial mixing and the denigration of mixed-race as unclean and inferior. Ancient Sanskrit texts, particularly the *Rig Veda*, which contain elaborate rules related to intermixing, interdining and intermarriage between Aryans and non-Aryans, as well as between castes, betray a deep-rooted Indo-Aryan suspicion of miscegenation. Colonial anxieties about preserving whiteness, notwithstanding pragmatic contingencies related to regulating white male sexuality through explicit or tacit encouragement of cohabitation or even intermarriage, were mirrored in the Hindu purity fetish and the *varna* theory, in which race was imbricated with colour and caste.[2] The overlap between these twin discourses of race, one pre-colonial and the other colonial, in the positioning and perception of mixed-race persons in India, has made mixed-race communities doubly stigmatized. Previously employed to refer to the British in India, since 1911 the term Anglo-Indian has been used to denote a:

> domiciled community of mixed descent, ... formerly known as Eurasian, country-born or half-caste, [which] forms one of the largest and oldest communities in the world, and continue to live in India as well as across a wider diaspora, particularly in Britain, Australia, New Zealand, Canada and the United States.
>
> (Blunt, 2005, p. 1)

Although eighteenth century colonial anxieties about mixed race originated in the biological discourse of miscegenation, whiteness and Europeanness was largely conceived as non-biological and performative in actual practice in the colonial Indian context. As Buettner points out, neither skin colour (or other biological markers) nor birthplace could serve to determine racial identities such as Europeanness and whiteness in late colonial India. Instead, they 'depended upon individuals displaying a combination of cultural, behavioural, occupational, and class markers deemed characteristic of a privileged racial identity, and which differed for men and women' (Buettner, 2000, p. 291). 'Europeans', were defined as including 'any person of European descent, pure or mixed, who retains European habits and modes of life' by successive government Codes of Regulations for European Schools (2000, p. 283). Buettner's view of whiteness, and Europeanness as performative rather than biological is complemented and supplemented by other studies on Anglo-Indians that foreground the significance of sports, music, dance, middle-class gentility and so on in the performance of Britishness (see Ward, 2004; Shope, 2004; Blunt, 2005; Mills, 2005; Bear, 2007; Mizutani, 2011).

This chapter aims to extend and complicate existing research on Anglo-Indians using data from 50 qualitative interviews conducted in the railway town of Kharagpur. It argues that while Anglo-Indians' aggressive retention of European habits, tastes and ways of life enabled them to stake claims to Britishness and disavow their Indian roots, their attempt to define themselves as a new railway caste propelled them into Hindu social hierarchies in which mixed races have been traditionally included in the fifth caste or in the category *avarna* ('classless').[3] It begins by showing that the performance of Britishness through sports, music and dancing, along with other forms of sociality, not only accorded Anglo-Indians honorary British citizenship during the colonial period, but also facilitated the production of a specifically Anglo-Indian subjectivity converging on the railway colony. It concludes that colony born or bred Anglo-Indians' self-fashioning as a new 'railway community' in relation to the Hindu category of caste paradoxically betrays their 'contamination' by Indian social hierarchies and forms of sociality that were stigmatized by the British.

Anglo-Indians, railways and the railway colony

Railways were primarily established in India in the mid-nineteenth century, first by the British East India Company, and subsequently by the colonial British government, to transport troops for wars and to export cotton to England. Recruitment to the Railways, until their Indianization in 1860, was largely from three groups of European ancestry,[4] who were assigned different positions in the highly hierarchized and racialized Railways structure. Unlike senior and mid-level positions that were usually assigned to Europeans and domiciled Europeans respectively, Anglo-Indians were largely placed in upper subordinate positions (Bear, 2007). From 1857, the Railways also built railway colonies with 'neat, ordered, enclaved housing and recreational complexes' in metros and in junctions on railway lines to produce railway towns that materially reproduced colonial hierarchies to 'convey symbolic meanings over and above their daily functions' (Kurd and Kerr, 2012, p. 104) and to 'inculcate a practical mastery of middle-class domesticity solely in their European employees' (Bear, 1994, p. 531). These railway colonies, between which Anglo-Indian families moved, were imagined as homes by Anglo-Indians who, unlike other Indian ethnic groups, could not trace their roots to a particular ancestral place or *des*.

Kharagpur, 125 km from Kolkata, was one such junction, built following the setting up of Bengal Nagpur Railways in 1888–1889, and serving as the headquarters of the South Eastern Railways, whose railway colony offers a textbook illustration of the colonial railway colony. While the majority of Europeans, domiciled Europeans and Anglo-Indians migrated overseas after the Independence of India in 1947, about 200 Anglo-Indian families, mostly former and some serving railway employees, continue to reside in Kharagpur. Of these, Anglo-Indians in service continue to live in railway quarters, while others have rented houses in the nearby Jhapatapur area and a considerable number have built houses in a semi-rural neighbourhood adjoining the railway lines, called Jhouli.

Interviews for this chapter were conducted with male and female Anglo-Indians between the ages of 45–87 in Kharagpur between July and December 2013 under the New Zealand India Research Institute project 'Anglo-Indians in Small Towns in India'. An attempt was made to balance the sample on the basis of age, gender, class and location. Participants came from three areas of Anglo-Indian settlement: the railway quarters, rented houses in Jhapatapur, and self-owned bungalow type houses in Jhouli. The majority of male Anglo-Indians were either employed in the railways in upper subordinate positions such as drivers, guards, foremen, and firemen, or superannuated after having served the railways in similar positions. The Anglo-Indian women interviewed were either formerly or currently working as schoolteachers in local missionary-run schools, or were homemakers. A third group consisted of younger Anglo-Indians, both male and female, who were enrolled in colleges.[5]

Peforming Britishness in the railway colony

In view of the emphasis on non-biological features in determining racial identity, both domiciled Europeans and Anglo-Indians aggressively embraced cultural, behavioural and class markers, such as certain forms of sport, music, dance, food and dress, in order to gain admission into elite British class circles. While the hyper-masculine culture inculcated in Anglo-Indians through physical training and participation in sport in boarding schools located in hill stations facilitated their contestation of racial degeneration theories and identification with British character and moral values (Ward, 2004; Mills, 2005), their exposure to certain forms of music, dance, dress and etiquette both in schools, homes and clubs equipped them to make cultural claims to Britishness. Narratives of Kharagpur Anglo-Indians reveal the extent to which the physical and moral qualities attached to the British were appropriated, through mastery of certain British sports, music and dance in the production of racialized, gendered, and even classed, subjectivities.

Sports and the production of British character and masculinity

Ward stresses the importance of sporting ability in those embarking on military, civilian or administrative responsibilities within British dominions and colonies and shows how these activities served not only as signifiers of physical fitness but also 'of personality, initiative and capacity for judgement and control of subordinates' (Ward, 2004, p. 74). More importantly, he maintains that 'sport also played a role in asserting Britishness throughout the Empire, and later, the Commonwealth' (Ward, 2004, p. 74). Drawing on British models of 'culture to define itself', sports thus became important as a means of visibly displaying 'British-like' behaviour for Anglo-Indians (Mills, 2005, p. 207). The mapping of Britishness onto sport and its suggestions of both strength of the body and of the mind is evident in the centrality of sport in Anglo-Indian existence in Kharagpur.

Athleticism appears to have been part of both Anglo-Indian male and female childhoods, and the prominence of sport in the railway colony illustrates one way through which Anglo-Indians affirmed their claims to Britishness.

> Now I'll tell you another thing, we had sports – hockey, football and boxing. And nowadays you see the children, they're all – the parents have no time for sports. But that time sports was – we had sports after school. We went to play hockey, football or we box – according to the season. So, lot of activities there.
>
> (Manuel Banks, 56)

Foregrounding the role played by British public schools in underlining the 'connection between sport, national character and imperial governance', Ward adds that this percolated 'to boys lower down the social spectrum' through popular culture (2004, p. 74). Even though Kharagpur Anglo-Indians were not being groomed to run the empire, but were, at best, to occupy upper subordinate positions, British officials encouraged sports in the firm belief that this would inculcate in them desired British 'virtues of team-playing, discipline and confidence' (Ward, 2004, p. 74).

> From the school days, you know, officers in those days. They were Englishmen. They would go to the games field and watch these children play and from that stand they started to eye certain children who were playing good hockey or good athletes and straight after school, they were given employment.
>
> (Olga Lamb, 87)

Several of the Anglo-Indians interviewed were state, or even national-level, hockey,[6] football or basketball champions and found employment in the Calcutta Port Trust (CPT), Calcutta Police or the Bengal Nagpur Railway on the strength of their excellence in sports.

Performing Britishness in a railway colony 199

Anglo-Indian recruits to the railways between 1956 and 1975 demonstrated skills, talents, and traits that defined the Anglo-Indian Railway fraternity, including sporting excellence, hands-on skills, a strong work ethic, discipline and personal integrity. Sports imbued them with the virtues of team-playing, discipline and confidence and they were held in high esteem by their peers and superiors for their punctuality, resourcefulness, and problem-solving skills. Anglo-Indians viewed themselves as running the Empire by taking on the responsibility for the smooth functioning of the railways: 'You see, because I worked, though we were not educated, we were eighth and ninth Standard boys but because we worked from the very bottom, we knew every part of the engine, knew our job well' (Robbie Cama, 74).

> Many drivers did some great things on the railways. They were daring drivers. They were so hardworking, some of the drivers, they made up time and they were very good at driving. Anglo drivers very good and competent. I don't remember their names. And they were loved whichever department an Anglo-Indian worked, he was loved but later on they lost that.
> (Manuel Bush, 70)

Although they occupied mid-level positions, they rightly viewed themselves as being entrusted with the efficiency and safety of the railways. Some of the drivers, guards and firemen discharged their duties even at the cost of their lives. Poignant stories were told of acts of commitment and heroism where such workers were burnt while trying to ensure that the system worked efficiently.

> ... what he'd done to save the lives of the passengers, he just destroyed vacuum. Destroyed vacuum means apply the brakes [to ensure a fire didn't spread]. When he got down, my father was wondering why the train stopped, ... and he (Johannes) just went running fully black up to my father. Guards used to wear, you know white uniforms, fully white uniforms. He just went running up to him and he put his hands on my father and said 'Ben, save me'. The way he was burnt, the skin from his palms went on his [Robbie Cama's father] coat.
> (Robbie Cama, 74)

Even though high positions in the administration were passed on to 'Indians' possessing formal qualifications, after Independence, the skills attributed to Anglo-Indians appear to have been recognized as indispensable even by the highest authorities in the Railways.

> Something which comes naturally to Anglo-Indians is a – you need little common sense. The Railways to work, you need common sense and a lot of what you call it? You have to foresee things.
> My job was safe working of a train. That was my job and I'm in charge of that train and they know – you go to him he'll tell you, 'You don't

> interfere with my work. You do your work, I'll do my work. No matter who the hell you are, you sent me to work this train. I am the boss of this train. You don't tell me what to do'.
>
> (Simon D'Silva, 56)

Thus, the physical culture of sport, with its emphasis of physical capability, prowess and team commitment, inculcated in Anglo-Indians refuted the theories of racial degeneration and produced a form of subjectivity that fortified their claims to Britishness and separated them from 'Indians'.

The culture of boxing among Kharagpur's Anglo-Indians, some of whom became acclaimed boxers at the national level, similarly essentializes the cult of masculinity through which they asserted their physical prowess. The boxing skills acquired by young Anglo-Indian men in British boarding and railway schools completely overturned the physical degeneration theory and strengthened the community's claims to Britishness.

> In Railway school, you had to box. You had to box. They put the gloves. They knew boxing…. In our school, boxing was a compulsory thing. We had three good boxers – Maxie Carr, Anto Marshall and Rozario. Anto Marshall – we called him the brown Bomber. He was known as India's best scientific boxer.
>
> (B. Bush, 70)

In addition to accentuating physical fitness, the culture of throwing physical challenges to settle scores practiced by Anglo-Indians expressed an aspiration to approximate the notion of British courage, fair play, openness and daredevilry that natives were believed to be lacking.

> The 'maar peet', the fights. Difference between an Anglo-Indian and a Bengali, I'm just comparing. The Anglo-Indian comes to the point and hits out and it's over. And the Bengali keeps arguing and arguing and it will never end.
>
> (B. Bush, 70)

Music, dance, manners and the production of British forms of sociality

While examining the production of middle-class British as 'civilizing agents' of the British in British India in the nineteenth century, Mizutani (2011) includes cultural refinement as the essence of middle-class British gentility, expressed through a dignified demeanour, as well as the production of certain forms of sociality maintained in the secluded spaces of the clubs:

> … islands of Britishness in the great Indian sea, to which the imperialists might withdraw whenever they felt a personal, social or ritual need: for a drink at the bar, for a stag dinner, for a dance, a horse show, a wedding reception or a game of bridge.
>
> (Morris, 2005, p. 57)

Excluded by the deliberate insularity of white clubs, domiciled Europeans and Anglo-Indians performed genteel British forms of sociality in their own clubs and in the Railway Institutes that formed the cultural hub of the Railway colonies. Apart from dance halls and clubs, the setting up of the railway institutes facilitated this performance, nurtured local talent, enabled musicians from all clubs to interact with one another and allowed for the staging of shows of musicians from overseas.[7]

The Bourdiesque notion of taste as a marker of class in certain fields, and as a determining factor in the establishment and maintenance of social hierarchy, is evident in the Anglo-Indian insistence on their refined tastes in music and dance. Deprived of political and economic power until 1834, Anglo-Indians used their cultural competence in the music and dance of the British elite to close the social gap to empower themselves, a process that was facilitated by the space of the dance halls that enabled the British, the American and Anglo-Indians to cross boundaries. Through embracing similar tastes in music and dance, Anglo-Indians aspired to cultural, if not political or economic, Britishness.

Tracing the emergence of ballroom and Western dance music in India in the first part of the twentieth century with the setting up of Railway Institutes and dance halls in the 1930s, Shope notes an appreciation for these styles of music particularly among Portuguese Goans and Anglo-Indians, and argues that 'for these two groups, it served to assert their identities as distinct from other South Asians and highlighted that their taste for music reached beyond the geographical boundaries of India' (2004, p. 167). For Kharagpur Anglo-Indians, as for those of Shope's Lucknow, music was a way of promoting respectability in the eyes of the British (Shope, 2004) and staking their claims to British musical tastes that helped them maintain their distinction from other South Asians.

> Anglo-Indians loved music and they lived in style.... Music was part of their life.... Music was there all day and the radio we used to get from Radio Ceylon – Lovely English Music. So, anyone's house you just, someone's blasting it but you had music. Music was their life.
>
> (B. Bush, 70)

Shope's analysis of issues of power relations maintained through the consumption of music in colonialism (2004, p. 167) is corroborated by the premium placed by Anglo-Indians on the possession of expensive electronic gadgets such as a gramophone or a radiogram, which served as signifiers of British middle class or elite Indian modernity.

> You walked into anyone's house – not good old days, my days, you'll find they had a record player. The gramophone which you had to wind it.... Those who could afford had a radiogram. No tape recorder. Later the radios came. You see, Panasonic – the big one, the first one which came. But previously we had radiograms, a record changer and some had gramophones.
>
> (B. Bush, 70)

The exceptional musical talent and highly popular professional bands emerging from Kharagpur foreground the relationship between the consumption and production of music and relations of power. Anglo-Indian residents nostalgically recall a number of popular bands such as that of Alex Saldanha, the Apaches, Louis Banks and others who performed largely rock and roll and country music, right up till the 1980s and 1990s.

In addition to professional bands, the presence of amateur musicians enriched the musical culture of the Anglo-Indians through their performances in private parties.

> I can't exactly remember the names of the bands but there were people who were very good musicians … all the famous singers and musicians at that time…. Whenever there's a show, if anybody called them if there was a christening party, if there was a birthday party, if there was a wedding, they would be called and they would play. But without money, those days … they never played for money, they played for music. These days musicians play for money.
>
> (Nina, 58)

This tradition of playing an instrument appears to have continued to the present.

> Bradley's the eldest. He's also a guitarist and a singer. Brett is a drummer actually, not interested in the music, guitars and he's a drummer. Third one is an all rounder. Calcutta even, he organizes shows, emcees shows and plays in the band, fourth one is also a singer.
>
> (Louisa Pinto, 70)

Dance was also an important marker of distinction. Anglo-Indians' loving reconstruction of the dances held at the South Institute in Kharagpur reflects the centrality of the performance of these dances in the performance of Britishness in which dress, table manners, dance and music played a significant role. While the Institute staged Britishness through screening English language films, indoor and outdoor games, British difference was articulated through particular forms of music and dance at balls, Christmas, and New Year dances, held at regular intervals throughout the year. Although the theme underpinning many interviews was the pleasure of dancing, the pride that Anglo-Indians take in their mastery of certain kinds of dance demonstrates the relationship between dance and the maintenance of social hierarchy. The dance floor served as a space where Anglo-Indians staked their claim to the cultural citizenship of a nation to which they were denied full and equal citizenship.

Central to the staging of particular forms of Britishness was the spacious dance hall of the railway institutes with their wooden boards that had springs beneath to facilitate dancing.

> They used to have spring boards I believe…. To make you jump a little more. Makes you feel more springy, more dancing. It used to serve the

purpose. It was all wood and along with that you used to have the Railway hospital. Plenty of Anglo-Indian nurses and they used to run a nurse's ball. That used to be in the month of September. So that was organized by the nurses.

(Robbie Cama, 74)

Railway institutes

Several scholars have commented on the importance of the racialized space of the railway institutes in performing British forms of sociality including dance, music, card games and drinking, from which Indians were completely excluded (see Shope, 2004; Mizutani, 2011; Roy, 2012). These institutes were open to British and Americans, just as some of the British clubs permitted Anglo-Indians opportunities to interact with the British on the strength of their mastery of Western music, dance, dress, table manners and etiquette. Anglo-Indians' performance of refined British manners and tastes, to assert their claims to Britishness and middle class British norms of gentility (often with the encouragement of the colonial authorities), accentuates the strong relationship between sartorial, cultural and culinary preferences and identity construction.

The convergence of British, Americans, and particularly Anglo-Indians, on the railway institutes in the performance of different forms of Britishness inscribes the Institute as an enduring metaphor for carefully preserved Britishness in the colonies. Nostalgic reconstructions of these leisure pursuits at the South Institute in Kharagpur foreground Anglo-Indian performances of middle-class Britishness.

> The Institute, the beautiful institute.... The South Institute. It was maintained till about 1975–76. After that whatever little Anglo-Indians left they migrated.
>
> (Lenny, 64)

> There were two institutes – one is the South Institute and one is the North Institute. Now in the South Institute, we had a bar where two brigades came and a big dancing hall. But we used to have pictures three times in a week – Tuesday, Thursday and Saturday. And once in a month, we used to have whist drives.
>
> (B. Bush, 70)

> Every day they had the bandstand out in the institute and the Band would play once a week. Local railway band.... A brass band with the trombone and they would play on the bandstand.
>
> (Olga Lamb, 87)

Mixed race as caste

While tracing the formation of the Anglo-Indians as a railway caste and its present predicament, Bear shows that domiciled Europeans and Eurasians were recruited in upper subordinate positions from the first operations of the railways in India. She asserts that the railways remained 'the only arena of the colonial state that continued to give preferential recruitment to domiciled Europeans and Eurasians to upper subordinate positions' despite the implementation of the official policy on Indianization as part of the effort to reduce expenditure on expensive and European and Eurasian labour (Bear, 2007, p. 9). This was confirmed by the residents of Kharagpur:

> But during my father's day, even during my time, most Anglo-Indians were in the Railways.... All types – foremen, maintenance, workshops, locomotives, carriages, bogies – we had for Anglo-Indians.
>
> (B. Bush, 70)

In her examination of the petitions made by railway workers to seek equal rights, Bear notices the fusing of *jati*[8] moralities with pseudo-scientific colonial 'biomoral hierarchies' that not only produced new forms of social distinction but also extended the idea of *jati* to the employment hierarchies of the railways.

The production of the Railways as a signifier of modernization and development by both the colonial and nationalist state was undermined by this line of reasoning, which appears to be predicated on the aptitude of certain groups for certain professions as posited in the traditional Indian caste system. Narratives of Anglo-Indians employed in the railways offer illuminating case studies of the way the hereditary system of 'father to son' functioned in Kharagpur.

> After independence all the drivers, there was a certain rule – father to son rule. As soon as the father finished, the son would be given the job. The son would be given the job but slowly they did away with that rule, father to son rule.
>
> (Ritter, 79)

The majority of Kharagpur Anglo-Indians found employment in the Railways due to their father or uncle having a connection with the Railways, even if they might not have been placed in the same position: 'My brother joined just because of that rule. If a person completed so many years of service, the son can be taken on' (Manuel Banks, 56). In their petition to the Simon Commission in 1928,[9] the Anglo-Indian Association, allying with other subaltern groups, argued for 'the protection and reservation of upper subordinate positions for Anglo-Indians in the railways, customs, post, and telegraphs, and constitutional safeguards for fifty years', which would provide the community temporary economic protection while enabling it to attain the level of educational qualifications achieved by other Indian communities (Bear, 2007, p. 10). At Independence, the Constitution of India granted Anglo-Indians reservations in the public services, such as the railways, post, and telegraphs, and the right to separate educational institutions for a period of ten years from 1950, and they were placed under the administrative authority of the commissioner of scheduled castes and tribes. The benefits of the quota system that guaranteed employment without the benefit of a formal qualification was the prime reason for the high school drop-out rate of Anglo-Indian males who did not see a reason to finish their education or go to college.

> 'Go to the local foreman tomorrow'. That easy it was to get a job. Today my girl, stand in the queue, put in your application, you may get a call. You may not get a call. Then there's a back door to get a call.
>
> (Radice, 80)

The majority ignored their parents' advice to:

> '... go to school. Work – you can always get a good job but go to school'.
> No, we totally refused because we were promised that we'll be appointed and made permanent. Every one of us. 17 of us Anglo-Indian boys never went to school. Above 15–16 years of age we all started working. Within three years we were all promoted.
>
> (Robbie Cama, 74)

This informal system of recruitment continued well into the 1980s in a modified fashion:

> Generally, our Anglo-Indians would go up to Class XII – intermediate we had that time. Then they would look for jobs. That time things were easy up to 80. Seventy or 80. After [that] our people started moving abroad, moving away from here. It's not different but it changed, the situation changed.
>
> (Manuel Banks, 56)

After the end of the ten-year period granted to Anglo-Indians by the Constitution to increase their qualifications to match other groups, sporting excellence was often employed as a criterion for recruiting Anglo-Indians, who might otherwise have fallen short of other eligibility criteria such as finishing high school or a college degree, as late as the late 1970s.

> Mr. Brown said, 'Keep the boy as goalkeeper and if he plays well, then he'll get the job. Anyway, I'll go to the football field and see his performance'.
> My mother said, 'And if he's not playing well, you don't have to give him the job. It's up to you what you feel'.
>
> (Mannie Longman, 54)

However, with the possession of the requisite academic qualifications becoming rigorously enforced for recruitment to the railways, Anglo-Indians' sporting talent ceased to guarantee railway jobs by the 1980s.

> I was a footballer in KGP. The whole lot of people in KGP who are working in the DRM [Divisional Railway Manager] Office thinks I am working in the Railway. I have been playing for the South-Eastern Railway. I played for the [unintelligible], I played for workshops, I played [unintelligible]. All promised me jobs but it didn't work out. I was thrown aside.
>
> (Mannie Longman, 54)

Many Anglo-Indians were either unemployed or forced to seek alternative careers: 'Yes, now of course most Anglo-Indians are changed but one main drawback – unemployment. All working privately. Very few are working in the Railways' (B. Bush, 74). The closure of preferential railway recruitment thus directly impacted the Anglo-Indian exodus overseas or to larger cities in India.

> Many of our Anglo-Indians have after that slowly, slowly they've started migrating abroad to London, America, mostly Australia, Canada, Britain. Slowly, slowly the population of Anglo-Indians, as they're migrating, many of the people have gone away abroad, left this small place to go to cities, bigger places for jobs, for studies.
>
> (Manuel Banks, 56)

The respondents voiced strong objections about the withdrawal of the quota system, and demanded a quota system for Anglo-Indians as a minority, along the lines of reservations for Scheduled Castes, Scheduled Tribes and some minorities in state-owned educational institutions and workplaces.[10] The reservations for Scheduled castes and Scheduled tribes was a belated gesture made by the independent Indian state to redress the centuries-old oppression of the lowest caste of *shudras* and the outcaste untouchables. Thus, Anglo-Indians' expectation to be accorded the same concessions ironically appears to have been predicated on the traditional Hindu practice of caste, in opposition to which European modernity has defined itself.

> We are considered minority but then no facilities, specialities or special cases – nothing of that sort. If you have to qualify and go for any exams, it is all General category, general basis. Qualify and if you qualify for it and you are academically well, then you get the post. There is no thing you are an Anglo-Indian, you secure any extra points there, nothing like that.
>
> (Louisa Pinto, 70)

The arguments made by certain Anglo-Indians about being deprived of opportunities as a consequence of the removal of the quota system that guaranteed employment in the railways also violates the defining principle of equal opportunity on which modern secular Indian democracy has been founded. It makes a case for Anglo-Indians by invoking the practice of caste hierarchy not only in public, but also in the domestic sphere: 'I thought that when I met an Anglo-Indian boy working in the Railway, I had a very nice little dream that I had met my own caste. My father wanted me to marry an Anglo-Indian' (Aurora, 60). Bear comments on the building of railway colonies by the British to inculcate middle-class domesticity in European employees, which served as key sites for the construction and contestation of European identity (1994, p. 531). However, the European idea of the nuclear family and the space of the couple is complicated in the context of Anglo-Indian families, with their co-option of the Indian structure of the joint family with similar kinship loyalties and support systems in their nuclear units. In recalling her early life in Kharagpur, Aurora explained how her husband's income supported the extended family:

> You know when you work on the Railway and you have a family to look after – especially my father-in-law had a big family: five sons and five daughters. And only two people working. My husband and the second number two.
>
> (Aurora, 60)

Although most Anglo-Indians were sent to boarding schools to complete their education and spent their formative years away from home, family bonds were strong between parents and children and between siblings. The support system that Anglo-Indians in the railway colony enjoyed through the extended families of parents and in-laws after marriage has a strong resonance with the practices of traditional Indian joint families, rather than with those of the European family. As in other Indian families, the elderly and the disabled are tended by family members despite their small incomes.

The practice of father to son recruitment in the railways and the incorporation of Indian family support networks produced a unique railway culture and subjectivity among Anglo-Indians. It is this railway culture that motivated several of the Anglo-Indians to retire in Kharagpur despite having the option of migrating overseas or to metro cities within India:

> We both feel and KGP people they feel, they feel. In KGP, even if they go anywhere abroad, because most of Daddy's friends who are abroad, they've come back and settled here. So that feeling is there. We're Kharagpuris. That feeling is there.
>
> (B. Bush, 70)

> An Anglo-Indian is always an Anglo-Indian – live up to that standard right up to his end.
>
> (Vinny Tally, 60)

Conclusion

Through examining the narratives of Anglo-Indians, this chapter looked at mixed race in the Indian context, in the railway town of Kharagpur. Defining Britishness in British India to be cultural rather than biological, it began by exploring the production of Britishness by Anglo-Indians through the performance of British sports, music, dance and forms of sociality. It followed by exploring the production of a unique Anglo-Indian subjectivity centred on sports, music, dance and manners. It found that these self-identifications made Anglo-Indians paradoxically reproduce the ancient Indian category of caste, stigmatized by the British.

Mixed race was considered as physically and morally inferior to 'pure' races in both European and Indo-Aryan miscegenation theories. However, racial categories such as whiteness and Britishness were not predicated on biological differences in the colonial context, but constructed in relation to cultural, behavioural, occupational or class markers characteristic of a privileged elite. Anglo-Indians' appropriation of British notions of masculinity centred on physical culture, work ethic and leisure pursuits, and reflected an earnest desire to disprove miscegenation theories and make claims to Britishness through exhibiting evidence of both physical fitness and moral integrity. Similarly, the appreciation and performance of British and American music and dance, facilitated through the training provided to Anglo-Indian children in convent schools, generous allowances provided by the railways to maintain middle class norms of gentility and the setting up of ballrooms, dance halls and railway institutes, enabled them to assume aesthetic and cultural parity with the British. Through emulating the leisure pursuits and tastes of the British and Americans, Anglo-Indians aspired to a British or European status denied to them by descent.

Although railways were produced as a signifier of progressive techno-modernity by the British imperial state, Anglo-Indians' self-identification as a railway community along the lines of Hindu caste divisions betrays a return to tradition and to the Hindu social hierarchies disdained by the British. In addition, their indignation at the withdrawl of the Anglo-Indian quota in the railways predicated on a dynastic logic appears to be antithetical to the vision of a casteless society underpinning the emancipating project of European and Indian modernity. By demanding reservations in government jobs, similar to those granted to oppressed scheduled castes and tribes by the postcolonial Indian state, Anglo-Indians become unwittingly complicit in their demotion from an aspirational Britishness and privileged in-betweenness to the position of the lowest castes in the Hindu caste hierarchy.

Notes

1 Buettner maintains that 'these alliances and the offspring resulting from them were increasingly condemned by the colonial authorities for two reasons: they not only fell outside the bounds of acceptable bourgeois respectability but also violated the growing desire for racial exclusivity' by the early 1800s (2000, p. 279).
2 Although *chaturvarna* (from Sanskrit, *chatur*: four; *varna*: colour) was a non-genealogical system of social classification based on a four-fold occupational division between brahmins (priestly classes), kshatriyas (warrior classes), vaishyas (peasants, cultivators, traders,) and shudras (service providers) in ancient Indian texts, dating back to the *Rig Veda*, ancient Hindu texts, including the *Rig Veda* often exhibit an overlap between colour and vocation. In some texts, class distinctions were predicated

on differences in skin pigmentation between allegedly light-skinned invaders called Aryans and the darker indigenous people called dravidians and dasyus (Ghurye, 1969, p. 46).
3 The unofficial acceptance of a fifth class, *panchama* led to the inclusion of those who are outside the system and, consequently, *avarna* ('classless') such as the untouchables and tribal groups. Although strictures related to intermarriage between Aryans and anaryas including both *dasyus* (indigenous people) and *yavana* (foreigners) did not prevent cohabitation, it was discouraged through demotion of the offspring of the unions between Aryan females and non-Aryan males to a lower class or outside class or *avarna*. On the other hand, non-Aryan women could be elevated to an Aryan status through marriage, and offspring of illicit alliances between Aryan males and non-Aryan females were admitted into the father's caste.
4 Buettner suggests that persons of European ancestry in nineteenth- and twentieth-century India, were classified into three broadly defined groups:

> the more affluent Europeans, who could afford to maintain ongoing contact with the metropole by undertaking periodic journeys between Britain and India; those who were European but had become 'domiciled' in India, and were usually far poorer than the transients; and the Eurasians/Anglo-Indians.
>
> (2000, p. 280)

5 Pseudonyms have been used for respondents and their age indicated against their names in brackets.
6 Hockey legends with a Kharagpur connection included Joseph Garibaldi, one of the eight Anglo-Indian members of the 1936 Berlin Olympics team, and Leslie Claudius, who won four Olympic medals in field hockey. Claudius's talent in hockey was spotted by Captain Dickie Carr during a practice session in Kharagpur during the period he worked for Bengal Nagpur Railway.
7 Shope (2004) effectively demonstrates that the railway institutes in Lucknow served as the hub for performance of music and dance and for different groups as well as for musicians to interact with one another.
8 'Jati, also spelled jat, caste, in Hindu society. The term is derived from the Sanskrit jāta, "born" or "brought into existence," and indicates a form of existence determined by birth' (*Encyclopedia Britannica Online*).
9 The Simon Commission was a 'group appointed in November 1927 by the British Conservative government under Stanley Baldwin to report on the working of the Indian constitution, established by the Government of India Act of 1919' (Encyclopedia Britannica Online).
10 The Scheduled Castes (SCs) and Scheduled Tribes (STs) refer to various groups of historically disadvantaged indigenous people in India.

Bibliography

Bear, L. (1994). 'Miscegenations of Modernity: Constructing European Respectability and Race in the Indian Railway Colony, 1857–1931'. *Women's History Review* 3(4), pp. 531–548.
Bear, L. (2007). *Lines of the Nation: Indian Railway Workers, Bureaucracy, and the Intimate Historical Self.* (Cultures of History.) New York: Columbia University.
Blunt, A. (2005). *Domicile and Diaspora: Anglo-Indian Women and the Spatial Politics of Home*. Malden, MA: Blackwell Publishing.
Buettner, E. (2000). 'Problematic Spaces, Problematic Races: Defining "Europeans" in Late Colonial India'. *Women's History Review* 9 (June), pp. 277–298.
Ghurye, G. S. (1969). *Caste and Race in India*. Mumbai: Popular Prakashan.

Hunt, J. (1863). 'On Ethno-Climatology; or the Acclimatization of Man'. *Transactions of the Ethnological Society of London* 2, pp. 50–83.

Jati. (2016) *Encylopedia Britannica*. Available at: www.britannica.com/topic/jati-Hindu-caste (accessed: 1 November 2016).

Kurd, J., and Kerr, I. (2012). *India's Railway History: A Research Handbook*. Leiden: Brill.

Mills, M. (2005). 'Community Identity and Sport: Anglo-Indians in Colonial and Post-colonial India'. In James H. Mills (ed.), *Subaltern Sports: Politics and Sport in South Asia*. London: South Asian Studies, pp. 205–216.

Mizutani, S. (2011). *The Meaning of White: Race, Class, and the 'Domiciled Community' in British India 1858–1930*. Oxford: Oxford University Press.

Morris, J. (2005). *Stones* of *Empire: The Buildings of The Raj*. New York: Oxford University Press.

Roy, A. G. (2012). 'The Remembered Railway Town of Anglo-Indian Memory'. *South Asian Diaspora* 4(2), pp. 139–158.

Shope, B. (2004). 'Anglo-Indian Identity, Knowledge, and Power: Western Ballroom Music in Lucknow'. *The Drama Review* 48(4) (Winter), pp. 167–182.

Simon Commission. *Encylopedia Britannica*. Available at: www.britannica.com/topic/Simon-Commission (accessed: 1 November 2016).

Varna. (2016). *Encyclopaedia Britannica*. Available at: www.britannica.com/topic/jati-Hindu-caste (accessed: 1 November 2016).

Ward, P. (2004). *Britishness Since 1870*. London: Routledge.

13 Sometimes white, sometimes Asian

Boundary-making among transnational mixed descent youth at an international school in Indonesia

Danau Tanu

Introduction

Much research on 'mixed race' identities to date has focused on particular national contexts or ethnic groups. In contrast, this chapter explores the experiences of a diverse group of 'mixed race' youth, who grow up as children of serial temporary migrants with childhoods that often traverse multiple national boundaries. They are popularly referred to as 'Third Culture Kids'. Consequently, their transnational experiences of being 'mixed race' vary with shifting contexts, as do their identities, adding a dimension of dynamism which can enrich and widen the field of 'mixed race' studies.

The scholarship on 'mixed race' experiences has recognized the need to move beyond a myopic focus on the US and UK. However, much of the scholarship remains narrowly focused within national boundaries. For example, Telles and Paschel's (2014, p. 895) comparative study of four Latin American countries shows that the experiences of individuals of mixed descent are specific to each national context and dependent upon 'nation-building narratives', 'popular understandings of race', and the 'incentives' available for identifying with one particular race category over another. In a similar vein, Hewett (2015) found that national narratives shaped the experiences and views of 'Indos' (of mixed European and indigenous descent) from the Dutch East Indies in diverging ways, depending on whether they remained in Indonesia when it became an independent nation-state after World War II, or fled overseas to the Netherlands and elsewhere. Scholars have also shown that the way people of mixed descent negotiate identities can change over time, in accordance with the evolution of national narratives as governments and policies change, as in Soviet and post-Soviet Kazakhstan (Ualiyeva and Edgar, 2014) or in Australia before and after the White Australia policy (Trigger and Martin, 2016). In each case, the research followed the trajectories of populations bound to the influence of national boundaries and policies specific to the territories within, even when comparisons are drawn between two or more national or temporal contexts.

This chapter takes a transnational view of a 'mixed race' population of (serial) temporary migrants who are exposed to multiple national contexts during childhood. Young temporary migrants experience a high degree of international mobility, usually due to their parents' work, either through living in multiple countries or among those who have. They often attend international schools where, due to their diverse backgrounds, they can be celebrated as poster children for an idealized future of a united global village. For example, at the time of Barack Obama's election to his first term as President of the United States, many teachers at the international school where the fieldwork took place, used their classrooms to highlight the multiracial composition of Obama's family to the students as though it signaled the dawn of a new post-race era.[1] Yet, many of their students who were temporary migrants found that their identities continued to be politicized on a daily basis, in a world fraught with social fault lines that run along racial, cultural and economic divides. This chapter draws attention to young temporary migrants of mixed descent whose experiences resulting from their (sometimes ambiguous) phenotype bring these fault lines into relief. They straddle contemporary versions of the so-called 'colour-line', falling on either side of it depending on the context in which they find themselves (Du Bois, 2007[1903], p. 3). Sometimes they become 'white' and sometimes 'Asian', or sometimes Japanese and sometimes Indonesian, with implications for their status within national and transnational social hierarchies, leading some to actively negotiate their identities on a daily basis. They are, as a result, acutely aware of the social processes of boundary-making, rendering them methodologically useful subjects for studying racial boundaries which may otherwise be invisible.

Over the last decade, 'Third Culture Kids' (Useem and Downie, 1976) and 'global nomads' (McCaig, 2002) have become increasingly popular as terms of identification among those who grow up with a high degree of international mobility in their childhood and teenage years. 'Third Culture Kids' was coined in the 1970s and became the subject of a seminal book published initially in 2001 (Pollock and Van Reken, 2009[2001]; for history of the term see Useem, 1993). However, it was not until 2007 that 'Third Culture Kids' entered the internet lexicon when a young man of mixed descent set up the first online community for those who, like himself, grew up internationally (Tanu, 2015). Brice Royer, who at the time was in his 20s, is a Canadian citizen and had lived in seven countries by the time he was 18 years old due to his father's career as a UN peacekeeper. His mother is Ethiopian and his father is of mixed French-Vietnamese descent. Royer started the online community because he had become chronically ill from the stress of not having a sense of belonging. After coming to terms with his mixed identity, which prompted his recovery, he wanted to reach out to others facing similar issues of belonging that result from serial temporary migration in childhood. Royer, with his international and multiracial background, is an example of a growing population of young people of mixed descent who are raised as serial temporary migrants and who are the subjects of this chapter.

The insights presented here are drawn from ethnographic fieldwork conducted in 2009 at an elite international high school in Jakarta, Indonesia. Apart from attending classes and socializing with students outside of class, I interviewed over 130 students, parents, teachers and alumni from the school. The school boasted a diverse student body with about 900 students representing over 60 nationalities. The students were drawn mainly from the families of expatriate professionals and from the local elite. While approximately 20 per cent of the students were Indonesian nationals, most were not and considered Indonesia as a temporary place of residence, regardless of whether they had lived in the country for one year or for most of their young lives. Many of the students, both foreign and Indonesian nationals, would have lived in two or more countries by the time they completed high school. Thus, the school was a convenient field site for conducting immersion research on (serial) temporary migrants, while remaining in one location.

This chapter focuses on the experiences of seven children from the school who are of mixed descent (six of whom were of high school age at the time of research). The chapter goes beyond the traditional American-centric binary focus of white and black (Ifekwunigwe, 2004) to include four of mixed Asian and European descent, and three of mixed Indonesian and Japanese descent. None are Indonesian nationals. Some participants were phenotypically ambiguous, while others looked distinctly Indonesian, which affected their experiences of navigating socially constructed racial and ethnic boundaries. Given that some of their mixed backgrounds do not fit neatly into conventional racial categories, this chapter uses the term 'mixed descent' rather than 'mixed race' to refer to their backgrounds.

It was common for students to have more than one nationality and to speak multiple languages. Despite their multilingualism, the major student cliques were formed based on the language they preferred to speak with friends: the English-speaking, Indonesian-speaking, Korean-speaking and Japanese-speaking groups. The English-speaking groups most closely reflected the dominant culture of the teachers – who represented 20 nationalities but were mostly from white-majority, English-speaking countries – and of the school as an institution. As a result, they were the ones who were perceived as most 'international' by the school administrators. It was also not uncommon for students to have parents from two different ethnic or racial backgrounds. Of the over 80 students interviewed, approximately 15 were of mixed descent. I highlight a few of their voices in this chapter. Importantly, these voices were presented to me within the context of Indonesia, where stereotypes surrounding intimate interracial relationships abound (see also Hewett, Chapter 14 of this volume).

Straddling racial boundaries

Prior to the formation of the Indonesian nation-state, the Dutch colonial administration legally sanctioned a racial hierarchy, which continues to linger in contemporary Indonesia in the form of a racialized social hierarchy. The racial hierarchy under the Dutch dictated that Europeans were superior, while foreign Orientals (such as the Chinese) occupied the middle ranks and the indigenous population occupied the lower ranks (Coppel, 2002). Sexual relations that transgressed these racial boundaries were mired, according to Stoler (1992, p. 551), in a 'tangled political field' of 'gender inequalities, sexual privilege, class priorities, and racial superiority'. In this context, the offspring of such intimate relations 'straddled and disrupted' the 'arbitrary logic' of the racial divides (Stoler, 1992, p. 550). In the Dutch East Indies, those of mixed European and indigenous descent had varying privileges depending on whether they were acknowledged by their European fathers as legitimate and accorded 'European' legal status or, if they were not acknowledged, accorded 'native' status (Stoler, 1992). Historically, those of mixed European and non-European descent were generally, across the world, perceived as having a lower status compared to Europeans, though where they were placed in relation to others, such as the indigenous population or migrants, differed from one colonial context to the next (Ifekwunigwe, 2004).

While racist hierarchies are no longer legally sanctioned, intimate relations across racial lines are still often politically loaded in contemporary Indonesia, with effects on the children born of such relations. For example, while living in Jakarta in 2016, I commonly heard young white men mention their use of Tinder, a smartphone application for dating, to find local short-term sexual partners, knowing that their whiteness elevates them to the status of, as one of them jokingly put it, 'God's gift to women'. Middle Eastern men also often claim that Indonesian women are 'easy' because they perceive Middle Eastern men as *bule* (slang for 'white people') due to their lighter skin and phenotype. There are also local women who prefer to date white men as they are perceived to be socio-economically superior. Given this context, interracial relationships are often met with suspicion. In Indonesia, stereotypes about relationships between Indonesian women and white men are particularly loaded with political, social, and moral insinuations due to the massive gaps in living standards and the colonial baggage of racial discourses.

One particular stereotype dominates perceptions regarding sexual unions between foreign men and Indonesian women – that the women were of disrepute and hankering after money. Although they may not form the majority of interracial couples, while doing fieldwork in Jakarta, it was not uncommon to see racially mixed couples comprising older, expatriate, white men with Indonesian women who were possibly 20 years younger and apparently less well off. The stereotype is that many of the women were either former maids or sex workers. Steve, a male white American teacher, who is married to an Indonesian woman, explains:[2]

> My wife and I noticed there's a huge difference. If we're out ... with our kids, we are treated with much more respect because we have a family, so we're legitimate. But if we're without our kids, people look at us totally differently. She's twenty years younger than me, so it just plays into all of those stereotypes.... It's more comfortable being out with our kids, for sure.

According to Steve, the stereotype is prevalent both among Western expatriates and local Indonesians though perhaps more so among the latter. Intimate 'interracial' unions occur within a 'highly complexly stratified space' whether it be in Indonesia (Leggett, 2007) or in other parts of Asia (Farrer, 2010, p. 89).

Indeed, these dynamics of racial hypergamy are supported by a socio-economic hierarchy with a transnational reach. As a result of the contemporary capitalist system, those who migrate from developed countries to less developed countries gain status with the move and often become part of the upper-middle class in the destination country. In Indonesia and elsewhere in Asia, these workers and their families are referred to as 'expats' (from 'expatriate') to mark them as working professionals on lucrative salaries that are calculated in stable foreign currencies. The label 'expats' stands in stark contrast to the label 'migrant workers', which is used for those who move from developing countries to more developed countries to work. 'Expats', whether they are from the West or other developed countries like Japan, form part of the transnational capitalist class that occupies managerial positions within multinational corporations (Sklair, 2001). Locals therefore assume that temporary migrants in Indonesia who look as though they are from developed countries are rich, and perceive them to be superior.

These perceptions were reflected in the gendered nature of the interracial couples whose children attended the international school in Jakarta. The mothers of the mixed descent students were usually local or from other developing countries, while fathers – who were often white, but also Japanese – were usually from more developed countries.

It would be naïve to assume that young temporary migrants of mixed descent do not have to navigate the 'system of racialized sexual stratification' that their parents' marriages are subject to while negotiating their own identities and place within that structure (Farrer, 2010). During fieldwork, there were five students in the three upper grades who were of mixed Japanese and Indonesian descent among the 15 or so students with Japanese citizenship. All five had Japanese fathers (and therefore Japanese surnames) and Indonesian mothers. While the two boys had no qualms speaking Indonesian and switching back and forth between hanging out with their Indonesian peers and their Japanese peers, the three girls socialized almost exclusively with their Japanese peers. All three girls were fluent in Indonesian, but they spoke only in Japanese or English at school and refused to speak in Indonesian. When I sometimes spoke in Indonesian to them, they would respond in Japanese or English.[3] I asked them about their language choices, but each time they pretended not to hear me. It was not until I interviewed two of the girls, Ellie and Aya, in private, ten months into the fieldwork, that they willingly explained why they had deliberately refused to speak Indonesian in front of their peers, especially their Japanese peers. They complained that they felt forced to do so to prevent their Japanese peers from perceiving them as Indonesian, and therefore inferior. By not speaking Indonesian, Ellie and Aya distanced themselves from Indonesia in order to retain the status associated with identifying as Japanese.

While the high school students used language to mark their distance from Indonesia, others used physical space to the same effect. Steve, the aforementioned white, American teacher, candidly shared his observations of his primary school-aged daughter's desire to identify as white. Lara dislikes visiting her mother's village in Indonesia, and when she does, Lara stays physically close to Steve as though to indicate she is white like her father and not Indonesian like her mother. On another occasion, when Steve made a self-deprecating joke about being the only *bule* or white person in the family, Lara would counter saying, 'No, I'm *bule*'.[4] No matter how many times Steve explained to Lara that she is '*campur*' or mixed, Lara would not accept it. Steve said that in Lara's eyes, 'She's *bule*. That's the way she sees herself'. For Lara, superiority was marked as white, male, urban and rich, like her father, in contrast to Indonesian, female, rural and poor, like her mother. Even as a seven-year-old, Lara recognized that she could elevate her own status by identifying with her father (Tanu, 2016, p. 446).

Lara's self-identification is in part a response to others' perception of mixed-race children. The often racially ambiguous physical appearance of young temporary migrants of mixed white and Asian descent led others to perceive them differently depending on the context: 'white' in Asia; 'normal' at international schools in Asia; and 'Asian' in the US. The following two stories illustrate such shifting identities.

Maura's mother is Filipino and her father is Italian American. Maura grew up almost exclusively in Asia, having been born in Indonesia. She moved to Thailand, Bangladesh, Philippines, then back to Indonesia, attending international schools for most of that time. According to Maura, the international school that she attended in the Philippines was made up mostly of children of mixed marriages and of affluent local families: 'Most of the kids are like me, mixed: half Filipino, half American kids. The majority of the population are Filipinos mixed with, like, a white, a Caucasian. My best friends were Swiss-Filipino, Singaporean-Filipino, American-Filipino'. Maura felt that she was part of the norm at her international school in the Philippines because a majority of her schoolmates were of mixed descent like herself. It was similar at the international school in Jakarta. Although those of mixed descent did not form the majority of the student body there, their presence was not unusual. Maura was part of the mainstream English-speaking groups at the school.

Meanwhile, outside the campus gates of the international schools that she attended, Maura became 'white' in Asia.

> I've lived in Asia my whole life, so I'm used to seeing Asians everywhere and, like, walking into an airport and being the tallest person in the airport, you know? ... When I'm in Asia I feel ... I guess 'cause I'm white I feel like ... it sounds bad ....

Maura hesitated, but continued after I asked her to go on: 'If you're white in Asia you have the sense of power because you're *white* in Asia. Do you get what I mean?'. In Asia, Maura felt that her ambiguous appearance led locals to perceive her as 'white', which enables her to draw on colonial discourses of race that construct 'white' as superior, as well as contemporary capitalist discourses that continue to construct 'the West' as superior.

But her identity and status shifts when Maura visits the United States, her country of citizenship.

> I hate being in the States. Whenever I go to the States ... I have cultural shock 'cause everyone's, like, white. It freaks me out ... When I'm in the States, everyone else is white. I am the same as them. So then, not only do [I] feel intimidated, they scare me. They're louder than Asians, they're ruder than Asians, they're yeah ... I kind of have an Asian mentality....

In the US, Maura's whiteness does not set her apart to mark her as more privileged than the majority of the population as it does in Asia. While she may still benefit from white privilege vis-à-vis other minorities in the US, her status is not as special as it is in Asia where she feels she can get away with making mistakes more than she can in the US. Having an 'Asian mentality' indicates that Maura sees others who are white in the same way that others perceive her while in Asia – as superior and more powerful. This makes her feel insecure in the US where she is intimidated by whiteness.

Further illustrative is the case of Tim, whose mother is Taiwanese and father is white American. Tim felt ambivalent about his identity. Tim was born in the United States; when he was four he moved to Jakarta; then to Kalimantan (an island in Indonesia) in second grade; back to Jakarta for fourth grade; repatriated to the United States where he enrolled in fifth grade at a public school for seven months; to Japan from fifth to eighth grade; back to Jakarta to finish eighth grade at one of the smaller international schools; then moved schools and enrolled in ninth grade at the international school where I was doing fieldwork. I met Tim when he was in twelfth grade in his last semester of high school. Due to his complex background and upbringing, Tim had developed a simplified answer to the question, 'Where are you from?' Tim claimed, 'I say I'm from the States. But my mom is Taiwanese.... That's usually what I do'. It does not, however, reflect how he feels about his identity. 'But, to me, I actually don't feel like I belong anywhere, like, home to me is where my family is', Tim explained. Defining 'home' as where the family lives is typical of young people who grow up in multiple countries because they find a sense of home in relationships (Pollock and Van Reken, 2009[2001]).

Meanwhile, the way others perceived him shifted depending on the context, affecting his sense of belonging. Tim found it difficult fitting in when he moved 'back' to the United States due to his ambiguous phenotype. He was in fifth grade at the time (about 11 years old).

> For some reason, I didn't want to be Asian. I wanted to fit in like an American student. I think that really affected me in some ways. Just because I look different and ... because I felt like people were looking at me, seeing how I was different, sort of.... It made me self-conscious.... It would be really hard for me to join games and stuff that they were playing because I felt like I wouldn't be accepted just because of the way I looked.... It would be hard

for me to talk to them because I'm scared they would judge me and be, like, 'Oh, you're stupid', or whatever.

In the US, Tim felt as though others judged him negatively based on the way he looked. In contrast, in Japan he felt that his peers accepted him precisely because he looked different.

It was really strange because in the States, I felt like I was Asian. But then when I went to Japan, I felt more Western in the way people were treating me. I felt more welcome[d] – like all the kids wanted to talk to me and wanted to know where I was from. They tried really hard to be my friends and I really liked that.

In the US, Tim felt that others saw him as Asian, and therefore he felt unaccepted, whereas in Japan, he felt his peers saw him as 'Western', which made him more worthy of their attention.

The way he thought others perceived him affected Tim's sense of confidence in approaching his peers. Tim related that moving to Japan was 'really nice'.

There were a few other American students, or Caucasian students, and we all mixed with the Japanese kids. Like, they would talk in Japanese sometimes to each other, but most times you could go over there and ask 'Hey, what's up?' And they'll be like, 'Oh, so and so …' and they would tell us. It wasn't like the States where I felt afraid to kind of go up to people and ask about stuff like that.

Meanwhile, at the international school in Indonesia, Tim was part of the most popular student clique among the English-speaking groups. Like Maura, Tim found that his status shifted downwards in the US and upwards in Asia.

Despite being seen as white in Asia, both Maura and Tim identified themselves as 'Asian' in their interviews. 'I'm an Asian', Maura asserted as she cited some Filipino cultural practices that she followed and the fact that her American father lives in Asia and 'can speak Filipino'. Not to mention, Maura views her father as 'American, but not really' due to his Italian ancestry, both justifying her sense of distance from being American herself, and therefore from identifying as white or Western, and reinforcing a stereotype of the typical American as Anglo-Saxon. Similarly, Tim said, 'Culturally, I consider myself more Asian than Western'. He went on to explain: 'I've lived overseas, basically my whole life, in Asia, and I feel I look more Asian'. For Tim, like Maura, his upbringing in Asia, and his physical appearance that did not fit into the stereotype of a 'white American', were reason for identifying as Asian.

But at the international school in Jakarta, Maura and Tim's own identification contrasted starkly with the way they were perceived by some of their peers. Their Asian peers, namely those who did not consider English as their first language and felt left out of the mainstream English-speaking groups, labelled them as 'white' or 'Western' in the same way that locals outside of the campus gates did. Additionally, even those in the English-speaking groups often labelled Tim (though not Maura) and his close friends as 'white kids' – half in jest – regardless of Tim and his friends' racial backgrounds because Tim's clique was seen as being high status due to the athleticism of its members. Although some of Tim's friends were Caucasian, his group also included African Americans, Asians, and others of mixed descent. Maura, on the other hand, was not part of the high-status clique and therefore was not accorded the label 'white' by others in the English-speaking groups. Thus, even within the school, high status was marked as 'white' irrespective of actual phenotype (Tanu, 2017 forthcoming).

However, not all students of mixed white and Asian descent at the international school shifted between being 'white' and 'Asian'. When I saw Shane, I did not realize that he was of mixed descent. He had been socializing with the Indonesian-speaking students when I visited their hangout area. I knew the group was diverse in that while most spoke some Indonesian, not all were Indonesian nationals. Some were from other Asian countries and some were of mixed descent. But when Kenji, who is of mixed Japanese (father) and Indonesian (mother) descent himself, told me about his mixed British Indonesian friend Shane, I told Kenji that I had not seen this friend of his before. 'Yes, you have', Kenji countered, 'The guy who passed us just now with the painting in his hand. That's Shane'. Indeed, as I had approached the group, I had seen a twelfth grader leave the hangout area with a canvas heading towards the school's art room. 'The guy with the black hair? But he looked completely Asian', I said, puzzled. 'Yeah, but his father is British, white', Kenji corrected me.

I later interviewed Shane and found that though Shane's mother was Indonesian and his father British, he considered himself more Indonesian than British. He had spent almost all his life growing up in Indonesia. 'Here in Indonesia, I can make conversation with anyone I see. From Bali to wherever I go, upper-class to lower-class, even *becak* (pedicab) drivers and the beggars', Shane gestured 'high' and then 'low' with his hand as he spoke. 'But then when I go to England, it's a different story. I don't really know what to talk about'. Speaking of the students who hung out in the English-speaking groups, including Maura and Tim, he said, 'When I hang out with them, I just don't feel that connection. It doesn't feel right. It doesn't feel comfortable'.

As with Maura and Tim, Shane spoke of his lack of a sense of belonging in the UK, a Western, English-speaking country that is majority white like the US. Unlike Maura and Tim, however, Shane does not attribute this sense of ill-ease in his country of citizenship directly to his Asian-looking phenotype. Even so, his explanation about his inability to make conversation in the UK suggests that it could be due to his lack of understanding about British cultural norms or a sense that, as someone who appears to be part of a minority population in Britain, there is a lack of interest on the part of others to engage with him, which echoes Tim's experiences. In contrast, Shane has an easy time engaging with Indonesians, but not because he is seen as white. When I met with Shane and Kenji one weekend at a beer garden off campus, which at the time was a popular teenage hangout for international school students and affluent locals, it was clear from his interactions with a security guard that Shane's sense of place and power in Indonesia is derived from the way he carries himself with confidence and authority as a member of the Indonesian upper-class.

Meanwhile at the international school, Shane used the term *bule* to refer to students in the English-speaking groups, such as Maura and Tim, as though he himself was of fully Indonesian descent and not in any way of white descent. Shane and his friends were part of the Indonesian-speaking group that saw themselves as high status on account of their family wealth (many of their parents were far wealthier than those of the other students). In fact, Shane and his male friends tried to assert themselves as being of *higher* status than the English-speaking groups, knowing that the transnational socio-economic structure dictated the superiority of the *bules* or 'white kids'. This construction of 'white' as superior did not sit well with Shane and his friends, who felt that the national Indonesian structure, in which the wealthy elite like themselves were superior, should take precedence. As for whether Shane saw himself as Indonesian because he looked more Asian, came from a wealthy family, or had not moved multiple times like Maura and Tim had, it is difficult to tell. Most likely, it is a combination of all those factors.

Whether they identified as Asian, Indonesian, Japanese, or white, the young people presented here seemed to have an intuitive sense of the social fault lines that they were navigating. Both Tim and Maura felt that 'white' is seen as high status and 'Asian' as low status because their understandings of racial hierarchies, whether they endorsed them or not, were reaffirmed through their lived experiences on a daily basis. In developing countries like Indonesia, the stark class differences amplify racial hierarchies, as illustrated in a telling description by Tim:

> One of the things that I find really strange is when I'm here [in Indonesia], most of the workers in McDonalds, in all these restaurants, are Asian. Then, going back to the States and ... giving orders to someone who is white or Caucasian is really strange to me. I feel it's, it's really weird. I don't know why. It's just, something about it is strange to me.

Growing up in an environment where class division overlaps with racial difference visibly reinforces the notion that 'white' is superior. And it does so powerfully, such that when the physical reality of another national context does not fall in line with this internalized notion, it feels 'strange'. When social hierarchies are reinforced daily through real-life economic hierarchies, it becomes powerful as it is internalized as habitus – 'a system of dispositions that incline actors to act, think, and feel in ways consistent with the limits of structure' (Bourdieu, 1986; Ortner, 2006, p. 109). Yet, even as he described the strangeness of seeing a white person in a low-level job, Tim seemed to feel uncomfortable – as suggested by his statement, 'I don't know why' – with the fact that he found it strange at all. Perhaps it made him aware that he had involuntarily and subconsciously accepted the racial hierarchy that he saw everyday, while he consciously felt that he should not. It would seem then that exposure to different contexts contributes to challenging the internalized system of racial and other social hierarchies. As Maura stated, 'When I think of hierarchy, the only reason they're higher than us is because they think they are ... and we let them'.

Conclusion: a transnational view

This chapter confirms that the mere 'presence of mixed people, even over long historical periods, does not indicate a declining significance of social boundaries, including racial ones' (King-O'Riain *et al.*, 2014, p. 277). Young mixed-descent temporary migrants' identities shift with their movement between Asia and the West. Their experiences reflect the racial and socio-economic boundaries that continue to exist, albeit from a transnational perspective.

The reflections presented in this chapter highlight three main points. First, mixed or otherwise, identity is embedded within a grid of social power structures, where race, gender and class, among other factors, intersect (Anthias and Yuval-Davis, 1992). There is no escaping the grid, yet its lines shift with context and can be negotiable. Those who are of mixed descent and have an ambiguous phenotype, like Maura and Tim, feel they are perceived differently – sometimes white, sometimes Asian – depending on where they are, with concomitant effects on their sense of power and belonging. Ellie, Aya and Lara actively strategized to align themselves with their higher status identity, Japanese and white respectively. Second, national and transnational structures intersect to complicate the power structure in a given setting, such that various actors are left to compete with one another to gain superiority. Shane used financial capital in the setting of the international school to challenge the transnational structure that suggests that white is superior, and attempted to replace it with a national structure that places elite Indonesians, with whom he identifies despite his British nationality, at the top. Third, these structures remain powerful because they are internalized.

Young people who are serial temporary migrants of mixed descent are methodologically interesting subjects from a Barthian perspective which emphasizes the importance of ethnic boundaries rather than the 'cultural stuff' contained within (Barth, 1994). In straddling social fault lines, their experiences bring these lines into relief as others place them on different sides of the lines each time they cross national boundaries or change social contexts. Furthermore, anchoring the research in an international school enabled exploration of the complexity of mixed-descent identities. The setting of the international school acted as a microcosm of a world where national and transnational structures converge in the context of a postcolonial, capitalist society to bear upon the socially constructed identities of young temporary migrants of mixed descent. In the international school, a cosmopolitan ideology of 'being "international"' normalizes the multinational, multiracial identities of the children of transnational professionals (Tanu, 2014, p. 2). But this normality is mediated by a transnational hierarchy that situates global powers with advanced economies, particularly former colonial powers, at the top and developing economies below them. The experiences of those introduced in this chapter show that the hierarchy is often racialized and ranked as white, then East Asian, then the rest. Their experiences also show that the position of mixed descent youth in this hierarchy shifts vis-à-vis the dominant population depending on the national context. This research offers a window into the way the racialized hierarchies of national and transnational contexts intersect, and how they cannot always be compartmentalized within national boundaries.

Notes

1 Barack Obama was born to a white American mother and black Kenyan father, while the father of his half-sister, Maya Soetoro, is Indonesian (Obama, 2004[1995]). Obama also spent a few years of his childhood in Indonesia and his sister has married a Chinese Canadian.
2 I have used pseudonyms throughout the chapter for all research participants to preserve their anonymity.
3 I am also of mixed descent: my father is Indonesian of Chinese ethnicity and my mother is Japanese. I speak English, Japanese and Indonesian fluently and used all three languages to conduct the research.
4 *Bule* literally means 'faded' in Indonesian, but is usually used as slang for 'white folks'.

Bibliography

Anthias, F., and Yuval-Davis, N. (1992). *Racialized Boundaries: Race, Nation, Gender, Colour and Class and the Anti-racist Struggle*. London and New York: Routledge.
Barth, F. (1994). *Ethnic Groups and Boundaries: The Social Organization of Culture Difference*. Oslo: Pensumtjeneste.
Bourdieu, P. (1986). 'The Forms of Capital'. In J. G. Richardson (ed.), *Handbook of Theory and Research for the Sociology of Education*. Westport, Conneticut: Greenwood Press, pp. 241–258.
Coppel, C. (2002). *Studying Ethnic Chinese in Indonesia*. Singapore: Singapore Society of Asian Studies.
Du Bois, W. E. B. (2007[1903]). *The Souls of Black Folk*. Oxford and New York: Oxford University Press.
Farrer, J. (2010). 'A Foreign Adventurer's Paradise? Interracial Sexuality and Alien Sexual Capital in Reform Era Shanghai'. *Sexualities* 13(1), pp. 69–95.
Hewett, R. (2015). 'Children of Decolonisation'. In *Indonesia and the Malay World* 43(126), pp. 191–206.
Ifekwunigwe, J. O. (2004). *Mixed Race Studies: A Reader*. Abingdon: Routledge.
King-O'Riain, R. C., Small, S., Mahtani, M., Song, M., and Spickard, P. (2014). *Global Mixed Race*. New York and London: New York University Press.
Leggett, W. H. (2007). 'Expatriate Ethnoscapes: Transnational Masculinity and Sexual Transgressions'. In R. Hutchison and J. Krase (eds) *Ethnic Landscapes in an Urban World*. Boston: Elsevier, pp. 223–246.
McCaig, N. M. (2002). 'Raised in the Margin of the Mosaic: Global Nomads Balance Worlds Within'. *International Educator* 2002(Spring), pp. 10–17.
Obama, B. (2004[1995]). *Dreams From My Father: A Story of Race and Inheritance*. New York: Three Rivers Press.

Ortner, S. B. (2006). *Anthropology and Social Theory: Culture, Power, and the Acting Subject*. Durham: Duke University Press.

Pollock, D. C., and Van Reken, R. (2009[2001]). *Third Culture Kids: Growing Up Among Worlds*. Boston: Intercultural Press.

Sklair, L. (2001). *The Transnational Capitalist Class*. Oxford; Malden, Mass.: Blackwell.

Stoler, A. L. (1992). 'Sexual Affronts and Racial Frontiers: European Identities and the Cultural Politics of Exclusion in Colonial Southeast Asia'. *Comparative Studies in Society and History* 34(3), pp. 514–551.

Tanu, D. (2014). '"Unpacking 'Third Culture Kids": The Transnational Lives of Young People at an International School in Indonesia'. PhD thesis. *Anthropology, Sociology and Asian Studies*. Perth: The University of Western Australia.

Tanu, D. (2015). 'Towards an Interdisciplinary Analysis of the Diversity of "Third Culture Kids"'. In S. Benjamin and F. Dervin (eds) *Migration, Diversity, and Education: Beyond 'Third Culture Kids'*. Basingstoke: Palgrave Macmillan.

Tanu, D. (2016). 'Going to School in "Disneyland": Imagining an International School Community in Indonesia'. *Asian and Pacific Migration Journal* 25(4), pp. 429–450.

Tanu, D. (2017 forthcoming). *Growing Up in Transit: The Politics of Belonging at an International School*. New York: Berghahn Books.

Telles, E., and Paschel, T. (2014). 'Who is Black, White or Mixed Race? How Skin Color, Status, and Nation Shape Racial Classification in Latin America'. *American Journal of Sociology* 120(3), pp. 864–907.

Trigger, D., and Martin, R. (2016). 'Chinese History, Indigenous Identity and Mixed Ancestry in Australia's Gulf Country'. In K. McGavin and F. Fozdar (eds), *Mixed Race Identities in Australia, New Zealand and the Pacific Islands*. New York: Routledge, pp. 12–20.

Ualiyeva, S. K., and Edgar, A. L. (2014). 'In the Laboratory of People's Friendship: Mixed People in Kazakhstan from the Soviet Era to the Present'. In R. C. King-O'Riain, S. Small, M. Mahtani, M. Song, and P. Spickard (eds), *Global Mixed Race*. New York and London: New York University Press.

Useem, R. H. (1993). 'Third Culture Kids: Focus of Major Study – TCK "Mother" Pens History of Field'. *NewsLinks*. Princeton. New Jersey: International Schools Services, p. 1.

Useem, R. H., and Downie, R. D. (1976). 'Third-culture Kids'. *Today's Education* 65(3), pp. 103–105.

14 Class, race and being Indo (Eurasian) in colonial and postcolonial Indonesia

Rosalind Hewett

Introduction

The histories and lived experiences of groups defined as 'mixed race' provide an important insight into deeper social currents and identities in different periods. Postcolonial scholars have tended to celebrate Eurasian populations as challenges to popularly understood categories often essentialized by colonial and postcolonial states (starting with Stoler, 2000). Yet in historical and contemporary Indonesia, where a confusing multiplicity of criss-crossing ethnic, racial and religious identities co-exist, Indos (Eurasians) are one group of many that illuminate the social and racial hierarchies of different periods. This chapter provides an historical overview of the position of Indos in Indonesia, beginning with late colonial society and ending with their involvement in popular culture in Indonesia today. It draws on Dutch and Indonesian language documentary sources and interviews I carried out in Indonesia in 2013. I argue that contemporary understandings of both class and race are relevant to discussions of Indos. I also suggest that the designation of Indos as an 'in-between' group is difficult to apply to the Indonesian context; first, because of the class divisions among Eurasian communities in colonial Indonesia, which led to them being assigned different labels according to their respective social status. Second, postcolonial Indonesian society consists of hundreds of ethnic, racial and religious identities, not just two discrete identities. In this chapter, the terms 'race' and 'mixed race' are used as interlocutors used them.

Defining 'Indo'

The word 'Indo' has had different meanings in different historical and cultural contexts. In its current usage, it can refer to Indonesians in general, or Indonesians of mixed descent. This second meaning has its origins in the Dutch term *Indo-Europeesch* (Indo-European), although contemporary understandings of the term tend to encompass a broader group than just those of European descent. Translating the term 'Indo' into English is problematic, not least because its nearest analogue in English, 'Eurasian', originated in contexts specific to British colonialism. Populations termed Eurasian in nineteenth century Asia were generally distinct legal groups within British colonial racial hierarchies, particularly in India, Hong Kong and Singapore (see Lee, 2004, p. 2; Teng, 2013, p. 6). These groups tended to be given special privileges as an 'in-between' group. In the Dutch East Indies, however, there was never a legal category for an equivalent group. The term Indo arose in the late nineteenth century to describe a sub-class identified not just for their mixed descent but also for their lower class position in European society (Bosma, 2010, p. 13; Stoler, 2000, p. 41), though it appears to have been used to describe people of mixed descent outside the European community. The term *Indische Nederlanders* (Indies Dutch, or Dutch citizens born in the Indies) was often used to describe wealthier members of the European community, including those who had local ancestry.

In 1854, the colonial government divided the population of the Netherlands Indies into *inlanders* ('natives') and Europeans, followed by a third category, Foreign Orientals, in 1925 (Fasseur, 1994). Each of these legal categories consisted of a confusing plurality of groups that defied the immediate racial connotations surrounding each term and was often tied to political interests. European status came to include Japanese, Armenians, former 'natives' granted equated European status (Luttikhuis, 2013) and Indos acknowledged by European fathers. In the nineteenth century, European status granted poorer families access to free medical care and a free European education (Penders, 1968, p. 148; Bosma and Raben, 2008, p. 270). Most Indo children attending European schools were from lower and middle-class families, while wealthier families sent their children to the Netherlands for an education. Only those with a European high school diploma could work in the colonial civil service. Thus, Indos with European status enjoyed more or less a monopoly on the lower and middle levels of the colonial civil service. Indos also frequently worked as soldiers and policemen, meaning that they increasingly became the face of Dutch colonial authority in the Indies (Wertheim, 1950, p. 67).

Many Indos were the children of poor soldiers and their concubines, or the illegitimate children of Dutch men and their 'housekeepers' (see Stoler, 2009). In the early twentieth century, wealthier members of the Indo community increasingly began to adopt more 'European' behaviour, such as speaking 'proper' Dutch and eating Dutch food, to distance themselves from poorer Indos and prove that they belonged to the European community (see Protschky, 2008). This phenomenon arose after new European arrivals in the twentieth century derided poorer Indos in terms that drew on popular understandings of race from Western Europe. Their opinions tended to belong to two streams of thought. The first stream drew on essentialized biological ideas suggesting that Indos embodied the worst of both races. The second stream explained the stereotypical characteristics often attached to Indos (like indolence) in terms of the environments in which they were raised. The 1919 edition of the *Encyclopaedie van Nederlandsch Indië* expressed this second view of lower-class Indos, explaining that they adopted certain characteristics because they were raised in indigenous kampungs (lower-class indigenous areas). It still described them in less-than-glowing terms as 'so-called "rough-paupers", the scourges of kampungs, [who] run illegal liquor houses and brothels ... and trade in young native and Indo girls. Through unscrupulous and other methods, they are so-called Europeans (thanks to false acknowledgements) ...' (Encyclopaedie van Nederlandsch-Indië, vol. 3, 1919, pp. 367–68). However, wealthy Indies families known to have mixed descent, such as sugar and indigo planters possessing huge tracts of land in Java and nutmeg planters in Ambon, escaped such criticism, suggesting that class was just as relevant as race in Dutch discussions of Indos during this period (Houben, 1992; Bosma, 2005, p. 68).

Most new arrivals from Europe tended to describe Indos as separate from *totok* ('pure') Europeans. Opinions among Indonesians towards Indos are for the most part unclear based on existing sources, but elite Javanese appear to have despised them, as Javanese feminist Kartini suggested in her writing in 1902 (Coté, 2013, p. 518). Her brother-in-law, Javanese intellectual Achmad Sosrohadikoesoemo, referred to Indos as 'Demi-rulers' unwilling to give up their privileged position in colonial society, who wanted to ensure that indigenous groups would never be schooled in the Dutch language, to ensure they could not gain employment in the colonial civil service, like Indos (Coté, 2008, pp. 278–279). It seems, then, that Indos were largely rejected from upper- and middle-class European society and from elite Javanese society. As a result, the Indo community withdrew into itself and fought to improve the position of Indos in the early twentieth century through social initiatives and organizations. This rise of identity politics was part of a broader trend in which groups defined as mixed in other European colonies in Asia, such as Anglo-Indians, formed organizations in the first few decades of the twentieth century to promote their social position above indigenous groups (Henry, 1986, p. 114).

Race, class and social boundaries

The Indo community of the twentieth century mostly aligned itself with European status because of the privileges that this status entailed. There were some notable exceptions, among them Ernest Douwes Dekker who, together with two Javanese intellectuals, Tjipto Mangoenkoesoemo and Soewardi Soerjaningrat, founded the Indisch Party in 1912, which they opened to all persons born in the Indies, regardless of their legal status. However, few Indos were willing to align themselves with groups defined as 'native', as Douwes Dekker promoted. Douwes Dekker and his co-founders encouraged former members to join the Indies organisation Insulinde after the Indisch Party was disbanded in 1913. When Insulinde changed its by-laws to open its membership to those who held native status, more than a third of its members, most of them Indo, resigned in protest (Van der Veur, 2006, p. 152).

From 1919 a new organisation, the Indo-Europeesch Verbond (Indo-European Alliance, IEV) positioned itself as the mouthpiece for Indos with European status. The IEV quickly became far more popular than the Indisch Party and Insulinde. Combined with the families of its members, the IEV could have represented between 20 and 25 per cent of the approximately 200,000 Indos who held European status before the outbreak of World War II (Van der Veur, 1955, pp. 229–231; Van der Veur, 1960; Meijer, 2004, p. 302). Besides social initiatives to improve the living standards of Indos, it also took a role in identity politics as the largest European party in the Volksraad (People's Council) (Van der Veur, 1955, pp. 300–301).

The IEV's conservative position on most issues brought it into conflict with Indonesian parties and nationalist leaders. In 1922, a commission of eight people, two of whom were Indo, revisited the question of salary levels. The commission recommended that the tripartite system of pay scales in the civil service be revived on the basis of 'standard of living', with a middle pay rate reserved for, though not exclusive to, Indos. Indonesian representatives in the Volksraad fiercely opposed the proposal. One nationalist, Soeroso, called for only two groups: those born in the Indies and those not born in the Indies. He called for Indos to join with the first group. However, IEV Chairman Dick de Hoog argued in response that Indos had a different definition to Indonesians of what constituted a reasonable living standard. Indos, he suggested, would never be willing to go without shoes, while this would be perfectly acceptable for Indonesians (Van der Veur, 1955, pp. 252–253). IEV calls for Indos to be given the right to purchase land while retaining European status brought the IEV into further conflict with Indonesian nationalists, particularly because it was supported in this push by fascist and conservative parties opposed to Indonesian emancipation.

In response, most senior Indonesian nationalists tended to exclude Indos from their definitions of who could be called 'Indonesian'. Future vice-president Mohammad Hatta as early as 1926 defined 'Indonesians' as those with native status (Elson, 2008, p. 78). The Indonesian National Party (Partai Nasional Indonesia), chaired by future president Sukarno, refused to grant Indos membership, declaring that they were not members of the 'Indonesian race' (Suryadinata, 2010, pp. 129–130). Future Prime Minister Sutan Sjahrir wrote in 1937 that 'the place occupied by the Indo in this society is changed ... Their privileged position has thus lost all support in society, and so that must also disappear' (Sjahrazad [Sjahrir], 1950 [1937], p. 138).

By the end of the colonial period, the Indo community had decidedly defined itself in both racial and class terms. Towards *totok* Dutch, it demanded the right to be considered a class of the European community. Towards Indonesians, many Indos defined themselves not only as different in terms of social status and living standards, but also as superior in racial terms on account of their European ancestry. One study in 1953 of recent Indo arrivals in the Netherlands asked participants about their relationships in Indonesia with *totok* Dutch. Many reported experiencing discrimination and being excluded from *totok* Dutch society. When asked about their relationship with Indonesians, most reported it to be good. Responses included, 'We were honoured and respected; they were afraid of us'; 'The lower-class Indonesians treated us as superiors, but intellectual Indonesians were our equal'; and, in one comment that illustrated the social and geographic distance between Indos and Indonesians, 'We visited them; they treated us with respect; they knew we were a little higher' (Van der Veur, 1955, pp. 132–133).

Race under the Japanese

When the Japanese invaded Java in 1942, the decision of the Indo community to align itself with European status became problematic for the first time. The administration consistently attempted to persuade them to renounce their perceived loyalty to the Netherlands. Most Indos, unlike *totok* Dutch, were not imprisoned on Java until the Japanese military administration began to implement a series of progressively stricter 'registrations' requiring Indos to declare the percentage of their Indonesian ancestry.

Among the small number of Indos who worked with the Japanese administration was P. F. Dahler, appointed spokesperson of the Kantor Oeroesan Peranakan (Office for People of Mixed Descent, KOP). Dahler made repeated appeals to Indos to consider themselves as Indonesian. In May 1944, Dahler addressed a gathering of Indos in Batavia to convince them to renounce their loyalty to the Netherlands and state they considered themselves to be 'Asian' (De Jong, 2002, p. 520). Another series of public gatherings called by the KOP for young Indo men resulted in an incident in the KOP compound on 15 September, in which the Japanese and Indonesian flags were torn from the front of the KOP building. Young Indonesians present considered the incident an insult to the Indonesian flag and people. The issue remained unresolved after the young Indo men involved refused to apologize (De Jong, 2002, p. 521).

The Japanese administration, in preparation for an Allied invasion, began to train young Indonesian men (*pemuda*) in paramilitary organizations to defend Java against an attack. Tensions between young Indos declaring their support for the Dutch and *pemuda* loyal to an independent Indonesia, an idea that in theory the Japanese supported to prevent the re-establishment of Dutch colonial rule, grew. One Dutch journalist described these tensions in a diary entry on 24 October 1944:

> [Youth] leaders have been instructed to spread the rumour in the villages that the Indo-European community is preparing an action against the Indonesians and Indonesians should therefore be on their guard.... In doing so the Japanese are sowing the seeds for massacres on a large scale.... Now I suddenly understand what has caused the verbal abuse of Indonesian street youth against Europeans passing by....
>
> (Bouwer, 1988, p. 297)

This diary entry was prophetic in its prediction of massacres. On 15 August 1945, Japan surrendered to the Allies. Two days later, Sukarno and Hatta, at the behest of *pemuda*, announced Indonesia's independence from the Netherlands.

Nationalism, violence and the citizenship question

In the following weeks, armed *pemuda* began to gather in public areas and harass local populations, among them Indos (Taylor, 2003, p. 367). In the midst of this, many Indo families returned to their pre-war homes and tried to resume their pre-war lives. As one Indo man who later left Indonesia wrote in his memoirs, 'Life at home was like the good old days' (Flach, 2005, pp. 75–76). The expectation of many that colonialism would return led, inevitably, to open conflict with armed *pemuda* supporting Indonesia's independence. One *pemuda* leader later described how many *pemuda* saw the return of Indos:

> The Dutch and Eurasian troops and civilians released from internment camps were now on the prowl, launching actions in many parts of the city, hoping to take back their old properties and even regain their old positions in government. We knew then we had to hurry and form a fighting corps before they had a chance to use the Allied forces to help them form a new Dutch government.
> (Padmodiwiryo and Palmos, 2016, p. 28)

Pemuda gangs in Java began to round up Indos and members of other groups popularly considered to be supporters of colonial rule (Hewett, 2016). They killed some families outright. Others were interned in prisons and camps, where they faced torture, starvation and death (see Frederick, 2012; Cribb, 2008). In response, young Indo men joined anti-Indonesian militias in Jakarta and Batavia, targeting Indonesian civilians and seizing Indonesian property (McMillan, 2005, pp. 86–88; Cribb, 1991, p. 58; Meijer, 2004, p. 250). Indos able to afford the cost of passage left for the Netherlands, but many more remained in Indonesia. Among those who remained were poorer families without the money to repatriate and those without Dutch citizenship. A small number – among them Douwes Dekker – opted to side with Indonesia during the Indonesian National Revolution (1945–1949) (Schumacher, 1995, p. 214).

The Dutch-Indonesian Round Table Conference, held in The Hague in August to November 1949 to resolve the Indonesian-Dutch impasse, granted Indos a two year 'opting period' to choose to take Indonesian citizenship. Almost all Indos delayed making a decision while assessing the political and economic environment of post-1949 Indonesia. As the post-war Indonesia economy languished in the 1950s, the media was keen to paint Dutch citizens as wealthy compared to ordinary Indonesians. Some Indos encountered discrimination and lost their jobs. The IEV in Indonesia encouraged Indos to assimilate, even as its senior leaders departed for the Netherlands and its Dutch branch opposed assimilation (Bosma, 2009, p. 96). The Dutch government also appealed to Indos to take Indonesian citizenship, most notably through High Commissioner Arnold Theodore Lamping who released a media statement for this purpose three weeks before the deadline to take Indonesian citizenship (Javabode, 1951, p. 1). The general reaction among the Dutch Indo community to these appeals was negative. By the end of the opting period, only around 30,000–33,000 Dutch citizens had decided to formally adopt Indonesian citizenship. Some did not inform relatives and friends with Dutch citizenship about their decision for fear of a backlash (Van der Veur, 1955, p. 414).

The Indo community remaining in postcolonial Indonesia was almost completely endogamous and had few ties with other groups ('De Sociale Positie',

1952, p. 19; Allard, 1955, p. 18). Increasing numbers chose to repatriate to the Netherlands throughout the 1950s, including migrants termed *spijtoptanten* in Dutch, or those who had chosen Indonesian citizenship but changed their minds. Their main reasons for repatriating were limited access to a Dutch education, decreased employment opportunities for Dutch citizens and anti-Dutch sentiment over the West New Guinea issue, which remained in Dutch hands despite pressure from the Indonesian government to hand it over to Indonesia.

In December 1957 the Sukarno government, reacting to a decision from the United Nations not to support Indonesia over the Netherlands New Guinea issue, expelled all Dutch citizens. The remaining Dutch in Indonesia – about 45,000–50,000 – boarded ships and departed for the Netherlands en masse (De Tijd, 1957, p. 5; *Nieuwsblad van het Noorden*, 1957, p. 1). Most of them were Indos. They left behind at least 10,000 Indos (Hewett, under review, p. 114). Among those who remained were former Dutch citizens married to Indonesians, illegitimate children, impoverished Indos unable to prove Dutch descent and children born to Indonesian mothers and Dutch soldiers during the Revolution. Pressures to assimilate increased with a ban in 1957 on Dutch language material, which most interpreted as a blanket ban on speaking Dutch. This ban was followed by legislation enacted in 1960 forbidding the use of Dutch in schools for Indonesian citizens. During the remainder of the Sukarno years, many families struggled to find work, particularly in the civil service.

Indonesians of foreign descent under the New Order

After Suharto came to power in 1966, pressures to assimilate increased as his New Order (1966–1998) government began to target groups they termed 'Indonesian citizens of foreign descent' (*warga negara keturunan*). The New Order forbade public discussions of ethnicity, religion, race and class. As a result, few Indos met for social gatherings on the basis of shared heritage. A presidential decree in 1967 announced that 'Indonesians of foreign descent' would be subject to 'a process of assimilation, mainly to prevent racially secluded lifestyles' (Keputusan Presiden Republik Indonesia, 1967, pasal 3–4). It encouraged Chinese Indonesians to change their names to more 'Indonesian' sounding ones. Indos also changed their surnames during this period out of fear that their property would be confiscated, and to avoid questions about their citizenship.

In some public discourse during the New Order period, Indos were contrasted with Chinese Indonesians as a 'model' minority. According to one New Order general writing in 1987:

> Assimilation of Indonesians of Chinese descent presents the most obstacles, as there are other factors beyond race, like economic, cultural and religious factors ... [but] Indonesians of European descent (usually called Indo-Europeans) easily became Indonesians if they intended to do so.
> (Suryohadiprojo, 1987, pp. 218–219)

In practice, many Indos used Dutch at home and were typically Christian, but few were involved in business, as were a small number of high profile Chinese Indonesians who became the target of the media and power-brokers.

Indos were largely removed from the public eye, except when they dealt with the bureaucracy. From 1978, like Chinese Indonesians, Indos who were born with a European birth certificate were required to provide a naturalization certificate (*Surat Bukti Kewarganegaraan Republik Indonesia*, SBKRI) to apply for marriage and death certificates, to register the birth of a child and to apply for a passport (Lan, 2012, p. 373). Some poorer Indos who had lost their documents during the chaos of the 1940s never applied for a naturalization certificate, meaning that technically they were not Indonesian citizens. This requirement, along with different legal provisions for Indonesians of foreign descent compared to those defined as *pribumi* (indigenous), was an ongoing reminder for Indos that they were considered a different class of citizens.

New identities after 1998

After the fall of Suharto in 1998, new identities and ethnic-based organisations began to emerge in Indonesia. Among them was De Indo Club, established for Dutch speakers in the city of Surabaya, and similar social gatherings for Dutch speakers held in other major cities like Malang and Bandung. These groups were often established with the support of Indos from the Netherlands and the United States who returned to Indonesia to retire or holiday. The division between *pribumi* and 'foreign descent' Indonesians remained in legislation until 2006, when a new citizenship law and a regulation on population administration removed both the SBKRI requirement and legal distinctions taken from colonial legal categories. By this time, however, the almost complete assimilation of the older generation of Indos during the Suharto years meant that few Indonesians were aware that Indos still existed as a group beyond the realm of popular culture, which I discuss below.

The attempts of Dutch and American Indos, themselves beneficiaries of a rise in identity politics in both nations, to promote a transnational Indo identity in Indonesia were limited to some extent by the diverging definitions of what it meant to be Indo between a former colony and a former metropole. In the Netherlands and among Indo communities who migrated to the United States, Australia and elsewhere, the term Indo generally means someone of mixed European and Indonesian background who was born in the Netherlands Indies or is descended from someone born in the Indies, speaks Dutch and has an emotional attachment to the Netherlands. In Indonesia, only a small number of Indos remaining from the colonial generation are able to speak Dutch, and few identify as Dutch or express attachment to the Netherlands. The term 'Indo' in Indonesian today is a broad concept encompassing those of mixed Indonesian and *bule* ('Caucasian') descent, and is usually associated with popular culture rather than the colonial past.

Indo faces in Indonesian popular culture

During the 1950s and 1960s, when employment options were few and discrimination towards Indonesians of Dutch descent was still common, some Indos turned to work in modelling and films, where they established a new tradition of Indo faces on-screen. Among the earliest and most prolific was Indo actress Suzanna (1942–2008), known for her 'skin as white as marble' and for being Indonesia's 'Queen of Horror' (*Tempo*, 17 February 2003, p. 78). From the 1970s, more and more Indos appeared in Indonesian films. In the 1980s, Indo models frequently appeared in advertisements for modern products and skin whitening cream that connected their lighter skin colour with wealth, modernity and cosmopolitan lifestyles (see Handajani, 2006; Prabasmoro, 2003).

By the end of the decade, producers' preference for an Indo look was particularly evident in Sinetron, or soap operas. This preference was controversial. One Indonesian academic, in fairly typical criticisms of the period, declared that Indos were inappropriate casting choices because of their backgrounds, appearance and, in some cases, limited Indonesian language abilities. He outlined two examples in which Suzanna played the wife of a village religion teacher and a Javanese goddess, inferring that Indos were not suitable to play a Javanese deity or a villager because their background and appearance marked them as modern and foreign (Depari, 1990, pp. 77–79). One Dutch author drew out a clearer relationship between appearance and class, writing that younger Indos in Jakarta 'associate[d] [lighter skin] with a higher social status and better humanity'. She also suggested that they linked skin colour to moral and intellectual quality: 'For them, poverty, a dark complexion and an inferior nature are not far apart' (Huisman-Carels, 1990, p. 55).

The argument that Indos were not suitable to play ordinary Indonesians reappeared in the mid-2000s, when the trend of casting predominantly Indo faces in Sinetron began to shift in response to public pressure and broader trends. Wider anti-Western sentiment emerged in the public debate about a proposed anti-pornography bill, in which proponents of the bill linked 'pornography' (loosely defined as revealing women's clothing and public displays of affection) to stereotypical Western morals and appearance (see Allen, 2007). At the same time, an influx of dramas from Northeast Asia redefined the stereotypical role of protagonists in Sinetron, which in the past often had been played by Indo women. In these Northeast Asian dramas, young female protagonists were typically lower-middle class or poor and hard-working, and rejected the materialism of their wealthy love interests (Heryanto, 2014, pp. 175–180).

Class, race and appearance

Popular Sinetron also began to produce similar storylines in which *pribumi* Indonesian actresses took leading parts and Indo actresses were often instead cast as antagonists of dubious moral calibre, while Indo men continued to be cast as wealthy, cosmopolitan love interests. The creative director of one leading Sinetron production house described the reasons for this in an interview in 2013:

Say, for example, we are doing a show on a girl who is being tortured who is poor, you cannot give an Indo look. An Indo look is usually more ... a bit rich, but if you are doing a drama of a rich person ... then it's okay to give an Indo look. But if poor, being tortured, coming from a low-class family then you prefer it to be ... a proper Indonesian look.

The idea that wealth and loose morals (especially in the case of women) are attached to Indo appearance is not just limited to Sinetron but also is evident more broadly in contemporary Indonesia in discussions of *bule*. *Bule*, or 'Caucasians', are often popularly imagined in contemporary Indonesia as wealthy cosmopolitans who have access to much greater social and cultural capital than most Indonesians, but they suffer from a lack of appropriate moral standards (see Schlehe, 2013). Books for Indonesian women like *How to Catch Mr Bule* reinforce the idea that marriage to a *bule* man means access to a life of wealth and privilege – if Indonesian women can negotiate the 'dangerous' moral environments of bars and hotels to meet these men (Erlinawati, 2008). The privilege attached to a *bule* appearance is not just limited to wealth, but also to the networks, transnational connections and opportunities expected to come with it, expressed in the common joke about Indonesian men married to *bule* women that they want to *memperbaiki keturunannya* ('improve their bloodline'). The stereotype that Indo children are *anak rusak* ('morally damaged' children) forms the nasty underbelly of popular contemporary understandings of Indo identity.

Despite the shift in popular culture, the children of mixed relationships are still commonly expected to become models and actors on the basis of their parents' backgrounds (Kebon, 2011). Indos who I spoke to from elite families, educated in international schools, rejected offers to work in the entertainment industry, declaring that this sort of employment was only for uneducated and poorer Indos. Children whose circumstances do not fit the stereotype, as one young Indo woman noted, struggle to adapt to societal expectations: 'you're *bule* but at the same time you're Indonesian, so you're kind of expected to be wealthy but you're not .... It's not as glamorous to be Indo because you look the part but you're not really living the part'. Employment in acting and modelling provides one relatively easy way for Indos from lower-class backgrounds to access higher salaries. As a result, the stereotype of Indos is locked in an endless loop in which Indos are expected to work in entertainment because they are considered attractive because of their access to social and cultural capital, and entertainment provides Indos who are not from elite families the access to social and cultural capital that they are expected to have.

Theories of mixed race

Research on mixed race outside Indonesia outlines the current international appeal of a 'Eurasian' or 'mixed race' look. It suggests that fear of miscegenation has been replaced by a recasting of Eurasians as cosmopolitan – that is, worldly, refined and sophisticated individuals able to negotiate a multitude of cross-cultural contexts and networks (Matthews, 2007). Over the last several decades, theories of mixed race have often celebrated a liminal, or in-between, position of the mixed-race subject. Many authors suggest that people of mixed race are able to transgress binary categories imposed by colonial and postcolonial structures because of their hybrid identities and positions (e.g. Ifekwunigwe, 2004, p. 14; Young, 1995).

But describing Indos as 'in-between' categories in colonial and postcolonial Indonesia is problematic given Indonesia's own complex hierarchy of groups defined along ethnic and racial grounds. The question arises as to what categories Indos are 'between'. Although racial ideas from Europe did gain some currency in the early twentieth century Netherlands Indies, they competed with existing legal structures, class and ethnic divisions that were marked by their plurality rather than uniformity. While popular ideas among the Indo diaspora suggest that Indos were and are situated in-between East and West, these two categories were imbued with a multitude of complex social and racial identities in the Netherlands Indies that sometimes aligned with legal status and sometimes did not, like the legal definition of Japanese as Europeans.

Indos also are imagined in a much more complex way in Indonesia today than simply bridging two categories. The concept of a Western world is encapsulated to some extent in the stereotypes and popular ideas attached to *bule* appearance. But the closest commonly held concept of an imagined Asian identity in Indonesia is the imagined religious divide between the Arab and Western worlds. In postcolonial Indonesia, those defined as Javanese have traditionally dominated politically and culturally. Groups from eastern Indonesia, Chinese Indonesians and religious minorities are often under-represented. The concept of 'mixed descent' applies equally to children whose parents are from different Indonesian ethnic groups and children who have one foreign parent and one Indonesian parent. Furthermore, a child with a Javanese mother and foreign father may be treated very differently to a child with a Papuan mother and a foreign father.

Hierarchies of race and ethnicity, imbued with essentialized class distinctions on the basis of one's ethnic background, often compete in different parts of Indonesia. Although stereotypes about *bule* are relatively consistent across Indonesia, the plurality of competing ethnic identities – for example, that the Javanese are *halus* (refined) and eastern Indonesians are *kasar* (coarse) – complicates discussions of Indos framed in terms of them being situated between two discrete racial identities. The idea that Indo children are 'morally damaged' relates far more to popular understandings suggesting that *bule* parents do not inculcate their children with appropriate religious morals, rather than essentialized ideas about mixed race that may have been evident in other, historical contexts. However, the continued casting of Indo men as wealthy love interests in Sinetron suggests that the essentialized idea that Indos have access to significant cultural and social capital through their foreign links still prevails in the popular imagination.

Conclusion

Indos in colonial Indonesia negotiated a complex system of overlapping social categories. On the one hand, the colonial legal system included them to the extent that it drew on social class and political understandings of who could be European. On the other hand, early twentieth century notions of race imported from Western Europe excluded Indos on the basis of either biological essentialism or the environments in which they were raised. The systems of exclusion that the colonial Indo community used to promote its collective interests above indigenous groups reflected these broader structures. After colonial social structures were dramatically revised, first under the Japanese and then in postcolonial Indonesia, many Indos remaining in Indonesia downplayed their European heritage in response to broader pressures to assimilate. But remnants of the Indies legal system and colonial structures remained, manifest in the requirement that Indos of former European status produce naturalization certificates in their encounters with the New Order bureaucracy.

One area in which Indos could relatively easily obtain employment during the post-war period was popular culture. By the late 1980s, with the rise of Sinetron, Indos were well and truly established as actors in Indonesian television, but some critics declared that they were not suitable to play lower-class or poor Indonesians. Indo celebrities benefited from popular beliefs that ascribed higher social class, wealth and modernity to pale skin colour, until a shift in Sinetron led to revised story lines in which female protagonists were generally portrayed as poor, hard-working and morally upright. Deeper undercurrents attached to *bule* appearance emerged publicly at this time, suggesting that *bule*, though wealthy, had dubious moral standards, particularly in the case of women. As a result, Indo actresses were more likely to be given the role of antagonists.

The social and cultural capital attached to being *bule* or someone of *bule* descent continues to influence the meanings surrounding Indo appearance in Indonesia. Young Indos from wealthy families in Indonesia today often reject the stereotype that they will become celebrities. Those from poorer families, however, often fulfil the stereotype by becoming actors and models to access the social and cultural capital that they are expected to hold by virtue of their appearance.

Discussions of Indos as 'in-between' two distinct racial identities overlook the complex legal, social and cultural identities of colonial and postcolonial Indonesia in which plural identities competed with each other and hierarchies – rather than binaries – of race, ethnicity and class determined social status. Contemporary social relationships draw on both the social and legal structures inherited from the Indies and broader global hierarchies of mobility, wealth and cultural capital attached to *bule* appearance. Race and class are just as relevant in discussions of Indos today as they were 100 years ago.

Bibliography

Allard, E. (1955). 'Laporan sementara tentang penjelidikan kemasjarakatan dari golongan Indo-Eropah jang dilakukan di Bogor tahun 1953'. *Bahasa dan Budaja* 3(5), pp. 3–22.

Allen, P. (2007). 'Challenging Diversity? Indonesia's Anti-Pornography Bill'. *Asian Studies Review* 31(2), pp. 101–115.

Bosma, U. (2005). 'The Indo: Class, Citizenship and Politics in Late Colonial Society'. In J. Cotë and L. Westerbeek (eds), *Recalling the Indies: Colonial Culture and Postcolonial Identities*. Amsterdam: Aksant, pp. 67–98.

Bosma, U., and Raben, R. (2008). *Being 'Dutch' in the Indies: A History of Creolisation and Empire, 1500–1920*. Singapore: NUS Press; Athens: Ohio University.

Bosma, U. (2010). *Indiëgangers: Verhalen van Nederlanders die naar Indië trokken*. Amsterdam: Bakker.

Bouwer, J. (1988). *Het Vermoorde Land*. Franeker: Van Wijnen.

Coté, J. (ed. and trans.). (2008). *Realizing the Dream of R.A. Kartini: Her Sisters' Letters from Colonial Java*. Athens: Ohio University Press.

Coté, J. (ed. and trans.). (2013). *Kartini: The Complete Writings 1898–1904*. Clayton, VIC.: Monash University Publishing.

Cribb, R. (1991). *Gangsters and Revolutionaries: The Jakarta People's Militia and the Indonesian Revolution 1945–49*. Sydney: Asian Studies Association of Australia in Association with Allen & Unwin.

Cribb, R. (2008). 'The Brief Genocide of the Eurasians in Indonesia, 1945/46'. In A. D. Moses (ed.), *Empire, Colony, Genocide, Conquest, Occupation, and Subaltern Resistance in World History*. New York: Berghahn Books, pp. 424–439.

De Jong, L. (2002). *The Collapse of a Colonial Society: The Dutch in Indonesia During the Second World War*. Leiden: KITLV Press.

De sociale positie van de Nederlandse blijversgemeenschap te Makassar. (1952). National Archives, Nederlands Commissariaat te Makassar 2.05.61.04 165. Den Haag.

De Tijd (1958). 'Razzia's en Arrestaties in Djakarta: Bepaalde Nederlandse boeken weer in Indonesië toegelaten', *De Tijd: Godsdienstig – Indonesiestaatkundig Dagblad*, 11 January.

Depari, E. (1990). 'Eurasian Faces in Indonesian Films'. *Indonesian Film Festival*, Jakarta: Indonesian Film Festival Committee, pp. 77–79.

Elson, R. E. (2008). *The Idea of Indonesia: A History*. Cambridge and New York: Cambridge University Press.

Encyclopaedie van Nederlandsch-Indië (1917–1939). The Hague: Nijhoff, vol. 1.

Erlinawati (2008). *How to Catch Mr Bule: Buku Panduan Bagi Perempuan Untuk Berkencan Dengan Pria Asing*. Jakarta: Gramedia Pustaka Utama.

Fasseur, C. (1994). 'Cornerstone and Stumbling Block: Racial Classification and the Late Colonial State in Indonesia'. In R. Cribb (ed.), *The Late Colonial State in Indonesia: Political and Economic Foundations of the Netherlands Indies 1880–1942*. Leiden: KITLV Press, pp. 31–56.

Flach, W. (2005). *Never a Dull Moment: The Memoirs of Willem Flach*. Sippy Downs, Qld: Maju Publications.

Frederick, W. H. (2012). 'The Killing of Dutch and Eurasians in Indonesia's National Revolution (1945–1949): A "Brief Genocide" Reconsidered'. *Journal of Genocide Research* 14(3–4), pp. 359–380.

Handajani, S. (2006). 'Female Sexuality in Indonesian Girls' Magazines: Modern Appearance, Traditional Attitude'. *Antropologi Indonesia*, 30(1), pp. 49–63.

Henry, R. J. (1986). '"A Tulip in Lotus Land": The Rise and Decline of Dutch Burgher ethnicity in Sri Lanka'. Unpublished MA thesis. Australian National University.
Heryanto, A. (2014). *Identity and Pleasure: The Politics of Indonesian Screen Culture*. Singapore: NUS Press.
Hewett, R. (under review). 'Indo (Eurasian) Communities in Postcolonial Indonesia'. PhD thesis. Australian National University.
Hewett, R. (2016). 'The Forgotten Killings'. *Inside Indonesia*, July–September. Available at: www.insideindonesia.org/the-forgotten-killings (accessed: 2 October 2016).
Houben, V. (1992). 'De Indo-aristocratie van Midden Java: De Familie Dezentjé'. In W. Willems (ed.), *Sporen van een Indisch verleden*. Leiden: Centrum voor Onderzoek van Maatschappelijke Tegenstellingen, Faculteit der Sociale Wetenschappen, Rijksuniversiteit te Leiden, pp. 39–50.
Huisman-Carels, S. (1990). 'Indische mensen in Indonesie'. *Jambatan: Tijdschrift voor de geschiedenis van Indonesia* 8(1), pp. 49–60.
Ifekwunigwe, J. O. (2004). 'Introduction: Rethinking Mixed Race Studies'. In J. O. Ifekwunigwe (ed.), *'Mixed Race' Studies: A Reader*. London: Routledge, pp. 1–36.
Javabode (1951). 'Woorden van Hart tot Hart tot de Indische Nederlanders. Hoge Commissaris Lamping over nationaliteitskeuze. Prijsgeving Nederlanderschap zeker niet laakbaar'. 8 December, p. 1.
Kebon, A. (2011). 'Stars and Stereotypes'. *Inside Indonesia* 103 (January–March). Available at: www.insideindonesia.org/stars-and-stereotypes?highlight=WyJpbmRvIiwiaW5kbyciLCInaW5kbyIsIidpbmRvJyJd (accessed: 2 October 2016).
Keputusan Presiden Republik Indonesia nomor 240 tahun 1967 tentang kebidjaksanaan pokok jang menjangkut warga negara Indonesia keturunan asing, bab II, pasal 3–4.
Lan, T. J. (2012). 'Contesting the Post-colonial Legal Construction of Chinese Indonesians as "Foreign Subjects"'. *Asian Ethnicity* 13(4), pp. 373–387.
Lee, V. (2004). *Being Eurasian: Memories Across Racial Divides*. Hong Kong: Hong Kong University Press.
Luttikhuis, B. (2013). 'Beyond Race: Constructions of "Europeanness" in Late-colonial Legal Practice in the Dutch East Indies'. *European Review of History: Revue Européenne d'Histoire* 20(4), pp. 539–558.
Matthews, J. (2007). 'Eurasian Persuasions: Mixed Race, Performativity and Cosmopolitanism'. *Journal of Intercultural Studies* 28(1), pp. 41–54.
McMillan, R. (2005). *The British Occupation of Indonesia, 1945–1946: Britain, the Netherlands and the Indonesian Revolution*. New York: Routledge.
Meijer, H. (2004). *In Indië Geworteld: de Twintigste Eeuw*. Amsterdam: B. Bakker.
Nieuwsblad van het Noorden (1957). 'Demonstraties in Djakarta: Vrijdag a.s. weer grote Nieuw-Guinea-meeting'. 11 November, p. 1.
Padmodiwiryo, S., and Palmos, F. (2016). *Revolution in the City of Heroes: A Memoir of the Battle that Sparked Indonesia's National Revolution*. Singapore: NUS Press.
Penders, C. L. M. (1968). *Colonial Education Policy and Practice in Indonesia 1900–1942*. Unpublished PhD thesis, Australian National University.
Prabasmoro, A. P. (2003). *Becoming White: Representasi Ras, Kelas, Feminitas dan Globalitas Dalam Iklan Sabun*. Yogyakarta: Jalasutra.
Protschky, S. (2008). 'The Colonial Table: Food, Culture and Dutch Identity in Colonial Indonesia'. *Australian Journal of Politics and History* 54(3), pp. 346–357.
Schlehe, J. (2013). 'Concepts of Asia, the West and the Self in Contemporary Indonesia'. *South East Asia Research* 23(3), pp. 497–515.

Schumacher, P. (1995). 'De coup van Ernst Douwes Dekker tegen de "Indo-pioniers" in Yogyakarta'. In W. Willems and J. de Moor (eds), *Het Einde van Indië: Indische Nederlanders Tijdens de Japanse Bezetting en de Dekolonisatie*. The Hague, Sdu Uitg., pp. 208–220.

Sjahrazad [Sutan Sjahrir] (1950). *Indonesische Overpeinzingen*. Amsterdam: Djambatan.

'Soekarno Blijft op Irian-Aanbeeld Hameren: Djakarta wil Aandacht van Interne Situatie Afleiden'. (1957) *De Tijd: Godsdienstig-Staatkundig Dagblad*, 6 December, p. 5.

Stoler, A. L. (2000). 'Sexual Affronts and Racial Frontiers: European Identities and Cultural Politics of Exclusion in Colonial Southeast Asia'. In A. Brah and A. E. Coombes (eds), *Hybridity and its Discontents: Politics, Science, Culture*. Hoboken: Routledge, pp. 19–55.

Stoler, A. L. (2009). *Along the Archival Grain: Epistemic Anxieties and Colonial Common Sense*. Princeton and Oxford: Princeton University Press.

Suryadinata, L. (2010). *Etnis Tionghoa dan Nasionalisme Indonesia: Sebuah Bunga Rampai, 1965–2008*. Jakarta, Penerbit Buku Kompas.

Suryohadiprojo, S. (1987). *Menghadapi Tantangan Masa Depan*. Jakarta: PT Gramedia.

Taylor, J. G. (2003). *Indonesia: Peoples and Histories*. New Haven: Yale University Press.

Taylor, J. G. (2009). *The Social World of Batavia: Europeans and Eurasians in Colonial Indonesia*. 2nd edition. Madison, WI: University of Wisconsin Press.

Tempo (2003). 'Suzanna: Syukur bisa menakut-nakuti Anda'. 17 February, pp. 78–79.

Teng, E. (2013). *Eurasian: Mixed Identities in the United States, China, and Hong Kong, 1842–1943*. Berkeley: University of California Press.

Van der Veur, P. W. (1955). 'Introduction to a Socio-political Study of the Eurasians of Indonesia'. PhD thesis. Cornell University.

Van der Veur, P. W. (1960). 'Eurasian Dilemma in Indonesia'. *Journal of Asian Studies* 20(1), pp. 45–60.

Van der Veur, P. W. (2006). *The Lion and the Gadfly: Dutch Colonialism and the Spirit of E.F.E. Douwes Dekker*. Leiden: KITLV Press.

Wertheim, W. F. (1950). *Herrijzend Azië: Opstellen over de Oosterse Samenleving*. Arnhem: Van Loghum Slater US N.V.

Young, R. (1995). *Colonial Desire: Hybridity in Theory, Culture and Race*. London: Routledge.

Afterword

Paul Spickard

'Eurasian', 'Anglo-Indian', 'Half', 'Double', 'Mixed', 'Indo', '*Haafu*', '*Métis*', '*Hunxue*', 'Chindian', '*Damunhwa*', '*Honhyeol*' – these are some of the names by which people of multiple ancestries are called across Asia's vastness and variety. These names suggest the richness of racial encounters in the many very different, hugely complicated places we choose to include in our idea of Asia. The deeply researched, richly imagined, and finely crafted chapters in this book offer up a dizzying array of different racial systems and mixed peoples who live within them. The insights to be found here are substantial.

As Zarine Rocha and Farida Fozdar point out, the study of people with multiple ethnoracial identities has languished with regard to Asia. Almost all the writing in the mixed race field is centred on the United States and the United Kingdom, and much of it is about the mixing of white and black in those places. White and black are not irrelevant racial categories in Asia, but they are not the main peoples who have confronted each other and mixed (or not), throughout Asia's long, complicated racial history. Rather, the mixers in Asia are mainly Chinese and Malay, Vietnamese and Khmer, Korean and Japanese, Mongol and Han, and a host of other Asian ethnic combinations. So, this volume is especially welcome as a first foray into the complex racial systems that have evolved in various parts of Asia.

The editors have very sensibly divided their book geographically, with four sections treating, in turn: China and Vietnam, Korea and Japan, Singapore and Malaysia, and India and Indonesia. There are many good reasons for this arrangement. If nothing else, it helps the reader keep track of what part of Asia the author of each chapter is talking about, as not many people are knowledgeable about social relationships in every part of this huge continent. It is useful to have Singapore analysed alongside Malaysia, for example, or Japan alongside Korea, for in each such pairing there are parallels and contrasts to be made between the racial regimes of neighbouring societies that may help us to analyse both.

On the other hand, there may be something to be gained by thinking about the chapters thematically. Let's see what the lineup looks like if we tweak it just a bit, to emphasize not geographical proximity but the kinds of encounters between peoples that these essays elucidate. In this brief afterword, I will divide the chapters analytically among four kinds of mixed situations:

1 mixed people who are the products of sex or marriage between colonizers and the people they have colonized;
2 mixed individuals who live in or have some claim to societies that do not recognize mixing and insist that all people there must be monoracial and behave in a monocultural fashion;
3 members of longstanding ethnic minorities that are defined by long-ago mixing and have maintained more or less bounded and intermediary communal identities over many generations; and
4 chapters that focus on the process of identity negotiation.

Of course, these are not four separate, sealed-off categories. Most of the chapters contain elements of more than one of these themes. But arranging them thematically in this way may help us see some patterns that otherwise would remain indistinct.

The colonizer and the colonized

The story in this imagined section is interaction between white colonizers (mainly men) and local Asian women and the children to whom they gave birth. Some chapters here feature Europeans, not Asians, as the main actors in colonial or semi-colonial situations. Emma Teng, in ' "A class by themselves": battles over Eurasian schooling in late-nineteenth-century Shanghai' (Chapter 1) portrays the struggles of mixed-race Eurasians for a place, not in Chinese society, but in the white, British-dominated international enclave that existed in deeply colonized Shanghai in the last third of the nineteenth century. As Teng argues, 'the "Eurasian Problem" exposed a fundamental contradiction in the status of Eurasians, who were despised and feared, on one hand, but also desired, needed, and partially privileged, on the other'.

On the other hand, in some instances of mixing generated by colonial relationships, it is local Asians who are the main actors. Still, the question at the core is, 'Will mixed people be accepted into local society?' only this time the society is that of the formerly colonized Vietnamese. In '*Métis* of Vietnam: an historical perspective on mixed-race children from the French colonial period' (Chapter 3), Christina Firpo describes the long history of interaction between foreign men and local women – French, but also African, North African, and Indian – during the French colonial period. She gives us a sense of the range of very different life experiences that Vietnamese *métis* have had, in Vietnam and in France, and of the increasing attitude of acceptance among the Vietnamese public that mixed people have encountered in recent years.

English-language international schools, such as the one in Jakarta, are indisputably colonial institutions, even if the years of formal colonial sovereignty have long passed. In 'Sometimes white, sometimes Asian: boundary-making among transnational mixed-descent youth at an international school in Indonesia' (Chapter 13), Danau Tanu explores the lives and identities of 'Third Culture Kids': mainly mixed-race, internationally transient youth at an elite international school. As she observes, such people's identities are in flux: they 'shift between being Asian and white, or being Japanese and Indonesian, depending on where they are living, [which language they prefer using with their friends], and who their peers are'. She sees them as experiencing ongoing racializations from different angles as they move from country to country, school to school, despite their relatively elite economic status. In Teng's chapter, it was white colonizers doing the deciding about who would be accepted among Europeans. In Firpo's, it was Vietnamese who were deciding whether *métis* would be admitted into Vietnameseness. Here, Tanu shows Third Culture Kids making places of their own, moving in and out of whiteness and other identities.

Mixedness in a monoracial nation

There are nations, especially in Northeast Asia, where the local ethos is decidedly monoracial and monocultural. Japanese, Koreans, and Chinese all cling to myths of ethnic purity that reach deep into their respective pasts. The pressures on mixed people (and on their non-local parents) in such places are quite intense. The master question in this imagined section is: 'Will mixed people be accepted as members of these monoracially-defined societies?' The answer is not encouraging in China, Korea, or Japan.

In 'Developing bilingualism in a largely monolingual society: Southeast Asian marriage migrants and multicultural families in South Korea' (Chapter 4), Mi Yung Park studies the language behaviour and skills of children whose fathers are ethnic Koreans and whose mothers are marriage migrants from Vietnam and Cambodia. Such children, Park reports, are called by the derogatory term *damunhwa*. They suffer prejudice, discrimination, and bullying, especially if they have dark skin. Park reports that, even if the mothers attempt to teach the children their native language, the pressure to conform to Korean standards inhibits the children from becoming proficient in their mothers' language.

Alexandra Shaitan and Lisa McEntee-Atalianis explore the identity status of Japanese mixed people in '*Haafu* identity in Japan: half, mixed or double?' (Chapter 5). They find that the *haafu* adults they interviewed are profoundly stressed by the marginal position they are relegated to despite their being native-born Japanese and their possessing deep knowledge of Japanese culture and language, although the degree of their inclusion depends somewhat on context.

'Claiming *Japaneseness*: recognition, privilege and status in Japanese-Filipino "mixed" ethnic identity constructions' (Chapter 6), by Fiona-Katharina Seiger, has quite a different slant than the other essays in this imagined section. The central figures here are mixed-race children of Filipino women and Japanese men – many born in Japan and others in the Philippines, but most raised in the Philippines either by their mothers or by extended family. These mixed-race young adults may not possess all the Japanese language and cultural skills of the older mixed adults Shaitan and McEntee-Atalianis studied, but they seem to have more readily claimed a Japanese identity, partly because of the high status of Japaneseness in the Philippines. Whether they can make that claim stick in Japan is a matter yet to be determined.

In 'Mixing blood and race: representing *Hunxue* in contemporary China' (Chapter 2) Cathryn Clayton's operant question is, can mixed people be included as full members of a monoracially self-defined Chinese nation? In her telling, the Chinese mixed-race story is especially complicated, because Clayton insists that Chineseness rests not so much on race as Westerners understand it (as a biological inheritance) but rather on several overlapping vectors of connectedness: kinship, centuries-long membership in a multi-ethnic empire, consciousness of shared 'blood' among a complex hybrid people who nonetheless all see themselves as Chinese, and so forth. Still, the deciders about mixed people's membership here are Chinese, even as the deciders for Shaitain and McEntee-Atalianis are Japanese, the deciders for Seiger are Filipinos, and the deciders for Park are Korean. They are making race-like judgments about whether or not mixed people will be accorded a place in the Chinese nation, based on features they interpret as permanent, irrevocable, and innate – whether they attribute them to biology or not is beside the point. Clayton takes us on a thought-provoking, suggestive, if somewhat dizzying tour of the history of racial thinking in China, demonstrating the value of exploring 'Asian' perspectives.

Enduring ethnic minorities derived from centuries of mixing

In ' "Our Chinese": the mixedness of Peranakan Chinese identities in Kelantan, Malaysia' (Chapter 9), Pue Giok Hun describes Malaysia's four-part, monoracial system, inherited from the British colonial habit of putting peoples in discrete conceptual silos: Malay, Chinese, Indian, and Other (including Europeans and Indigenous people). In amongst those groups, however, Pue brings to light the several communities of Peranakan peoples who live in peninsular Malaysia – people who are descended from centuries-old intermarriages between Indigenous people and Chinese, Indigenous people and Arabs, Indigenous people and Indians, Indigenous people and Thais, and several other pairings. Focusing on the Peranakan Chinese community in Kelantan, she lays out the markers of Peranakan identity and performance, including particular mixtures of Malay and Hokkienese inherited languages, and the changes that are occurring in current Peranakan generations.

Two chapters explore the dimensions of identity in India's Anglo-Indian community, a separate ethnic designation that arose in the late eighteenth century out of families with British colonizer fathers and Indian colonial subject mothers. Anglo-Indians amount to a prototypical long-term community that possesses an enduring, intermediate, mixed identity – like Peranakans in Southeast Asia or *métis* (mixed communities of European-Indians) in Canada. In stereotype, Anglo-Indians aspired to Britishness; adopted British manners, morals, clothing, language, food, and religion; took on mid-level functions in the British empire; and found themselves frustrated and shut out of what they hoped would be their British racial patrimony.

In 'Is the Anglo-Indian "identity crisis" a myth?' (Chapter 11), Robyn Andrews's answer is emphatically yes. She objects to the widespread assumption that Anglo-Indians, past or present, experience angst or identity confusion. These, she implies, are fictions not unlike the tortured mulatto myth common in American literature – tropes created to soothe the consciences of the master class. Her conclusion: 'while Anglo-Indian identity is fluid and changing, it is not in a state of crisis'. In 'Performing Britishness in a railway colony: production of Anglo-Indians as a railway caste' (Chapter 12), Anjali Gera Roy analyses a group of contemporary Anglo-Indians from a different vantage point. She portrays Anglo-Indians as pursuing expressions of European culture aggressively in order to claim a measure of Britishness. But she also shows some who were associated with railway work moving in the direction of a Hindu category of caste simultaneously. This is complicated stuff.

Rosalind Hewett, in 'Class, race and being Indo (Eurasian) in colonial and postcolonial Indonesia' (Chapter 14), describes the related but distinct dynamics for the generations-long Indo (Eurasian) community in the Netherlands Indies (later Indonesia). As in India, an in-between group of people with European fathers and local mothers grew up during the Dutch colonial regime. Hewett argues, however, that such people were not a simple, intermediate, biracial class. Rather, she sees more complicated calculations of class, race, phenotype, performance, and cultural capital hierarchies at work, defining people's social position and relationship to European status.

Negotiating mixed race

Caryn Lim explores mixed-race identity negotiation in 'Being "mixed" in Malaysia: negotiating ethnic identity in a racialized context' (Chapter 7). She finds that different mixed individuals employ different strategies when confronted with the four-part monoracial discourse of Malaysia's officially decreed racial system. Some choose a single monoracial identity, though this may be difficult to live out consistently. More probably shift among identities depending on the compulsions and advantages offered by different social contexts. And some attempt to step outside the official racial labelling system entirely.

Rona Chandran attacks the same social system from a slightly different angle in 'Chinese, Indians, and the grey space in between: strategies of identity work among Chindians in a plural society' (Chapter 8). Instead of surveying the entire population, Chandran concentrates on those people who are specifically mixed Chinese and Indian (locally: 'Chindians'). The government insists on classifying them as either monoracially Chinese or monoracially Indian depending on the identity of each person's father. Both Indian and Chinese communities will grant a measure of acceptance to Chindians, but they frequently insist on performance criteria such as language and foodways. The people Chandran interviewed adopted several different strategies for negotiating ethnic identity spaces for themselves, ranging from full participation in a single community to identifying with neither group to insisting on access to both.

With 'Eurasian as multiracial: mixed race, gendered categories and identity in Singapore' (Chapter 10), Zarine Rocha pulls this thread to a close. In Singapore as in Malaysia, one of the legacies of British colonialism is a fixed racial category system. Singapore has the same four big categories, but it also recognizes a multitude of subsidiary groups. One of the categories recognized in Singapore is 'Eurasian' – which in patriarchal tradition originally meant the offspring of a European father and an Asian mother. Rocha unpacks the complex, gendered, and sexualized ways that mixed race is interpreted, enforced, and performed in contemporary Singapore.

The figure of the Eurasian here brings us full circle to where we began with this imagined rearrangement of the chapters of this fine book, back to Emma Teng's contemplation of Shanghai's Eurasian population in the nineteenth century. The insightful essays in this volume have taught me a lot – but not nearly as much as I still want to learn – about the enormous variety of racial systems, and therefore of mixed-race experiences, that are obtained across the broad expanse that is Asia. I am hopeful that many of these chapters' authors will soon be turning out books that take us in more depth into each of these complex mixed-race encounters. There is a feast of ideas and information here for students of race, of mixed race, and of human social interaction.

Index

affective labour 24
African-American 35, 37
Afro-Asian, African Asian 46, 53, 57–60
Alford, E.F. 28
alignment: dis- 87–9, 93
Althusser, Louis 118, 129
Amerasian Homecoming Act 60
ancestry 2, 5, 11–12, 39, 56, 94, 99, 107, 118, 122, 125, 196, 209, 218, 223, 225, 227–8
Anglo-American values 28
Anglo-Indians 179–81, 184, 187, 195–7, 226, 269
ascription: by the other 87, 90–1, 93; by self 84, 87, 90–1, 93–4, 99
assimilation 42, 69, 77, 82, 145, 148–9, 158–9, 181, 192, 229, 230–1
Australia 12–14, 56, 167, 169, 175, 192, 195, 206, 211, 223, 231, 236–7
authenticity 11, 40, 125, 129, 164, 166
avarna 196, 209

Bazé, William 58, 61
belonging 1–7, 9–12, 22, 37, 57, 70, 88, 92, 94, 105, 107–8, 128–9, 134–6, 138, 140, 162, 169, 170, 172–3, 188–90, 212, 217, 219, 221
Bengal Nagpur Railway 197, 198, 209
bicultural identities 68, 77
biethnic 133–7, 141–3; biethnic identity 133–4, 139, 142
bigotry 29, 35; *see also* discrimination
bilingual 72, 74, 78–9, 86–7, 153, 165; labour force 24
bilingualism 8, 67, 69, 71, 73–5, 77–9, 241
biracial 5, 57, 84, 163, 243; *see also* mixed race
black 1, 5, 35–6, 45, 59, 83, 158, 182, 199, 213, 222, 239

Blasian 39
blood 2, 5, 10, 11, 22–3, 37, 42–8, 82, 99, 104–5, 107, 137, 149, 163, 184, 242; blood tie 44; mixed-blood 7, 10, 37, 39, 163; bloodline 37, 233; *see also xue*
boarding school 20, 22, 23–4, 56, 197, 200, 207
Bonney, Catharina Van Rensselaer 20, 24
boundaries 29, 67, 121, 125–9, 135–6, 165–6, 180, 212–14, 221–2, 226
Buettner, Elizabeth 28, 196, 208, 209
bule 214, 216, 220, 222, 231, 233–5
Butler, Judith 118, 121, 125, 129

capitalism 37, 41, 215–16, 221; global 40–2, 109, 215
caste 19, 23, 24, 84, 184, 187, 195–6, 204–9, 243
categorization 4, 11, 38, 53, 67, 121, 128, 132–4, 141, 143, 147–8, 150, 153, 162–6, 168–73, 182–3; *see also* classification
census 5, 12, 31, 54, 129, 133, 163, 165, 186, 193; census forms 129; national census 5, 133, 163, 186
Chambers, J. 26–7
Chan Ah Yuen 26
charity school 25, 27, 31
Chevrotière, Henri Chavigny de la 54
children's home 24–5, 31
China 5–11, 20–3, 26, 28, 30–1, 35–48, 148, 150, 173, 239, 241–2
Chindian 5, 6, 8, 11, 126, 132–43; *see also* Machindian
Chinese 7–8, 19–24, 35–43, 44–7, 62n30, 98–9, 117–22, 126–9, 132–4, 137–8, 139–43, 148–57, 164–7, 213, 240–3; children 20; Indonesians 230–1, 234; mothers 23, 27, 29–30, 35

246 Index

Chineseness 31, 35–9, 41–3, 47, 147, 157, 242
Christian 23, 186, 188, 231; Christianity 164
Cina kampung see Peranakan Chinese
citizenship 10, 21, 40, 46, 54–6, 58, 76, 86–7, 100–1, 108, 111, 117, 188, 191–2, 196, 202, 215, 217, 219, 228–31; dependent 21, 29, 31
civilization 28, 37, 42, 46
Clarke, Brodie 25–6, 28–9
Clarke, Louisa Augusta 26
class 9, 10, 12, 19–31, 42, 52, 54, 67–8, 77, 99, 107, 171, 192, 196–7, 200–1, 203, 207–9, 214–15, 219–21, 224–35, 240, 243
classification 1–6, 10–12, 19, 37, 40, 54, 62, 88–9, 99, 120, 129, 132–3, 143, 162–6, 169–70, 173–4, 208–9, 243; *see also* categorization
clerks 24
collective identities 7, 19, 184; *see also* communal identities
colonial domesticity, ideals of 197
colonialism 5, 6, 9, 11, 184, 224, 229, 238, 244
community: communal identities 119, 240; feelings of 83, 169; online community 212
contact zone 31
cosmopolitanism 4, 6, 19, 31, 38–9, 126, 172, 221, 232–3
Critical Mixed Race Studies 36, 38
culture 3, 47, 89, 91–4, 101–5, 122, 125, 127, 128, 138, 143, 149–51, 157, 168, 197–8, 200, 207–8, 241, 243; cultural practices 55, 124, 188, 218; cultural symbols 136, 137, 138–40; culture and language 68–9, 138; *see also* custom
custom 11, 105, 126, 135, 137–9, 155–7, 164, 168

Dalat 56
Damunhwa 5, 67–8, 239, 241
De Batie, Eugène Dejean 54
Dekker, Ernest Douwes 226, 229
descent 2, 4, 7–11, 38, 40, 44, 83, 90, 99, 104–7, 111, 120, 123, 134–5, 147–9, 158, 162–7, 171–4, 179, 183–4, 187, 192, 195–6, 208, 211–16, 219–26, 228, 230–5, 240
diaspora 192, 195, 234
Điện Biên Phủ 52, 57–9
discourses 5–9, 21–2, 30, 36–7, 41–5, 47, 60, 69, 74, 82–3, 86, 93, 100, 108, 117–19, 128, 147–8, 157–8, 163, 195, 214, 216, 230, 243
discrimination 8, 47, 67–70, 76–7, 108, 111, 120, 132, 158, 163, 184, 227, 229, 232, 241
dissonance 4, 163
diversity 1–3, 5–12, 31, 38, 43, 67–8, 78, 82–3, 99, 127–8, 132, 142, 148, 157–8, 162, 168, 173, 180, 186, 189–90, 211–13, 219
double 5, 84, 87, 90–1, 93, 239
Dover, Cedric 19, 22, 31
Drummond, W.V. 30
Dutch East Indies 22, 211, 214, 225
Dutch language 226, 230–1

Ecole de La Providence 26
Ecole des Enfants de Troupe Eurasiens 56
Education Committee 26, 30
Ellis, Francis 28–9
embodiment 3, 4, 7, 22, 89, 94, 118, 120–1, 163–4, 225
empowerment 19, 26, 201; disempowerment 2
essentialization 106, 128, 167, 192, 183, 200, 224–5, 234, 235
ethnic boundaries 3, 125, 129, 135, 180, 213, 221
ethnic identity 72, 74, 77–8, 84, 98–105, 110, 117–25, 128, 133–40, 143, 149, 157, 179, 183–8, 241, 243; and belonging 3, 5; claims 5, 85, 98, 104
ethnicity 1–5, 8–9, 11–12, 44–6, 54, 67, 69, 75, 77, 82–3, 87–9, 94, 99–100, 104, 109, 118–29, 132–43, 147–8, 151, 158, 162–3, 173–4, 180, 183, 189, 192, 222, 230, 234–5
eugenics 30, 45, 182–4
Eurafricans 57
Eurasian 5–7, 11, 19–25, 30–1, 38–9, 45, 53–6, 162–73, 183–4, 186, 195, 204, 224, 233–4, 239–44; battle 20, 25, 27, 28, 31; in Indochina 54–7; in Malaysia 11, 164; problem 7, 21, 22, 25, 30, 240; in Singapore 19, 162–73, 183–4
Eurasian School 7, 20–31
European 2, 5, 7, 20–4, 26–30, 37–40, 45, 54, 99, 158, 162, 164–7, 173, 183–4, 186, 192, 195–7, 201, 204–9, 211, 213–14, 224–8, 230–1, 234–5, 240–3; identity 195–6, 207; men 20, 23–4, 28–30, 54, 164, 184, 195, 214, 225, 243–4; status 30, 208, 225–8, 235, 243; women 28, 54

Index

exclusion 20–1, 23, 26–31, 45, 47, 59–60, 69, 135, 141, 148, 152, 162, 164, 167, 170–3, 180, 184, 201–3, 208, 227, 235
expatriates 21, 23–4, 26, 28–31, 111, 213, 214–15
expulsion of children 20, 25, 26
extreme case formulation 88
extrinsic elements 148–9

fair play 21, 28, 30, 200
family 38–9, 55, 72, 105–7, 185, 187, 207, 217
family structure: Vietnamese 55
Fédération des Ouvres de l'Enfance Francaise d'Indochine (FOEFI) 57–9
Filiation 30–1, 100, 104, 107–10
flexible identities 3, 19, 100
fluidity of identity 3, 5, 9, 44–5, 85, 94, 100, 117, 128, 135–6, 143, 157–8, 173, 180, 243
foreign community 19–20, 82, 225
Foreign Orientals 213, 225
French Indochina 53–6

gender 2, 5–8, 10, 12, 31, 35–6, 110, 118, 121, 155, 158, 162–6, 170–4, 182, 186–7, 197, 214–15, 221, 244
generational change 152, 156–7, 231
Geneva accords 57–8
geographical location 181, 188–9
globalization 7–8, 31, 39–40, 150, 157, 180, 184
gutter children 21, 29–30

haafu 5, 82–4, 88–90, 94, 95n2, 239, 241
half-caste 19, 23–4, 84, 186, 195
Han (Chinese) 37, 41, 42, 44, 46–7, 239
Han Suyin 43
Hanbury, Thomas 23; Thomas Hanbury School and Children's Home 25–6, 29, 31
Hapa 82, 86, 94, 95n1
heritage language: development of 68–70, 72–7
hierarchies of race 2, 3, 9–10, 19, 21–2, 30, 99, 140, 158, 170, 172, 196, 213–15, 220–2, 224–5, 234–5
Hindu purity fetish 195
home 23, 68, 72–4, 91, 101, 165, 189–91, 217
homogeneity 8, 10, 40, 62, 67, 82, 104, 157, 168, 182, 186, 190
Hong Kong 19, 21, 24, 225
hunxue 35–9, 45–7; *hunxue'er* 38–9, 43, 45–7

hybrid degeneracy 7, 22
hybrid vigour 7
hybridity 11, 40–3, 127, 167; hybrid identity 87, 91, 126–7, 186, 234
hyphenated identities 166, 186

identification 3–9, 11, 19, 39, 43, 87, 89–91, 98–9, 102, 106–7, 122, 127, 136, 138, 140, 147, 153, 157–8, 172, 181–2, 186, 197, 208, 212, 216, 218; external 3, 7; personal 108, 125, 162, 168; social 100, 153; verbal 136, 138, 140
identity: crisis 9, 82, 179–92, 243; fluidity of 3, 5, 9, 85, 94, 100, 117–18, 128, 135–6, 143, 154, 157, 173, 180, 243; markers of 138, 139, 150, 153, 156; politics 9, 107, 226, 227, 231
identity work: strategies of 8, 132–3, 136, 138, 142–3
illegitimate, illegitimacy 27, 29, 53, 108, 225, 230
immigration 1–2, 6–9, 39, 45, 59–60, 62, 67–70, 74–7, 98–9, 101–2, 105, 108–10, 134, 150, 166, 185, 187–9, 191, 193, 197, 203, 206–7, 211–16, 221, 230–1, 241; *see also* migration
in-between 82, 94, 132, 148, 166, 208, 224, 234–5, 243
in-group 58, 135, 143
inclusion 11, 19–21, 23, 28, 30–1, 40, 153, 157, 167–9, 188, 209, 241
India 5–11, 19, 21–2, 57, 148, 164, 177, 179–81, 183–5, 225, 239, 243
Indian 5–9, 38, 52–3, 56–7, 117–23, 125–9, 132–4, 136–41, 143, 147–8, 164–5, 168–9, 171, 179–93, 195–208, 240, 242–3
Indian-Asian 53, 57–8
Indisch Party 226
Indische Nederlanders 225
Indo 211, 224–6, 232–3, 235
Indo-Aryan 195, 208
Indo-Europeesch Verbond (IEV) 226–7, 229
Indonesia 9, 211–15, 224, 228–31, 234–5
Inlanders 225
instrumental use of identity 106, 118–20, 128, 154
Insulinde 226
intermarriage 41–3, 148–51, 166, 195, 209n3, 242; *see also* marriage
International Settlement 20, 27
interpellation 118, 121, 128
intersectionality 10, 157, 163
intrinsic elements of identity 148–9

Index

Japan 5, 82–3, 93–4, 98–100, 102–5, 107–10, 215, 218, 241
Japanese: culture 82, 87–9, 91–2, 99, 107; identity 83–4, 87–9, 90–2, 98–100, 101–2, 212, 215, 241–2; invasion 228, 235; language 86, 94, 106, 213, 218; society 8, 82, 86, 901, 100, 107, 241; *see also* Japaneseness
Japanese-Filipino Children (JFC) 98, 100–3, 105–7, 110
Japaneseness 98–100, 103–4, 106, 108
jati 209n8
justice 21, 23, 28, 30

kampung 155, 225
Kang Youwei 45
Kartini 226
Kelantan 147–8, 150–1, 157
Kharagpur 197
kinship 35–6, 42–3, 44–6, 156, 242
Korea 7, 36, 67–70
Korean language 67–70, 73, 77–9

labels: ethnic 11, 67, 82–4, 86, 94, 123–4, 128–9, 134, 147, 164, 166, 173, 224; racial 84, 127, 147
land ownership 191
language: and identity 11, 36, 68–70, 77–9, 86, 94, 103, 117, 121, 137–9, 143–4, 153–4, 164–5, 185; loss of 68–9, 77–8
legitimate offspring 27, 53, 61n8, 214, 225, 230; *see also* marital status of parents
lineage 2, 42, 45, 55, 82, 89, 102–3, 105–7, 153
Lorde, Audre 21
Lou Jing 35–9, 43, 46–7

Malay 5, 38, 117–25, 133–4, 139–43, 147, 149–56, 164–5, 240–2
Malaysia 117–19, 132–3, 142–3, 147–9, 164, 242–3; Peninsular 149–50
Malaysian identity 117–18, 121–9, 133–4, 142
marginal identities 162–3; 'marginal man' 3, 103, 135, 172
marginalization 7–8, 19, 82, 165, 183, 241
marital status of parents 53
marriage 41, 54; international 67, 76; mixed 149, 151, 209n3; *see also* intermarriage
marriage migrants 67, 76, 241
mestizo 98–100, 111n3

métis/métisse 52–5, 57, 59–60, 240–1; legal classification of 10, 54, 61n17
migration 39, 59, 98, 108–10, 150, 185, 188–9
miscegenation 22, 195, 208; anti-miscegenation legislation 184; constructive 30
mixed: descent 7, 40, 134–5, 163, 166, 171–2, 179, 195, 211–13, 216, 222, 224–6, 234; heritage 5, 19, 67, 147–8, 163; identities 4, 40, 170, 182, 191, 212, 242; parentage 20, 36, 82–3, 134–5, 164, 182–3
mixed ethnic identity 135
mixed race 3–7, 37, 46, 103, 110, 148–9, 157, 162–4, 179, 182–3, 187, 191, 204, 211–13, 224, 233–4, 243
mixedness 3, 11–12, 36–7, 110, 148–9, 157, 162–3, 173, 241; *see also* mixed race
monoethnic 8, 142
monoracial 36, 45–6, 240–3
multi-ethnic 37, 142–3; children 67–70, 82
multicultural families 67–8
multiculturalism 10, 79
multiracial 4–5, 47, 84, 162–4, 172–3, 182–3, 211–12; model 164–6, 172–3; movement 19
multiracialism 164–6

national identity 117–18, 125–6, 164, 172–3, 180–1
national service 168
nationalism 67–8, 104, 142–3, 192n2, 228–9
nationality 29, 46, 86–7, 89–90, 101–2, 108, 111n9
natives 21–2, 29, 200, 225
Netherlands Indies 55, 211, 225–7, 234
"*Như chưa hề có cuộc chia ly*"/As Though Never Separated 52, 57–8
Nihonjinron 82–3, 88, 104
Non-Governmental Organizations (NGOs) 100, 102–5, 111n10

Orientals 213–14, 225
orphans 21
other 45, 54, 73, 85, 88–9, 164–5
othering 47, 84, 187
out-group 135–6

passing 59–60, 100
paternal inheritance 30–1

patrilineal 36, 42–4, 55, 133, 143, 164–5, 173
pemuda 228–9
Peranakan 134–5, 147–9, 149–50, 157–8, 242
performativity 118, 121–2; performance of identity 103, 118, 122, 196, 208, 243
phenotype 10, 46, 135–6, 139, 212
Philippines, the 69, 98–100, 110, 216
politics of recognition *see* recognition
Pomfret, David 21
popular culture 59–60, 107, 150, 198, 232–3
positioning 83, 85–7
post-colonial 162–4, 186, 224, 234–5
post-racial 4, 31
power 2–3, 94, 162–3, 202, 216, 221
prejudice 26, 37, 69–70, 77–8, 171, 241; *see also* discrimination
pribumi 231–2
privilege 22, 54, 98–9, 107–9, 111n10, 164, 196, 208, 214, 233; economic 123; political 117, 225
Probst, E.A. 28
protection societies 55–7
public/private identities 172
purity *see* racial purity

Qing Dynasty 41
questioning identity 88, 94, 139, 217

race theory 44–5, 148, 182, 195–6
racial: binaries 19, 235; categories 4–5, 117–18, 133–4, 147, 163–4, 166–7; hierarchy 21–2, 30, 99, 158n5, 213–14, 220–1, 224–5; intermediaries 24; purity 3, 19, 36, 90, 143, 180, 241
racial mixing 12n3, 22, 195
racism 37, 158n2, 184; anti-black 35–6
Ratepayers' Meeting, Shanghai International Settlement 26–30
recognition 4–5, 19, 102–5, 107–9, 166
reference groups 133–8
religion 117–18, 132, 143, 151, 156, 230
respectability 21, 29–31, 201
Ridley, H.N. 22
rights 19, 28, 30, 54, 98–9, 103, 110, 111n8, 117, 204

Royal Asiatic Society 25

St. Xavier's School 26
Shanghai Municipal Council 25, 30
Shanghai Public School 20, 25–30
Sinetron 232–5
Singapore 134, 163–7, 183–4
Social Identity Theory 134
social media 39–40, 147, 188
social status 46, 99–100, 120, 224, 232, 235
Society for Protection of Abandoned *Métis* Children 56
Sosrohadikoesoemo, Achmad 226
South Institute 202–3
South Korea *see* Korea
stance 83–6
stereotypes 21, 27, 76, 132, 136, 148, 171, 187, 213–14, 234
Stoler, Ann 20–2, 214, 224

television 43, 52, 154, 156, 235
terminology 4–5
Third Culture kids 211–12
Thorne, Cornelius 25, 29, 30
totok 226–8
transmigration 6
transnational identities 10, 102, 211–13, 221–2, 231

varna 195, 208n2
Việt Minh 57, 59
Vietnam 52–3, 58–60; Democratic Republic of 58–9; Republic of 58
Vietnam war 57–60; end of 59
violence 58, 228–30
Vũ Trọng Phụng 55

Wakaf Bharu 150–2
Whiteness 7, 31, 45, 57, 195–6, 208, 214, 217, 241
worlds: best of both 4, 31, 103, 142; worst of both 4, 103

xue (blood) 37–8, 43–6; *hunxue* 37–9, 45–7; *xuetong* 37–8, 45

Taylor & Francis eBooks

Helping you to choose the right eBooks for your Library

Add Routledge titles to your library's digital collection today. Taylor and Francis ebooks contains over 50,000 titles in the Humanities, Social Sciences, Behavioural Sciences, Built Environment and Law.

Choose from a range of subject packages or create your own!

Benefits for you
- Free MARC records
- COUNTER-compliant usage statistics
- Flexible purchase and pricing options
- All titles DRM-free.

Benefits for your user
- Off-site, anytime access via Athens or referring URL
- Print or copy pages or chapters
- Full content search
- Bookmark, highlight and annotate text
- Access to thousands of pages of quality research at the click of a button.

REQUEST YOUR FREE INSTITUTIONAL TRIAL TODAY | **Free Trials Available** We offer free trials to qualifying academic, corporate and government customers.

eCollections – Choose from over 30 subject eCollections, including:

Archaeology	Language Learning
Architecture	Law
Asian Studies	Literature
Business & Management	Media & Communication
Classical Studies	Middle East Studies
Construction	Music
Creative & Media Arts	Philosophy
Criminology & Criminal Justice	Planning
Economics	Politics
Education	Psychology & Mental Health
Energy	Religion
Engineering	Security
English Language & Linguistics	Social Work
Environment & Sustainability	Sociology
Geography	Sport
Health Studies	Theatre & Performance
History	Tourism, Hospitality & Events

For more information, pricing enquiries or to order a free trial, please contact your local sales team:
www.tandfebooks.com/page/sales

The home of Routledge books

www.tandfebooks.com